Light in the Valley

Light in the Valley

THE STORY OF CALIFORNIA'S
COLLEGE OF NOTRE DAME

by

MARY DOMINICA MCNAMEE,
S. N. D. de N.

BERKELEY   Howell -North Books   CALIFORNIA

992113

LIGHT IN THE VALLEY

Centennial Edition

———

Printed and bound in the United States of America
Library of Congress Catalog Card No. 68-21402

Nihil Obstat: Reverend Lyman A. Fenn, S.S., *Censor Librorum*

Imprimatur: Joseph T. McGucken, S.T.D., *Archbishop of San Francisco*

The *nihil obstat* and *imprimatur* are official declarations that a book or pamphlet is free of doctrinal or moral error.

No implication is contained therein that those who have granted the *nihil obstat* and *imprimatur* agree with the content, opinions or statements expressed.

Published by Howell-North Books
1050 Parker Street, Berkeley, California 94710

To

SISTER ANNA RAPHAEL FITZGERALD

ACKNOWLEDGMENTS

The list of those who have made research for this volume both possible and enjoyable is lengthy. Among those to whom the author stands most indebted are Clyde Arbuckle, City Historian of San Jose; Paul R. Teilh, County Clerk and Recorder, Santa Clara County; J. R. K. Kantor, Archivist, University of California; Dr. Edwin A. Beilharz, Chairman of the History Department, University of Santa Clara; A. V. Wildblood, Western Title Guaranty Company, San Jose; Rev. Arthur D. Spearman, S.J., University of Santa Clara; Dr. C. Albert Shumate; Directors of Relations with Schools Keith Merrill at U.C., Berkeley, and J. Price Gettinger at U.C., Davis; Richard Barrett, *San Jose Mercury-News;* Rev. William N. Abeloe; Dr. F. M. Stanger; John A. McCone; Anita Truman; Mary E. Valla; Mrs. Lucretia Little; Mrs. E. P. Schlichtman; Mrs. Arthur C. Townsend; Thomas M. Storke; W. E. Gledhill; and many others.

Barbara Grimstad of San Jose and Mr. and Mrs. David H. Locke of San Mateo deserve special thanks for preparing copies of the manuscript.

Foreword

Almost a decade ago, the author of this important volume published her *Willamette Interlude* which chronicled the coming of the Sisters of Notre Dame de Namur from old Belgium to that land "where flows the mighty Oregon." It was evident to this reader that the story of these Sisters in Oregon, 1844-1851, had three things to commend it as it was recorded by Sister Mary Dominica: there was a genuine felicity of style and this was joined with mastery of the germane fact; most of all, though, it was a delight to note the honest and frank approach which was so evident in its pages and which served as but another satisfactory sign that the day of the hopelessly pious and annoyingly edifying account had passed: indeed, this aspect of the volume caused me to write of it in a review that "we see here another verification of the fact that the history of religious groups is best told by letting the facts speak for themselves without retreating to the high ground of self praise or glorification of a given community." Now that the same competent and gifted author has given us a sequel to *Willamette Interlude,* it is a pleasure to record that the same qualities are evident all throughout its interesting pages.

The history of the apostolic and educational activities of the daughters of Mère Julie in California from 1851 until now are of the very warp and woof of the California Catholic story. Sister Mary Dominica has chosen to bring this story to 1923 when its Belmont phase was inaugurated. It is hard to see, though, that any important or significant phase of the intervening years has been neglected; written with affection and yet with a critical sense, the whole volume emerges as the right account written, it would seem, by the right person. Among the features which merit commendation is the manner in which the author relates her story to the broader picture of California and local history. Absence of this orientation has resulted in some other such accounts emerging as unsatisfactory and insufficient literary efforts. To return to the matter of frankness, the readers' attention is called to chapters 10, 14, and 17 among others where I hope they will share my delight in the "open end" approach to the matters treated there. I feel it no exaggeration, then, to say that this present volume worthily records the works of the Sisters of Notre Dame in California. It should encourage others to engage in like arduous and persevering research, which shall, it may be hoped, result eventually in the splendid sort of mature and measured historical account found in *Light in the Valley*.

JOHN BERNARD McGLOIN, S.J.
Professor of History
University of San Francisco

December, 1967
San Francisco, California

Author's Preface

This volume is not prompted by nostalgia, nor is it an attempt to enhance the actors in its pages. Still less is it intended to invest the present College of Notre Dame with a romantic past. The present college is of yesterday, its beginning a burst of energy that in a way recalls the surge of enthusiasm that marked the second decade of the early college on Santa Clara Street in San Jose. In those days a small group of Sisters, secluded and tradition-bound as they were, turned their eyes to the future. Though they would not have employed the expression, those Sisters seemed to understand the evolutionary nature of learning and thought. Those of them who reached old age were saddened by later acceptance of the formal and static, or of the notion that intellectual movement is all one with rebellion.

When at the end of the century, Sister Anna Raphael Fitzgerald adopted changes advised by educators, she accepted along with undeniable improvement, a rigidity of curriculum that failed to consider human development. What she gave up was, in fact, more in accord with the finest educational thought of today. But willingness to change proved her progressive spirit, a characteristic shared by Sister Mary Xavier Mills and others, one which made them as truly pioneers as were the Belgian Sisters who crossed two oceans in a small ship in 1844.

This volume is the story, too, of the California Province of Notre Dame, of which the college was also the central house. This story is not merely a background accompaniment. Its purposes need no comment, but the telling provides biographical opportunity, which will, I hope, be welcome to Sisters, alumnae, and friends of Notre Dame on the Pacific Coast.

MARY DOMINICA MCNAMEE, S.N.D. de Namur
Professor Emeritus
College of Notre Dame

January, 1968
Belmont, California

Contents

Part One   Learning for Pioneers
  CHAPTER   1   Line of Willows   1
            2   Mutiny, Brigands, and Angel Cohorts   16
            3   Prizes in a Blue Tent   33

Part Two   The Quickening
  CHAPTER   4   Brick and Polished Pine   45
            5   Gathering of Minds   60
            6   Señoritas, Yanquitas, and Others . .   77

Part Three   Reaching to Maturity
  CHAPTER   7   A Degree of Importance   92
            8   Daughters of the Valley   108
            9   Uniforms and Rules   120
           10   Study Plans and Books   131

Part Four   Filling the Corners
  CHAPTER 11   Blessing from a Southland   146
           12   New Workers in the Field   161
           13   Evening of the Valiant   170

Part Five   Second Noble Woman
  CHAPTER 14   Dawn of a Lovely Day   182
           15   Donors and Foundations   199
           16   Hearts Brave in Peril   214

Part Six   Tide of Achievement
  CHAPTER 17   A School's Assessment   230
           18   Music of Merit   244
           19   The Printed Image   257

Part Seven   Farewell and New Beginning
  CHAPTER 20   Old San Jose   268
           21   Beckoning to Belmont   281

Notes   296

Bibliography   325

Index   327

CHAPTER 1   LINE OF WILLOWS

*T*wo Belgian Sisters of the Congregation of Notre Dame de Namur, self-effacingly clad in modest lay attire, looked about them as the carriage that had brought them from San Francisco on this April day in 1851 jolted into the young State of California's fledgling capital city. Pueblo San José had been founded by the Spaniards in 1777 as the first secular community in the province of California. A sleepy settlement during the years of Spanish and later Mexican rule, it was chosen by the Americans at the constitutional convention of 1849 as the state capital. In the following year it was incorporated as the City of San Jose.[1] Still known familiarly as the "pueblo" despite its newly acquired status as an American city and its dignity as capital of California, it was generally drab and offered little promise to the strangers that April, for it could boast only a handful of houses and stores, these for the most part hastily and poorly constructed.

Through the springtime bloom of mustard that had grown to biblical proportions, the two Sisters could glimpse one of the few inviting home scenes in town, the adobe residence of Don Luis Peralta, with orchards extending along San Augustine Street.[2] The pious-minded Don had built that small house half a century earlier; he was now 97 years old and for him the place had taken on the sacred nature of a Spanish family dwelling. Here he lived, in this last year of his life, with his spinster daughters, Gertrudis and Trinidad, for whom he intended that life should be "free from the storms of this world and from evil-inclined persons." If others thought their father mad, his daughters knew him as a saint who, during this time of the great gold rush to California, warned his sons against gold-seeking and asked to be placed on the "hearse that is used for my fellow men, the Indians."

1

The storms of life, nevertheless, were besetting San Jose. The disorderly first session of the California Legislature the previous year had been accompanied by a building boom which began to subside with word that General Mariano Guadalupe Vallejo had offered a site for a new state capitol at Benicia, and in February of 1851 the legislators had passed the law which sealed the doom of San Jose as California's capital city.[3]

Sister Loyola Duquenne and Sister Marie Catherine Cabareaux had come from the Willamette Valley in Oregon where, with a few companions, they had made two beginnings since 1844. At St. Paul they had built a home and school for orphans and French-Indian children and, at Oregon City, a Young Ladies' Boarding and Day School. The work there was now being carried on by their colleagues while the Superior, Sister Loyola, and her companion were in California to meet four new missionary Sisters en route to San Francisco by sea, and also to investigate the need and possibility of opening a new foundation to minister to the swelling population of the gold rush state.

San Jose, once a Spanish pueblo, and then briefly an American boom town and capital city, was certainly not as promising a site as the Sisters might have hoped. It is little wonder that they felt hesitant about making a foundation in such a place, whether or not they knew of its rejection as capital.

What worried them more than local aspects, however, was their previous commitment, or rather it was that their divergent attitudes toward that commitment accounted for an increasing strain in their mutual relations. A start in California might necessitate their withdrawal from Oregon, a possibility which for some time seemed attractive enough to Sister Loyola, but surely a source of something close to anguish to Sister Marie Catherine. As gold seekers left the Willamette for California, Sister Loyola saw new opportunities there; she was suffering, perhaps, from a growing discouragement and certainly from her increasing inability to maintain amiable relations with Archbishop Blanchet. Her companion saw only the native and

French-Indian children for whom she believed they had left Belgium in the first place.

Actually the missions begun by the Sisters of Notre Dame in Oregon were not completely untenable in 1851. It is true the California's trumpet call to the gold fields had drained off the valley's population, and that missionary priests had thought it better to start new centers where a growing and unshepherded population had special need of care. But it is also true that a returning wave of miners, successful or disillusioned, had set in. In little Portland many of these were taking on the role of producer to meet the needs of California miners, and lumber mills were springing up along the Columbia to supply homes and stores for San Francisco. For a time, St. Paul and Oregon City seemed by-passed, though there was always some activity in the latter. After the Sisters' heavy labor in both places, their withdrawal now seemed regrettable indeed. Most of that little band of the first of all Sisters in the Oregon country regretted that departure as did Sister Marie Catherine.[4] They would have agreed with the first American civil governor of California who, recalling Oregon years with the wisdom of hindsight, said of that era that they had all passed through trials that had "tested and established" their patience and that their condition was much better than earlier; in all, he thought they should have been content.[5]

Wisely as well as virtuously, Sister Loyola and Sister Marie Catherine refused to allow their difference of opinion to amount to estrangement. For aside from their relationship as religious, these two enjoyed a friendship based on mutual recognition of fine characteristics. Still Sister Marie Catherine could not have failed to note Sister Loyola's decision to meet the third group of missionary Sisters in San Francisco herself, instead of following the directive of the Sister Provincial of Cincinnati to send a "trusted person" there to meet them. As the journey was at best troublesome, Sister Loyola might have been expected to follow the suggestion, and added to Sister Marie Catherine's bewilderment over this matter were her superior's cryptic references to messages from the restless Father Anthony Langlois, for

whom future apostolic plans held so great an attraction. Thus
when Sister discovered in San Francisco that Bishop Alemany
had asked her Superior to make a foundation there, she was not
surprised, and not even at the further disclosure that the invitation had been made through Father Langlois, who had even
offered to pay traveling expenses of Sister Loyola and a companion. In fact, said Sister Marie Catherine, describing their
reception by Father Langlois, he quite "ignored," by which she
meant was unaware of, the real purpose of the Sisters of Notre
Dame in coming to Oregon.

Still there was a slight evasiveness in Father Langlois' greeting in the name of the absent Bishop when the two Sisters
arrived on that last day of March in 1851. For one thing, he
seemed to wish to avoid the subject of the foundation about
which he had been so enthusiastic. Thus the Sisters settled
down to await the Bishop's return and the delayed arrival of
their new missionaries with no special interest beyond their
prayers and a forced comparison between their outdated street
costumes and those of ladies of the city. This embarrassment
did not, however, prevent their making a few excursions with
members of the family of Judge Patrick Barry, who on hearing
of the Sisters' presence in the city, had hit upon a plan of their
own for a Sisters' school on Presidio Heights. Perhaps prudence
in the face of this suggestion from the laity prompted the Sisters to point out the rampant growth of poison oak in the area
as a deterrent. It was well they did so, since they presently
discovered that Father John McGinnis, then establishing St.
Patrick's Parish, had recently invited the Daughters of Charity
of St. Vincent de Paul to open a school, and that neither he nor
anyone else considered San Francisco large enough for two
simultaneous foundations. Then subsequent events added to
Sister Marie Catherine's bewilderment over this lack of diocesan coordination. On Bishop Alemany's return to San Francisco, she sat with only her conjectures for company during his
conference with Sister Loyola, who finally rejoined her without
however satisfying her curiosity by so much as a word. But
since no allowance had been made for wholesome curiosity in

Sister Marie Catherine's training, she made an effort to leave the future in her superior's hands. Try as she would, however, she could not prevent the escape of certain slight revelations of her state of mind.

A series of these revelations, it seems, followed Sister Loyola's announcement that the two should visit San Jose presently on the advice of His Grace and at the earnest request of Martin Murphy, Jr., of Rancho Pastoria de las Borregas. Sister Loyola could see plainly that not even their joyous reception by Mrs. Murphy was blotting out her companion's mental picture of reproachful dark eyes in the Oregon Mission, of families lapsing into the state in which the Sisters of Notre Dame had found them. Not even the story of the Murphy-Townsend-Stevens Party could completely distract Sister Marie Catherine.[6] The crisis that forced her to speak out her mind was the tour of San Jose, its purpose to select a school site. As they jogged along in the Murphy carriage, Sister Loyola ventured a cautious query. How was Sister impressed by the possibilities? Sister answered frankly, even heatedly, in French, grateful that Irish Martin Murphy could not understand her words. How, she wanted to know, could they even consider the matter without their higher Superior's permission? To her horror, she observed that Martin Murphy was laughing; his youth in Quebec had made him an understanding listener. But despite his laughter, Sister was certain that the good man must be shocked, since he knew that Sister Loyola was her Superior. Perhaps to set matters right, she approved of the frontage on Santa Clara Street, pointing out the line of graceful willows that marked the course of the old *acequia,* and noting that the spot might be an ideal location for a boarding school. Relating this event and her swift change of mind, Sister recalled a convenient dream she had experienced somewhat earlier of a line of hills beyond which lay a new mission for her Sisters. Even her sensible life seems, in fact, to have been dotted with such useful visions.

Good will thus secured, Sister Loyola now began to utilize her companion's business ability, including her in plans made with the advice of Father John Nobili, S.J., when he shared his

meagre breakfast of bread and coffee with them after early
Mass in the Santa Clara Mission. These plans included the first
few of a series of land purchases on Santa Clara Street. Checking them off on the White Survey of Peter Davidson's holdings,
one sees that the Sisters hoped to obtain a solid frontage on this
line.[7] For though, when the Sisters arrived, Santa Clara Street
was little more than a pathway, unsure as yet of its direction,
its function of connecting the center of the pueblo with The
Alameda, and thus with the Santa Clara Mission lent it distinction and promise. More than that, Martin Murphy, Jr. and
the "Senators," Sister Marie Catherine's group title for the few
civic leaders or professional men other than medical doctors,
even then foresaw its future importance as a thoroughfare. The
Capital "boom" had produced a lively transfer of property in
this area. To take advantage of this opportunity, owner Peter
Davidson had marked off a dozen lots fronting the future artery
on the north, from Davidson Street east to a canal known as the
acequia, and measuring fifty Spanish varas in depth with 25 in
frontage, *poco mas o menos,* a qualification that appears to
have been quite necessary at the time. He had disposed of all
of these lots except two before the Sisters arrived, but he still
possessed the large, unplotted section that lay between them
and the Peralta property to the north, an area reaching from
Davidson Street to the meandering line of the *acequia.*

When a few days after their first visit to the site, the Sisters
purchased fifty feet of frontage on Santa Clara and this large
back area, the *acequia* rather than the willow border, was a
considerable motive. This waterway, some four feet wide, running in a zig-zag northwestern line, connected a pond fed by
the Arroyo Tulares de las Canoas with a branch of the Guadalupe River, and was one of a network of such *acequias.* To the
Sisters this water source was a blessing before their first well
became a more convenient supply. After that improvement, the
little lake that adorned their campus was a reminder of water-
toting days.

Value of land and other values, too, for that matter, fluctu-
ated rather temperamentally in those days, but no doubt the

"Senators" advised the Sisters that $4000 was not too high a price to pay for their first real estate acquisition. And the fact that they paid it off, together with many other obligations, during their first four years in San Jose, seems at variance with tales about their destitution. They purchased the remaining frontage lots of the tract, it would seem, as soon as their boom time investors were willing to part with them. The initial deed indicates the first frontage acquired was Lot 30, which the survey, recorded in 1855, presents as 25, not 50, varas wide, a correction necessitated, no doubt, by earlier hurried measurements during rapid turnover. Thus the Sisters' first neighbors on Santa Clara Street were Levi Goodrich on the east and Judge Joshua Redman on the west. Within a few months pioneer Elisha O. Crosby sold the Sisters Lot 27 for $200, an example of a drop in value, and Levi Goodrich deeded over Lots 28 and 29. Before long, Job F. Dye sold the Sisters Lots 24, 25 and 26 for $3000, and Davidson deeded the remaining frontage to the west. Finally Judge Redman relinquished Lot 36, thus completing the frontage.[8] If it seems regrettable that the line did not run to San Pedro Street, an achievement which might have led the way to a future rounded city block, we should recall that bordering on the *acequia* was the Sisters' goal as it had been Davidson's.

At the same time the Sisters of Notre Dame acquired the Davies property along the north line of Santa Clara Street west of the Davidson Tract to allow for the full expansion of their school. The Sisters' first purchase in this section was from Jonathan Parr, their interest being two or three small buildings which stood on his property, and which they at once moved into their own building area. Next Charles White deeded to the Sisters his holding in the section, a free gift on his part.[9] The same is apparently true of Martin Murphy's large lot. The Sisters held the Davies tract until 1864 when Guadalupe Peralta, her sister Maria Dolores Castro and Juan Castro signed over their holdings in consideration of $6700.

Further titles, east of the *acequia*, indicate later attempts to square off that side of the campus. These titles show the irregular lines of the early *suerte* holdings and such old pueblo names as Amesquita and Alvirez. The result of all this rounding out is shown in the city chart of San Jose, 1884. In all, the length of the real estate name run for the Sisters of Notre Dame in those early days would indicate that as both grantor and grantee, Sister Marie Catherine needed all her business acumen, as well as a share in the confidence with which Sister Loyola countered her lapses into "cowardice."

Sister Marie Catherine can scarcely be blamed for one such lapse as she began to realize the disappointing returns on the appeal for donations inaugurated by the "Senators" for the benefit of the Sisters' building fund. The Murphy family contributed $500; all other honored pledges amounted to some $800. With the best of will, several promises could not be met. Clearly money was scarce in the area, but to Sister Loyola this fact only proved the abiding necessity of a successful boarding school with its appeal to the wealthy of distant places. And local good will was at least encouraging. There was Paula Suñol Sainsevain, for instance, offering the Sisters a lovely christening robe in lieu of money. They converted this piece of exquisite needlework into a communion cloth, their first chapel treasure. But trust in the future was strengthened for both Sisters by Father John Nobili's advice and example. In Santa Clara, he was planning an educational center with confidence that its success would be in proportion to its necessity. Further, he was not awaiting approval, of which he felt certain.

The sense of timeliness was enhanced for the Sisters when they accompanied the Murphy family from Murphy's Station, the present Sunnyvale, to the Santa Clara Mission on Palm Sunday morning. For as Bishop Alemany pontificated on that historic, mid-April occasion, his Franciscan deacon and Jesuit sub-deacon furnished dramatic background for his announcement that henceforth both the mission and the church in San Jose would be in the hands of the Jesuit Fathers.[10] For the proposed Notre Dame foundation, this change meant assurance of zealous instruction for both Sisters and students. On that Palm Sunday, too, the Sisters made first acquaintance with local families, all repeating the desire of the Murphys for a school. Foremost among these was the San Jose family of Thomas Kell, an English-born immigrant to Quebec, who had there married Margaret, daughter of the elder Martin Murphy, and whose name was to become a benediction in Notre Dame of San Jose.[11]

The Kells now welcomed the two Sisters to their new home on the Almaden Road until they should be settled. But here the guests could not help realizing the inconvenience they were causing as their new friends had to abandon spring work in their fields to drive them into town. Their next move was to the residence of the Charles White family, where Mrs. White was accommodating a few boarders. But as Sisters have always been inclined to convert their immediate surroundings into cloister, these two arose each morning at an unthinkable hour so as to assist at early Mass in Santa Clara. They stepped carefully, of course, on the poorly laid floor, but seemingly the more softly they stepped, the louder were the creaking reports of their footfalls. Then striding along The Alameda, they would forget those anxious moments at the sight of the sunrise on great expanses of wild mustard like paintings between the willows planted some fifty years earlier by Franciscan Father Minister José Viader.[12]

To those sturdy Belgian women the morning trek on The Alameda perhaps seemed a bracing jaunt. Certainly they preferred it to attending the local church, a barnlike, neglected structure built half a century earlier for the convenience of pueblo dwellers and still attended by a Mexican Franciscan. On Holy Thursday the Sisters were shocked at the squalor, the lack of preparation, the jostling and pushing for first places at Communion. Sister Loyola wept over the irreverence. If teaching Sisters were needed in any place, she said, it was surely San Jose. Mrs. White's other boarders, however, did not, it seems, appreciate the creaking of floor boards at so unearthly an hour, and the Sisters sensed the fact. Their search for another lodging ended in a short stay in the home of Don Antonio Suñol, where good Dolores Bernal Suñol, with her old-world picture

of Sisters, provided something like the convent situation.[13] Still
that hospitable home, which perhaps approached more closely
than most the idyllic picture of Spanish California, seems not
to have met with Sister Loyola's approval.

Fortunately through the good offices of Father Nobili, the
Belgian Dr. Peter Van Caneghan offered a little hospital which
was vacant at the time. Here the Sisters were housed, comfortably as well as canonically, until their first quarters on Santa
Clara Street were ready for them. From this location, they
made exploratory tours, each time confirmed in their preference
for a site removed from the center of things.

For the area verging on the plaza was not pleasant. Deep
ruts in the streets told of their condition during the winter
months. Stagnant water still lay in front of the converted adobe
home of J. D. Hoppe which, bizarre as the Sisters considered it,
furnished some relief from the general drabness and disorder.
It was witness, as well, to the talent of Levi Goodrich, architect,
carpenter, contractor all in one.[14] This fact was not lost on the
Sisters, nor on the city of San Jose when it turned to the construction of public buildings. But for the moment, with building material so hard to come by, Goodrich was employing his
talent in making the best of existing structures.

Unavailability in other lines was the Sisters' worst problem.
With so much walking about, they had worn their knitted wool
stockings threadbare, but there was not an inch of worsted in
the local stores with which to darn them. Their wardrobe (they
were still in lay attire) called for replacements, but they could
find no suitable yardage. When they set about securing supplies
for their future convent and school, they found themselves
always purchasing the last of the stock, trying to match cups,
plates, knives, and forks that bore any likeness in pattern and
size. Thus Sister Loyola was forced to go to San Francisco on
shopping tours, combining with this activity not very successful
efforts to increase her building fund. With hope for their watch-
word, they stocked the little hospital with supplies and trusted
for housing. They began to teach, too, on the same small scale.

Sister Marie Catherine gave lessons in the Suñol home until classes were opened on Santa Clara Street.

Even though teaching seems not to have been Sister's strong point, she met this challenge with zeal and a degree of enjoyment. Setting out each morning, she gathered up an unnamed and very recalcitrant little French girl who pouted and screamed before succumbing to Sister's persuasive French argument. Arriving at the Suñol home, they found an elegant breakfast awaiting, which may explain why the spoiled darling behaved obligingly during classes. Sister now introduced the señoritas, Encarnación, Antonita, and Francesca Suñol, to "the principles of writing" and other matters, at the same time enscribing their names in the first Notre Dame roster in San Jose. Whatever the principles were, the señoritas probably began on the same level as did the little French girl. Quite possibly Sister had to show them how to form letters and spell simple words, adding avidly to her small store of Spanish as she did so.

This haste of the Suñol family to acquire the "principles" is at first a bit baffling; learning was the declared ambition of the Murphys and the Kells, whose minds had been denied their rights by law in their native land, and by the demands of struggle for survival in Quebec and Missouri. But Spanish mothers, as the Sisters were to learn, preferred art and needlework for their daughters, along with seclusion that would protect them from acquaintance with the hated Yankee. In this household, however, eagerness for books may well have been due to the influence of young Pierre Sainsevain, who had married Paula Suñol in 1845. A member of the Constitutional Convention at Monterey at 31, he had been noted all along for his intelligent and constructive attitudes. In the Suñol household, he would have stressed the value of education as he did in other instances.[15] In any case, Paula's younger sisters learned rapidly and well; seemingly they could not get enough of the "principles." Doña Dolores saw to it, of course, that teacher and scholars were properly sequestered from the pleasant din of the famed Suñol hospitality. Here where the grand tradition was honored, where sea captains and supercargoes rode down from

San Francisco as a matter of course, where a guest might expect fine horse and silver-mounted saddle, as well as a servant guide to clasp his spurs, not so much as a tinkle disturbed the schoolroom.

Certainly the Sisters must have observed something of the grand Spanish tradition since they were in general very alert women. They possessed the same material for striking description as did Grandma Bascom, who presents the silks and jewels of her friends, the señoras, in contrast with their sordid adobes. Such matters were worldly; it seemed there was no need of their acquaintance, and here lies the great weakness in old mission reports. Ignoring background, the missionaries hastened to fit all into their own picture. Letters and annals made good reading inasmuch as they were success reports in adaptation to the missionaries' own way of life with its bias of angelism. In those early days teaching would have been better served had the Sisters known why Spanish mothers insisted on their daughters being separated in classes from "las Americanas," if they had read aright the grieved look in Spanish eyes. They mistook for innate goodness the shyness of the señorita always overshadowed by madre or dueña. They left unexplained the Spanish girls' unwillingness to learn English or to participate in musical entertainments. They accepted the loathing that caused *sangre pura* to despise and be despised by the families of the *fundadores* as a matter not to be questioned. They failed to discover that a sad mood might be instantly cured by a horseback run in the cattle roundup. In this aloofness from their milieu, the Sisters missed the beginnings of wholesome social change. For at the same time Mrs. Bascom was employing her leisure time to encourage social events.[16] But such local problems were not for Sisters.

One exception to this attitude, and this became the special interest of Sister Marie Catherine, was the cost of living with its unaccountable variations. Baffled by it all, Sister uses the word "exorbitant" again and again, though it did not apply so generally in 1851 as it had a little earlier. If $32, or two ounces of gold dust, seemed too high a fare for the stagecoach journey to

San Francisco, Mrs. Bascom had paid almost five times that amount as boat fare for herself and small children down the bay to Alviso in 1849. And when Sister moaned over the high cost of food, she was, no doubt, thinking of life on the Willamette, where the farm at St. Paul supplied so many needs. Still, scarcity, especially of building materials, presented greater problems in the pueblo than did high prices, greater problems, in fact, than the Sisters had experienced in Oregon City, where the little stores had been longer established and were within easier reach of shipping. One must make allowance, besides, for Sister Marie Catherine's sense of drama. Sister Loyola's purse was not likely to be "without a penny," nor even reduced to the "25 cents" of tradition, a metaphor more than likely borrowed from St. Teresa of Avila, who also possessed a high dramatic sense. The exaggerated tradition of poverty has presented, for instance, wretched hovels as homes for the Sisters in both St. Paul and Oregon City. In both instances, truth comes as a surprise. Certainly for a time, housing was a serious problem in San Jose. Sawmills, (the nearest was William Campbell's on Saratoga Creek) had been deserted in the gold rush. Lumber brought by sea, as well as the prefabricated house, made difficult and costly entry to the pueblo by reason of added transportation down the bay and over the unspeakable Alviso-San Jose road.

In this last difficulty, Levi Goodrich proved an invaluable friend. His first feat was to complete a long, narrow adobe house that had been started on one of the newly acquired lots, its back wall along the street broken by small, high windows. Two inner walls divided its length, and its poorly made tile roof was unfinished. Goodrich finished the front, connected the rooms with a long corridor, and completed the tiling. Next he moved some two or three small frame buildings, probably from the Jonathan Parr property, into the same area. One of these, long known as the 1851 House, became the Sisters' first convent, and for that historic house, this removal was the first of three, a simple matter, since it was fitted together like parts of a puzzle, the whole held firmly by means of wooden pegs. In 1923 foreman Augustine Barbieri numbered all parts for reassembly at Belmont, where the house served as a museum. He repeated the process in 1937, when the house was removed to the new provincial center at Saratoga to continue the same service. With floor space at a premium, this sturdy building, with its one long room and stairs at the back leading to an attic in which a tall person could stand erect only under the rooftree, served all purposes by day, housing in turn almost every known Notre Dame activity.

Sister Marie Catherine also describes a barn which Goodrich converted into a temporary kitchen and dining room, but while such adaptations were going forward, he was also laying the foundation for a two-story house, which for lack of lumber was not completed for some months. Into this assemblage of shacks, among which the 1851 House wore a palatial air, the Sisters moved the odds and ends of furniture and household gear that they had been storing in the hospital. In one little unit they settled their first boarder, three-year-old Johnny Townsend, his Irish nurse, and an Indian servant girl from the Townsend household. This arrangement was the Sisters' act of gratitude to Dr. Van Caneghan, guardian of little Johnny since the death of his parents, Dr. John Townsend and his wife, in the cholera epidemic of 1850.[17] As young Moses Schallenberger, administrator of the Townsend estate, compensated the Sisters generously, their kind act turned out to be an encouraging arrangement. And the three made no comments on the rugged situation, but neither apparently did any of the other first boarders, girls who brought finery in strong leather trunks, but were willing to live from pillar to post, to climb over wooden benches, tuck their knees under planks stretched over wooden horses, and serve their dinner into a soup plate.

Preparing for their first boarders, the Sisters worked about the place long into the late summer evenings. Levi Goodrich worked long hours, too, and others dropped in to lend a hand. To the Sisters, it was reminiscent of their building days on the Willamette. There, however, they had lacked the good will and competence that they now found in builder Goodrich, the competence he had gained in New York, as well as a reputation for construction of houses with graceful bay windows. The good will was the result of his admiration for the Sisters and the fearlessness and industry with which they met pioneer conditions. Some time after the arrival of the four new Sisters, he remarked to friends that he knew of "six fine women in this town." Then he told them about the Sisters on Santa Clara Street.

When 26-year-old Sister Marie Alenie Thewissen and her three companion missionaries entered the Golden Gate on the *Sarah Sands* late in June, 1851, they expected to be met on landing by certain "responsible persons" who would lead them, they had no idea by what route, to Oregon City.[1] They had no real notion of its location; it was near the Columbia and safely separated from the wild gold fields and the even wilder San Francisco. That was the important thing. As leader of the group Sister Marie Alenie had been charged with the responsibility of reaching that destination. In Namur some nine months earlier, the Mother General of the Sisters of Notre Dame, Mère Constantine, bidding ten missionary Sisters farewell, had given a special warning to the four destined for the Oregon Mission; on no account must they yield to an invitation to remain in San Francisco. In Cincinnati, Sister Superior Louise had repeated the injunction. San Francisco was just not a proper place for Sisters.

In sending a mission group of ten Sisters to America in the summer of 1850, the Mother General was fulfilling a promise of six to Cincinnati. With the exception of Sister Marie Alenie, she was wisely leaving to Sister Louise the selection of those who should join the Oregon Mission, for this plan would leave Sister Louise free to supply the younger mission with Sisters of longer American experience and better knowledge of English.[2] Sister Marie Alenie was not alone in her desire to go to Oregon; it would seem that at least half of the ten cherished that wish, to say nothing of several eastern Sisters who considered the North Pacific area a genuine mission land and Ohio much too civilized. The ten who set sail from Antwerp on the *Fanny* September 4, after a long wait for wind, were mostly quite young and inexperienced.[3] The scribe of that three-week voyage to

New York was Sister Marie Alenie herself, beloved by all, as gentle and saintly. If she was a little too gullible, she was still a good leader by reason of her sweet approach to life.

This group of missionaries had to embark upon its voyage without the usual guidance of an experienced missionary. However, said Sister Marie Alenie, the captain of the *Fanny* was a pious man; that was clear from his willingness to credit the prayers of Mère Constantine with the long-awaited wind. Besides, the generosity of Lady Laura Petre, the future Sister Mary of St. Francis,[4] made first-class cabin passage possible for the ten Sisters, a thoughtfulness which afforded Sister Marie Alenie a sense of security from the dangers of a mutiny in the reality of which she still believed when writing her story years later. And if her nine companions were not equally credulous, they must have crossed the Atlantic in a state of suppressed merriment. For the captain, if pious, was humorous as well. As soon as his special charges had recovered from their first experience with *mal de mer,* he regaled them with seagoing tales. Had they ever heard of casting lots? Well, on his very last voyage, that custom had been honored. When the food failed, the lot fell upon the cabin boy, a clever fellow who at once mounted the highest mast and remained aloft until he sighted a sail. Divine Providence! But the comfort in that happy ending was presently shattered by danger close at hand.

As the Sisters sat chatting with the captain one evening after supper, a grim-faced officer appeared carrying a large lantern which he presented to each Sister in dour silence. Quailing at its skull and crossbones surmounting the inscription "Prepare for death," Sister Marie Alenie turned to the captain, who muttered the word "Mutiny" with heavy resignation. But the Sisters were not to fear. He had ordered guns and pistols loaded for emergency, and an array of sharpened knives and daggers as well. Best of all, he had discovered exactly when to expect the break. The Sisters must then take to their cabins, and at the psychological moment, he would have two cannon fired. He did, said Sister, and the wicked scheme was foiled, but the Sisters, she added, kept a wary eye on the deck for the

remainder of the voyage. In fact, Sister considered the great
storm they experienced a mere trifle compared to the machina-
tions that were certainly going on below. Finally, she says, the
harassed captain put on a show of might, sabres, and all. For
the benefit of posterity, she sets down the date as September
18, 1850, after which she dismissed the matter, though just to
make sure, she recommended it to "the whole Celestial Court."

She was not worried by the storm, which raged on through
the last lap of the voyage. There was no malice in it, only the
finger of God. How foolish to fret when one was ready to die;
besides, Heaven had given them a captain who could deal
cleverly with a waterspout as well as a mutiny. Thus minded,
she recorded those days in good Ancient Mariner spirit. After
the blast, succeeding calm was perfect milieu for a great whale
that would certainly have upset the ship had not the Good God
suddenly attracted its attention to some more interesting object,
and thus left the Sisters to contemplate the sunset. Next a good
wind sprang up behind, six to eight knots an hour, Sister says
in approved sailor fashion. That was a blessing, as according to
the captain, the "mortal enemy" was again on the warpath, and
constantly bothering him with questions about the ship's log.
To deceive them, he explained, he was increasing the number
of knots recorded daily on the slate. Thus believing the ship
almost in sight of harbor, they would hardly contemplate an
attack.

Disembarking at New York, the Sisters found carriages
awaiting them at the plank of the *Fanny*. As they set off for the
house of Archbishop John Hughes, whose kindness had thus provided for them, they caught a final glimpse of the terrible muti-
neer and his crew, striding along with dufflebags on their shoul-
ders, but fortunately heading in another direction, and leaving
Sister Marie Alenie to America and its strange ways. Her first
astonishment was the reaction of the priest who received the
group in the absence of Archbishop Hughes, and who met her
request that the ten might make a short spiritual retreat by
taking them instead to visit the convents of the city. Retreats
marked the stopovers of missionary Sisters, as well as imme-

diate searching for a Father Confessor. Besides, sightseeing
and visiting, even of convents, formed no part of their travel
plans. They enjoyed the tour, however, which included points
of interest other than the convents, since it was all marked by
episcopal blessing. They enjoyed, too, the hospitality of the
Sisters of Charity while awaiting the arrival of Sister Louis de
Gonzague, superior of the recently established first foundation
of Notre Dame in Boston.[5]

Sister Louis de Gonzague, guided the group through a series
of shocks and wonders. They rushed through the bustling city
to the Hudson River steamer, where by a seeming miracle, their
baggage awaited them. Aboard, Sister jotted down a few notes
about the interesting Babylon they were leaving, a jostling,
informal place where car conductors wore citizens' garb. Up
the river, she found Albany a bit more conformed to urbanity,
but, alas, the good dinner served in a nice hotel in that city was
a mere pause before return to what seemed a general absence of
the amenities.

As the New York train bore them westward, flurries of early
snow drifted into the car through its broken window. But even
here chivalry lived; a gentleman arose, hung his coat over the
aperture, and took to pacing in the aisle to keep warm. An
Archangel Raphael in person, said Sister Marie Alenie. Buffalo,
she found, outdid New York, where at least, she had not seen
pigs wandering about in the streets. Much as she loved all
animals, she preferred the Belgian custom of not permitting
livestock to promenade with people. Buffalo was Bedlam, with
its bus drivers shouting above the din, but in some remarkable
way, Sister Louis de Gonzague knew which one to hail, and
presently the group was lodged in a hotel to wait out a four-day
storm on the Lake before taking steamer to Sandusky.

Sister's odyssey took a more civilized and comfortable turn
when a second chivalrous knight appeared, as did also the former pastor of the Notre Dame Sisters in Toledo. Because of
both, it seems, the travelers presently found themselves in a
palace car, all fares paid. Still as nothing is perfect on earth,
Sister now regretted the high speed of this elegant train, which

blurred the lovely country scene and so deprived her soul of inspiration. But as her disappointments never amounted to frustration, she soon found new sources of wonder, which she set down in facile French notes interspersed with attempts at English expression. If dedication to the Oregon Mission was her first responsibility, conquest of the English language was her second.

In the Sixth Street Convent in Cincinnati, the ten missionaries resumed community life and settled down to a protracted guessing game as to which of them should go on to Oregon, that is, all except Sister Marie Alenie, who knew that she was not intended to remain in "the United States," which she considered "too near Belgium in civilization." Her covoyager, Sister Marie Donathilde Lempereur, was one of the three selected by Sister Louise. The other two had lived in America since childhood and so were English speaking. And now with the appointments made, intensive preparation began, and this for Sister Marie Alenie included hours of piano practice, for according to Sister Louise, her talent would be needed in Oregon City.

When the four were setting out at last on the evening of Easter Sunday, 1851, their baggage addressed to the little city on the Willamette, Sister Louise again repeated her injunction not to accept any invitation to stop short of their destiny. Their purpose was to strengthen the Oregon Mission, she said, not dreaming that on that very Sunday Sister Loyola was laying plans with the Murphys and the Kells for a foundation in San Jose.

The four Sisters began their long journey to Oregon by going east to New York, where they were to board the steamer for Panamá. In New York, Sister Louis de Gonzague confided them to the care of Father Eugene O'Connell, the future Bishop of Grass Valley, who had also assumed the guidance of two California-bound Dominican Sisters.[6] Aboard the coast steamer *Empire City*, the six Sisters donned their religious habits and kept their rather summery lay attire for Colón and Panamá City.[7] Again Sister Marie Alenie pursued her English exercises, that is when not meditating on Atlantic or Caribbean waves, or laying foundations of her lifelong friendship with the Dominican Sister Louise.

Though many a journal relates a mid-century crossing of the Isthmus, few approach Sister Marie Alenie's calmness as she sets her array of pistols, knives, and scheming natives against the Providence of God. Though she views danger with awe, it is the reader's heart that skips the beat, not hers. The crossing, it would seem, was her favorite thriller, but a thriller laced with humorous bits.

At the entrance to the Chagres River, she said, an Indian-manned boat, she calls it a canoe, picked up the Sisters, together with Father O'Connell and a certain Mr. and Mrs. Heffernan. A group on the shore called to them not to land as murderers were lying in wait of them, the warning followed by the sight of ten naked Indians rowing towards them and armed with knives, daggers, and bundles of dried roots, a rather detailed picture in view of the approaching darkness. But as suddenly a certain Jewish Doctor Rabbe, with a few other gentlemen, appeared rowing rapidly to their rescue, all of them armed with pistols, and here one can tell that the pistol was fast becoming Sister's most trusted weapon. The rescuers commanded the Indians to row the travelers ashore, which order they obeyed at once, being really cowards at heart. And with that observation, Sister passes with womanly concern to the state of her voluminous cotton dress, dried in masses of wrinkles after the rain. She regretted appearing thus even in the makeshift inn where they sought shelter and had their first taste of food since morning.

The cowardly Indians kept up a deafening din nearby, but Father O'Connell assured the Sisters that he and Mr. Heffernan would guard the door with pistols. This arrangement left Sister Marie Alenie undisturbed to meditate on the joys of sacrificing one's life for the "conversion of the American nation," as well as to solicit the protection of the Celestial Court for the coming day. With that unfailing help and the visible aid of their "Angel," Doctor Rabbe, well-acquainted with the route

as he was, the group next morning boarded a river steamer, one
"considered superb in those days." Their enjoyment of the gorgeous Isthmian view from the deck was suddenly shattered by
a command that the ladies go below. The Sisters obeyed at
once, but the inquisitive Mrs. Heffernan had to see what was
going on. In a few moments, however, she, too, fled in horror as
a number of murdered bodies floated by on the river. These, the
captain told them later, were the messengers who were bringing food to working crews and had been ambushed by brig-
ands. The workers, he said, were leaving because of hunger,
and improvement of the route by the government of the United
States was thus being delayed.

Presently the captain had troubles of his own for, the river
being low, his superb steamer went aground in deep sand, an
accident which caused a delay of three days. Now as provisions
ran low, the Sisters of Notre Dame felt impelled to sacrifice a
real treasure, a box of fine tea sent by Sister Louise to the
Sisters in Oregon. But the brief delay brought enjoyment, too,
as the passengers made little exploratory trips ashore for closer
views of cascades and tropical flora. Next the passengers were
rowed to Gorgona to prepare for the overland stretch, which
meant setting up a caravan that included some additional
members, and securing good pack animals and an experienced
and reliable guide. Perhaps the cost astonished Sister Marie
Alenie, since she recorded it, $64 for four mules and transpor-
tation of baggage to Panamá. She had a greater worry, though,
as some of her companions had been made quite ill from river
water, among these Father O'Connell, who seemed near dying.
Again she placed all in the keeping of the Celestial Court,
especially those on the sick list.

The caravan started with courage, unaware for the most
part that mules tend to establish their own pace. Thus the rid-
ers soon found themselves often out of sight, and even hearing,
of their nearest companions on a winding and precipitous
mountain path. At a jutting, craggy turn Sister Marie Alenie
realized her isolation with a sense of panic. Perhaps sensing her
fear, her mount suddenly bolted and threw her. Worse, she

could not immediately extricate her foot from the stirrup, swollen as it was from poison oak. So this was to be the manner of her sacrifice. And here in her story she allows herself one of those romantic and flattering revelations found in old memoirs. This, she says, was the happiest day of her life, which had never known an unhappy one, and yet she was apparently glad enough to be rescued, and that without serious injury.

Some time later Sister had reason to consider her accident a minor adventure when an unnamed member of the party, who had gone on ahead, fell into the hands of bandits. Father O'Connell and Mr. Heffernan discovered him robbed, badly beaten, and bound to a tree to die. The poor man recovered with the help of the doctor and the assurance that he was among friends, for the group presented him with his fare to San Francisco. Sister passes in mirthful vein to the next occurrence. Rounding a bend, she and a few others discovered the almost severely proper Sister Aloysius Richeat caught up in the branches of a tree by the folds of her billowing lavender skirt, her mount walking placidly away from the scene of her distress. This tiny Sister was rescued with no loss of dignity, and it is quite improbable that the incident was later mentioned in her presence.

At Panamá, Sister saw their boy guide for the first time since setting out; he had considered it his duty to keep in the lead, it seems, without concerning himself about who followed and who did not. But now she was feeling less and less concerned with affairs; in fact, she was growing quite ill with Panamá fever. Seeking for her a more comfortable place than the noisy, disorderly inn, her companions found a small and destitute contemplative convent, where a few poor Sisters cared for her, supplying the only known cure, hot tea and brandy. For the cloistered nuns, her illness was a blessing; awaiting her recovery, her companion Sisters stocked their depleted larder. Grateful to be rid of aches and fever, Sister Marie Alenie joined in preparations to board the *Sarah Sands*, the west coast Empire City Line steamer.[8]

If this "iron" steamer was itself interesting, its throng of prospectors' families was more so. Always a good mixer, Sister Marie Alenie was soon learning the hopes and fears of wives and children on their way to rejoin husbands and fathers who had gone ahead to make fortunes. Both she and Sister Louise found scope for mercy and friendliness, neither of them inhibited by the prevalent notion that the good nun must carry with her a cloister. For Sister Marie Alenie, this experience aboard the crowded *Sarah Sands* is a sort of preview of her life in the West.

Loving the beautiful, she was enraptured with San Francisco Bay but shocked by the sight of buildings, squalid and ravaged by fire. Loving people still more, she forgot both scenes when relatives or friends of some of the passengers came aboard bringing sad news of husbands who had met violent deaths, or lost all at the gambling table. She was all compassion for the recipients of such tidings, and for the city as well in which men could kill their fellow men and not be arrested. This city was, after all, just as her retreat master in Namur had described it. How fortunate that she and her Sisters were going on to Oregon!

According to Sister Marie Catherine's account, pioneer J. B. Ward sought out the Sisters and presented them to Bishop Alemany and his Vicar-General Father Anthony Langlois. To his cordial welcome, she says, the bishop added casually that the four Sisters of Notre Dame were also to remain in California, where they would find abundant scope for their zeal. Sister Marie Alenie's well-rehearsed reply was equally respectful and firm; she and her Sisters were bound for Oregon City where Sister Loyola would be awaiting them. In that case, the Bishop said, he still thought he could claim at least two of them for his diocese; surely Sister Loyola would agree to that arrangement. And as Sister Marie Alenie again demurred, he laughingly handed her Sister Loyola's letter which bade all four to remain in San Francisco, where she would presently meet them and accompany them to San Jose. Where the others are concerned, one may write it down as California's gain, but it is less easy to dismiss the case of Sister Marie Alenie. She would have been the very one to hold the foundations in Oregon. She would have understood the character and troubles of Archbishop Blanchet. She would have loved that land of tall trees and full rivers, of abiding greenness and timid wild life. She would have taken every little French-Indian to her heart. Instead, her name became a blessing in San Jose and Marysville.

Ashore the Sisters found the recently fire-gutted city even less deserving of the name than it had seemed from the deck of the *Sarah Sands*. They were shocked at the bishop's San Francisco residence, a hut, Sister Marie Alenie called it, in which her head touched the ceiling and the furniture comprised a cot, a few chairs, and a small table, with a little statue of St. Dominic. Here at the bishop's suggestion, she wrote to Sister Loyola to announce their arrival, and noted that he dispatched her letter by a messenger on horseback. Not even a dependable mail service in this land of gold! But presently she and Sister Catherine Strubbe found themselves in the comfortable and well-appointed home of French Consul Patrice Dillon, knowing that their two companions were lodged with equal hospitality in the household of Judge Patrick Barry.

So it seemed that though the condition of streets was unthinkable, carriages were quite nice, and that at least some ugly exteriors belied interiors of a certain elegance. Yet some of the noisy, sordid atmosphere penetrated even such a home. At night the air was filled with "cannonading and discharge of artillery." Had they escaped mutiny at sea only to be caught up in war on the Pacific Coast? Sister Catherine explained Independence Day, but surely California could not be included in the "States." How could the States wish to hold this land with its disorderly populace and lack of thrift? Surely one could not class New York and Ohio with a country in which gambling was a chief occupation. Sister Catherine was equally puzzled about California's fitness for statehood. Perhaps the Dillons found it no easier to explain. At any rate, they set aside political questions when Sister Loyola arrived presently from San Jose.

"Here," wrote Sister Marie Alenie years later, "was that noble woman, so full of courage, energy and zeal," and in listening to her new Superior's plans for a boarding school, she quite forgot about wilderness and distance from civilization. In reality she admired order and the amenities and Sister Loyola was aiming at both. For the time at least, Sister Marie Alenie was in complete accord with her. And for her part, Sister Loyola must have been pleased with this youthful Sister, who though professed only four years, had "boarding school experience and a knowledge of music." The other three might have seemed to fall under Mère Constantine's promise to send "persons noted for virtue rather than for intellect," as befitting a wild, new country. Sister Marie Donathilde was plainly the "good housekeeper." Sisters Catherine Strubbe and Aloysius Richeat answered her request for American teaching experience. Sister Marie Alenie, besides being youngest and most talented in the group, was also best endowed with family prestige and cultural opportunity.

This sweet-faced Sister, her naive and gentle look broken by glances of quick wisdom, was Virginie Thewissen, child of a successful merchant, John Hubert Thewissen of Maestricht, and Marie Ida Henrietta de Fooz, descendant of a noble family at the Austrian Court, one that boasted several priests and nuns and at least one bishop. At the age of four, she was sent to the Sisters of Notre Dame in Namur, and under their care developed into the typical good little Belgian schoolgirl, adept at the deep curtsy and respectful "oui, ma soeur." If in her early teens she indulged in a few injudicious imitations of St. Aloysius, such as placing a mattress of straw on her bed, however she managed that, and persuading selected friends to join her in prayer kneeling on the stones of the cellar, that was the result of overzealous instruction, or of unwholesome books for children. But such practices were soon abandoned, for Virginie was a normal and happy girl for one whose childhood had been disrupted by war.

Her memoir recalls refugee life in Flanders, return to a pillaged home and her mother weeping over the loss of her family coat of arms, and then the joy of Belgium when Leopold I accepted the throne. Then a last uprooting brought the family to Liége and Virginie to acquaintance there with Sister Marie Catherine, who talked often of foreign missions and of Oregon in particular. But alas, after that period of bracing interest, Virginie was sent to boarding school again, this time in Visé, a spiritual hothouse in which forty adolescent girls lived in devout seclusion, each receiving personal instruction in piety, and edifying their peers with bits of spiritual gossip. It speaks volumes for Virginie that despite this experience, she developed into a humble, happy young woman, rather than a sanctimonious prig. If an occasional vestige of perfectionism appears now and then in her notes, there are no such traces in her living. Her two recorded visions are a modest number for her time of writing. No doubt Virginie's friendship with Sister Marie Catherine saved her from a life of sterile piety. Whatever the influence, she entered the novitiate of Notre Dame in Namur a few months after the sailing of *l'Infatigable*, and from that time the mission in the West was like a star.

Tall, gentle-natured Sister Catherine Strubbe, who wrote no memoir and probably never expected a vision, had emigrated from Germany with her parents as a child.[9] When the family settled in Cincinnati, she became a pupil of the Sisters of Notre Dame. Her teaching experience was in the "German School," staffed by Sisters of Notre Dame, in the predominantly German quarter of the city. She spoke English well, if with a slight accent, and was in general well prepared. Her one teaching drawback, and Sister Loyola no doubt noted it, was her shyness. But refined and accustomed to American ways, she would be an asset in the boarding school, and her German classes would be small and easily managed. If Sister Catherine lacked the qualities of an educator, she possessed in a high degree those which make community livable. A little photo presents her guiding the steps of almost blind Sister Marie Catherine, her smile a study in loving reverence for this first pioneer. She outlived all the other pioneers, and Sister Anthony, S.H., who loved her dearly, made use of her clear memory in her ac-

count of Notre Dame's early western history in *Notre Dame
Quarterly*.

Little, keen-eyed Sister Aloysius Richeat, also German born,
had spent her girlhood in the boarding school at Sixth Street
in Cincinnati, and seems to have been entirely separated from
her German background.[10] Her exact English speech and her
knowledge of mathematics, together with her unfailing self-
assurance, gave promise of a successful, if rigorous, teaching
career. By nature she tended to exaggerate the Belgian ideal of
the good religious, a fact which prevented her from making Sister Catherine's sweet and gentle contribution to convent life.
Yet Sister Loyola must have read dependability and order in her
cool young eyes, and with the adolescent Californian, both
Spanish and American, in mind, those qualities must have commended the newcomer to her.

Because she remained so briefly in California, Sister Marie
Donathilde fades completely from the picture.

With this beginning of a faculty, Sister Loyola proceeded
with her plans to open school in August. Appointing Sister
Marie Alenie as mistress of the boarding school and first
teacher, and Sister Aloysius as teacher and mistress of order,
she laid the foundation of the model Belgian girls' school. The
first choice was temporary; Sister Marie Alenie would be
needed to build up a department of music. Sister Aloysius
would have been the ideal selection in any boarding school of
the century. For decades she performed her charge in a meticulous, almost military fashion that seemed a sort of ubiquitous
extension of her unimaginative classes in algebra and geometry.
Never unprepared herself, she could not tolerate lack of pre-
paredness in others, as her reports to Sunday "Lines," a sort of
weekly Dean's List, attested. Yet if she rarely smiled, neither
did she scold, and if she uttered few words of sympathy, she
was the Good Samaritan of many an occasion. Long afterwards she performed the duties of Superior in the convent in
Marysville, with a mere nod toward the social aspects of the
charge, but with total dedication to the smooth running of
household affairs. A patient at St. Joseph's Hospital in San

Francisco in 1906, she rose from her bed as soon as the great earthquake had subsided, secured dustpan and brush, and was presently found by the nurses sweeping up plaster that had fallen from her ceiling.

Sister Loyola's teaching plans become clear only as she began to transfer Sisters from Oregon to San Jose. Then her new curriculum presented a departure from that of her first boarding school, the change representing, no doubt, the advice of the Jesuit Fathers and adaptations made by the Sisters of Notre Dame in Cincinnati. There would now be emphasis on mathematics and language, the latter an ethnic necessity. For here the idea of yielding one's native tongue was in general unwelcome; the school ought somehow to present education in the student's language. With French, Spanish, and English heard commonly, there was a tendency to become at least bilingual as a practical matter. Thus Sister Marie Catherine began again to study Spanish with the help of the good Suñols and the Peralta daughters, sending off to Mexico and Valparaiso for textbooks. At this point she must have realized her linguistic limitations, but she was always ready to try the difficult and to get things started.

With the first opening day set for August 4, the work of preparing living quarters became more laborious, and to Sister Marie Alenie, suddenly attacked by a great nostalgia for Namur, the changing and reassembling of furniture to gain floor space became a trial. The attic dormitory depressed her, as did the makeshift chapel which would have to serve at least two other purposes. The large rooms, the long corridors of the mother house persisted before her mental vision, and in them the smooth-working community. The mood was probably due to fatigue as Sister was perhaps the least hardy of the group. It passed, however, and she presently found herself amused as Sister Loyola airily commissioned her to plan on teaching art as well as music. The boxes of art materials and music intended for the school in Oregon City were still en route around the Horn, and she was awaiting the arrival of the first piano. Before opening day, Sister Loyola's trips to San Francisco had netted school supplies including Sister Marie Alenie's needs. And though she had not been successful in fund collecting, she brought back with her the four first boarding students.

Judge Barry's daughter Emma, it seems, set the new school off to a brisk and intellectual start by signing in first. Hard-working as well as bright, she had already formed habits that her co-workers found difficult to emulate through her life as Sister Marie du Sacré Coeur.[11] Her bent toward studies is explained by her background. Her father migrated from Ireland to North Carolina at 18 and commenced the study of law with Judge Gaston of Raleigh. On the advice of his brother, Bishop John Barry of Savannah, he established himself in Louisiana, where he soon became District Attorney. There he married Emma Carr, daughter of a lawyer and descendant of early French settlers, and herself an unusually well-educated woman for her day. Young Emma was in fact caught between pressures of Barry zeal, for both father and uncle exploited her quick mind, and of the erudition of a mother who taught her to read in Latin and Greek as well as in French and English. A sample of the child's eagerness to learn is her attack on the Spanish language when the family was detained at Panamá by her mother's illness; in fact, according to her biographer, she was doing quite well with this language when she came to Notre Dame. Her determination appears in other matters, too, one being her vocation. Even her very pious parents, it seems, insisted, as did many others, that a daughter should weigh the matter for some years. Emma, who had cherished the idea of becoming a Sister since her childhood visits to the Religious of the Sacred Heart in her southern home, obeyed dutifully, turned down several good offers of marriage, and entered at 24. She faced life sternly; "not too genial," said outspoken Maria Lucas, who still commended her other fine qualities.

Her sweet-natured if less determined friend, Eugénie Van Damme, daughter of a secretary in the Belgian Consulate in New York, was glad to have teachers who knew her native Brussels and who, like herself, found difficulties in the English tongue.[12] The other two of these "firsts," whom Sister Marie

Catherine always referred to as "the Irish girls," were Mary
Foley and Mary Fuller. Sister was probably correct about the
nationality of the former, though nothing is known of her except that she excelled in "crochet." The second, however, was
the child of Englishman John Fuller and his Spanish wife, Concepción de Avila. Sister was deceived by her ready use of English, an unusual thing in homes with Spanish distaff side, and
this Mary used her linguistic blessing then and later to good
advantage. She counted among her friends General Mariano
Vallejo, Robert Louis Stevenson, Bret Harte, and Mark Twain.
As wife of Charles Watson Grant of Boston, and in her own
right, she was always socially prominent. A successful enter-
tainer, she loved to relate her school years at Notre Dame, of
her father paying her tuition and stage fare in gold dust, of
her childhood home, the first house in San Francisco, she
claimed, to be fitted with glass windows. Like Eugenie, this
Mary was a frequent visitor at Notre Dame long before the
existence of an organized alumnae association. It was at least
partly due to Mary's devotion to her Alma Mater that so many
noted persons visited the school in its early days.[18]

The honor of being first enrolled traditionally accorded to
Emma, Eugénie, and the two Marys, has often been disputed,
and no doubt Sister Loyola had inscribed in her book the
Suñols, the Murphys, and perhaps the Whites, some weeks
before. Besides, opening day had not yet acquired its later
character of precision; because of communications and a sort
of habitual local tempo, things were bound to be *"poco mas o
menos."* Through the beginning years, the Sisters could only
hope that the final sentence in their prospectus, which pointed
out the value of prompt registration, would catch the eye of
parents. Through the weeks of that first August, 26 boarders
and twenty day students were enrolled. Before the completion
of the two-story house, it would have been impossible to house
a larger number. At its completion, the number rose to forty,
and the original makeshifts were released for classrooms and
living quarters. But in two years Sister Marie Catherine recorded sixty boarders and forty day students, and once again

crowded space and great inconvenience. It is clear that the
Sisters might count on as many boarders as they could house,
but day students would be limited to those within walking
distance. Many of these last, too, were entered as boarders,
since residence seemed to their parents the ideal plan of
education.

And now Sister Loyola announced her intention of returning to Oregon City, where under her leadership in 1848 the
Sisters of Notre Dame had set up the boarding school. She left
Sister Marie Catherine in charge of the foundation at San Jose,
for the period of her absence, and promised to bring two or
three Sisters back with her. As she set out alone on the hard
trip back to Oregon, at the far edge of a wilderness, she was
commended to the care of the Angels by Sister Marie Alenie,
who felt she had reason to trust them. Besides safe conduct
through perils of mutiny at sea, storms and Isthmian precipices,
the Angels had brought her courage in her hours of sadness.
Sister Marie Alenie was becoming as sturdy a pioneer as Sister
Marie Catherine.

CHAPTER 3 PRIZES IN A BLUE TENT

---

*T*hough Sister Marie Catherine's progress in Spanish was slow during the following six months, she was an undoubted success in finance and leadership. In December she reimbursed Sister Superior Louise for traveling expenses of the four missionaries from Cincinnati to the West, and still closed her accounts with a small surplus. A more difficult accomplishment was maintaining general good disposition in their haphazard existence, though everyone realized that Sister's planning was logical and directed to general comfort. Reaping now the fruit of experience at St. Paul, she divided a room by stretching muslin over a frame so taut, that covered with wallpaper, it deceived the most discerning eye, a feat which she relates with gusto. And though so extremely diffident about assuming responsibility, she could express her mind decidedly to any who upset good order.[1]

"Don Juan," the gardener, whose tendencies matched those of the company he kept, stood quite in awe of Sister Marie Catherine. To keep matters under control, she had set a curfew somewhat too early for this convivial soul, and had forbidden, besides, all entertainment of his friends on the grounds, an extension of cloister that he and his pals found galling. Making her tour of the place with Sister Marie Alenie one evening, Sister detected movement in the tall mustard and felt certain that Don Juan was breaking the law. To Sister Marie Alenie, the skulking figures were marauders armed with bows and arrows, or perhaps pistols. Thus she stood horrified as her companion dashed into the mustard screaming, "Police!" and by way of sanction, "Calaboose!" But presently Juan's Mexican friends crept out of their shelter, and dashed across the *acequia* and out of sight, bearing with them the evening's good cheer, and leaving Sister Marie Alenie to marvel at the courage of Sister Marie Catherine and to ponder over western depravity.

33

No doubt Juan joined his pals at a safe moment, nor would he and his friends have guessed the solemn words inspired by the incident in Sister Marie Alenie's notes. The poor neglected Mexicans and Indians, she wrote, were not to be blamed for murders and other crimes. They were untaught, and when strangers deprived them of their lands, plunder seemed their only means of livelihood. She must pray for "a more settled form of government," her ideal being, it would seem, one that would send all grasping newcomers back to "the States" at once. But she was most distressed to hear that "criminals," such as Juan's tempters, lying in wait with their bottles in the mustard, were generally regarded as Catholics. For with all her sweet charity she was steeped in the prevailing unecumenical notion that evil customs should be somehow attributed to those of other creeds.

Sister would have been astonished to learn that the progress of her little group was causing like distress in a nearby quarter. For as the Sisters converted old boards into school benches, the Reverend Isaac Owen was including in his statistical report for 1851 a troubled plea to Dr. J. P. Durbin of the Methodist Episcopal Missionary Board on behalf of "Bro. Bannister's San Jose Academy." If only the Board, he wrote, would send a strong man and a good teacher, "the right sort," the school would "maintain itself," and the group would "hold ground in this valley." The "Catholicks," he said, had already established a "female Institute in San Jose, and were collecting a large number of young ladies, and girls, into their school."[2] Brother Bannister had little need to worry about competition from the Sisters of Notre Dame, nor did Sister Marie Alenie have reason to fear the ill opinion of those of other creeds. For from the beginnings established timidly by Brother Bannister has arisen the present University of the Pacific, and from Sister Alenie's day, unfriendly opinion has never deterred non-Catholic parents from enrolling their daughters at Notre Dame. Governor and Mrs. John McDougal were happy to leave their niece Ella with the Sisters when the capital departed from San Jose, and to enroll their daughter Susan with her two years later.[3] Eva

Bascom, too, was an early student whose locally notable non-Catholic family had nothing but praise for their daughter's school.[4]

In time Sister Marie Alenie discovered the fine good will of such families and ceased to worry about the honor of her fellow Catholics. But the long life of this interfaith touchiness is due, no doubt, to the fact that it was nourished in hearts of such good will as a point of loyalty. It was probably virtue that prompted the warning in the *California Christian Advocate* that the Sisters in San Jose were obliging their non-Catholic students to follow chapel exercises with the added implication of proselytizing. And certainly it was fear that motivated Sister Loyola's defense in the *Daily Alta California*.[5] It was better, according to the saintly Father Peter de Voss, S.J., to have no education at all than one not based on principles of Faith. By this argument he hoped to coerce Daniel Murphy by means of indirect appeal to his father, Martin Murphy, Sr., to whom he offered Archbishop Alemany and the Council of Baltimore as authorities. For Daniel was sending his stepsons, children of his wife, Mary Fisher, by an earlier marriage, to a school other than Santa Clara College, perhaps because, like some of the third generation Murphys, they objected to the discipline of a Jesuit school.[6] The phrase "Protestant school" which meant any outside the fold, was as dread a specter as the phrase "Catholic school," and even so sensitive a soul as Sister Marie Alenie lived in fear of it.

Such fears arose, of course, from lack of knowledge, which would have discovered for both sides bonds of sympathy. That same lack prevented for some years a wholesome public attitude on the part of the Sisters. Leading persons were important only inasmuch as they were kindly disposed to them. They fail to remark, for instance, that Susan McDougal was daughter of the governor who succeeded Peter Burnett. And if Sister Marie Alenie is careful to give Peter Burnett his title, she pays this tribute as to a kind friend of her Sisters in their Oregon days, and because his daughter Letitia, the recent bride of Caius Tacitus Ryland, would scarcely have failed to impress Sister with her father's historical and political importance when she came to Santa Clara Street for her weekly piano lessons.

One would like to have a recording of Sister's encounters with that beautiful but formidable young woman, whose name appears as "Lady Ryland" on two numbers in the Ryland music collection presented to College of Notre Dame many years ago by her family. For lovely Letitia shared the Burnett habit of prolonging for hours debates set up at the breakfast table, arguments the conclusion of which usually appeared as her conviction in the opening sentence. She enjoyed, through a generous life span, the frail health of a Dickensian heroine, a feat which is perhaps another facet of her determined character. Her younger sisters, Romieta J. and Sally C. Burnett, enrolled among the first day pupils at Notre Dame, must have enlivened Sister Marie Alenie's classes in religion since, in this field especially, the Burnetts were deadly debaters.[7]

By reason of these and other encounters, Sister Marie Alenie acquired a fair command of English during that year, and despite heavy labor, her health and spirit improved greatly. For, as Sister explained, such expedients as rising at four in the morning so as to avoid working late into the night, failed to bring actual relief. The laundry presented the greatest difficulty, as long as they had to carry water from the *acequia*. Even with well and pump, they still carried in huge buckets of water to boiler and tubs. From the washboards, they hastened to the chapel for mass at 6:30, and from thence to their daily routine, a schedule which never grew monotonous, what with such incidents as rain pouring in through loosened tiles of the adobe roof and streaking freshly laundered bedspreads with mud. But as Sister Marie Alenie observed, it did not kill them. They met the challenges with young vigor, managing always to have well-cooked nutritious meals and a bundle of nicely folded and ironed garments on every bed each Friday. They were bringing order out of chaos. Even their pupils were sharing this happy mastery over things as they seized boards and "horses" that had just served as their dinner table and converted dining room into art studio. And whenever things seemed a bit overstrenuous, or verging on the impossible, they looked for comfort at the two-story house nearing completion, and hoped to have it in nice order before Sister Loyola's return.

In the spring of 1852 Sister Loyola returned from Oregon bringing with her Sisters Mary Cornelia Neujean, Aldegonde Delpire and Norbertine Vereux, her covoyagers of 1844, their transfer made possible by the closing of the foundation at St. Paul. The last two were not teachers, but they were both ingenious and strong. Before leaving her homeland, Sister Aldegonde had learned weaving. She could set up a loom, its bolts and chains no mystery to her, and her homespun had provided many a Willamette native child brought to St. Paul, a deerskin tunic her sole garment, with an equally durable woolen dress.

Sister Norbertine, a lonely soul inclined to querulous moods, was blessed with a green thumb. If the legend that she planted a thousand trees on the Willamette leans to the epic side, certainly the account books show that her gardens and fields supplied both houses in Oregon, and insured some little income as well. Besides, Sister loved to plot out flower gardens and border them with shrubs; in bringing her to San Jose, Sister Loyola had an eye to landscape gardening.

Sister Mary Cornelia's transfer was in line with the specific directive of the Mother General. In the summer and autumn of 1851 Mère Constantine had addressed three strong-opinioned letters to Sister Loyola who probably received all of them before returning to San Jose. From these letters it becomes clear that Sister Loyola had presented her plan to abandon the Oregon mission entirely, and that Mère Constantine was worried about the changing plans.[8] She decided that Sister Mary Cornelia should be Superior of the new house in San Jose; this choice was a definite order and with no temporary clause. That Sister Loyola failed to note its finality and for two years continued to exert leadership in building and organizing the school was probably due to Sister Mary Cornelia's humble interpretation of it, but clearly, in appointing her to this more promising post, the central government was transferring leadership to her. A subsequent letter, in fact, indicates regret that the leadership of the western mission had not at first been placed in the hands of Sister Mary Cornelia.[9]

Sister Marie Catherine's welcome to Sister Mary Cornelia is charged with admiration. Recalling their years at St. Paul, she rejoiced to see her reinstated in superiorship. Knowing herself as few mortals know themselves, she handed over authority to her old friend as most fitting, happy at renewal of their former relationship. For the time, Sister Loyola would bustle about, arranging and controlling matters; that seemed natural enough, but she would eventually return to Oregon and beyond that Sister Marie Catherine was too present-minded to conjecture. Her chief concern was sleeping quarters. Through the months of Sister Loyola's absence, boarders had been drifting in, announced or otherwise. There were forty or more that spring, and another year would perhaps double that number. The two-story house was soon overtaxed, and the older girls were again housed, merrily enough it seems, under the rattling tiles of the long adobe.

Now Sister Loyola began to talk of a large brick unit, the first of a full-grown plan. Her talk was all of that plan now when she was not engrossed in preparations for the closing of the first session; it was important to make that as impressive as possible, a two-day "exhibition" with "fair specimens" of work from all classes.

In dry California summer weather an outdoor closing presented only the problem of lack of shade trees, but as usual Sister Marie Catherine was quick to solve it. Since the departure of the capital from San Jose, large tents were more readily available than were knives and forks. With unhoused crowds flocking in at the opening of the first session, pueblo women had hastily stitched together these tents of canvas or blue jean cloth, Grandma Bascom's famous Blue Tent, which served as the first Baptist Church in the valley, being perhaps the most spectacular.[10] Sister secured one of these tents, and Don Juan knew a period of well-supervised employment during which a stage was constructed for performers and instruments, with benches facing it for the audience. As space could not have allowed for

the presence of the pupils, sitting in white-clad decorum while
awaiting their turns, they must have stood in silent lines outside
until a signal bade them enter for their first deep curtsy. In that
first audience were the Murphys, the Kells, the Picos, the
Suñols, all the local families, and of course the "Senators."
Notre Dame's annual Exhibition was launched. The tent soon
gave place to a great outdoor stage; the audience a few years
later numbered some 1200 and the city hotels were overcrowded
as parents and friends arrived from great distances to enjoy mornings of music and declaiming, afternoons of drama, and most of
all, as Sister Marie Alenie said, "to see their darlings decked
with crowns and medals." The prizes were conspicuous; crowns
heavy with silken oak leaves and actual size acorns, though
adding little to girlish beauty, were well worth a parent's journey from Sonoma or Santa Barbara; so were the runner-up
prizes, mostly books of an edifying nature, dated and autographed by the Sister Superior.

Between exercises the fond parents were invited to view the
specimens of penmanship, school work, needlework samplers,
designs in needlepoint, crayon drawings and water colors "executed" by their offspring. Even in that first year, Isabel Ramírez, at the age of 12 years, completed a little masterpiece in
bright threads on white watered taffeta. In its gold setting and
frame it hangs in Ralston Hall at College of Notre Dame, as
distinguished in a room of rare antiques as is her ancestral line.
And as Isabel stepped up for scholastic honors at that first
closing, none could have missed her look of maturity and seren-
ity. If the Sainsevains were present, they would whisper the
identity of this first little student of Notre Dame from Southern
California. For Pierre Sainsevain acted as local guardian of
Isabel and her brothers, Francisco and Juan. Their maternal
great grandfather, Cornelio Avila, had assisted the early Padres
as Majordomo General. His son, Francisco, had built the old
Avila Adobe, in 1818, now a State Historical Monument. In
1830 Francisco's daughter Petra married Juan M. Ramírez, who
founded the Ramírez Vineyard where Union Terminal in Los
Angeles is now located.

Isabel displayed such unusual promise that her godfather, Louis Vigne, generously paid her boarding school bills at Notre Dame. Francisco became a brilliant lawyer and editor of the first Spanish newspaper under the American regime. Assisting him in his office, Isabel acquired knowledge which helped her especially in her future role of adviser to Italian immigrants in the expanding wine industry of the Los Angeles area. Examining her needlepoint, one is not surprised at the successes of its maker; there is about it a loving care, and total impression rarely found in the work of a 12-year-old.[11]

The College today treasures also the exquisitely stitched sampler done by Fermina Sanchez for that same closing. Fermina appears to have been an older sister, or perhaps an older cousin of Refugia, Calendaría, and Guadalupe Sanchez, who were almost certainly the daughters of Don José María Sanchez and Encarnación Ortega. For girls like Fermina, that opening year at Notre Dame meant a fleeting brush with culture before they settled down to married life. For such the sampler was a reference book of needlecraft, a great page of patterns worked out fully but with total absence of creativity. Yet in its use, both hand and eye were trained in precision, as artistic taste was developed in color, space, and proportion. Like needlepoint, the sampler was at first considered a branch of art and was thus directed by Sister Marie Alenie, whose experience had been reproduction of finished copies. In fact, Sister was a bit nonplussed when Sister Loyola suggested arranging real fruits and flowers as models in lieu of pictures of still life. She did allow pupils of obvious talent to paint from objects themselves, not subjectively, of course, but as nearly as possible as a camera would produce them. For herself, however, and for most students, she thought copying the suitable approach to art. That parents, friends, and reporters shared this idea is clear from their generous praise of art pieces that were obviously copies. They were so lavish in praise of everything in fact, at that first closing, that the reputation of the fledgling school was doubtless better served by it than by any number of ads in the *Daily Alta California*.

The Sisters' most serious problem was that as yet they had done nothing for the poor Spanish-speaking children of the pueblo. Yet this was their acknowledged first duty and, before returning again to Oregon in June, Sister Loyola discussed plans for a "poor school" with Sister Mary Cornelia, as a project parallel with her dream boarding school, the financial success of which would make it possible. With their Belgian background, these two Sisters easily accepted the idea of complete separation of "free school" children from both boarders and paying day pupils, an idea heavily underlined in this instance by the attitude of both groups toward the poor Spanish Californians of the pueblo. For the children of these families then there must be a special building as well as special teachers; separation must be complete. And there were other families, not to be included in this lowest social group, people who did not live in squalor and who maintained traditional dignity. These Sister Loyola classed as "land-poor," too proud, she said, to accept education with resident or day boarders without paying the full tuition, and her plan for these and all the less well off was to be realized later in Notre Dame Academy.

The plan for this separate day school fell in conveniently enough with the feeling of the Belgian Sisters about "externs." They would have approved of it, in fact, for paying day-boarders as well, as furnishing a milieu of greater seclusion for their resident pupils. For these last, their adolescence steeped in a piety enhanced by at least some share in the religious life of the Sisters, would emerge, the latter hoped, as an elite Christian womanhood. Except on their rare outings, they would know only Sister-supervised recreations, and would thus be saved from "the world." The training did not foster religious vocations, which for many years were few. It very often did produce the pious maiden-lady, a fact which did not have for the Sisters the psychological implications which it carries today. Such a woman, it seemed to them, would bring otherworldliness to her position as social leader; she would organize culture and charity; she would lead her social peers away from frivolity. While a fond mother would add finery to her daughter's trousseau, the boarding school was making of her a dignified, gracious and pious matron or, and it perhaps seemed a step nearer perfection, the ornament of the parental house, with these common notes intensified. And since this experience of total unworldliness was denied to the best of "externs," their parents were advised by the Sisters to give them if possible at least one year in the boarding school. It may be noted here that although, as Sister Marie Alenie observes, a number of both "American and Spanish young ladies" took somewhat unkindly to the notion of boarding school as the highest good, many parents were in fairly complete approval of it. The times were inclined to wildness, and even despite their own gold-getting and gambling, they viewed with alarm certain tendencies in their offspring which seemed to call for the training and seclusion of boarding school.

Reporting matters to the Mother General, Sister Loyola stressed the need of a school for "externs" as well as for the children of the poor. These were things hoped for as compared with the already-achieved success of the boarding school. In a few months this last had won a wide reputation; "everyone speaks of it all over California." Though it stood in need of more teachers, it had made a fine beginning. Buildings and enlarged staff will bring the daughters of all the wealthy families in the West to San Jose.[12] This was certainly true. But it was also true that the school on Santa Clara Street had at the moment greater assurance of success than had most investments in the valley. Since the debacle of the state capital, money was flowing toward San Francisco. Loans for a local venture were difficult to obtain, a circumstance which might make building difficult if not impossible.

It was well for the Sisters that Martin Murphy, Sr., had enough faith in their enterprise to assume risks for its benefit. Rich in lands, this generous friend was, as his will reveals, a man poor in money. One dry winter like that of 1850-1851 could render cattle, his chief source of income, unmarketable, and at best his animals lost weight in the long trek on foot to San Francisco. Thus it is entirely probable that he mortgaged a section of his land to help Sister Marie Catherine acquire property in the spring of 1852. Then as that loan of $2000, without interest, was not enough, he responded to Sister Loyola's appeal on her return from the North with a like sum, its interest to be applied to the tuition of his granddaughter, Elizabeth Yuba. These two loans were, in fact, only the beginning of a long series of Murphy loans which made possible the development of Notre Dame in San Jose. Until weighed against economic facts, the interest paid by the Sisters on these later borrowings may tend to present Martin Murphy, Sr., in a less generous light. With an understanding of these facts, however, he easily resumes his traditional role of benefactor. Certainly his willingness to help contributed to Sister Loyola's trust in the future of her venture when she set out once more for Oregon after that first June closing of her school.

Affairs were disheartening in the tall white house in Oregon City. There the two teachers, Sisters Mary Aloysia Chevry and Mary Bernard Weber, were prostrated by a fever which Sister Marie Catherine sets down as malaria. Nine of the remaining 12 paying boarders had just announced their departure. Sister Loyola might have straightway abandoned the Oregon venture had she not determined to dispose of property there before the final break. In February, however, she made a hurried trip to San Jose, transferring two more Sisters to the new foundation and leaving in charge, during her absence, Sister Mary Aloysia, whose sorrow over the departure of the Sisters from the Willamette Valley and sympathy with the trials of Archbishop Blanchet are recorded in her first letter to the Mother General from California.[13]

Returning again to Oregon City, Sister Loyola found the archbishop's annoyance intensified by her failure to advise him of her absence, and this discovery spurred her will to rapid action. The dispatch with which she carried out an auction sale and found homes for her orphan charges is a tribute to her ability. By mid-April all was in readiness for the departure of the Sisters of Notre Dame from the Willamette Valley.

Sister Mary Aloysia and her companions left Oregon sadly, remembering the hard work, privations and obstacles that had attended their work in building the missions at St. Paul and Oregon City, and most of all the children there whom they had come to love. Their hope eventually to return was still nourished by Sister Mary Cornelia some years later.

Archbishop Blanchet, too, was saddened by their departure and long clung to a hope of their return. His payments made on Sister Loyola's sometimes unreasonable demands testified to his desire to win good will. These payments, the auction and the sale of the big white house in Oregon City all come as a shock to anyone who might be under the impression that the Willamette Valley had been deserted.

One can only regret that Sister Loyola did not see fit to leave some of the Sisters to continue the work begun there, and rejoice that others soon found it possible to relight the torch.

CHAPTER 4   BRICK AND POLISHED PINE

*A*ttracted by the sound of the stagecoach late one afternoon in April, 1853, one of the older girls rushed to a window with unladylike eagerness and beheld Sister Loyola getting down with three strange Sisters. With equal precipitation she shared the news with her companions, and suddenly the value of street windows as points of vantage rose to new heights. For once, there were no Sisters about to point up such lack of decorum, for they themselves were converging from all points with even greater speed though with less noise at the street gate. Their grand welcome of the travelers afforded the window viewers brief excitement before all disappeared into the convent enclosure, leaving pupils to their customary world of conjecture, and somewhat unfairly, considering that their stampede had warned Sister Marie Catherine of the exciting arrival.[1]

For one of the new arrivals, Sister Mary Aloysia Chevry, the moment was charged with shock as well as joy, as she noticed the "pallor and thinness" of the Sisters in San Jose. These, she saw, had been reliving their building days in Oregon, painting, hammering, scrubbing, washing and ironing, with scant regard for rest. She had as quick an eye, too, for scholastic difficulties and shortcomings, as well as immediate opportunity to assess them. Assuming authority, which Sister Mary Cornelia yielded to her without hesitancy, Sister Loyola assigned the more advanced classes to Sister Mary Aloysia and Sister Mary Bernard Weber, and these included the Spanish pupils, since the lay Spanish teacher had recently withdrawn. Both Sisters had been studying that language for some time, but of course with accentual results quite foreign to native ears. Thus in her class in mathematics, Sister Mary Aloysia found herself helpless. Her attempts to convey numerical truths in French or English were futile, even with girls who were beginning to exchange other

45

than scholastic matters in either or both. In the classroom the "Spanish Young Ladies" were adamant; they must be taught in their ancestral tongue. Willing even to help their teacher in this matter, they wrote Spanish mathematical terms on the board and pronounced them patiently for her since they found her "muy simpatico." They greeted her efforts with high approval and bewildering runs of class comment. It was thus give and take until closing day after which Sister obtained such competent tutoring that autumn found her reading stories *en español* to pleased juniors, and generally accepted by all the señoritas.

But Sister Mary Aloysia found more serious problems. Writing after the closing, she relates the fiasco of the first public examinations undertaken somewhat precipitously by Sister Loyola. In these, she said, the children were "embarrassed," and the teachers "entirely humiliated." For many of those girls of 12 or 14 were just learning to read and write, and under pressure to produce the impossible, their teachers had set certain questions to be learned, a preparation which was the general practice of the day. But as the examiners saw fit to ignore the question lists, the pupils for the most "answered badly in the two languages." A glance at the list of inquisitors may help somewhat to explain the general wilting, for kind Father Peter DeVoss, S.J., whom the pupils considered a friend, could scarcely offset Vicar-General John F. Llebaria, Ex-Governor Burnett, and French Consul Patrice Dillon. In their hands chemistry, astronomy, and "uses of the globes," could become formidable. As group after group went down under the assault, it was not the examiners, but the parents who looked disappointed and grim. To soften the stark truth, Sister added with her abiding humorous tact that by afternoon the audience had come round to a kinder view of the matter. The examiners, some of them said, had gone a little too far; perhaps they could not have answered all of their own questions. However, next morning's conferring of prizes "reconciled all." Yet Sister did not rescind her own estimate of the pupils' responses. There was great need of better teaching.[2] Facing truth squarely, she would not disapprove of the public examination, as some did, as not proper in a girls' school, nor did she offer any serious excuse for the failure, and she had matured beyond the notion that only pleasant reports must be made to the mother house.

But the reporter of *San Francisco Daily Herald* was quite carried away.[3] Describing the assembled student group, he declared that none would believe "such an array of youth and beauty could be seen in California." Examination responses he commended as "exceedingly prompt and creditable," a statement which more likely described the glib answers of Sally Burnett and a few others about whom Sister Mary Aloysia entertained no worries. Amanda Brannan, he wrote, "gave proof of a high order of talent" as she dramatized the "Mother of Moses" in a piece translated from the French. And the same star also read "a letter of condolence from one friend to another on the death of a mother, which in sentiment and diction was equal to anything from the pen of Mrs. Hemans." Spanish names listed for special praise in this report ring like evening chimes of California's halcyon days: Isabel Ramírez, Dismas Fernández, Isabel Castro, Lucía Valencia, Hilarita Reed.[4] A few, like the two Isabels, excelled generally; but most clustered around needlework, tapestry, and drawing, in which accomplishments, as Sister Mary Aloysia said, "the Spaniards carried all before them." The cynosure of this array was Isabel Castro's drawing of the Castle of Fontainebleau, which according to the *Herald*, "excited the admiration of everyone who saw it."

Though Sister Loyola agreed with Sister Mary Aloysia about the school's actual needs, she could not have been other than pleased and impressed with that second closing, which though held in a great tent, had drawn 600, among them leaders of both San Jose and San Francisco. Heading the list of distinguished guests were, "Ex-governor Burnett and lady; the Baron Bendenleben; Mons. Dillon and lady; Mons. Pinet and lady; Mlle DeBoom; Judge Hester and lady; Judge Barry; Samuel Brannan, Esq.; Signor DeLeon; C. T. Ryland and lady; Signor Ainsa; Signor Suñol . . ." And all of the 600 had carried away the 18-inch broadside program, proof of culture on Santa

Clara Street and reminder of high-phrased, original dramatic bits by Mary Fitzgerald, Mary Barry and other Americans, as well as piano numbers "executed" by Señorita Virginia DeLeon, Francisca and Antonía Suñol, and Francisca Ainsa, whose soulful eyes gave no promise of the possibilities they found in "Ben Bolt, Variations," "Evergreen Waltz," and "Saratoga Schottisch."[5] In all, that program maintained delicate balance between instruction and delight; no doubt all enjoyed the moment of relief afforded by Amanda Brannan's solo, "Coming thru' the Rye," set amid the moralistic scenes entitled "The Value of Time."[6] And if that broadside commanded respect, Sister Loyola's ambitious printed booklet of prizes offered still greater reason. Seven pages of winners and runners-up made an impressive total for a school just completing its second year, and considering the tendency of parents to agree to the justice of awards made to their offspring, there seems little wonder that the former day's failure of the glib response was soon forgotten. Those old enough and fortunate enough to recall academy school days, will understand the peaks of excitement that marked "Distribution of Prizes." Rows of schoolgirls might sit still as statues. Sisters might appear sweetly unconcerned. All knew these external attitudes were deceptive as they were proper, as parents present, especially fathers, gave more appropriate responses.

The two-day performance, with added days of travel for guests who came from distances, seemed time well spent considering the school's attainment in so short a period. The guests could form some estimate of the rate of progress as Sister Loyola showed them the foundation of the first brick unit of her campus plan, a foundation of great redwood piles, selected as being most impervious to dampness. Those interested might view the full plan, drawn that spring by Architect Kerwin. For the first unit, Sister Loyola had secured large loans from Peter Davidson and Martin Murphy, Sr., to cover initial cost, risks which appalled Sister Marie Catherine and the other Sisters. It seems unlikely that any of the Sister's trusted friends would have considered great expenditure as yet advisable.[7] What led her finally to accept a more modest building scale was her new architect's astonishment and refusal to proceed on such extravagant lines, a fact recorded by Sister Marie Catherine with some relief. To her the stately first unit that did arise seemed risk enough. Sister Mary Aloysia must have shared this relief. Her chief worry was passage money for Sisters that she hoped Mère Constantine might find it possible to send. For that alone, she said, they would need a mine in their garden.[8] But insisting that such views arose from lack of trust, Sister Loyola proceeded. Through 1854 her indebtedness reached $49,000, and despite the success of the boarding school, payments were for a long time mostly interest.

Other than monetary difficulties, too, attended the construction of the first unit. With what seems a strange lack of central responsibility, the brick mason, who also furnished the bricks, was paid by the Sisters, as was also the carpenter. Thus one finds in the convent accounts such items as $160 for two large doors. Yet full responsibility for the construction lay in the hands of the architect-builder, who, as it turned out, had "so many irons in the fire" that he failed to give Notre Dame's new building sufficient attention. It was perhaps this neglect that seemed to warrant the degree of supervisory privilege assumed by the Sisters. At any rate, it was fortunate that they had had a similar experience in Oregon City. The most serious problem was the chapel wing. Here complicated measurements quite puzzled the builders until Sister Loyola and Sister Marie Catherine arrived, rulers in hand, to clear up obscurities.[9] They must have regretted not having their good friend, Levi Goodrich, in charge, and it is gratifying to note that his name appears later on in Notre Dame construction.

Fortunately, problems lay mostly in matters of construction. The boarding school, despite its living quarters, began to run with smoothness after the arrival of the last Sisters from Oregon. The staff was still far from sufficiently large, but all were resourceful workers toughened by experience on the Willamette. Those not adapted to teaching founded and headed the "charges," a division of responsibilities that resulted in easy and reliable functioning of household departments.

Thus smiling Sister Francisca Gernaey established the bakery which through the following decades supplied community and boarding school with fine white bread, with breakfast cornbread that became a tradition, and with delicious rolls and desserts. Often in the earlier years, the huge bins in that bakery were filled with flour received as tuition, and it was Sister Francisca's duty to keep an account of these deposits as also of payments in butter. Besides, Sister's charge included management of the boarders' dining room, or refectory, as it was called. In a small adjoining room she cut thick slices of her golden-crusted loaves before each meal and patted generous helpings of butter with her grooved wooden paddles. From the door of this sanctum, she reviewed the servers, young Sisters and Novices, arriving from the kitchen with large trays, each awaiting her smile of approval. She supervised table setting, too, a simple, unadorned matter in those days, with stress on immaculate linen and the art of "spotting" it between bi-weekly changing. Even after a fall which left her unable to stand erect, Sister Francesca carried on her charge, to the end smiling on good servers and on every pupil who came to thank her for some favorite dish.

Tall and placid Sister Odelie Golard, who had devised little dresses that caused orphans on the Willamette to strut about like peacocks, in San Jose turned her hand with equal skill to the production of schoolgirl uniforms that conformed, a little belatedly, to current fashions. Uniforms included headgear, and as it turned out, Sister Odelie's special talent was hatmaking. In the first years, of course, it was rather a matter of bonnets, the girls procuring the desired "shape" in the milliner's shop, and Sister applying the modest decor. When the hat replaced the bonnet, Sister undertook the entire production, fitting each girl, regardless of facial contour, with a wide-brimmed shape of buckram, or such, which she covered with silk or satin, adding a few loops of ribbon. No flowers, no plumes. In the old pictures, the maid of the lovely locks, holds her hat, as a rule, coyly in her hands. Others, not so blessed by nature, don the hats jauntily, often a bit recklessly, for the photographer, as though, after all, the daredevil might be fully as intriguing as the beauty. Of course the arrangement may have been the photographer's notion, a fancy akin to that of posing subjects of all ages perilously on one foot, the other crossing it at an impossible angle.

Be that as it may, Sister Odelie considered both gown and hat slightly on the dressy side, as became an outfit worn only on Sunday, but without ministering in any way to vanity. Young ladies, she believed, should never appear ostentatious. To prevent so great an evil, Sister gently aided the reluctant maidens to lay finery away in their trunks, folly not to be donned again until they were departing for home. If this Sunday dress regulation drops heavily into the Blue Law category, daily dress, though not uniform, was also hedged about by all known negatives. After six days of such apparel, Sister Odelie's hats must have seemed even "a little dressy." But if this invasion of one of woman's cherished realms of interest met often with young western resentment, calmly smiling Sister Odelie, herself, according to all reports, did not encounter it. She was, it seems, quite a favorite.

Sister Aldegonde Delpire, a more stolid and less ingratiating soul, headed the charge then known as "dortoirs," and later often referred to as "blankets." Sister's almost Amazonian build and strength fitted her well for the several duties included under either title, the most onerous perhaps being the weaving of woolen blankets for community and boarding school. Sister had learned the craft in Belgium in preparation for the Oregon Mission where a decade had made her an expert. In San Jose her loom produced a supply of fine blankets that outlived the century, the last of them grown a ripe corn color. Until stooped with years, Sister Aldegonde supervised the making of mattresses, which were taken apart when they lost their rounded contours, their contents cleaned and "teased," probably with *teasel,* on a huge spike frame. This monster, together with the loom and large spinning wheel, were retired at last to a dark corner in "Egypt" where they were pointed out to new novices to the last days of the college in San Jose. But weaving and mattress-making were for Sister Aldegonde's quiet hours. Her exacting responsibility was care of the long dormitories, the cleanliness of which the starched white alcove curtains were obvious symbols. These curtains, hanging in precise pleats, told of hours of bleaching in summer sun, of "pulling," folding, and mangling, of finishing with old-fashioned irons, all under Sister Aldegonde's watchful eye, as along with Sister Odelie and Sister Francisca, she laid the foundation of Notre Dame's ménage.

Another who set the stage was Sister Mary Albine Gobert, the little sunbeam of the voyage of 1844 whose smile was said to resemble that of Blessed Mère Julie. In her office of infirmarian, that smile facilitated administration of her *médecines*, and made amends, too, for her inability to master the English language. The smile, it is true, gave place to slightly raised brows at unasked, and certainly uninterpreted young American or Spanish opinion, and Sister's strong index finger pointing to the obnoxious *médecine*, counseled compliance without further observation. In her second responsibility, the embroidery room, Sister probably found little reason for the dictatorial approach. Here she dealt mainly with the artistic señoritas. In that room too, Sister was following her own bent as she embroidered with golden thread the first of the elaborate chapel vestments, which over the years came to be a rich and varied treasure. Besides all this time-consuming work, Sister wrote long newsletters to Namur.

Also a scribe, seemingly better educated than Sister Marie Albine, was Sister Laurence Lejeune. In San Jose, Sister Loyola appointed her teacher, probably of the younger boarders. Sister was Notre Dame's first annalist in the West, writing of course in French, which perhaps suffered in translation. Glints of humor, however, recall her good letters from Oregon to Namur, and make the loss of her original annals regrettable. Her early illness and death perhaps account for her quite complete oblivion in California, beyond a shadowy tradition of sweet gentleness.

Her voyage companion, Sister Alphonse Marie Vermuylen, now joined forces with Sister Marie Alenie in establishing a music department with somewhat greater promise than had appeared on the first closing program. With her upper middle-class background, good general education, and special musical training and ability, this Sister would have graced any academy of the time. Besides these advantages, the administration of her father's estate after his death had given her business and legal experience that made her a decided asset despite her frail health. She assisted Sister Marie Catherine in the business office as she did Sister Marie Alenie in music; in fact, she assisted everyone, the one charge which she set up and headed being the little book store known as the *dépôt*. But poor health may account only partly for Sister's place in the background; she possessed Sister Mary Aloysia's delicate thoughtfulness of others; her appreciation of her Sisters amounted to reverence. Even her youngest pupils recognized this attitude, for one thing in the care with which she wrote their names, the least of them deserving her most careful and artistic airy tracery.

Another of the final arrivals from Oregon City, Sister Mary Bernard Weber, daughter of a prosperous and well-educated German family, though as humble as Sister Alphonse Marie, was much more vigorous and likely to take the initiative.[10] Still, for all her ability, she, too, managed a degree of self-forgetting; she took so to heart the advice not to boast of one's family that after 24 years in the West, she left no trace of her ancestral name, merely her religious signature here and there, a few references in Archbishop Alemany's letter book, and in Marysville, a general if somewhat vague reputation for charity. In 1856 she built the towered brick house in Marysville, styled in that throwback to Gothic that marked many early Victorian edifices, too ambitious many said later, not recalling that Marysville at that time held much greater promise than did San Jose as the site of a large boarding school.

Whatever the reason, Sister Mary Bernard was transferred in 1872 to New England, where none even dreamed of her fine work in the Sacramento Valley until, on a visit to her convent,

Bishop Eugene O'Connell told of her humility as well as her
success. But again she suffered eclipse until recently a faded
memoir, the work of a lifelong admirer, was restored and has
come to light. Here she appears as the friend of thousands of
New England factory girls, a woman whose wisdom was sought
by bishops and pastors, but who found time to correspond with
the Reed daughters of Marin and to encourage literary endeavor in San Francisco. Whatever classes she may have taught
in San Jose, her presence there was certainly a blessing, and her
English, no doubt still strongly accented, was certainly not a
barrier to understanding. In San Jose Sister Mary Bernard may
have shared Sister Marie Catherine's misgivings about risks and
indebtedness, as she shared in the general labor of the brief
holiday, only a little more than a month, in the summer of 1853.
For the prospect of increased enrollment now necessitated re-
adaptation of "sheds" abandoned when the first convent was
completed.

At sight of the progress made on the palatial new building,
girls signing in for the fall semester could well put up with
crowded quarters for a while. Some of them, perhaps the majority, and certainly those housed in the old adobe near the
street, began to anticipate the coming transfer to the great
brick house with a degree of regret, as they assessed its distance
from the entrance. It was at least amusing that the adobe windows should keep Sister Marie Catherine and Sister Marie
Alenie in a state of perturbation shared less obviously by Sister
Mary Aloysia and Sister Mary Bernard. There was, for instance,
the last St. Patrick's Day, a holiday for the Murphys and Kells,
but as gratefully enjoyed by the de Haros and the Valencias. In
the midst of their hilarity, a young Irishman, with "a drop too
much," as Sister Marie Catherine explained, looked in from the
street, smiled approval, and declared that never before had he
beheld such beautiful young ladies, and if the much-chap-
eroned señoritas ran shrieking, they were probably less sincere
than were the giggling Americanas on this occasion. For all of
them the massive house in preparation must have promised cur-
tailment of possibilities; at a glance one could see that it was

planned for central control. After all, there was something to be
said for the status quo, for with a bit of good fortune one might
be housed in one of the less closely supervised, if more uncom-
fortable, scattered units, in which one enjoyed a sense of
freedom.

Still a great deal of excitement and fun attended the actual
moving into the new building during the Christmas holiday,
which the majority spent at school in those pre-railroad days.
The Sisters, especially Sister Marie Alenie, found somewhat less
enjoyment in the process, exhausted as they were with removing bits of plaster from pine floors and waxing them, the
latter the less back-breaking task, but both performed in early
morning hours and after classes, with endless washing of windows as a change. But it was worth all the labor to have the
girls housed in large, airy dormitories and well-lighted classrooms, and to possess at last a chapel worthy of the name, one
that bore some resemblance to the church at the Mother House.

That this likeness might be some day more complete, the
chapel wing was elevated some four or five feet above the first
floor level to allow for future vestibule, grand portico and descending steps. It would then constitute a separate unit, joined
to the main building only by a side entrance. But for the time,
there could be neither vestibule nor portico. Instead, wide steps
descended into the long main corridor in what was hoped to be
a temporary arrangement. The dream of a grand facade persisted for decades, and an architect's drawing of a later date, a
plan that was never realized, was first inspired by Sister Loyola.
The arched windows had to wait years for their stained glass,
too. But in all it was a lovely chapel, deserving somewhat the
flattering description of reporters, who did not realize how far
it fell short of the "church" in Namur, but who knew enough
of western building problems to appreciate the Sisters'
achievement.

The entire new construction was, in fact, at once the pride
of San Jose. Public officials brought important visitors to see
this "finest school for women in the West," as Richard Henry
Dana called it.[11] Guests were amazed at the long avenue of

corridor and stately parlors in the main building. Some considered the exterior austere, and so it was for years, before the wide, unadorned space beneath the Attic gable over the front entrance was finally broken by rich baroque adornment. By present-day standards, the interior of the living and school quarters was severity itself, with cold, white-plastered walls, monotonously varnished woodwork, and polished pine floors, the only relief the warm, bright colors in the tiling. Almost nothing except the tufted mattresses in the dormitories spoke of comfort, and that to be interrupted, alas, by the bell at six. Yet once established in this milieu of bright good order, the girls began to share in the general admiration. Even the basement dining room seemed elegant when they recalled scrambling over rough boards for their places at dinner.

Before the erection of further brick units, the little two-story frame convent, by no means an architectural ornament, kept its place between the west end of the new building and the street front, housing the lower classes, play rooms, and parlors. The adobe and other small houses were now demolished or removed from the front area, and plans for a beautiful garden were at once under way. In the midst of moving, Sister Mary Aloysia and the older girls organized Notre Dame's first Christmas and Epiphany dramatic productions. Thus play and crèche and tree, and jolly jester as well, gave impulse that year to traditional activities that no Notre Dame student today would willingly miss.

At the same time, Sister Marie Alenie was laying the foundations of Notre Dame's western novitiate. When Australian Annie Walsh applied as first aspirant, Sister Loyola, somewhat eagerly assuming the Mother General's permission, appointed Sister Marie Alenie first Mistress of Novices and assigned novitiate quarters adjoining those of the professed community on the third floor, a sort of half-story, in the new house. Here Annie was soon joined by Canadian Margaret Daley, whose prospecting brother had amassed quick fortune in California and enthusiastically persuaded her to come and enjoy the Promised Land with him. And recalling that she had once expressed a wish to become a nun, he had added as an after-thought that there was a wonderful community and school in San Jose. Margaret arrived in San Francisco only to discover that her brother had been killed by robbers. Recovering from the shock, she asked his good friend, James Enright, to conduct her to the Sisters of Notre Dame. Thus in the new novitiate, Annie and Margaret were clothed and given the respective names of Sister Mary Julia and Sister Mary Stanislaus.[12] They were professed together in the summer of 1856, the first products of Sister Marie Alenie's gentle and wholesome, if somewhat abstracted training. This last quality seems not to have affected any of her disciples, as her life pattern, friendly and utterly charitable, certainly did. But friendly as she was, she still seemed to dwell in a happy sort of solitude, and many of those most deeply influenced by her came to do the same. Like her, they would not have dreamed of today's whirl of organized activity; they would not have considered today's flood of original ideas as inspirations to be enacted for the furthering of the Apostolate. Sister Marie Alenie probably never gave a thought to public relations, which would have seemed to her an artificial concept.

In San Jose Sister Marie Alenie set the ideal of the happy novice, who eats well, sleeps well, and contributes to community entertainment, characteristics which in time came to mark the Californian Sister of Notre Dame. It would perhaps have worried this first novice mistress to see a community silently watching television or movie. She would have seen in this a threat of passivity with its accompanying danger to charity. Participation was aided, of course, by the richly varied experiences of that little group recalled in tales of *l'Infatigable*, *l'Étoile du Matin*, *The Fanny*, the Panamá Crossing, and girlhood days in East Canada and Australia. Sister Alenie, it seems, yielded to none in the telling of tales, yet when recreation hour ended, none slipped so easily as she into the land of the spirit. She was quickly and kindly available for the novice who needed her help, but in those work-filled days there was little time for problems and perhaps less likelihood of their arising. With all her respect for the individual, she still feared "occupation with self," an attitude which places her spirituality somewhat in contrast with that of her teacher, Sister Marie Catherine. Physical illness in others she met with complete sympathy; it was largely her solicitude for pain and overweariness that set the note of charity in those hard-working days.

Still despite that prevailing charity, a growing tension marked the early months of 1854. Preoccupied with planning, obtaining loans, and a thousand other matters, Sister Loyola failed to notice her own growing impatience, her frequent response of disdain for what, to her, seemed foibles. There was, for instance, her expressed annoyance at Sister Alenie's tender attitude toward all living things including garden worms. But perhaps her chief cause of irritation was her own unadmitted recognition of the dangerous financial situation in which she had involved the community. For all her insistence that an increasing enrollment could be counted on to pay off indebtedness, she must have seen that business reverses might cause a decrease instead, in which case loss of her fine new building could not be prevented. Mère Constantine's letters indicate that the Sisters had written of their worries, probably when Architect Kerwin was insisting on a less ambitious plan. They indicate, too, that the community felt less peaceful than through the quiet months of Sister Mary Cornelia's leadership.

Mère Constantine was astonished to receive word of this lack of peace, since she felt that she had made it quite clear that Sister Mary Cornelia's appointment was to be permanent. She was also concerned over complaints made to her by Archbishop Blanchet to whom Sister Loyola had addressed an itemized claim based on expenditures made by the Sisters at the mission at St. Paul on the Willamette. Peace in the community and cordial rapport with pastors and ordinaries were with Mère Constantine desiderata that ranked above her wish for moderation in expenditure.[13] She decided the time had come for action and transferred Sister Loyola to Cincinnati, with instructions to depart at once with Sister Marie Donathilde.

Yet the Mother General realized, as did the pioneer Sisters, the superficiality of Sister Loyola's foibles. If any of her co-workers had failed to see the grandeur of her character before word of her transfer broke in San Jose, they would have then corrected their earlier estimate. When a forceful Sister, who has long played a leading role, accepts a non-administrative status happily as well as humbly, and especially when she takes up her subordinate tasks with zeal, she displays at once high nobility and deep spirituality. That the community on Santa Clara Street fully appreciated Sister Loyola's true worth is manifest in their sorrow at her departure for Cincinnati. There under the calm and wise leadership of Sister Superior Louise, she employed her fine constructive abilities to the full, notably in the building of the beautiful chapel at The Summit. And here no doubt she found in architects and builders a greater sense of responsibility than she had in carpenters on the Willamette and in Architect Kerwin with his many irons in the fire.

CHAPTER 5 GATHERING OF THE MINDS

*A*s the Nicaragua Route boat carried Sister Loyola and
Sister Marie Donathilde eastward across the lake, they
caught site of five Sisters of Notre Dame on the passing Pacific-
bound boat, but failed to attract their attention. These five,
Sister Loyola knew, were Mère Constantine's response to her
petitions and those of Sister Mary Aloysia, a generous response
at least numerically. If she entertained a doubt about suitability
of the new Sisters to her foundation in San Jose, their identity
would have dispelled it.[1]

Fortunately for the new boarding school, two members of
this fourth *colonie* had been raised and educated in England,
and would thus present no linguistic difficulty to young Americans beyond variations in accent. The older of these, Sister
Mary of St. George, Helen Bolton, born in Kells, Ireland, in
1830, into a family in which children were reared strictly and
educated earnestly, had been sent early to "the best academies"
in England. Before 1850, this would mean that she had known
the training of the Benedictines or Augustinian Canonesses. In
either case, Helen made the acquaintance of the Sisters of
Notre Dame in Liverpool, entered the novitiate in Namur in
1851, and was sent back to Liverpool while still a novice, there
to direct the diocesan orphanage. Sad to say, the disciplinary
ability of which Sister gave evidence in this appointment won
for her high approval, a fact which established her, while still
young, in the habit of setting a standard, short of the attainment of which it was not well to fall. With sharp eyes and firm
mouth, Sister Mary of St. George still looks compellingly from
a faded photograph, her tense hands displaying annoyance at
the camera's delay, her direct glance promising little tact. You
could depend on her to give an unvarnished appraisal, recalled
Marie Dillon Lally of the class of 1883, adding that she classi-

60

fied scholastic performance with truthful epithet, and was a favorite with the conscientious. Mention of her name, said Marie, divided the school into camps.

Still, most admired Sister's honesty; even Maria Lucas, often the recipient of Sister's less flattering remarks, admitted that she had her good points though she "wasn't very cordial." Studious Mary Frances Redmond, it seems, saw only the good points. "How she loved and defended her girls!" wrote Mary. "What pride she took in her class! What a rich, pungent, sparkling wit was hers!"[2] Less successful students treasured her occasional praise, too, as through nearly four decades as first teacher she set a standard of attainment for all, on which later times would frown as impossible. And Sister would have accepted the charge; she believed that education was for those who could and would bear the rigors, an educational credo to which the college adhered tenaciously long after Sister's death. The college diploma became the coveted mark of high merit, nor did so high a standard tend to decrease the enrollment; in fact, it was considered good fortune to have spent a year or two in a school that maintained it, even though one did not complete the course. And Sister Mary of St. George's intransigence was offset by Sister Mary Aloysia's sweet understanding as head mistress of the boarding school. This was an excellent arrangement since these two disparate characters produced a balanced harmony by their mutual high esteem. A large bronze plaque dedicated to these two Sisters, bears witness to that harmony.[3]

Three years younger than Sister Mary of St. George, Sister Aloyse of the Cross, Hannah Jenkins, entered the novitiate with her in 1851. Even at 18 Hannah displayed a blend of strength, sweetness, and fine manners. Hers was no conscious acquisition of personality and poise, but she dried a child's tears, or hung the coat of an ailing old priest near the fire, with reverence and a sense of privilege. When she answered the doorbell and found there a beggar bearing the sign "Dumb," she inquired with pity outrunning reflection, how long he had been so afflicted. And she was not annoyed when, quite overcome by her sympathy, he replied, "Forty years, Sister." She merely explained to him that moral failure is worse than physical affliction, and sent him away with an alms. In her admonition, this denizen of Skid Row must have sensed her firmness, as her students always did; in her classes even the negligent and distracted performed her assignments.

Little is known about the education of this fine teacher except that the Jenkins family was outstanding in Liverpool and devoutly Catholic. Whether or not she was sent to one of the old academies, she would certainly have had excellent instruction in her own home. When the Sisters of Notre Dame opened a small select day school at Islington Flags in 1851, Hannah, just past her 18th birthday, was one of the first enrolled and quite likely she may have spent a few months in the small boarding school added to the establishment a few months later, this as a preparation for her entrance in the novitiate in Namur in December.

Sister Maria Theresa, first headmistress of the new school at Islington Flags, was a daughter of the cultured Parry family, and one of a line of gifted young English Catholic women who entered the Notre Dame Novitiate at Namur and who presently returned to their homeland to teach the less fortunate girlhood there. Thus Hannah Jenkins' year under the care of Sister Maria Theresa was a further step in an education well begun. Certainly during that year, Sister Maria Theresa and her school made at least two great contributions to the teaching life of the future Sister Aloyse of the Cross, and so to the new school on the outpost of American life. For as teacher of English in San Jose, Sister set her mark of clear, lucid, if somewhat stylized writing, on the young Fitzgeralds and Annie Mills, on Catarina Den and Frances Miller, and many another. This was writing founded in literature which she taught them to understand and love. It was a narrowed world of literature, to be sure, and its boundaries may well have been the walls of her father's library, but the method of its imparting, like the manner of teaching to write, must have been the work of Sister Maria Theresa. And astronomy, a stressed interest in school days and teaching years of the pupils of Sister Aloyse of the Cross, is more than likely a result of her days at Islington Flags where Sister Maria Theresa's Jesuit brother, a noted astronomer used to lecture.[4]

Beginning with the days of Sister Aloyse of the Cross, astronomy and botany were Parnassan hillsides on which the poets of Notre Dame in San Jose staked their claims, though young Annie Fitzgerald required all Nature for her province. She developed a Donne-like attitude that brought out the best in her when she wrote, for instance, of a flaming gas light. She was deeply impressed, too, by Sister Mary of St. George, who taught chemistry and physics with gusto and an occasional touch of comedy, her favorite bit being to engage some over-ladylike miss in a tug of war with Madgeburg hemispheres to illustrate atmospheric pressure. The wedding of science and poetry became a lifelong interest of Annie Fitzgerald, who for more than half a century transmitted this enthusiasm to generations of Notre Dame students as the unforgettable and beloved Sister Anna Raphael.

Sister St. George's wit and the humor of Sister Aloyse of the Cross were in contrast with the character of their somewhat somber traveling companion, Sister Aurelie, the tall, dark-eyed Jeannette André, born and reared in South Belgium just over the French border. As she too, entered in Namur in 1851 she may have gained her fairly good command of English from her two missionary companions.[5] How much Spanish Sister Aurelie knew when she opened the "Poor School" in San Jose is problematic, but from that docile group she would certainly not have experienced the resistance to a foreign tongue offered by the señoritas. Nor would Sister have understood resistance. She knew what was good for the pueblo's needy children, and from the first, both they and their parents trusted in her judgment. Her school, one of the original little one-room houses, stood close to Santa Clara Street on the edge of the *acequia*. For some years it kept its first title in strong witness to class distinction. Then as even Sister Aurelie could not withstand democracy forever, it became the Day School, as distinguished from the day academy. Finally it acquired St. Joseph as patron and under his tutelage became a parish school in a large brick building. But in old age Sister Aurelie used to point out with pride her first little school, which after diverse uses and moves, settled at last beside the 1851 House near the entrance at Santa Teresa Street, a homely little structure made lovely by a climbing white rose.

Artistic in a painstaking fashion, Sister Aurelie spent endless hours adorning the chapel for feast days. As sacristan, she expected the same exactitude from her novice assistants, who came to know her distrust of tasks done too quickly, for the speedy worker was certain to meet Sister Aurelie at the first cut corner and to be greeted by her look of shocked surprise. Sister Aurelie's perfection viewed religious poverty as demanding for instance the burning of altar candles to mere stubs. Still, she lacked the pride of perfectionism; when one humorous chaplain arrived early for Mass, his pockets bulging with candles, his arms filled with wood for the meager sacristy fire, she laughed and acted on the hint.

The two other arrivals of 1854 formed each in her own way strong contrast to Sister Aurelie's stately dignity. Sister Marguerite de St. Pierre Baltus, a tiny Luxemburgian, professed in Namur in 1849, was as completely unprepossessing as she was active and responsible. The last qualities at least fitted her for the post of head portress, which she held for 34 years. The second of these, the rotund and unworried Sister Brigitte Van Houtvelot, was professed in Namur just in time to join the fourth *colonie*. In calm and slowgoing fashion she gave years of excellent service as cook and baker, mostly in San Jose. A contented soul, her one recorded resentment was aroused by the lay attire that she and her companions were obliged to don for the final stages of their journey. This regulation she considered a trick of the demon himself.

These five Sisters acquired a fairly clear picture of their future mission from Father Michael Accolti, S.J., who accompanied them on the Atlantic crossing and escorted them to the Berkeley Street Convent of Notre Dame in Boston. Sister Mary of St. George and Sister Aloyse of the Cross had started the usual voyage journal in collaboration, but found in the Hub

City the same lack of exciting content for their pages as they had experienced on the high seas, since Sister Superior Louis de Gonzague considered sight-seeing worldly even in staid Boston.[6] When however, they set out for the station to board the train for New York, the coachman, guessing at their neglected cultural opportunities, drove them to the depot by a circuitous route, pointing out historic spots with no regard for British sensibilities, and also with none for the passing of time. Worse, too, in his distraction, he delivered his charges to the wrong station, so that there was nothing to do but return them to the convent which they had so recently left with farewells "as if for eternity." Whether or not the travelers commented on Boston Common and the State House, they certainly were on time for the next train. From this point the journal moves rapidly, its bits of suppressed merriment, unspoiled by the usual pietistic milieu, though all five are recorded as displaying the most proper missionary unconcern during an ugly Atlantic mood on the trip down the coast.

The Nicaragua crossing presented even more unsettling tests of courage, incidents passed over quickly between lovely nature pictures and hilarious moments. Now the caravan is saved by the quick thought and courage of a certain Father Gallagher, who seems to have replaced Father Accolti as guardian, and without whose presence of mind the party would have been dashed over a terrifying cliff. In the next paragraph, however, they are all brought to the brink of starvation by the absent-mindedness of the same hero, who supposedly had charge of travel provisions. When at last the Sisters with their companion Sisters of Mercy enter a "sumptious hotel," they appear more like a group of "Bohemians," and so are glad enough of descending darkness. Once inside, they are given candles, in bottles instead of holders, as well as a single pitcher and towel for morning ablutions. Called to breakfast next morning, they find only three chairs and "all else in accordance." Their next grand hotel lacks even windowpanes, so that one and all rejoice to see the lovely Pacific at last, and a steamer waiting to receive them. Sight of the distance between water's edge and ship causes the usual concern, but Sister Aurelie, "grande et forte," explains that porters will carry all aboard; the important thing is to select one with mighty muscles and thus avoid being dropped into the Pacific.

As all pioneer Sisters considered it a mark of Heaven's blessing to arrive at journey's end on a feast of the Mother of God, this journal notes entering the Bay of San Francisco on December 8, 1854, Feast of the Immaculate Conception, and that in time to assist at Mass. It notes, too, that among the several visitors who welcomed the Sisters that day, the most gracious was Archbishop Alemany. But no welcome could have matched that accorded the new missionaries in San Jose where their arrival solved a problem to general satisfaction. Awaiting their coming, Sister Mary Cornelia had assured the Sisters that one of the new group would be assigned to replace Sister Loyola; she felt that their unanimous desire to see herself in charge arose from gratitude, and as the letter which the Mother General sent with the new Sisters made no mention of the matter, she asked each of them in turn to tell her which one had been appointed. She refused their explanation that they had expected to find her in office, until when some weeks later Sister Laurence Lejeune received a letter from Mère Constantine stating that her appointment of Sister Mary Cornelia as superior in San Jose had not been temporary in 1852.[7]

Then began an era of calm and stable control that evoked the best in everyone, though for some time Sister Mary Cornelia herself was plagued by the sense of incapability which she had acquired in Oregon. Mère Constantine treated her complaints gently at first, assuring her that all was well since she was receiving no more troubled letters from San Jose. Finally, however, she wrote a last stern rebuke which ended Sister Mary Cornelia's doubts and initiated an era of community life that has always been referred to as a sort of Golden Age.[8] This was the leadership, stable, wise, and loved, for which mission-minded Mère Constantine had been waiting. Without hesitation she now encouraged Belgian volunteers for California and asked Sister Louise to send Sisters from Cincinnati to insure for the West a good quota of teachers who could begin classes without a language difficulty.

And now Notre Dame in California entered a decade of remarkable development. The faculty was increased by Sisters of ability from Belgium and Cincinnati. Cultured young women of established East Coast families entered the novitiate in San Jose, there to strengthen the forces of a few exceptional young pioneers.

Sister Mary Gonzaga Von Aschen, gifted in oil painting, and a generally able teacher, arrived from Cincinnati in 1858.[9] With her came her fellow novice, Sister Kotska Dehan of Boston, whose name was to become a benediction in both Marysville and Santa Clara. Nature and training had combined to make her the perfect elementary teacher, especially of boys. And though the Belgian notion frowned on the Sister as teacher of boys beyond seven years, Sister Kotska pleaded successfully to keep them through the grades, at least where she happened to be teaching. In and out of season she inspired them to develop their talents; in later days many a successful business and professional man, as well as many a priest, came in person or wrote to thank her.[10]

Third in this group was Irish-born Sister Mary Victoria Barry, who had not quite completed her novitiate in Cincinnati when they departed for the West. Small and delicately beautiful, but assured in manner, her mathematical ability was recognized at Cincinnati and her qualities of educational leadership were destined to serve Notre Dame well in California.

Another youthful trio arrived from Belgium in 1862, a year that marks a peak in Notre Dame's missionary development, since this group traveled as far as Panamá with the second contingent of missionaries to the new foundation in Guatemala. Their coming marked a sort of conquest in that they had made the entire journey wearing their religious habits. There was, in fact, general rejoicing over the matter, for to most Sisters even altering their habit, to say nothing of setting it aside for secular dress, seemed unthinkable.

The extrovert of this last three, twenty-year old Sister Marie de St. Albert Lefèvre, was little inclined to such conservatism. Bright and vivacious, and blessed besides with a green thumb, Sister St. Albert became an enthusiast for the house at Marysville with its city block for garden. Here on the rich soil of a one-time ocean floor, Sister developed her talent. Through the next three decades, ranchers and gardeners of the valley admired her profusion of citrus trees, figs, pomegranates and grapevines as well as the 36 varieties of choice roses that covered her long arbor. Specialists exchanged ideas as well as rose slips with her, as her dedication established a tradition. But besides directing the gardener and pruning roses, this incredible Sister milked two cows daily and gave a hand at "common work" in the house. How she found time to become so thorough and interesting a teacher is a mystery. She had had, certainly, a much better preparation in English than the first missionaries, a fact which aided her natural eagerness as she plunged into the American scene. Nothing seemed to daunt her; crippled by a fall, she continued to teach with tremendous vigor, and as head teacher in the day academy in San Jose in the 1890s, she soon acquired an enviable reputation. With her courage and sense of justice she stumbled now and then into minor troubles which prudence might have avoided. Yet on such occasions her superiors found her humble and yielding. As one of her pupils said, "Everyone loved Sister St. Albert dearly."[11]

The second of this group, on the other hand, Sister Marie de Ste. Thérèse Klausen caused some worry for a time because of her great timidity, and this despite the finesse of her training and her regal beauty and charm. This timidity may have resulted from her unhappy relations with an overly strict stepmother, but whatever the cause, her superiors at San Jose found her as fearful of taking over responsibility as her companion was eager and unafraid. And yet this daughter of a wealthy family, her lovely voice and musical talent highly developed, should have had at least a measure of assurance. So it seemed to Sister Mary Bernard, who reported to Mère Constantine that Sister Ste. Thérèse would not, or could not, play or sing before the students. The mother general rather caustically replied directly to Sister Mary Cornelia, reminding her of the restriction in force in Belgium which prohibited Sisters playing or singing in public or even before students. For despite her general tendency toward adaptation, Mère Constantine was regrettably adamant in matters of this kind. Sisters were not to display their talents; girls were to be taught, not entertained. In America, she said, girls were too prone to make a great noise with instruments. As to Sister Ste. Thérèse, she advised patience and understanding for the development of her abilities; she quite failed to see that encouraging her to perform would help her to overcome inhibitions. Neither the Mother General nor the superiors in California foresaw the brilliant contribution that this gifted Sister would make to the future college.[12]

Gentle Sister Marie Euphrasie, the third of this trio, replaced brusque Sister Aloysius as Mistress of Order in San Jose, being thus the second instance of a Belgian music teacher who somehow failed to fit into the scene in the West, this to the mother general's very real annoyance. If Sister had taught singing in the academy in Philippeville, why was she not acceptable to young Americans? And, with a touch of sarcasm, if Californians were too far advanced for Belgian Sisters, she trusted there would soon be vocations among them, since Belgium seemed unable to produce what was needed in America. Perhaps the difficulty in this instance was the English language. At any rate, Sister never succeeded as a teacher in California, which seems to have been a blessing, for she became instead the sort of housemother that Sister Mary Cornelia so much desired. Everyone, it seems, loved this motherly Sister who was never too busy to discuss shoes or gloves or the décor of one's alcove. It was partly the resulting happiness that justified the increasingly high reputation of the school at the beginning of its second decade.[13]

The addition of these eight Sisters between 1854 and 1862 made possible the foundations in Santa Clara and San Francisco in 1864 and 1866. In answer to Father Michael Accolti's request, a small group began to commute to Santa Clara on the daily stage. Here they taught in a mere shack beside the Mission until they purchased the Alexander Forbes home in 1872 and made it the nucleus of Our Lady of the Angels Academy, a successful boarding school, despite an unfortunate financial dispute which ended sadly for the Sisters.

The foundation at Mission Dolores was at the invitation of the Reverend J. Prendergast, later the Vicar General. Here too, the beginnings were humble. Don Timoteo Murphy of San Rafael offered Sister Mary Cornelia property on Market Street, but she preferred the present site on Dolores Street. Here the Sisters opened classes in a small building intended for a seminary and used off and on, it seems, as a boys' school. Its chief advantage was a chapel. Progress was so rapid here that Mission Dolores Notre Dame soon stood second to the foundation in San Jose.

Notre Dame's success in this era parallels California's striving for cultural advancement in the 1860s, that decade of efforts, often too ornate to be genuine, to announce in poetry and architecture that the West had cast off its mining day rudeness, and was beginning to vie with eastern centers. Yet the strivings were often valid, and though the boasting might quaver on a childlike note, there is no mistaking in it a sincerity and strength which compares well with the sentimental weakness of the century's end. And despite their seclusion, Sister Aloyse of the Cross and Sister Mary of St. George must have noted these educational and cultural yearnings. They must have taken comfort at new ambitions and at the simultaneous grouping of Sisters of fine minds coupled with exceptional teaching ability. Few schools of the time experienced such good fortune in this respect. For Notre Dame, it provided an impetus and standard, a tradition and an inspiration.

A facet of this impetus was the literary stamp set by Sister Aloyse of the Cross on Annie and Marcella Fitzgerald, and on Annie Mills and Frances Miller, just when San Francisco was dreaming of volumes of local poetry. From her these and others learned the meaning of poetry, of adaptation of sound, of economy and unity. For months they worked over poems, or essays, in which forms they became equally skilled. Better still, the two Annies, and others who dedicated their lives to the work of Notre Dame, learned Sister's teaching methods. For these young teachers, writing was of first importance; they would spend hours with a single student, explaining and criticising.

Annie Fitzgerald (Sister Anna Raphael), and Annie Mills (Sister Mary Xavier), were teenage Canadian girls when they were first enrolled at Notre Dame in San Jose. How much formal education either had previously is not clear. Both completed the course at Notre Dame, and Annie Fitzgerald taught for a time under the direction of the Sisters before entering the novitiate. From the first, both were marked for leadership as educators. They were not relatives though they had several common Canadian connections. The Fitzgerald story forms part of the Martin Murphy saga. When Johanna, daughter of the elder Martin Murphy was widowed by the death of Patrick Fitzgerald in Frampton near Quebec, she acted on her father's advice to bring her family to the Santa Clara Valley, where he furnished them with a ranch near Gilroy. The poetic name Mossy Landing, acquired by this place later on, gives little hint of Johanna's difficulties there in early days, and the absence in the school lists of her daughters' names for long periods after their first registration is quite likely due to her need of their assistance at home. The names of the older sisters, Mary and Johanna, appear on the boarding school roster shortly after the school opened in 1851, but no doubt because of expense involved, the two younger were not enrolled until 1853.

From the start, Annie and Marcella gave promise as poets, and Annie's scientific bent must have delighted Sister Mary of St. George. Here was the ideal encyclopedic mind, meeting place of the disciplines. Her photograph in her early twenties indicates a sturdy young woman, peaceful and pleasing though not beautiful, her maturity emphasized by shawl and bonnet, which in contrast with the jaunty plumed hats of her young relatives in the group, bespeaks her freedom from worry over appearances. And for all her lack of cultural advantages, for all the toil of her girlhood, she presents a sensitive dignity that is independent of good looks and elegant outfit. No wonder that, without looking for distinction, this girl should win it early and maintain it through life.

Annie Fitzgerald made her first acquaintance with prominence when President Abraham Lincoln was assassinated. Arriving at the lodge one morning shortly after that tragedy, she learned that the Sisters were also threatened by local treachery. As there was a sprinkling of Southerners in both community and school, it was not too surprising that some gossip should recall earlier expression of sympathy with secession. And now gossip had added rejoicing over the death of the president within the convent walls and the failure of the Sisters, in their ignorance, to drape the lodge doors with black, confirmed the rumor. Friends of the Sisters, suddenly alarmed by threats to burn the convent and drive out the supposed traitors, advised a public expression of sorrow. Levi Goodrich offered a suggestion. At closing programs he had noted the ability of Notre Dame girls as verse-makers, and he was sure that the city fathers would be grateful for a poem to be included in their memorial plans. Annie penned a dirge of tremendous eloquence, the effect heightened by her Alma Mater's need. Editor J. J. Owen of the *Mercury* read it himself at the end of the city's memorial ceremony. The Fifth Regiment's salute of three rounds of blank cartridge served as resounding echo. Before noon, the *Mercury*, with the long poem in full, was sold out, but the deeply impressed editor ordered black-bordered broadsides of the dirge run off so that all might have copies. That day Annie Fitzgerald's name was inscribed among Western bards. When she entered the novitiate a little later, the young school's educational impetus acquired its strongest contributing force.[14]

As her family arrived somewhat later from Canada, Annie Mills was fully 16 when she and her sister Katherine came to Notre Dame. In 1856 their brother John settled in the lovely Woodside area above Stanford, for he was attracted by lumbering possibilities in the redwood forests. Satisfied with location and prospects, John sent for his mother and sisters who then came by way of Panamá, the usual route of migrating East Canadians at this time. The site of the Mills home lies across the Portolá Road from Searsville Lake, and following the turns of the woodside roads, one finds also the sites of their related Canadian families, the Duffs and the Doyles.

Unlike Sister Anna Raphael, Sister Mary Xavier left few poems, letters, or science notes to tell her unusual story. Even her educational notes were destroyed in the earthquake of 1906. But Sisters who dealt closely with her used to recall her brilliant mind (superior even to Sister Anna Raphael's, they insisted), her shy disposition, her dislike for any kind of ostentation, her abiding love of truth and justice. Less sensitive and more dominant characters caused her pain, not on her own account, but because of the proneness of these traits to injure charity and justice. Still if her co-workers found her slightly too inclined to sadness and worry, her students loved her as a lively and inspiring teacher. Old and young found her attractive, and that despite the marring of her otherwise fine face by a childhood accident when she was tossed by a steer that she attempted to ride. None seemed to notice her badly flattened nose, nor the somewhat nasal tone that resulted from that fall. What all did remark was her captivating smile, her way of holding complete attention. Sister Aloyse of the Cross saw her gifts, and as the first superior of Notre Dame's foundation at Mission Dolores in San Francisco, she asked Sister Mary Cornelia to send this brilliant young Sister to head her staff.

In a somewhat less inspiring manner, Sister Marie du Sacré Coeur Barry made her strong contribution to the upsurge of the second decade, and this to the surprise of none. For since the first appearance of Judge Barry's studious child in 1851, she had been more or less counted as "one of ours," and this despite her long delay in entering the novitiate. Completing all the available classes, she also assisted for a time as a lay teacher. When she did enter, it seemed reasonable to expect a general raising of standards. As a teacher, she was, by all accounts, tremendously respected; certainly her assignments were rarely slighted.

About the time of Sister Marie du Sacré Coeur's profession, another home-tutored daughter of the South applied for admission to the novitiate. Studious habits, pursuit of truth and wisdom, had made of Elizabeth Shaw of Battletown, Virginia, a student of theology and Sacred Scripture, all of which was taken for granted in her intellectual family circle until she began to mention her attraction to the Roman faith. Then hoping that time would bring about a greater tolerance in her parents and friends, Elizabeth decided to visit her older sister in San Francisco for a few months. Johanna Shaw Wright, wife of the brilliant young lawyer and future judge, received Elizabeth gladly and with a sympathetic understanding of her spiritual searching.[15] It may have been through the Wrights that she made the acquaintance of the Sisters of Notre Dame. At any rate, she found the help she needed in the convent in San Jose and especially in the person of Sister Aloyse of the Cross. Entering the novitiate late in 1865 as Sister Mary Philomene, she began at once her life as teacher, her fine intellect and rare spiritual charm winning the least likely young westerners. "An aristocrat and a lady," said Maria Lucas with enthusiasm, "a learned lady and a lovely soul." High praise that from outspoken Maria, for whom aristocrats and learned ladies had little appeal, except the rare few on whom she herself bestowed the titles. Sister Mary Cornelia considered this young intellectual, "a gift of God," as also did young Sister Anna Raphael, who profited by her learning as she perhaps took on unconsciously something of her gentle poise.

The Sisters applied the epithet "gift of God" likewise to Mary Bridges of Boston as being not of their own training but something of a surprise package on the part of a loving Providence. As a small child Mary had come to the West by way of Panamá and had spent her girlhood in the gold country, and in Marysville, where she came to know the Sisters of Notre Dame. Her education before her novitiate days was desultory, but when she entered at eighteen, on New Year's Day, 1865, the gift of God was recognized almost at once, it seems, as something of a genius. Apparently all set upon her directly to teach her whatever of the "branches" she may have lacked. In later years, as Notre Dame's first school examiner, she was at home in all departments, nor was her knowledge in any of them a mere smattering. But her great gift was teaching and the preparation of teachers. Sister Mary Genevieve's name carried almost the sanction of Sister Anna Raphael's, said a contemporary Sister who had learned much from her. She could bring anyone to learn anything, said another. Like Sister Anna Raphael, she never ceased to study. Past middle life, she mastered Italian in order to read the original *Divina Comedia*.

Though Mary Ann, eldest daughter of the much traveled Michael J. Comerford family, shone with a quieter light, her contribution to this forceful era was still very significant. She and her sisters were among the earliest pupils at Notre Dame and their names appear often on the prize lists. In the upper classes, Mary Ann, and her more brilliant sister Catherine, must have been sources of joy to both Sister Aloyse of the Cross and Sister Mary of St. George. Through life Catherine was friend of Sister Anna Raphael, and almost as noted as a naturalist. Mary Ann entered the novitiate directly from school and pronounced her vows as Sister Mary de Sales in 1861, at the age of twenty, that relatively early age indicating in those days that both her parents and teachers considered her very mature. She was the "solid teacher" type, which meant that her pupils always had the answers. Her contribution was the image of meticulous, methodical, and consistent work. Yet she must have offered some inspiration; the tradition attached to her name bears the mark of admiration, a mark never accorded to the uninspiring.[16]

The pace-setting decade of the 1860s had, of course, its limitation. Art was a bit trivial; the level of music was not very high. It was in the "branches" that the full momentum gathered, as students were plunged into history, literature, and science, and into the logic of debate and essay. Study was earnest; one could not attain to it in a slouching position, nor might one substitute "I think it is thus," for "It can be proven thus." Everything was discipline; even the tyranny of rhyme somehow braced one for further encounter. Teacher and student might pontificate, and they did, but they reached their high pinnacles by logical steps. The late century day of the florid word had not yet beguiled them. And the word "branches" was of happy use, for each flourished for the good of the tree, no one at the expense of the others. The soil was the contemporary desire for culture and the special abilities of the two Sisters from England whose training had given them so much to offer the new school. Added was the providential grouping of young Sisters who received with joy the gifts of those two and brought others of their own as well. The resulting intellectual impetus at that early hour in the school's history was the fountainhead of an intense tradition, one strong enough to insure resurrection after weaker periods — the common lot of educational endeavors.

An immediate effect of this concentration of intellectual energy and ability was the movement begun shortly after 1860 to acquire a college charter. The result of this endeavor is the impressive document which ornaments St. Mary's Hall at Belmont today. Dated June 20, 1868, it bears the signatures of California's tenth governor, Henry H. Haight, of Superintendent of Public Instruction, O. P. Fitzgerald, and others. Its ornate penmanship is the work of L. M. Fernandez, Instructor at Santa Clara College, where this art held place with high studies. The date places College of Notre Dame as the first chartered college for women in the State of California. It marks also a step which the first Sisters could not have taken. From their days in Oregon they had known the importance of incorporation; their little academy on the Willamette had been properly chartered. Their incorporation in San Jose, dated June 11, 1858, as Academy of Notre Dame, obtained through the good offices of C. T. Ryland from "the members of the Incorporated Society for educational purposes," accorded them the status beyond which they would have had no further expectation at the time, even though a college charter had then been obtainable. The year 1868 is the great turning point; it is unlikely that many women's schools in America possessed so strong a claim to the title "college" as the first Academy of Notre Dame in San Jose.

---

*I*t was fortunate for the school on Santa Clara Street that the teaching impetus which gathered after the first years of its existence should have been accompanied by an increase in the number of very able students enrolled. And this good fortune is underscored by the contemporary handicap presented by the cosmopolitan nature of the student list. The campus picture of a century ago did not present minorities bent on acquaintance with the prevailing language and culture nor, on the other hand, a majority eager to understand foreign origins.

The Spanish señoritas constituted a minority large enough to build the wall which they erected, its effectiveness increased by the pity they felt for the Yankee lack of sense of family and establishment. And the wall was stronger by reason of the way in which *sangre pura* and that rendered inferior by native strain, could forget these distinctions in the face of American intrusion, in some instances in the face of American injustice. Actually the Sisters were slowly weakening the barrier. They performed, for instance, the miracle of bringing the De Haro sisters to share living quarters with the "Yanquitas" and without repugnance. The secret of this success, no doubt, was the common chapel and common prayer, and the lives of the Sisters must have helped to end old enmities.

Besides, it must have mollified the señoritas to find that at least some of the non-Spanish were also non-American, that Eugenie Van Damme, for instance, was having her own struggle with the language that gave the Yankees so great an advantage, and that she, too, at times felt out of place among them. Still such girls had no bitterness to forget; they had only to meet the challenge of strangeness, and if they spoke French, they were at ease with most of the teachers. There were some, too, who like the Van Houten sisters, Margaret and Lavinia, were Americans by birth but whose childhood milieu was strongly European in character, daughters of a "better class" seeking greater opportunities. When the progressive Dutch John Van Houten settled in New Jersey, his success as a farmer only whetted his desire for adventure in California. There, even before the discovery of gold, good fortune attended him as a buyer and seller of cattle; by 1852 he was well established in San Francisco and sent for his family to join him. On their arrival, this strict member of the Dutch Reformed Church brought his daughters to the Sisters in San Jose, where began a family loyalty of long duration.

Both girls left excellent scholastic records; Margaret was one of the finest of the early students and versatile as well. Her paintings done at Notre Dame were entered and honored in the First Industrial Exhibition of Mechanics Institute in San Francisco. Two of these are treasured at Notre Dame today, a crayon drawing of Sister Loyola's first building unit, and a watercolor of the Van Houten family crossing the Isthmus of Panamá in 1852. About both there is a refreshingly original note that makes one regret the loss of her "pastille," "Head of a Lady with Light Brown Curls," which the report calls "beautifully done."[1] Margaret is, in fact, as well represented in Notre Dame Archives as is Isabel Ramírez. Margaret's notebooks and texts are guides to the teaching of Sister Aloysc of the Cross and Sister Mary of St. George, and the lasting value of that teaching is well attested by her lifelong pursuit of literature and history, as well as by her geological collections. Like Isabel, too, Margaret handed down her feeling for her Alma Mater. When her daughter made a generous gift to Notre Dame's Memorial Chapel in Belmont, she was repeating her mother's earlier gifts to Notre Dame in San Jose. Margaret's strongest bond with her Alma Mater was, no doubt, her classmate, Sister Anna Raphael, though in later years she corresponded with Sister Anthony, S. H., supporting zealously and contributing to *Notre Dame Quarterly*.[2]

However the señoritas classified the Van Houtens and others from distant parts, they had no doubts about the local girls, who returned from occasional home visits laden with good things and plenty of grist for their mills of chatter. It was this chatter that tended most to aggravate the state of cold war, for though the señoritas who lived nearby enjoyed their share of such visits, their own net results in information were confined more or less to their group, whereas Sally Burnett, the Murphys, and the Kells always seemed to include the general group in their impartings, as though taking for granted that all wanted to be informed. That was the way with the *Americana.* Her noisy talk of new stores in San Francisco, of vessels in the harbor, of epic tales from the Isthmus, were irritants to smoldering dignity. So much contributed to her annoying assurance; mining successes, life in a wooden house, and worst of all, confirmed ownership of large land grants still known by their resounding Spanish titles. And while the Sisters may not have thus diagnosed the American girls' chatter and ready reply that often carried a note of pertness, they were worried by both, and were thus prone to see piety and docility in the graceful curtsy and sibilant "Si, Hermana."

For while the American girl was more or less herself before the Sisters, the señorita seems to have presented an angelic front. Sister Mary Aloysia probably never saw a Spanish girl in a tantrum, which was no doubt the basis of her notion of a "Castilian Province of Notre Dame" on the Pacific Coast.[3] The Americans inspired no such hopes, it seems; they were not being protected from "the world" as were the Spanish girls. There was, for instance, Sally Burnett, whose parents might have been expected to insist on her being enrolled in the boarding school instead of residing with friends, or perhaps with the Rylands, and attending as a day student, her head filled with all the flattery and excitement of San Jose's rising social circle, of which the double Burnett wedding of 1860 was one of the first brilliant functions. Yet this young socialite was gifted and a fine student; her ratings show an industry that her father must have commended.[4]

Whatever the Spanish girls thought of them, the daughters of Martin Murphy, Jr. did not rate as Americans in the Sisters' eyes. They and their cousins, the Millers, belonged in the Canadian group with Annie Fitzgerald, their cousin, and this despite the claim of the eldest, Elizabeth Yuba, of being the first American girl born in California. Though Elizabeth was only seven when her family settled in the Santa Clara Valley, she knew her distinction and could boast of her narrow escape in crossing the Yuba river, when her father had fastened her to the pommel of the saddle so that her mother might better manage the reins. When the horse stumbled, they were carried with the current until the animal regained his footing. That incident explained her middle name. She and her two little sisters, Mary Anne and Ellen, or Nellie, were the darlings of the school, the unspoiled children of good and sensible Mary Bolger Murphy. Always a paragon of "Good Conduct" and "Politeness," Elizabeth needed some time to win her high standing in classes. Her sisters, not so generally good, were still among those commended by Sister Mary of St. George.[5]

Slightly older than Elizabeth Yuba, her cousin Mary Frances, daughter of James and Ann Martin Murphy, was born as the family crossed the plains, and so could make her own claim as pioneer. She and her younger sisters appear occasionally on the early prize lists. There were unrelated Murphys, too which must have been a bit confusing on closing days, except to relatives, since only initials appeared on the programs. Thus Martin Murphy's younger daughters seem constantly in competition with others of the same first letters, so that a piano duet by one set of initials is followed by a second duet by another set. Only their fond parents could have made things out. These early Murphys stand at the head of a long line of Notre Dame students bearing their name, not all of them, however, as tractable as Elizabeth Yuba, and Mary Anne, and Nellie. And with equal frequency appear the related names of Miller and Kell.

Ann Kell, the daughter of Thomas and Margaret Murphy Kell, and her younger sister Mary Ellen, were beloved children at Notre Dame by reason of their parents' kindness to the two first Sisters in 1851. Their mother, independent as most of the Framptonians, paid for Ann's tuition by working at the convent, for the first few years of this family, as the Sisters knew well, were not easy. Sister Anna Raphael's sister Mary, must have had Margaret Kell as well as her own mother in mind when she wrote years later of the latter's enduring bravery. Ann herself had crossed the plains in the largest train, 53 wagons, to that date, 1846. As eldest daughter, she shared her family's trials, one the death of her brother, Thomas, who was killed with his uncle, Bernard Murphy, in the *Jenny Lind* explosion. The Sisters held Ann, and all the Kells in high esteem, rejoicing at their later prosperity and at the leadership of Ann Kell Colombet as an alumna.[6]

Other local girls at Notre Dame wore their own more recent pioneering with considerable pride. One of these, Annie McGinnis, had made the Isthmus crossing with her widowed mother at the invitation of friends in San Jose. Annie came to school fresh from her trek from New Orleans, ready to tell one and all about the crossing and how she was carried on the back of a native while her mother jogged along on a donkey. Whether or not Annie was one of the noisy Americans, she was soon a leading student, her accent affording delight to the southern Sisters. Boarding school days over, Annie married Jacob Gardiser, a prominent San Josean. She raised a family of 12, and of course, sent her daughters to her beloved Alma Mater. These missed the joys and escaped the rigors of boarding school by attending the new day academy, but like their mother they became strong alumnae as well as loyal and leading San Joseans.[7]

Another fine local student was Sarah, daughter of the Judge Craven P. Hester family. A full-blown pioneer at nine, Sarah found crossing the plains with the forty-niners somewhat dull, since her father, caring little for gold, talked only of fine, fertile valleys and such a home as he was soon to build on the Alameda. Sarah's mother, Mrs. Martha Hester, later made amends for this romantic failure by bringing the Hester Rose to the Garden City. It was something to know that all the Hester roses in the area had sprung from the shoot for which she had asked as a special favor on a visit to old Mission San José. Sarah and her little sister Laura fitted well into the picture of old Notre Dame. Their love of writing must have delighted Sister Aloyse of the Cross. Sarah's diary, running through twenty years beginning with her overland trip, testifies to her love of the written word. And all her life, Laura found joy in both writing and speaking of the pioneer era. Her special interest was pioneer mothers, for whose honor she campaigned vigorously through 1914 for a bronze monument to be displayed during the Panama Pacific Exposition held in San Francisco in the following year.[8] But she spoke as often of the pioneer Sisters, too. Many a student assembly listened with rapt attention when she addressed them at the invitation of Sister Anna Raphael or Sister Anthony, S.H. In their own school days, the Hesters, along with Sally Burnett, the Branhams, Elizabeth White, and Susan Bascom, belonged to that gay, sub-deb group that studied French and chemistry and English literature, their heads filled betimes with social gossip.[9]

One who must have stood aloof from the *Yanquitas* in her pride of family and race was Catalina de Danglada y Munras, that is if pride of her family in general may be taken as a key to her character. Catalina's grandfather, Estevan Carlos Munras, began his career as a Spanish diplomat to Peru and received for his service in that post the great Rancho San Francisquito in Monterey County. Here in 1807 he brought his bride, Catalina Manzaneli y Ponce de Leon, and established that independent sort of existence that ignored the Mexican era, and which Mexican rule wisely enough left unmolested. Daughter and heiress María Antonía Munras married Don Rafael de Danglada, and their child, with such an array of claims to distinction, was proud to be listed at Notre Dame as "A Spanish Young Lady" who knew no English, whose family had taken no oath of allegiance to Mexico, and who was generally disdainful of Americans. In her broken periods of school life, Catalina pleased her teachers and picked up more English than she had intended. When she married Thomas Jefferson Field, he probably was never allowed to forget that he was privileged to join a great Spanish family. Certainly her daughter, another María Antonía, came in her turn to Notre Dame steeped in that proud tradition.[10]

If the De Haro twins, Carlota and Candelaría, stood aloof from the American girls, their attitude was understandable. Who could blame them for recalling the murder of their twin brothers, Francisco and Ramón, by Kit Carson's men at the end of the Bear Flag Rebellion, when the deed could no longer be classed an act of war? Listed among "The Spanish Young Ladies," these girls were fully 18 when given their first taste of school life. But if they were ill at ease with the *Yanquitas*, they loved the Sisters, delighting Sister Mary Aloysia by winning "first crowns" in conduct. Besides, their semi-annual report cards, the only extant curricular evidence for the separate Spanish division, indicate that they gave general satisfaction. They would not have done otherwise, for they, too, had a proud lineage to honor. Their father, Francisco de Haro, had been Alcalde in San Francisco. Their maternal grandfather, Antonio Sánchez, whose name is also immortalized by a street in that city, had been commandant there.[11]

Close competitor of the De Haro sisters in the good-behavior category of ratings was Francisca Suñol, though it seems that Don Antonio's daughters, perhaps because of Sister Marie Catherine's initial lessons in their home, were listed in the "American" classes. Competition in this group was perhaps too much for them or perhaps they were just artistic señoritas. At any rate, they aimed at prizes in the fine arts and penmanship. Antonita was the school's songbird for a time, and Francisca's large, gold-framed needlepoint of Benjamin Franklin is a treasure at College of Notre Dame. Francisca was a worker though, coming out with first crown for diligence in the "branches."[12] Diligence was that halo-conferring, democratic honor which lessened the advantage of such as Sally Burnett. It was the great equalizer, being a requirement for the school's highest honor, "Superior Class of Good Conduct." The plan was Sister Mary Aloysia's, and no doubt met with the approval of Sister Aloyse of the Cross. If Sister Mary of St. George sniffed at it, she did no more than sniff.

Such another standard was "Order and Neatness," a fortunate thing for such girls as lovely Rosaría Palomares, daughter of Francisco and Margarita Pacheco Palomares. For when Narciso Suñol, brother of the Suñol girls, returned from studying commerce in Bordeaux to establish himself in the Suñol Valley, he married Rosalía or Rosaría, as she was later known, who had at least top marks in order and neatness to commend her as housewife. Rosaría seems to have been a cousin of Concepción and Benedita Palomares, whose board bill was sometimes paid in produce. After their names stand the substantial items: "1 boeuf, $32; 1 oxe, $40; cheese, $22.50." These sisters were not prize winners, though in 1855 Concepción managed a second crown in the Good Conduct list. After that supreme effort, their names disappear from the roster. Perhaps these sisters preferred rounding up cattle on the great rancho of their prosperous father, who paid bills in good round sums as well as in "1 boeuf."[13] Scholastic matters came none too easy to some of these señoritas, among them Dolores Noë, who found herself at 17 a bit too adult or at least too set in her ways, to work up any great enthusiasm beyond a slight dabbling in music and of course in embroidery.

Perhaps such dabbling was all that Guadalupe Gardano Noë expected of her daughters. Hers would seem to have been a mañana household; a certain Mr. Beaver had to collect the Noë boarding school bill, a forgotten detail, no doubt, since it was paid in full at a reminder. Yet the name of Noë marks another San Francisco street. The Valencias, too, belonged to the class from whom diligence, as abstracted from results, could not be expected with any certainty. Five of them entered and left the Spanish School with dependable irregularity. Apparently they were not gentle señoritas, and their unpaid bills, placed with little result in the hands of Mr. Beaver for collection, recall other irresponsible Valencias. They could not settle down as did Guadalupe Castro to a life of politeness and fine intentions. It was enough for Guadalupe to sit smiling as her sister Isabel bore away the prizes.

Sister Marie Catherine Cabareaux standing before a painting of *l'Infatigable* painted by an unknown artist for Notre Dame Hall shortly after its erection in 1884.

The 1851 House, the numerals above its entrance hidden by roses, stood near the Santa Teresa Street entrance through the last years of the College in San Jose.

Sister Aurelie's "Poor School" (above) served as San Jose's first parish school before the erection of the two-story brick St. Joseph's Parish School, which in 1906 became Notre Dame High School.

(Left) Painting of Elizabeth Schallenberger Townsend, wife of Dr. John Townsend, with their son Johnnie, Notre Dame's first resident pupil. This painting, the work of artist Anthony Long, has recently been donated to Ralston Hall in Belmont by Mrs. Arthur C. Townsend, wife of the late son of Alumnus Johnnie.

Community photo taken before 1880. In the front row, beginning second from left, Sister Odelie Golard, Sister Mary Aloysia Chevry, Sister Mary Cornelia Neujean, Sister Marie Catherine Cabareaux, Sister Alphonse Marie Vermuylen, and Sister Norbertine Vereux. Sister Aurelie André is center in the third row.

John M. Murphy and his daughter Mollie. Mollie's pioneer mother, Virginia Reed Murphy was a close friend and admirer of Sister Anna Raphael.

Martin Murphy, Jr. was in many ways Notre Dame's greatest benefactor. These two sons of Martin Murphy, Sr. continued his personal interest in the school.

Pueblo de San Jose Setiembre

Señora Doña Petra Avila

Meis muy queridos Papasito y Mamasita

My Dear God Father

Ysabel Ramirez

Querida Amiga,

Mon cher Parrain,

Ysabel

Isabel Ramirez Pelanconi-Tononi, Notre Dame's first pupil from Southern California, aged 20. At 12, Isabel wrote interesting letters in French, Spanish and English. Her correspondence includes well-known pioneer names, one of these Sister Marie Catherine, her beloved teacher.

Pueblo San José, 20 Octubre - 1853.

CUENTA DE LA Señorita, Isabel Ramirez.

Por la Entrada,	$	
" 6 Meses de Manutencion y enseñanza, hasta el dia 15 de febrero -	150 " 00
" " Lecciones de Musica,	36 " 00
" " " Dibujo,	24 " 00
" " Lavadura de Ropa,	35 " 00
" " Uso de la Ropa de Cama,	
" " Medico y Medécinas,	5 " 00
" " Gastos	15 " 00
	$ 265 " 00

With her linguistic ability, Isabel Ramirez seems to have fitted well in the English speaking classes. This bill was a statement in Spanish for the information of her parents.

COLEGIO
de las
HERMANAS de NUESTRA SENORA.

Sta. *Carlota de Haro*

Conducta, *Muy regular*

Aplicacion, *Constante*

Salud, *muy buena*

	Discrp.	Dev.	Lugar.		Discip.	Div.	Lugar.
Buena Conducta - -	8	1	2	Historia Santa - -	10	1	2
Aplicacion - - - -	10	1	3	" Antigua - -			
Ciencia - - - - -	"	"	1	" Moderna - -			
Doctrina Christiana -	33	1	2	Idioma Francesa - - -			
Lectura - - - - -	10	1	6	" Inglesa - - -	16	1	8
Ortografia - - - -	"	"	2	Labores de aguja - -	36	1	
Gramatica - - - -	"	"	3	Orden - - - - -	65	"	10
Geografia - - - -	"	"	3	Civilidad - - - -	"	"	2
Escritura - - - -	43	"	33	Musica vocal - - -	16	"	15
Arithmetica - - - -	10	"	5	Piano - - - - -	19	2	18
Estilo - - - - - -	"	"	2	Dibujo - - - - -	18	1	9

City of San José,

Noviembre 29 , 1853. *S. Loyola Sup.*

Carlota de Haro's report card, gift of Mrs. Anita M. Truman to the archives of Notre Dame. This report points up the complete separation of Spanish speaking students in the school.

Ida Haraszthy as a young woman. This brilliant daughter of Agoston Haraszthy married Major Henry Hancock. Hancock Hall, in the Allan Hancock Foundation at University of Southern California, is a memorial of Ida's cultural efforts for Los Angeles.

Below, are the daughters of pioneer John Reed of Marin, Inez (left) and Hilarita (right).

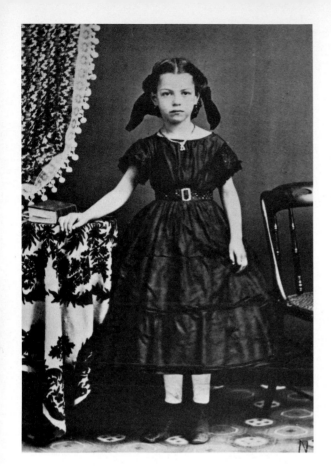

Isabel Arguëllo, descendant of two governors, left her palatial home in Santa Clara and enrolled at Notre Dame to win the Notre Dame diploma in 1874.

Elizabeth Landers, below. This beautiful Irish girl "just walked away" from her monastic school in Ireland to join her father in California, and imediately found herself in boarding school at Notre Dame. "Lizzie" was a favorite with teachers and classmates, and one of Sister Anna Raphael's outstanding nature students.

Until recent times the little wooden clapper known as the "signal" was the symbol of authority. The teacher who could control with the faintest click was considered the finest disciplinarian.

Don Antonio M. Pico's daughters, Petra and Vicenta, were students of sorts, and might have been much better had they not fitted in so well with the young society set of San Jose. Don Antonio, son of José Dolores Pico, had been a member of the Constitutional Convention in Monterey at the age of 41, and his wife, María de Pilar Bernal, was from the first a shy but friendly member of the little group that formed around the Bascoms, McDougals, and Burnetts. The Don was forward-looking politically; he was a Lincoln Elector in 1860. Petra and Vicenta were aggressive, too, and as they fluttered in and out of the boarding school, Sister Mary Aloysia would hardly have written them down as Castilians. For though they displayed great pride in their family story, they always kept an eye on the main social chance, not troubling to become candidates for school honors.[15]

They seem, in fact, to have been quite the opposite to their classmates, the Vallejos from Mission San Jose, the docile and studious Encarnación, Guadalupe, and María Teresa de Jesús. These, too, knew family pride; their father, Don José de Jesús Vallejo, was son of Don Ignacio Vallejo and María Antonía Luga, and brother of the famous General Mariano Vallejo. This family accepted historic evolution wisely; once Commandant of Pueblo San José, Don José became later its first U. S. Postmaster. His wife, the good Luisa Soledad Sánchez, reared her daughters in piety and dignity.[16] María de Jesús, the best endowed of the family, was described in her later life as a Sister of Notre Dame as favoring her military forebears in appearance, but as very generally resembling her kind and gentle mother.

Other daughters of dons who had thrown their lot with the Americans were Victoria Pedroreño and Concepción Estudillo from Southern California, names that head a line of Pedroreño-Estudillo-Wolfskill relatives on the records of Notre Dame. Bright, prize-winning Victoria was already honoring her lineage in 1854, with no need of separation in the Spanish group. Her father, a Spanish merchant, had been a member of the Constitutional Convention. A scion of Spanish royalty, he had studied at Oxford University as an exile. From there he had gone to

Peru, and then in 1838 to Old Town, San Diego. Eight years
later he set out with Don Santiago Argüello to aid Commodore
Stockton. Thus his daughter's knowledge of English and her
intellectual prowess are not surprising. Victoria's mother, Antonía, was the daughter of Prefect Antonio Estudillo, who was
perhaps responsible for the presence at Notre Dame of this
bright girl and her almost equally bright cousin, Concepción
Estudillo. At least he paid for the education of both, as well as
of Victoria's younger sisters, Ysabel and Elena.[17]

With some exceptions Spanish girls with non-Spanish sur-
names, children of fathers who had jumped ship, and of mothers
who were determined on a Spanish-speaking household, came
to boarding school in a state hovering between puzzlement and
resentment. Teresa and Josefa Livermore, from the great Livermore Rancho, Las Positas, knew no English when their father,
Robert Livermore, presented them to the Sisters. They were
rather spoiled, and satisfied with an occasional award in
"crochet" and penmanship. In this they were repeating their
father's own youth. With no love for his trade apprenticeship,
he had joined the navy at 16, only to desert ship. Yet he was
"the sailor lad" who became wealthy, secured two land grants,
and the general reputation of honesty. Later he brought his two
younger daughters, María del Milagro and Antonita, to Notre
Dame. Like their sisters, these two were not given to rigorous
study hours. It would seem that their mother, Josefa Higuera,
had as little use for the intellectual woman as for the language
of the Yankees.[18]

But occasionally the English or New England father carried
out his will, setting the stamp of progress on the household in
general. Such was the case in the family of Robert Walkinshaw,
a Scot, who married Francisca Gamiz in Mexico, settled in San
Jose, and there took charge of the New Almaden Quicksilver
Mine. He built a fine home in the area of Mountain View, where
he maintained the hospitable life of a country gentleman, complete with a pack of hounds. Thus his daughters, Roberta and
Francisca, arrived at Notre Dame knowing the fine points of
hunting and were generally well-poised despite their dubious

English. In a short time they had taken the linguistic hurdle, and Francisca especially, worked up an impressive scholastic record. Francisca was, besides, the school's best mannered student, the Miss Notre Dame of today. Thus Robert Walkinshaw's decision in 1858 to take his family to Scotland was a disappointment to the Sisters. But after the father's death a year later, the family returned, and the two younger girls, Josefa and Guadalupe, came to Notre Dame where they gave complete satisfaction, without however quite keeping the pace set by ambitious Francisca.[19]

Julian Hanks was another non-Spanish father who seems to have asserted his authority in favor of the English language; his daughters, Rebecca, Sofía, and Ann, were enrolled in the English-speaking classes in the earliest days at Notre Dame, where without spectacular results, they worked tirelessly to honor the name of their adventurer father, who with that other shipmaster, William Fisher, had left Connecticut, sailed around the Horn, and settled in Lower California. In Miraflores, Captain Hanks married Isabel Montaña, a señora not so adamant as others, perhaps, since her children bore Anglo-Saxon names. At any rate, Captain Hanks, as master of the ship *Maria Theresa,* brought his family to California in 1845, and was established in San Jose the following year. He and Isaac Branham were partners in a sawmill on Los Gatos Creek, and as a leading citizen he represented his area at the Constitutional Convention in Monterey in 1849. A successful rancher, he still yearned for the sea, and finally set off again for Lower California, again as shipmaster, and perhaps with the intention of settling property interests there. Family tradition says the voyage was made during the Maximilian uprising, and that the British sank his ship under suspicion of bringing aid to the enemy. His family took deep root in the Santa Clara Valley, and the network of Hanks-Fisher-Ceseña-Colombet-Murphy connections is of fascinating interest to the historian.[20] Simple and gentle, the Hanks girls had no thought of their historic importance. They were country youngsters whose father brought them to the Sisters, no doubt in a rough wagon, and paid their tuition in

1855 with "10 bags of flour," and the balance in cash, and for another session, with "2 oxes." Rebecca was a good student; her letter to classmate Isabel Ramírez indicates a friendly, sensitive, and intelligent nature.

A spectacular member of this mixed group arrived at Notre Dame from Santa Barbara shortly after the coming of Sister Aloyse of the Cross and Sister Mary of St. George. It seems clear that they singled out this bright and rather aggressive ten-year-old for special challenge, for she escaped quickly from the classification "Spanish Young Lady," and won prizes on every side, a real danger to the brightest Americans. This was Catarina Den, medalist at the end of her seven years at Notre Dame. Her father, Dr. Nicholas Den, landed at Santa Barbara from the *Kent* in 1836, and there acquired his vast Rancho Dos Pueblos. His bride, Rosa Hill, daughter of Daniel Hill of Boston and Rafaela Luisa Ortega, could speak no English when they were married in Santa Inez Mission, nor could the Doctor speak Spanish. In the home, in fact in the neighborhood, Little Catarina heard nothing but her mother's native tongue. Thus it is not surprising that at each summer's end, Doctor Den entrusted his daughter to the care of the captain of the steamer *Seabird* to be returned to Notre Dame in San Jose. Catarina was patently a spoiled darling at ten, a fact which accounts for her failure to be named even once in the "Superior Class of Good Conduct" list. Perhaps she insisted on being the center of things; her biography, compiled by her daughter in the sentimental vein of the late century, is a monument of self-esteem; all its eight full-page photographs are of Catarina herself. Its title, *Swinging the Censer,* seems particularly appropriate. There is no mention of the Sisters of Notre Dame in all its pages. Still in later years, in Santa Barbara, Catarina made amends. She was happy then to have a place of honor with the Sisters at commemorative ceremonies, occasions which had become her chief interest. At such functions, Catarina could be counted on for a rousing speech. Her great love was Santa Barbara's Spanish setting, and she often included her hiding of fugitive Edward McGowan in the cornfield.[21]

A small group from Oregon rounds out the picture of early Notre Dame. There was Harriet Pambrun with her French-Canadian and Indian heritage. In a way, her school days in San Jose continued her life in the boarding school in Oregon City. Enrolled as a senior student, she was one of Sister Marie de Ste. Thérèse's first vocal students. For Harriet, whose mother was a child of the forest, the school in San Jose offered, besides classes, a series of finishing touches before her return to the North and such a wedding as would befit the daughter of a Hudson's Bay agent. The finishing touches were perhaps less necessary in the case of Margaret Rae, granddaughter of the Hudson's Bay Co. empire builder in the Pacific Northwest, Dr. John McLaughlin.[22]

From Oregon, too, came little Annie Burns, one of the numerous Burns family, immigrants from Ireland and a relative of the Sisters' friend, Hugh Burns of Oregon City, who paid the bills of poor children whom he brought to Sister Loyola's new boarding school there.[23]

Other girls came down from Oregon, mostly of half-Indian parentage, and probably all on the advice of Archbishop Blanchet. These would want finishing touches, too, or perhaps they just missed Sister Marie Catherine and Sister Mary Aloysia. And both of these would be able to explain their moods to the young, energetic new Sisters who looked for intelligent and orderly results of their teaching. These girls, with their large dark, searching eyes, and coarse black hair, with their straight, slender lines surrendering to plump curves, lacked the pliant piety of the "Castilians." Perhaps they lacked sentiment and gratitude as well; they pass out of the ken of companions and teachers, taking with them a little music and singing and other graces.

It was certainly otherwise with Louise Provost, niece, or more likely cousin once removed of Archbishop Blanchet. Just as the last Sisters of Notre Dame were leaving Oregon for California, Charles Provost arrived there from Quebec with his young family. His wife, a Blanchet, died at Panamá, and it was well for his four children that the Archbishop was at their journey's end to receive them. The Archbishop sent the oldest child, Louise, to the Sisters in San Jose and taught her three brothers in his residence himself. From the first list on, the name of Louise Provost stands close to, sometimes ahead of that of Emma Barry. Like a true French-Canadian, she loved music and singing, but she was an enthusiast about every class, about the school and the Sisters. One of the first to complete the academic course in San Jose, Louise accepted Sister Mary Bernard's invitation to help in the newly opened school in Marysville where she taught with great success until her marriage in 1858 to John L. Auzerais, the son of a Normandy farmer who had given his children the best education possible. Two of these, Charles and John L. opened a successful business in Valparaiso, the latter remaining there while Charles went on to establish the Mariposa Store in San Jose. When John joined his brother, the store was only a first step in his career as a leader in local business. Auzerais House, of which San Joseans were justly proud, was only one of the ventures by which he aided city development. When he died suddenly in 1888, his name was one of the best known and most respected in the Santa Clara Valley.

And with the name of Louise Provost Auzerais, Notre Dame associates another complex of prominent families. Her son, John E. Auzerais, married Minnie McLaughlin, daughter of Banker Edward McLaughlin, in the private chapel of the McLaughlin home on Reed Street in San Jose. Her daughter, Louise Aimée, married Banker Edward T. Sterling with Vicar General F. X. Blanchet of Portland officiating. Her beautiful granddaughter, Aimée continuing the ancestral Normandy name, married Dr. Milton B. Lennon. Her Sterling granddaughters, Madeleine and Marie Louise, were later Notre Dame graduates. Louise herself, one of the valley's most esteemed women, seemed to draw closer to her Alma Mater with the passing years. Sister Anthony, S.H., called her "Grandmother of the Notre Dame Alumnae." To the younger Sisters, she was an organizer, an example of loyalty, but to the pioneers she was a last link with their Oregon mission. Certainly she was one of Notre Dame's splendid women, and the saying that "nothing but good was known of the Auzerais clan" was no doubt due in large part to her long presence among them.[24]

In the school, her example as a mature student helped to break down the cultural barrier; as the señoritas saw her perfect herself in the English language they realized its advantages as well as its inevitability as the common tongue. But other factors, too, led to the abandoning of the "Division of Spanish Young Ladies" and the attempt to conduct parallel classes for these. Certainly the new Sisters objected to this double effort. There was also a social factor. In a predominantly male society the attractiveness of the señorita was enhanced. Brothers and friends of the American girls wanted to meet their sisters' classmates. Among the Spanish young people American dance steps were competing with tradition. At least some unyielding madres began to relent, but whether they did or not, the change had set in, and even Sister Mary Aloysia realized that after all she could not hope to intercept every fervid note that entered the lodge after a holiday, well secreted between the pages of Yankee textbooks.

At the end of its first decade, Notre Dame in San Jose had established its character as a cosmopolitan school with stress on friendliness. To Sister Aloyse of the Cross this was a gratifying trend. It fostered a common outlook, a healthy competition in "the branches."

CHAPTER 7   A DEGREE OF IMPORTANCE

*J*he end of the first decade of the Sisters of Notre Dame in San Jose may be seen as a point of departure. The decade had brought success which was clearly only a beginning. The faculty was acquiring unforeseen strength. The aim of the boarding school was crystalizing; whatever other activities would be developed from it as a source, its own focus would be advanced teaching. For growth in population and a more settled and centered approach to mining, especially in the Comstock, was increasing the enrollment of older students. Nor was there need of advertising; Notre Dame was known in Virginia City and Gold Hill by people who had not read of the "Society of Ladies, who, in Europe and the Atlantic States, are devoted to education."[1] And advised by good friends, the "Ladies" were aware of their opportunities.

If they were caught napping politically, so that they needed the *Dirge* of Annie Fitzgerald to set things right, we need not be surprised; much of the loyalty to the Union which marked the close of the war was of the overnight variety. At the outset, only seven of the 53 newspapers in California had supported Lincoln. Businessmen advised neutrality, and one short-lived Governor, J. B. Weller, in 1860 saw California as potentially a "mighty republic" on the Pacific.[2] Besides, politics did not seem a necessary study for even learned ladies. And that being the case, the Sisters may be excused for failing to note that Union Democrats had joined with Republicans in 1862 to form a strong Union Party, and for missing the significance of Peter H. Burnett's advice quoted in the San Jose *Mercury*.[3] If they were bewildered by slogans of "hard money," and "worthless U. S. notes," they had none of the journals read by teachers today.

Perhaps a greater lag is evident in the Sisters' understanding of social change. Their memoirs make no mention of settlers

facing eviction and threatening civil war. Hearing about such
disturbances, the Sisters prayed for a "more settled form of
government," without realizing that Governor Downey's coun-
selling and compromise moves pointed to acceptance of an
inevitable changeover in property holding. They still looked
to a miracle, not to social evolution, to help them acquire the
Peralta estate which would round out their property. Sister
Marie Catherine prayed long for this miracle, taking care first
to place the statue of good St. Anthony, which ironically was
the gift of Gertrudis Peralta to the Sisters, high in a tree facing
the desired orchard. Gertrudis herself had declared that San
Antonio would have a care for the Sisters' wants, but it had
taken over a decade to convince her that the orchard was included in this list. It was a comfortable wooden house in Santa
Clara that made the adobe in which their father had died seem
less a sanctuary. Their change of mind was part of a general
change of which the lists of Sheriff's sales in the county, and
other chaotic signs were symptoms. But to Sister Marie Catherine it was a miracle.

The development to which the Sisters were completely alert
was in communications, a matter in which any improvement
would help their boarding school, and make branch houses
possible. Each step in this field was a blessing, the first being
the telegraph between San Jose and San Francisco. An archival
treasure of Notre Dame is the telegraphed inquiry of John Van
Houten about the health of his daughter "Maggie," dated November 1, 1856. Maggie had worried the family in San Francisco by failing to write. Is she sick? No doubt she was taken
to task by the Sisters and made speedy amends by letter on the
next northbound stage. Then within another five years New
York was suddenly as close as San Francisco, and orders for
books or apparatus might be telegraphed directly, thus ending
the need of scanning the long lists inserted in the newspaper
by book-dealer A. Waldteufel after the unloading of ships. This
was an exciting improvement. For if the San Jose *Mercury*
found it necessary to explain to its readers why messages were
recorded in the West apparently earlier than their time of send-

ing in the East, there must have been some local debate on that subject, not, to be sure among the girls of Sister St. George's science classes, who knowing the "uses of the globes," could have disposed of the problem clearly and succinctly. That progressive teacher read the newspaper without fear of "worldliness," and quoted to her class the prediction that soon, because of transcontinental telegraph, Pony Express would be "cast aside as a slow horse." Yet for all but brief messages, the "Pony" was the Sisters' wonder of the age as they waited through the decade for the last spike to complete the rails. It meant that a letter from Sister Louise in Cincinnati, usually including one from Namur, would arrive in a few weeks.[4]

Yet news sped from coast to coast long before it did from point to point in the West. One could not send a telegram to Marysville, which might as well have been at the end of the earth. Mère Constantine complained in 1862 that it took two and a half months for a letter to come from that point to New York and only about three weeks more to cross the Atlantic from there to Namur. Perhaps no American longed for the transcontinental railroad as did Mère Constantine; it would draw the western houses into the orbit of Cincinnati, and she had no thought as yet of setting up a western provincialate. Despite her admiration for Sister Mary Cornelia, she betrays in her letters a fear of western independence. She chides Sister for seeming indifference about visiting Namur when the railroad would make it possible, but age was telling on her, and the great unsettled American scene was trying her patience.[5] The residents of the Santa Clara Valley had lost patience, too, over the matter of rail communication between San Jose and San Francisco. Almost three years had passed since the granting of the railroad permit, when the first trains ran in January, 1864. Then amid the general rejoicing perhaps the enthusiasm of Notre Dame students passed unnoticed. They could now make the trip in two hours and ten minutes on the railroad built through the enterprise of the Irish foundryman Peter Donohue, father of Mary Ellen, one of the students.[6]

When the overland trains arrived some four years later, it was the Sisters' turn to rejoice. At last the arduous Isthmus crossing had passed into history. But for Sisters, as for all, the overland train cut off the last claim to pioneering. Even then a bit of epic grandeur began to mark those who had risked earlier distance and danger. But to all the "last spike" meant much more than future convenience. It promised an economic stability in the West that its "hard money" boast alone could not assure. Because of that promise, the Sisters saw signs of business progress in their city, and in those signs they read assurance of their own. Through that decade, the San Jose *Mercury,* a daily since 1861, gave enthusiastic notices of such developments as Auzerais House, "that new and splendid hotel," of Ryland Block, and the new Santa Clara County Court House. And there were smaller notes of progress in both ads and editorial comment. The first dental chair, in which "the victim may be raised or lowered," caused a stir in 1865, when Dentist J. J. Menefee installed one in his office at First and Santa Clara Streets. In the light of such scientific advance, the Sisters ordered a chair a little later for their infirmary, and in this deceivingly upholstered contrivance, victims, students as well as Sisters, were raised and lowered until well after the turn of the century.

Above all, there was the matter of a local bank. San Francisco's Bank of California, boasting a capital stock of $2,000,000, "paid up in gold coin," was an incentive for Editor Owen's declaration that San Jose needed a bank, since it had, in fact, "attained that degree of importance," a conclusion he might easily have drawn from his own announcement of a few days earlier that the city was now out of debt.[7] As the editor, and certainly the Sisters, hoped, San Jose's first bank was founded in 1866, the Knox and Beans Bank, on Santa Clara Street. Two years later it was incorporated as Bank of San Jose, its president T. Ellard Beans. Before another decade the city boasted two additional banks, McLaughlin and Ryland's, and the San Jose Savings Bank. The City Directory of 1874 called all three "palatial," a statement that certainly indicates a "degree of importance." For the Sisters, this was all symptomatic of stability. They could overlook as well as solve the difficulties of two sets of values for hard money and paper notes, transactions made easier by the experience of evaluation of gold dust and barrels of flour. If they needed a standard of comparison, they had it at hand in financial statements such as the San Jose *Mercury's* listing of donations in a charity benefit under separate headings, Gold and Greenbacks, making it clear that the larger paper donations were only apparently more generous, nor allowing it to be forgotten that the East was gaining in the matter of exchange. For this was the topic of continued bitterness, and even so peace-loving a man as Editor Owen had to admit that western metal was the "most difficult proposition to reconcile with loyalty to the Nation."

As the decade advances, the Sisters' business books indicate growing financial acumen. They were studying trends and weighing risks against reality. In the five years beginning with 1859, the annual income from the boarding school rose from $19,000 to over $30,000, this rise followed by a levelling off to $25,000 later in the decade and through the following, a turn explained by decrease in tuition in keeping with postwar decline in the cost of living, not as may seem, by a falling off in the student group, which was actually growing rapidly. In general, this decline in costs had less to do with postwar economy than with a settling from the uncertainties of earlier mining years with their lack of response to the laws of economy. Decline in living costs between the years 1851 and 1866 may be judged by these entries in the Notre Dame account books: flour from $7.50 a sack to $5.50 a barrel; butter, from 50 cents to 37½ cents a pound. And in the latter year the price of the best beef cuts was down to 12½ cents a pound. These are, of course, local quotations, and in both cases, wholesale, or at least at some reduction. Building costs were lower after the war, and the steady migration to the West brought skilled labor into less fantastic ranges.

And now the new names on the roster brought the added assurance of payment in hard cash and well ahead of time, whether their fathers were mine owners or businessmen in the centers of Mother Lode or Comstock. First came Jane Bowers of Gold Hill, Nevada, and Rose Morgan of Columbia. Then several from Washoe, Silver City, Grass Valley, Downieville and Virginia City, the greatest number from the last. Clara and Flora Sharon made their first appearance from Virginia City, recalling easily at first their less affluent childhood in San Francisco, and replacing these recollections with dawning awareness of great wealth. Some of the new girls came and went, like flashing gold or silver comets, with astounding outfits picked up in San Francisco en route to boarding school, but with manners that had not improved as their parents moved from town to town in quest of riches, with boarding houses for temporary homes. Some, like Ada Ellis and Viola Dyer from Carson City, were "Notre Dame girls" from the start, enthusiastic and grateful. And there was also Mary Atchison from Virginia City, excellent student and later an excellent teacher. She and Mary Frances Redmond of Marin were the only winners of the college diploma in 1872, an honor hitherto bestowed on only three others.[8]

Clara Sharon, petite and charming in the upper school, set her sights on top grades and so won "crowns" and other distinctions, including a prize for bookkeeping, the last subject being the suitable choice of a number of very wealthy daughters, perhaps with Papa's advice. Clara was last listed in 1869; then her father sent her to Paris for a continental finishing off. Returning, she married Yale graduate, Francis Newlands, who set up a law practice in San Francisco. Archbishop Alemany performed the ceremony in the grand Sharon home on Sutter Street. But this brilliant wedding was to be quite outdone by that of her vivacious younger sister Flora, who left no trace of very great scholastic effort. Flora won no prizes, her one high academic moment being her essay "On Street Beggars." Her real prize was, as Mrs. Fremont Older had pointed out, her marriage to Sir Thomas Fermor-Hesketh, San Francisco's "first fashionable international wedding," though the ceremony had for its setting the fabulous Ralston House at Belmont.[9]

The Sisters heard of all this splendor; that was worldliness. And because their students knew of this aloofness, perhaps, they sent no invitations to their Alma Mater. The wedding photographs, the betrothal ceremony in the college chapel, were for the future. An occasional forecast of that friendlier day brought the pious-minded former student back to Notre Dame for a sort of brief retreat before her wedding day. And after this preparation for her new state in life, the bride-to-be was called for by her fiancé whom she happily presented to Sister Mary Cornelia and her teachers. But this was the exceptional instance. The departing student was assured of the Sisters' prayers, of a welcome whenever she should return to visit, but in the days before the alumnae association was formed, visits were not frequent. Seeming indifference was part of the wealthy girl's rush from the convent campus to achieve sophistication. It needed travel and other advantages to be at ease with Nob Hill elegance fenced with bronze, or with the blaring grandeur of extravagance on the Peninsula.

That was the problem of adjustment faced by Jenny Flood, who drew first prize in bookkeeping, as could properly be expected of an heiress who wished to keep track of her new millions. She worked hard at piano, too, in preparation for her coming year or two of study abroad. Music came with less ease to practical Jenny, it seems. She played no exhibition solos, but managed a part in "Johann von Paris" with seven others at four pianos. When at last she returned from Europe, she was charming and finished to a degree that attracted the rather irresponsible son of General Ulysses Grant. After that unfortunate romance, she settled into an energetic spinster life filled with charitable causes and the social life of Linden Towers.[10]

Mary Ellen Donohue, daughter of millionaire Peter Donohue, the foundryman and railroad builder, could not trace her fortune to gold or silver. Her immigrant father and his brothers, James and Michael, were "kings of iron." Peter and his second wife, Anna Downey, sister of the Governor, paved the way to splendor; Mrs. Donohue used to be driven about in an elegant glass coach. And Mary (she was Mamie at Notre Dame) fulfilled her parents' desires when she married Baron Henry von Schroeder in New York.[11]

And there were the Hastings sisters, Clara, Ella, and Flora, also conscious plutocrats, proud of their father's distinction as first Supreme Court Justice in California. Iowa-born Clara could remember gold rush scenes, as well as arguments when little Benicia was competing with San Jose and Sacramento in the race for the capital. When Clara registered at Notre Dame in 1863, her father's immense fortune was already made, questionably said many. Whether or not she heard these innuendoes, Clara set about learning music and cultivating her fine voice, in preparation for studies in Paris and Germany, but gained only a bowing acquaintance with other studies. For half a century Clara was a society leader and chief holder of her father's vast estates. Outliving her age group, she long enjoyed the title of "last of the belles of pioneer days."[12]

There were others of this new-made heiress class through the second and third decades at Notre Dame, some of them a bit haughty, and demonstrating no great admiration for such eager intellectuals as Sister Mary Genevieve, but willing to drop deep curtsies to Sister Marie de Ste. Thérèse because of her courtly bearing and the whispers they heard of her lineage. Still, in later years, the first formal alumnae invitations brought most of them back to their Alma Mater.

The second decade brought also a fine group of less plutocratic but more scholastic-minded students. Not even Sister Mary of St. George could have asked for a keener, more logical mind than that of Mary McHenry, Justice John McHenry's daughter, who even as a junior, foreshadowed her own brilliant successes in every class. With ease, Mary outstripped her aunt, Bessie McHenry and her sister Emma. In fact, she challenged all comers without wishing to do so, or noticing her achievements. She was a sweet, outgoing girl, one of the few to sense the deep kindness that underlay Sister Marie Catherine's brusque exterior. Recalling the pangs of her first days away from home, Mary told how her longing centered about her pet cat, and how unable to find a gentle feline about the convent,

Sister substituted a canary in a cage. The anguish past, Mary was swept into studies, and despite her veiled, almost poetic look, decided to become a lawyer.

Graduating from Hastings Law School in 1882, Mary "brought down the house," as Emma put it, when as speaker of her class she swayed the crowded Platt Hall in San Francisco. But her successfully begun career was suddenly ended when she married artist William Keith, and thus became subject of humorous verse about lady lawyers in the *Argonaut*. The three McHenrys kept in touch with Notre Dame. Since Bessie's coming there in 1857, the names of the early Sisters were household names. But it was Mary who set down her recollections in after years. She recalls how she impulsively decided to be a Catholic, but how the Sisters told her she must have the consent of her parents, and how her report card once bore the shocking appraisal "a little self-willed." Even then she could hold her own, a trait that through life made her at ease with intellectual celebrities, including the historian Mommsen, with whom she enjoyed good conversation.[13]

Two other San Franciscans were Alice Lander and Sarah Webb, sole winners of the college diploma in its first two years of existence, 1866 and 1867. In both instances the honor was bestowed in anticipation of the charter, and this being the case, it is safe to say that no others since that time have had to work so diligently for their achievement. All eyes, one might say, were upon them, as well as upon the Sisters, who would risk only their most likely to succeed. With these came a beautiful Irish girl, who loved nature study most of all and won every botany prize without fail. This was Elizabeth Landers, who came well prepared from an Ursuline academy in her homeland, from which she had been abducted by her uncle at the request of her father, who had discovered that a fortune made in the West was not enough without his "little girl." At the very thought of sending this tender bud into the dangers of wild San Francisco, her mother's relatives immured her within convent walls, where she studied and perhaps lived happily enough. Still at her uncle's suggestion, she walked calmly away, boarded ship for New York, made the Panamá crossing, at last joined her anxious father, and soon found herself happily at work in boarding school once more. Lizzie was a very general student, liking all "branches," but her school above all. She married John O'Brien of San Francisco, and her descendants are still in Notre Dame schools. Dorothy O'Brien, Alumna of of 1931, is her granddaughter.[14]

Through the 1860s, the school's student list shows a sprinkling of army daughters. Colonel B. Lathrop's daughter Virginia, an outstanding student and later an able alumnae organizer, was one of these. Another army daughter was Helen Hensley, whose father was Major Samuel J. Hensley, a civic leader in San Jose. Helen wrote with ease and fitting phrase. Her *Quarterly* articles are a delight whether she tells of a school closing or of the exploits of her remarkable parents. From babyhood she had heard of her father's part in the Chiles-Walker crossing of the plains, of his leadership in the Bear Flag Revolt, and of his army title won for Mexican War service. But his civilian life was as distinguished; for one thing he was largely responsible for the development of the California Navigation Company on the Sacramento River. And Helen was equally proud of her mother, Helen Crosby Hensley, daughter of pioneer E. O. Crosby of San Jose, for in Washington Secretary of State William H. Seward had allowed her to hold the document which admitted California to the Union.[15]

With equal desire to educate his daughters well, General H. A. Cobb enrolled Zoë and Eugénie, who seem to have lacked the ability that carried their father from post to post up to his appointment by Governor Haight as Major General of the forces in California, and that won for him in civil life two elections as President of the Board of Education in San Francisco. Zoë lingered long in the grammar division without ever reaching the higher classes. She puttered with bookkeeping, one of the few upper school subjects open to those who failed to pass the grammar examinations. It was perhaps as well for her that she never reached the sanctum of Sister Mary of St. George. Yet Zoë had ambitions of her own. Sister Marie de Ste. Thérèse accorded her highest honors in vocal in 1869, and gave her the title role in "Flora's Festival" the spectacular operetta of that year. Slightly more successful in classes, Eugénie was something of an instrumentalist. At least on exhibition day the General could be proud. For then the morning's bright intellectual record tended to lose luster in the afternoon's flowery appeal to the senses. One rose wreath in an operetta might touch off more thunderous applause than that accorded to all the crowns of excellence.

Most of the crowns were being won, in fact, by girls who came to Notre Dame with less spectacular claims than great fortune or paternal high position. Middle class Catherine Mahoney of San Francisco finished with a fine collection of crowns; her highest honors were in literature. This explains the welcome she received in the new literary circles of her city, where she founded the Caedmon Club, and like her poetic husband, D. W. Nesfield, contributed to the literary offerings of the era. Her tribute to her friend, Sister Anna Raphael, in *Notre Dame Quarterly* presents an example of clear, forceful prose, of logical development and fulfillment around a central note of praise.[16]

Mary Pulsifer followed in Catherine's steps as collector of honors and as the school's best writer. But botany and geology were her delights then and through her remarkable life. Perhaps day scholar Mary and her sister Martha disliked boarding school; their names disappear when they complete the senior class, but before long Mary's reappears as a collector of California flora. Always in touch with Sister Anna Raphael, Mary vied with her in corresponding with noted scientists. In exchange for her collection of western flora, Austrian Botanist Karl Beck sent her his collection of algae and his autographed photo, both of which her family presented to the college after her death. In 1909 Sister Anthony, S.H., hoped to dedicate a number of the newly founded *Quarterly* to this alumna, so widely known "in the world of science." Regrettably she did not carry out this plan, for such an article would have preserved data on the family of Mary Pulsifer Ames, whose one appearance in Notre Dame Archives is the notice of the baptism of herself and her sister, in the chapel, January 13, 1900.[17]

Because of the extensive Miller-Kirk Collection the name of Josephine Miller has been accorded a scientific prominence at Notre Dame which she herself must have often disclaimed, since research and painstaking identification were the work chiefly of her husband, Joseph Kirk. Effort was, in fact, hardly necessary for this youngest of the Marin County Millers; it was enough that her name was linked so closely with that of the Martin Murphys, and that her sisters, Catherine, Ellen Independence, Frances, Theresa, and Julia had made records for perfect conduct at Notre Dame before her name was added to the list.[18]

Of these, surely the brightest, the most pious, the superlative in all good respects, was Frances. Her strong point was the essay, didactic and stilted. But with travel and pursuit of the arts in Europe, she acquired some naturalness. Perhaps her friendship with Ina Coolbrith helped to free her from perfectionism. At any rate, she was in constant demand as a guest speaker, and Miller Hall became famous for her entertainments, her art collection, and her ability as a critic. Art and music were her constant pursuits though in her early days at school, none of her teachers would have suspected ability in either. Frances did well enough as a child to manage a part in the 16-hand "Electric Polka." The Sisters would have counted on her ability to write, as well as on the use that she made of it.

Sharing her father's intense interest in orphan boys, she contributed articles regularly to Reverend D. O. Crowley's *St. Joseph's Union*, published from his Youth's Directory in San Francisco. Cultured Father Crowley, with an eye on the intellectual as well as on the underprivileged, made a point of encouraging writers. In Fannie de C., her *nom de plume* since school days, he found a contributor ready to discuss Political Power, Education, or Rights of Women, and to adorn her work in due season with allusions from Bacon, Shakespeare, or even Horace. And if on occasion, in her most convincing lines, the skeleton of a Bacon period shows through, that was Sister Anna

Raphael's basic training asserting itself. At any rate, what Fannie could always rely upon was good position with relation to footlights, a fact which both in school days and later may account for the eclipse in which her sisters seem to have moved. But they were fine alumnae, the best of Notre Dame girls, and so were greatly loved by the Sisters.

In a way, Fannie's shadow perhaps also obscured the four delightfully unself-conscious Redmond sisters Mary Frances, Bertha, Agatha, and Meida, all fine students; the older two won the college diploma in 1872 and 1873. The Redmonds were late arrivals at Notre Dame, and so well-started toward erudition that after her usual severe entrance examination, Sister Aloysius assigned the older two to the senior division. The family had settled late in Marin County, for Irish merchant John B. Redmond had been won to the joys of rural life only in 1864, when a large acreage near Novato Corners attracted his attention. Here he established a successful dairy farm and comfortable home from which his daughters were soon journeying down to Notre Dame with the younger Millers and others from Marin. Few girls enjoyed boarding school as did the Redmonds, especially Mary Frances, who four decades later recalled such delightful incidents, such lovely memories of the Sisters. An outgoing girl, with no selfish ambition, she attained a higher record than did perfectionist Fannie Miller. And certainly she enjoyed her young life, noting down her reasons for happiness. There was Sister Ignatius lighting the gas on gloomy evenings and lighting young hearts with the passing greeting as well. Sister Philomene was so kind that some girls "formed the idea they were relatives of hers." And how Sister Mary Cornelia robbed "parting of bitterness" when parents had said goodbye.

A much admired school friend of Mary Frances was Sophie Ward of San Leandro, a girl as given to declaiming and causes as Fannie Miller, but sweeter and more pliant. If the younger Sisters admired her scholastic qualities, the pioneers smiled upon her as the child of kind J. B. Ward, who had come aboard ship to offer them assistance in a strange new port. Sophie inherited his goodness and ability, as well as the wisdom of her mother, Arcadia Concepción Estudillo. She brought to the debating class something of her father's range of interests. It is unlikely, however, that her teachers would have foreseen what came to be her dedicated subject. As the wife of Colonel J. J. Tobin of San Francisco, Sophie became an ardent supporter of Irish Home Rule, her speeches often ending with her heart's desire, to be present at Ireland's first national parliament. If this goal was denied her, she scored a greater though unplanned achievement; through life she affected others so deeply in her casual conversation as to be constantly quoted. When the Redmonds arrived at Notre Dame, Sophie was detained at home by the illness of her mother. Before she returned, classmate Mary Frances knew her well. Everyone, she says, knew and quoted her opinions. The Davis girls of San Leandro made, it seems, no such impact, and their names in the lists are so lost among others of the same name, that identification is hazardous. A few of this name represented the East Bay in its beginnings of urban life. With these and Sophie Ward came the fine student Grace Riddle, born in Massachusetts, who seems to have been in the guardianship of the local Estudillo family.[20]

When Flora Sparks arrived from Santa Barbara in 1862, she was registered as a "Spanish Young Lady," since only in that language could she explain that her State-of-Maine father, Isaac Sparks had spent his boyhood in St. Louis, that he had come west as a hunter and trapper, that the Mexican government had granted him the great Huasna Rancho of five square leagues in 1843, and that he built and managed one of the first stores in Santa Barbara. Like Catarina Den, Flora was adaptable. Before long both she and her sister Rosa were following regular classes, though without Catarina's perseverence and love for learning. The Ormats, Francisca and Mary, arrived later as did Manuela Burke. They were all Catarina's friends, but the record seems to indicate that none of them came with a high resolve to walk in her footsteps.

At the same time a sprinkling of pioneer daughters came down on the new peninsula train from areas north of the Bay. One of these, Lizzie Yount from Napa, apparently got on well,

without being spectacular. And from Sonoma came the Haraszthy sisters, Ida and Otelia, who used to be met by their famous
father at the little steamboat landing at Sonoma Creek and
thence driven to their palatial Pompeian home at Buena Vista
Vineyards, where today stone pillars and foundations recall one
of the chief centers of Californian social life in the early American period. When Agoston Haraszthy entered his daughters at
Notre Dame, he wished them to follow the full course, to study
music, and especially to learn chemistry, since after less propitious starts, he had discovered on the sunny slopes of the Sonoma hills, acres well adapted to the pursuit of scientific viticulture begun by his family in his native Hungary. Ida's success
must have pleased him; certainly she delighted Sister Mary of
St. George. Through the next four years, she won top honors in
science, even surpassing Catarina Den. These two were rivals
in most classes in which both names appear.

   If international relations had held its present day scholastic
importance, the Haraszthy girls would have presented a remarkable case history, even though the school in those days
never lacked daughters of political exiles. For Agoston Haraszthy, usually styled "Colonel," had served at 18 as Royal Guard
under Austrian Emperor Ferdinand, then as private secretary
of the viceroy of Hungary, and later as leader of the Bacska,
before casting his lot with Louis Kossuth in the plot for Magyar
independence. With his beautiful Polish wife, Princess Elea-
nora de Dedinski, he had led the life of an exile in Wisconsin
and on the plains, searching always for likely climate in which
to raise the Zinfandel and other favorite wine grapes. Thus Ida
had tasted something of the hard life before the family settled
in the Valley of the Moon. Otelia was less given to studies, or
perhaps to boarding school, but Ida completed the course with
honors and then accompanied her father to Europe where he
had planned an extended tour in preparation for his report on
viticulture. During his months of travel and record making,
Ida studied music in Paris. Returning she married Major Henry
Hancock, who had served like her father in early sessions of the
California Assembly. Hancock Hall in the Allan Hancock Foun-

dation at the University of Southern California in Los Angeles, stands as a memorial of Ida's zeal for the advancement of music and culture in the South, just as the Foundation itself sponsored by her son, Captain G. Allan Hancock, stands for the development of marine biological research in the interest of humanity.[21]

Notre Dame expanded immeasurably because of Frances Miller, Sophie Ward, and their contemporaries. For whether they arrived from Mother Lode or Comstock, or from thriving San Francisco, they brought financial security and the prestige attached to names that were certain to confer strength and leadership. The young Sisters realized the value of such prestige in their work of building up a school for women, which would fulfill the new intellectual ambitions of the West as well as their own ideal.

*T*hat their boarding school roster should represent so many distant places was proof to the Sisters that Notre Dame had established a high reputation even in its second decade. What afforded them perhaps greater satisfaction was the growing appreciation of their work on the part of local influential families. In evidence of their approval, parents were accepting without demur the requirement that their daughters spend at least a year in residence on the campus. And most of the local students accepted this and other regulations with good grace and increasing attachment to their school.

Susan McDougal was of this loyal number. In her later school days, after her family had left the adobe on the plaza and moved to Belmont, Susan returned each term to Notre Dame, even after the death of her schoolgirl cousin Ella, daughter of the thoroughgoing adventurer, Colonel George Mc-Dougal. As an older student Susan sensed the importance of her family history, and could tell a good story in her turn. Her favorite tale was of her Uncle George buying up herds of cattle to supply American troups during the Mexican War. When somehow the American Government forgot to reimburse him, he staged a sit-down strike on the steps of the Senate in Washington, and this failing, went off to retrieve his fortune in South America, there bestowing such abundant good will upon the Patagonians as to win from them the honorary title of "King."[1]

The McDougals' friend, Sarah Donald, mounted the stage at Donald Station, the future Hillsdale, with her mother's injunction not to leave the vehicle at wayside stops ringing in her ears. And this animated girl obeyed the command as a child of fine upbringing and discipline. Singing and dancing as a child of six on the ship *Witch of the Waves*, on the voyage around the Horn, had not spoiled her. She knew she must honor her forebears. She was great-great granddaughter of Matthew Thornton, signer of the Declaration of Independence

and patriots were usual in her family story. A good general student, Sarah enjoyed especially the heated Civil War arguments,
the excitement of mail days, and the stories of Sisters who, like
her, had come around the Horn. In her final year, 1864, this
general favorite of teachers and companions provided high
excitement herself by eloping in the Christmas holiday with
George Winthrop Fox, a young lawyer from Maine. At Sarah's
request, her husband purchased and enlarged the Redwood
City inn which had so intrigued her as forbidden ground in
her stagecoach days. Here she became a lifelong civic leader,
which seems to have been the emerging pattern for early Notre
Dame girls. Sarah was a social leader, too, charming with her
lovely presence the first balls held in Ralston's mansion in
Belmont.[2]

A younger group of San Jose social belles reached the upper
school about mid 1860s, among them Mary Rhodes and her
sister Margaret, daughters of Judge A. L. Rhodes, who was
one of the first to erect an elegant home on The Alameda, near
that of Judge Craven Hester, so that these may be said to have
started the trend to gracious suburban living that was to line
that road with beautiful dwellings. Mary could recall crossing
the plains in 1854, and the party's meeting with John Trimble
at the Humboldt River and changing its direction at his advice
and his praise of the Santa Clara Valley. At Notre Dame, Mary
was in line for prizes, and Margaret followed fairly well in her
footsteps. During the holidays they enjoyed local social affairs;
Mary usually was described in the news notes as charming and
beautiful. In 1869 Alfred Barstow of the U. S. Postal Department claimed her as bride, a fact which explains perhaps her
failure to remain for the new college diploma, a disappointment
certainly to the Sisters.[3]

They were not to be disappointed by tiny Alice Younger,
who appears on the list in 1864 with her older half-sister,
Florence Inskip, already a social butterfly. Besides being a very
bright child, Alice became a sensation among her peers, when
with her entire family she was baptized in St. Joseph's Church
in 1866. It was a distinguished occasion by reason of the promi-

nence of Colonel Coleman Younger and his wife, Augusta
Inskip Younger, and because the honorable Peter H. Burnett
acted as sponsor for the two adults, with C. T. Ryland and his
wife standing for two of the children. Alice and little Augusta
Younger reached upper school only in the following decade.
Alice herself became a poet of local note, at least in her father's
eyes. As President of Santa Clara County Pioneers, he had her
poems read at meetings and published forthwith in *The Pioneer*. Genius or not, Alice was studious. She had a right to be
so, for despite certain oddities, such as passing the hat among
invited guests to pay the musicians at a dance, Colonel Younger
was a man of great intelligence. Both he and his wife led the
movement to recapture early western history. Mrs. Younger
especially was a favorite speaker at historical meetings.[4]

After the opening of Notre Dame Select Day Academy in
1867, the Youngers and others of their standing appear alternately on its roster and that of the boarding school. The Rylands, Ada and Norma, were among these, both studious girls,
who honored the Burnett-Ryland tradition despite lacunae in
school sessions caused by their mother's invalidism. Perhaps
enforced absences prevented their working for the college
diploma, or it may have been their fondness for music, for in
those days the overzealous musician was not considered suitable as a candidate for an intellectual pursuit; such a one was, it
would seem, off on a side track. Ada and Norma were both lovers of music though their tastes differed. Ada's music collection
points to her fondness for such artists as Parepa Rosa and Neil-
son. She collected autographs, too. "Dors Dormi Prue" is there
with the singer's photo pasted on its cover. Norma gathered
rollicking pieces, though she may have been merely enlivening
her classical collection. Between cultural trips to San Francisco,
the Rylands entertained frequently in their beautiful home on
North First Street. From childhood they were often in the public eye, for their father was one of San Jose's leading developers
and public donors. Ryland Park was his gift as well as his idea,
and lovely daughter Ada played a leading part on its opening
day. As director of San Jose's Associated Charities, her name

became a benediction in the Santa Clara Valley. It was also sadly connected with romantic tragedy, for her sense of obligation to her ailing mother prevented for years her marriage with handsome James Findlay. Then when after Mrs. Ryland's death, the wedding day was set, Ada herself died of a heart attack on a visit to Denver.[5]

The daughters of an equally civic-minded San Josean, Francis Lightstone, were listed as lower school day boarders before the opening of the Select Academy. This Bavarian had fled from political disturbance, first to Oregon, then to the Santa Clara Valley. Declaring that he wished peace and freedom, and not gold, he threw his energy into the building of San Jose, became its second city treasurer and organized and headed the first municipal fire department. He married Spanish Juanita Soto, who apparently had no prejudice against English, since her little girls arrived at Notre Dame using it glibly. They were gay children, always finding places in school dramas and music feasts. At one closing two of them set a happy theme with a rousing duet, "Welcome to Vacation." And the youngest, Juanita, read an essay dubiously entitled, "A Rambling Thought." In the senior classes she did no rambling; the pride of the family, she won the college diploma with flying colors.[6]

An early French colony, transplanted from Chile to the Santa Clara Valley, is represented in Notre Dame's lists by such names as Pillot, Poulin, and Petit. Three years before the discovery of gold Julian Pillot brought his Spanish wife and three small daughters from Santiago. In the late 1850s he enrolled Emelia and Heloisa in the Spanish division. Among the family treasures is an ornate birthday greeting for Madame Pillot done by Heloisa in lovely ink design. But this family took so readily to all things American that the younger girls, Clorinda and Matilda, entered the Day Academy with no language problem. The star of this family, Heloisa, was soon winning awards in French and English classes. Heloisa married San Jose's first Chief of Police, James V. Tisdall. Clorinda married Aloysius Benoit, and their descendants have honored Notre Dame down to the present.[7]

Born in San Jose in the year 1851, Sidone Poulin did not share her family's odyssey from Paris to San Jose, with brief sojourns, each planned as final, in Chile, Mexico, and Los Angeles. In San Jose, her father, Auguste Poulin, found at last the object of his search, a flour mill on the Guadalupe River with dam and water wheel. Strained through silk screening, the flour was so far from white as to give his property the name "Orange Flour Mill." But San Jose had another attraction for the Poulins, a well-established school, and when Eugénie Poulin entrusted Sidone to the Sisters, she made her purpose clear and definite. With her will thus doubly fortified, Sidone became the soul of application. When she left Notre Dame she spoke English, French, and Spanish fluently.

Among the Chilian arrivals was the interesting little Irish-born Mary Petit, whose adventuresome French father had taken his family from France to South America in search of a fortune, and at word of gold in California, had hurried them thither, only to be stricken with cholera in San Jose. After his death, his Irish wife, Eleanor Nugent, married Swiss pioneer Eugène Veuve. Thus Notre Dame student Mary Petit, in close touch with at least three national elements, was perhaps the school's most efficacious unifier, since she also lived in close acquaintance with the local Spanish families. Her first home was the adobe of Doña Juana Pacheco. The name of Veuve became a symbol of civic development, for Eugène Veuve gave up his early dream of mining and established his trade of watchmaking in partnership with Jackson Lewis. Mary's half-brother, William Veuve, married her school friend, Jennie Wilson and this strong Huguenot name again appears in the Notre Dame roster when they enrolled their daughter Vida.[8] Jennie had been in the boarding school, and at least occasionally up for honors, but not so constantly as her classmate, bright Sarah Hardesty, nor Viola Dyer, whose family moved from the Comstock to the mines of New Almaden.

It seems unbelievable that places within minutes of the heart of the city today were then at the end of the world by reason of bad roads. San Francisco was far more accessible in

that second decade than were New Almaden or McCartysville.
A great lumber wagon returning empty to the latter point
would convey Frances Jarboe home for a holiday, bumping her
about as though she had not won a crown for application,
completed a fine tapestry, and performed skillfully with seven
others one of the admired pieces for four pianos.[9] But it was
worth it. Lizette Steirlin and her sisters thought so as they
bumped over what is today's smooth road that bears their family name. Seemingly those rugged trips encouraged studious
purpose. Lizette especially brought to her studies much of the
energy displayed by her Swiss father, Christopher C. Steirlin,
in his restless search for better mining areas and finer ranches.[10]

The younger daughters of Martin Murphy, Junior, reached
the upper school in the second decade. Mary Ann might be
styled a plodder, but Ellen, the "Nellie" of Mary Atchison's
acclaim, came nearest to emulating the achievements of their
sister, Elizabeth Yuba.[11] Nellie worked industriously for a good
senior record, and then as the beautiful wife of Joaquín Arqués,
led a life of equally beautiful charity in San Jose. This "best
liked" school girl was certainly one of the most loved and
admired women in the city. Her cousin Mollie, daughter of
John M. and Virginia Reed Murphy, started well, perhaps because of the deep friendship that always existed between her
mother and Sister Anna Raphael. She ended her first term in
boarding school winning a beautiful leather-bound prayer book
for Excellence, a prize long treasured by her mother, a woman
of fine intelligence who in her later years contributed very
readable articles to *Notre Dame Quarterly*. And her gift of clear
statement was a blessing, for as a 13-year-old member of the
Donner Party, Virginia Reed had a tale to tell.[12]

The unspoiled children of caretaker Louis Pinard moved up
through the divisions in the second decade with decorum and
industry. Their names, Selina and Flora, Marie and Léocadie,
are like flowers in the award lists. The last two became Sister
Mary Clara and Sister Madeleine de Pazzi, traditions of goodness and zeal. The Pinard dependability was not surprising; as
his children acquired their education, Louis Pinard was before

them as example, Notre Dame's indispensable factotum through three decades, at his dignified best when as coachman he directed the ways of the Sisters' black carriage horse, Montezuma.

From Santa Clara, Ysabel and Solita Argüello, granddaughters of Governor Luis Argüello and Doña María Soledad Ortega, were enrolled in the boarding school by their father, José Ramón Argüello. The welcome accorded these serious-eyed, dignified little girls by Sister Mary Aloysia was no doubt the warmer because by that year the ranks of her "gentle Castilians" had grown thin. Well-trained and unspoiled, the Argüellos set about the work of education, making no fuss over restrictions which kept them on campus when they might have been enjoying their palatial Santa Clara home with its third floor skating rink and ballroom. Ysabel received a medal or two, once was accorded a crown, and finally the college diploma in 1874. They were pious girls who revered their aunt, Concepción Argüello, as a Beata, at the same time interpreting her story in the full light of romance. Ysabel herself furnished her school with a bit of romance when she married Nicholas Constantino Den, Catarina's brother, in 1877. She honored her beloved teacher by naming her daughter Mary Aloysia, but did not forget to add Concepción for the Beata whom she thought of as duly canonized.[13]

The story of Concepción Argüello should, one would think, have presented to those bright, imaginative young Sisters more inspiring material for exhibition day than thin operettas about flowers, or dramatic sermonettes labored over by graduates. What an oration Catarina Den could have spun out of her protection of Ed McGowan![14] But both teachers and students were still too near such stirring events, which it seemed to many had best be forgotten. The great need they felt was for the smooth and polished, for the capturing of sophistication. What the Sisters saw as they studied their lists was an increase in types and origins as well as in numbers. They saw in the local names the strength and dependability that warranted continuing Sister Loyola's building dream.

By means of smaller new loans in the latter part of the first decade, the Sisters had minimized the burden of larger sums borrowed earlier and so reduced heavy interest. By 1860 nearly $57,000 had been paid off on land purchases and borrowing, and $33,000 was on hand as well. The way was clear for the second unit, the large central building with Attic roof and classic main entrance that soon became a pictured feature of San Jose architecture.

This time Levi Goodrich was architect and builder, with Michael Kenny as master mason, and it would seem that this time, too, Sister Marie Catherine's role of general supervisor was accepted by all. In fact, when Theodore Lenzen continued the program a few years later, he was glad to begin with Sister's sketches. One result of her leadership was a unified quadrangle of buildings, all wide and roomy, with each area easily accessible from the others. When the work was completed in 1863, newsmen and city fathers declared it an ornament to the city, though some criticized the street wall which cut off part of the view.

Sister Marie Catherine's plan included continuous verandahs lining the court formed by the wings, to serve as passageways for all students except seniors, who because their particular Parnassus was located opposite the chapel entrance, quite aloof from the classroom block, claimed the privilege of a long march through the tiled front corridor. This procession afforded them at least a sidelong view of Thursday afternoon guests, mostly families of their companions, in the parlors on either side of the front entrance. Such peering was, of course, not becoming a young lady, and was rewarded, should Sister Mary Cornelia happen to be seated opposite the open door, by a grieved and unbelieving glance. If the eyes belonged to Sister Mary of St. George, however, the glance was summer lightning with the thunder appropriately reserved for the expectant moment following study hour prayer.

The east wing, really a large L that doubled existing floor space, was devoted to the resident students, who cheerfully took their last meal in the chapel basement and then helped carry piles of dishes to the bright new dining hall in the enlarged north end of the new unit. It was inviting by comparison with their last quarter, but one should not envision soft, pretty drapes and matching chairs. Green roller blinds, drawn with meticulous exactitude, and long tables flanked by round-backed oak chairs, spoke rather of the barracks, but the waxed pine floor was a mirror, and if the white plastered walls seemed too austere, one had only to trace the rich oak graining in the wainscoting and doors. Adjoining this room, the "Hall" promised to bring closing exhibitions indoors. Here at last was a permanent platform for performers and instruments. But almost at once this room proved inadequate. It was too small for the increasing number of visitors, and, what was a calamity in the eyes of the Belgian Sisters, the girls had to stand outside awaiting their turns to perform, or to be called for honors, instead of entering two by two, curtsying deeply, and sitting like white marble statues, hands folded and without a twitch. Parents and friends missed the big tent with its elbow room, but since it had been disposed of, and another could not be obtained, the Sisters had a large stage erected in the court for the next closing, and used the hall for art and scholastic exhibits. All went well to the end of the final rehearsal. Then just as the last student stepped down from the stage, the plank framework collapsed. No one was injured, not even the recently installed director of music, James Lawrie, who risked his life to save a piano.[15] The Sisters removed the exhibit to a couple of classrooms and prepared the hall for the entertainment. They worked well past midnight, Sister Marie Catherine wrote, and then snatched a brief rest in view of their role next day as cheerful hostesses. That was the end of outdoor closings, but it was also the beginning of a dream that was finally realized in Notre Dame Auditorium, or Music Hall as it was first known.

In this progressive second decade, large audiences, public examinations, and news reporters in attendance were no more acceptable in the mother house in Namur than they had been when the first Sisters set sail for America. Oratorical display

MENDING

Lady-like Deportment

California State Telegraph Co.

OFFICE,— 25 SANTA CLARA STREET.

ALL COMMUNICATIONS STRICTLY CONFIDENTIAL.

Write Plain.—Use no Figures.—Give full Address.

OFFICE HOURS, 8 A.M. to 8 1/2 P.M.   SUNDAY, 9 to 11 A.M., 3 to 5 P.M.

San Francisco Nov 1
1856
1. 10 PM

Sister Superior

Is Maggie ill

She has not written

A. A. Van Houten

Large gold medals were early added to the array of crowns and other prizes. As the century advanced with heavier stress on manners, the great medal for "Lady-like Deportment" became the enviable award.

Plain sewing and mending were required of all, and wealthy girls vied for the annual medal for mending.

Telegram dated San Francisco, November 1, 1856. Miner and cattle trader A. A. Van Houten inquires about the health of his daughter Margaret.

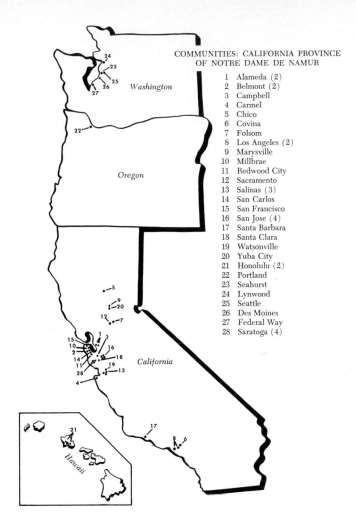

COMMUNITIES: CALIFORNIA PROVINCE
OF NOTRE DAME DE NAMUR

1 Alameda (2)
2 Belmont (2)
3 Campbell
4 Carmel
5 Chico
6 Covina
7 Folsom
8 Los Angeles (2)
9 Marysville
10 Millbrae
11 Redwood City
12 Sacramento
13 Salinas (3)
14 San Carlos
15 San Francisco
16 San Jose (4)
17 Santa Barbara
18 Santa Clara
19 Watsonville
20 Yuba City
21 Honolulu (2)
22 Portland
23 Seahurst
24 Lynwood
25 Seattle
26 Des Moines
27 Federal Way
28 Saratoga (4)

SISTERS OF NOTRE DAME DE NAMUR
THE CALIFORNIA PROVINCE

In 1803 two dedicated Frenchwomen established a new teaching congregation at Amiens in France. The inspiration, a departure in keeping with the needs of the post-revolution milieu, resulted from years of suffering and prayer on the part of a shopkeeper's daughter, Marie Rose Julie Billiart. Her friend, Françoise Blin de Bourdon, a young noblewoman, who had escaped execution by the downfall of Robespierre, contributed her fortune to the venture. Both saw that the new Christian educator must not be hampered by monastic characteristics, and both realized the need of educating the poor.

Because of failure of local clerical authority to accept their ideals, these two leaders and the first members of the congregation left France in 1809, and settled in the Diocese of Namur in Belgium, where they were warmly welcomed. From that center, the work of Notre Dame de Namur has spread to all the continents.

The California Province of Notre Dame de Namur is one of five in the United States. The map indicates the development of the province since the first foundation in San Jose in 1851.

Returning to her Alma Mater, Rebecca Ord Peshine
donned lovely costume and lectured to the students on
Spanish and Mexican days in California. Her interest
awakened a strong Mission movement at Notre Dame.

Mrs. Myles P. O'Connor, benefactor of Notre Dame and
foundress of Notre Dame Institute in San Jose.

Dollie McCone, Elizabeth Howell, and Mary Conway, the entire Class of 1885, styled themselves "The Funnies".

Sister Mary Bernardine Tivnan,
Provincial Superior, above, and
Sister Anna Raphael Fitzgerald
at right.

Articles of Incorporation

IN-CORP-OR-A-TION
OF THE
College of Notre Dame San Jose, Santa Clara County
OF THE
CALIFORNIA.

The application of the Visitors of the College known as the Academy of Notre Dame of the County of Santa Clara having been presented to the Board and it appearing that the proposed trustees are suitable persons and that the proposed College has properly, accurately, twenty thousand dollars, and that the requirements of law have been in all respects complied with, is hereby ordered, under, by the State Board of Education that said College be incorporated under the name of **The College** of **Notre Dame**, with all the powers and privileges conferred by law upon such corporations, and that the persons designated in said application to be the Trustees of such College.

Witness the hands of the undersigned, being a majority of the State Board of Education this 20 day of June A.D. 1868.

H. H. Haight, Governor.   **AUGUSTUS TRAFTON**

O. P. FITZGERALD, Supt. Pub. Instruction.   **S. J. C. SWEZEY**

JAMES DENMAN   **W. T. LUCKY,** Prin. State Normal School.

MELVILLE COTTLE   **J. H. BRALY**

I, **H. L. Nichols,** Secretary of State of the State of California, do hereby certify that the foregoing is a true and correct copy of the Declaration of Incorporation of said College, and the annexed, the original of this on my office.

Witness my hand and the Great Seal of State of this on Sacramento the

H. L. Nichols, Secretary of State.

State of California
DEPARTMENT OF STATE.

the first charter granted by the State of California to a women's college.

The object was poise. The long skirt only pointed up the grace. Gym and gym suit were unheard of. Dress was Sunday wear for picture-taking day, with most taking advantage of permitted after-Easter dresses.

Croquet. Little girls wore "shakers" to prevent freckles.

The Class of 1893, with leader Julia Farney in the foreground, is more interested in the camera than in the game. Note train on dress of tennis player.

and public debate were still thought of there as likely to break down maidenly reserve. The local clergy, the city fathers if they were friendly, a patron if such existed, might be invited to "Distribution of Prizes," and of course, the Sisters should be present. Musical numbers, biblical themes in dramatic form, were in order on these occasions. The important thing was the display of perfect manners and an almost impossible self-control. Yet local opinion was loud and adamant on the subject of display of talent and scholastic attainment. Once started, the great exhibition was demanded, and with fine tact and docile insistence, Sister Mary Cornelia won grudging assent from Mère Constantine, who still tried to prevent its spread in new foundations. It was not necessary, she admonished Sister Aloyse of the Cross, when the house at Mission Dolores neared its first graduation, for young ladies "to make a show of themselves," adding "that is for boys."[16] She regretted that such a custom had made a foothold in San Jose, where the crowd swept in and enjoyed "a sight rarely excelled in beauty."[17] Unfortunately, schools of Notre Dame subsequently founded in California carried out the Belgian prohibition against public closing exercises.

The throng that gathered for the closing of 1863 approved the austere elegance of the parlors, the bright and airy classrooms, the studios, glassed-in music rooms, and the shining, waxed pine floors. The succession of white-curtained dormitories on the second floor, each under the aegis of a heavenly patron, was a delight to good housekeeper visitors who today would find it an unrelieved Arctic scene. The single warm effect was afforded by the long, lower-corridor tiling with its brilliant border design. Uniting the new and older units, it imparted a rich and elegant spaciousness, and if Sister Marie Catherine indulged in pride on any score, it was in this.

But before long the additional space was found inadequate. During the following year the enrollment rose to 262, with 176 residents and 86 "Select Day Pupils." From then on, the lists show a steady increase in the latter group in keeping with the growth of the city population; in 1870 this number stood at

200. Now the necessity was for greater dining area and more classrooms. And as the local group grew larger, the notion of separate classes for these students asserted itself, and it would seem that in this matter there was a consensus among the teachers, even though repetition of instruction would result. Thus in 1866 Notre Dame Select Academy was erected. As if to emphasize separation, this unit stood on the eastern edge of the campus facing Santa Clara Street, and shared neither court nor connecting verandah. Local day students would henceforth enter by a special gate. They would dine at separate tables and share only the science laboratories. At the time it would seem that no one took offence at the separation; no one saw in it an attempt to establish a higher social status for resident students, since daughters of leading families were enrolled in the day school. When Editor Owen toured the new addition, he spoke in glowing terms of the progress that it indicated.[18]

The Select Day Academy was scarcely completed when Sister Mary Cornelia proceeded with the construction of a larger student dining room and kitchen, again according to Sister Marie Catherine's planning. Parallel with the front line and 150 feet long, this unit closed the quadrangle. Well-equipped infirmaries for both Sisters and students occupied the second floor, for with hospitalization then almost unheard of, this provision was essential. From this upper floor, an enclosed arcade known as the "Bridge," spanned the fifty feet separating the new dining room from the end of the north wing. Henceforth girls with real or imagined illnesses crossed the "Bridge" to obtain remedies and sympathy, always feeling that they had in some way penetrated the mysteries of the Sisters' quarters, and that having accomplished this feat was well worth a cold and the taking of a few pills.

Serious illness was unusual in the boarding school, a fact that marks the death of Bessie Byrne as stark tragedy. Bessie, beautiful in a flower-like way, and so sweet-tempered that all loved her at once when she arrived at Notre Dame early in 1868, was the child of pioneer Garrett J. Byrne of Cupertino. Eager as she was beautiful, Bessie was the delight of every teacher. With her brief illness, ending in her death on March 14, she became the touching legend of the school. She was, of course, "too good to live," a notion believed in those days almost as an article of faith, and not entirely complimentary to those who carried on. She was the "Angel of Notre Dame," for this eschatological confusion was also common enough. Sister Anthony, S.H., immortalized both Bessie and her father in the *Quarterly* by quoting a lengthy sketch of the pioneer from the *Leader*, and by giving in full Sister Anna Raphael's "Asleep 'mid the Lilies," a romantic effusion inspired by the flowers around Bessie's bier. Sister Anna was, of course, still young enough in those days, to toss off a dirge on notice. But only Sister Anthony would have quoted it in full in 1910, and remark besides, that "never did the Death Angel steal away a purer pearl."[19]

The "Bridge" with its curtained windows and long, flattened arch beneath, became the beauty spot of the otherwise unrelieved quadrangle, the wistaria that mantled its roof cascading down over windows and arch. The latest complex presented an architectural departure, its windows high and narrow, and with arched top and keystone. Constructed after the severe earthquake of 1868, it was so well reinforced, that the great disaster of 1906, especially destructive in the San Jose area, left it intact. Its completion marks the end of an ambitious decade; the two last units together cost well over $87,000, a large sum at the time, even for a school that was tasting prosperity.

*A*s subsequent years benefited by the scholastic stirrings of the second decade at Notre Dame, so were they deeply marked by its modus vivendi, its set of ideals for training of heart and will accepted then as indicating "the spirit of Notre Dame" for all times and places, the hallowed phrase strengthening the entrenchment of even small customs. If the entrenchment was itself regrettable, so would some of the customs be in any era, bearing as they did the Jensenistic stamp of the Belgian school of the century. Up to the 1930s, for instance, students on the junior college level were required to wear a uniform. Until that time, they entered and left the chapel in line. For too many decades, their behavior in the presence of visitors on the campus displayed the inhibition of small children warned to be seen and not heard. They stood in what was considered silent dignity, as though the give and take of conversation might seem boldness on their part.

Transplanting of Belgian ideals in American schools was deliberate on the part of educational leaders in both countries; programs, announcements, and lists of regulations printed for the boarding school in Namur were used as models in Cincinnati and San Jose. But it should be noted that in the mid-century these ideals were fairly universal; young Sisters coming from leading families in the Eastern States found nothing objectionable in many of them. If they saw wisdom in yielding to pressure for public closing exercises, they felt, on the other hand, that chaperoning of adult girls, censorship of their mail, and similar restrictions were both good and proper. The sad thought is, of course, that such regulations should have persisted in boarding schools and academies so long after their general discontinuance.

Persistence in this is accounted for by proximity of the students to a community that had come to prize semi-cloistered characteristics, even to their extension into the lives of students, and that at a time when the concepts of human liberty and dedication seemed hopelessly unable to discover this kinship. It was certainly an approximation of cloistered life, for instance, to allow students no other home vacation than the Christmas holiday, even after transportation had made more frequent vacations possible. It was by special concession that boarders who lived in the area were allowed to visit their homes once a month, and even this privilege was rescinded at times. A graduate of 1897 recalled rarely being allowed to visit her home a stone's throw away. Visitors might spend an hour with students on Sunday morning, or two hours in the afternoon. Thursday afternoon was assigned for parents' visits, which supposedly should end at four, and parents were asked "not to infringe easily on these rules."

Perhaps the most severe thwarting of liberty of spirit lay in the regulating of correspondence. All letters were subjected to "the Superioress of the Institution."[1] Even letters home were first written in a notebook on Sunday afternoon in study hall. Read and "corrected" by the Sister in charge, they were next copied on stationery, supposedly examples of copperplate and correct phrasing. "My Revered and Respected Parents," was a salutation understood to indicate an excellent parent-child relationship. Souls in extreme turmoil could, of course, smuggle a letter out, or they might wind up the elegant verbiage with such a volcanic burst as Mollie Murphy's "if you don't come and get me, I don't know what I'll do." Mollie's letter offers an example of surprise ending. She is writing to tell her parents about prize day, as well as to demonstrate her great improvement in penmanship. Considering her report card of a few months earlier, with two failures and general effort "only middling," her parents stood in need of some such comfort. In this instance, it is fine to note, the study hour Sister allowed the discrepancy of that letter to pass, as did Sister Mary Cornelia, if she saw it at all. At any rate, Mollie spent the weekend with her parents at Mission San Jose where they were vacationing. And her subsequent "Testimony of Diligence" would suppose general improvement in studies.[2]

Perhaps only a few advanced young minds were irked by having books and other publications subjected to faculty approval, under which searching light many a promising romantic tale, begun on the local train, could be withdrawn to remain until visiting day and then handed to one's parent with suitable admonition concerning the dangers suffered by the youthful mind when exposed to such enticements. Most realized that immediate surrender was wise; concealment, even under one's mattress, endangered hope of making the Good Conduct list. To those who cared less for the honor, the risk seemed worth while, a fact that accounted for the shelf of follies set discreetly high in the office of the Lady Superioress.

Cloister influence on boarding school life was certainly responsible for compulsory and routine attendance at chapel devotions. Daily mass at six in the morning and Sunday afternoon vespers were shared with the Sisters, and the school's separate devotions were obligatory. Some loved the routine, at least in retrospect and with a touch of nostalgia; others recalled that prayer was forgotten when the spell of routine was broken.

Membership in the school's sodalities was the reward of good behavior, and for Catholic students a requirement for graduation as well. Thus Maria Lucas, whose flippant retorts now and then left the Belgian, and even the American, Sisters quite speechless, found herself deprived of membership at the outset of her final semester. But by dint of her persuasive gifts and an apology here and there, as suggested by Sister Mary Cornelia herself, Maria was reinstated and maintained membership until the college diploma was safely in her hands. That, she said, was the longest continuous membership in her memory. Maria lived to see young people assume leadership, unherded and with enthusiasm. Commenting on the great differences between twentieth century youth movements and the marshaled sodalities of her schooldays, Maria added that her teachers were subject to their era; some of them, she thought, would approve of the changes.

Maria delighted to recall her school wardrobe, and the efforts the Sisters made to fend off worldliness, her almost racy comments in lively contrast to the staid wording of the old directives. She remembered seeing the large, colored "shaker" prescribed for the younger girls somewhat before her time. That, she said, was intended to avoid "sunburn," a condition, which if not downright unwholesome, at least proclaimed the hussy. Older girls, of course, did not romp about, at least not beyond the requirements of croquet, for which a wide garden hat was prescribed. Uniform dress, appearing first in the regulations of 1864, was for many years a matter for Sunday wear only, an attempt, it may be, to keep Sunday best at its simplest. This first list includes a dark blue merino dress and "sack," a waist-length circular cape, with brown kid gloves and a straw bonnet, and outside of chapel wear, a silk apron.

For a long time, however, indecision brought about unpredicted changes, not all of them recorded in the prospectuses. There was the red plaid coat, for instance, remembered with a certain nostalgia. The Sisters often made slight concessions; their concern was a degree of contentment consistent with modesty and unworldliness. Thus in the third decade, with what seems an attempt to follow advice given with less art than good will, the directive calls for black alpaca dress trimmed with green, a grey felt hat, and green kid gloves. This outfit is quickly followed by the same dress minus trim, with black hat and dark gloves, and as if for relief, a white hat for daily wear, the flopping headpiece seen in playground photos. It is good to know that after Lent an Easter outfit was permitted, provided it was simple enough. But each little fashion milestone marked only a truce in the war between Puritanism and feminine vanity. Before 1873 it was clear to the girls at Notre Dame that austerity of dress might be mitigated by a liberal display of jewelry, hence the new prospectus warns of retrenchment to breastpin and earrings. And when these became overspectacular, the war was taken to the parents who were now asked not to furnish their daughters with adornment of any kind. Perhaps the result was too drab for even the faculty to bear; at any rate, the ban was lifted, and the campus was gay henceforth with bangle and locket.

The reign of merino and alpaca failed to achieve uniformity of design, for as the school grew in numbers, Sister Odelie and her helpers were able to supply only those coming from great distances, and who could not thus be expected to have had a preview of the ideal. Nearby applicants and their mothers visited Sister Odelie, viewed the model, and took their yardage to a dressmaker, together with their more or less faithful description. Madame Alice Bassler made these Notre Dame dresses for years, and Madame Sarah Lorcea made reasonable facsimiles of Sister Odelie's hats. Both were located conveniently on Santa Clara Street and both were approved by the good Sisters, but the students at times expressed less complete satisfaction.

At last the enterprising Class of 1883 decided to take a revolutionary step at least in the matter of the dress, leaving the hat for a second reforming project. Maria Lucas, Marie Dillon, and Minnie Urie planned a rendezvous in San Francisco after the Christmas holiday. There they agreed on a pattern and material and went together to an expert dressmaker. Wearing the results of their endeavor, they boarded the southbound train and finally appeared before Sister Mary Aloysia, assuring her that she was now viewing a uniform acceptable to all. It was one of her last beautiful acts to approve. No wonder, said Maria, still a bit ecstatic at 96 over the triumph. For after all the dress was simple enough with its wide plaited ruffle at the hem and its silk frogs down the front. But the question was far from closed. A few years later the photographs show floor length skirts and angular bertha effect with rather startling rows of ribbon trim.

Toward the end of the century a "summer uniform" relieved the oppression of May and September, when Sunday was honored by long, dark skirt and waist of white lawn, its long sleeves and high, choking collar being miseries dictated by current style, and endured as such. At last arrived simultaneously the notions of uniform for daily wear and as a school symbol. That was the origin of the Peter Pan, furnished by Stull and Son-niksen of San Jose, still in dignified black, with white embroi-dered school emblem on the sleeve and detachable white "Dickie," the wearing of which became the badge of fidelity, the *sine qua non* of the good Notre Dame girl. The silk apron, or sometimes sateen, was retained for years, as enduring an article of wear, almost, as a Sisters' habit. Time brought slight adaptations to the Peter Pan, chiefly in length of skirt, but it was always the same recognizable Notre Dame dress, approved of by mothers, teachers, and wearers. The newcomer was fur-nished with two, when good John Mackey called on Sister Madeleine Marie Brennan for orders at the opening of classes. One was for Sunday and high occasions, when a large light blue hair bow, and gloves imparted a natty air. Besides, in and about San Jose, on car and commuter train, the Notre Dame Peter Pan was soon established as a status symbol.

In dress as in other matters there was never much student control. Maria Lucas' victory was perhaps unique. The one recorded attempt at group action was a request made to Arch-bishop Alemany for permission to waltz. Pre-holiday warnings against this diversion were casting gloom on their young lives. In the eyes of their teachers, dancing, especially waltzing, was performance for the primrose path. And since such gravity might suggest questioning at return from the holiday, attain-ment of the good conduct list could easily be endangered. Even sodality membership. Even graduation itself. Whoever may have thought of episcopal appeal, it seemed nothing short of inspiration. The Archbishop was so good and kind; he must surely sympathize with the request. Thus it was tactfully and humbly appended to student good wishes for Yuletide. The Archbishop's reply was cordial but disappointing; the girls might "dance out of the sight of men," and as a general direc-tive, they should follow the advice of the Sisters; as good young women, they "would not like anything else."[3]

It would be quite useless to like anything else in view of Mère Constantine's more remote control. She disapproved

strongly of hiring "masters of music and dance." She was out-
and-out opposed to "gymnastic lessons." The young need exercise, she concedes, but let it be "befitting." In some of the
Belgian convents, she adds, the girls make their own beds, and
even sweep their own rooms.[4] At Notre Dame in San Jose, the
girls had always made their beds, but except in the general
commotion attendant on moving into a new unit, none of them
had ever swept or dusted anything. No doubt Sister Mary
Cornelia wrote with her usual tact to her higher superior. At
any rate, her boarders continued their life of ladies, never so
much as wiping a dish. And at some point a gym, or rather a
calesthenics teacher, must have come to give initial lessons,
after which the more lithe of the Sisters directed groups in the
fantastic management of wands, and hoops, and clubs. Lawn
tennis, it would seem, made its unvigorous appearance on the
campus without benefit of lessons. In one faded picture, two
damsels of Victorian curves, both with hats and ground-length
skirts, one boasting a slight train, stand facing each other like
statues, and holding rackets on high in impossible vertical
positions. The gym suit, even its earlier billowing forms, was
in the dim future; as was also the wicked serve, the smash
return, and the score board. The game, like the calesthenic
drill, was for grace and poise, qualities immortalized in large
photographs in which older girls strike dramatic poses and
minims in ungainly Mother Hubbard aprons and sunbonnets
hold flower-entwined hoops awkwardly aloft. The concept
"sport" was nonexistent. The closest approach to vigor was the
brisk walk before breakfast, recommended by teachers, chiefly
as an outlet of energy before the long morning classes. And as
a break before evening study hours, there was the time-honored
walk "in the country," girls two by two, oldest to youngest, and
with two Sisters bringing up the rear.

In early years, the "country" meant usually The Alameda,
the full length of it if time permitted, including a visit to the
Santa Clara Mission. Sister Marie Catherine tells of a somewhat
stormy encounter with Judge Joshua Redman in Santa Clara
when the leaders of the line, with or without intent, drifted

into his apple orchard. With apology, the Sisters reclaimed
their charges, and the mollified judge signified his forgiveness
next morning by driving to Notre Dame with a huge box of
apples for the girls, a gift which he repeated now and then in
friendly manner. In later years the walk often terminated at the
Willows, the ten-acre orchard near the present Sacred Heart
Church, purchased by the Sisters as a source of fresh fruit and
vegetables.

Suitable pleasure trips came to include picnics to Strawberry Farm by bus, or to a lovely spot with the unlikely name
of Penitencia Creek. Mary Frances Redmond recalls these outings, which came to include a train trip to "the Belmont of
Ralston's days." Afternoon walks, too, were directed to more
broad-minded destinations including Turner's Bakery and
Cook's Grove in Santa Clara. In the first the girls might regale
themselves with Santa Clara Crackers and Paradise Sodas.
Large helpings of luscious strawberries and cream awaited in
the second.[5]

The year was broken by occasional student entertainments.
There were music evenings, original dramas, often Biblical, all
of these marking special feast days. That of the Foundress,
Julie Billiart, and the Patroness of Music, St. Cecilia, were next
to Christmas itself. But the Superior, the mistress of boarders,
and the first teacher were honored on their respective feasts,
and on these, in the matter of chapel adornment, the distinction
between canonized and uncanonized was so negligible as to go
unnoticed. With the coming of electricity, the magic lantern
show made its appearance, the sputtering carbon arc light competing with the speaker for attention. Entire classes sponsored
these programs of pictured historical and Biblical lore. These
and the musical and dramatic programs were printed in the
annual prospectus as evidences of educational progress. But
increasing elegance of costume and richness of orchestration
could not compensate for ingrowing. Until almost the close of
the century artists and lecturers were rarely invited to Notre
Dame, a fact in keeping with Mère Constantine's fears of "outside" dangers. At one time she disapproved of allowing a priest

to lecture to the students about his apostolate. Priests meant well, she admitted, but they did not know what was best "for us." She disliked Sister Mary Cornelia's quoting of episcopal opinion on school or convent plans. As a warning, she cited examples of communities cut off from their mother house because of differences between bishops and higher superiors.

One of these differences was in regard to titles to property, and here it would seem Archbishop Alemany was for a time somewhat confused or ill-advised. Mère Constantine's letters indicate his interpretation for some time, of the Council of Baltimore on property held by religious, as of universal application, in which case titles to property purchased by congregations under papal jurisdiction would have to be handed over to their local ordinary.[6] Actually the Archbishop had not been troubled about the matter at first; he had assured Sister Mary Bernard, says Mère Constantine, that the Sisters' property in Marysville was not affected by the decree.[7] But plans for the foundation at Mission Dolores apparently produced second thoughts. In all it was not a serious dispute. Archbishop Alemany's problem was sincere, and Mère Constantine's worries over the "famous decree" are better understood in the light of loans made by the house in Namur in the case of many an American foundation.

The same years brought requests for foundations in California's and Nevada's mining areas, and these, as in the case of Bishop Eugene O'Connell's request for Sisters in Virginia City, often involved sending the Sisters "on diverse missions," a stipulation unthinkable to Mère Constantine with her notions of stability and enclosure. Sisters of Notre Dame, she insisted, could not "follow the mines around." But the matter of the Virginia City mission weighed on her mind; over a year later she noted with relief that the Sisters of Charity had gone there. Her zeal was still strong, but there must be no departures. In San Francisco, "day and free schools" were permitted, but her Sisters must refuse to take over a home for working girls.

There were other signs that the desire of the foundress, Mère Julie Billiart, to see her congregation develop in the milieu of universal love, was losing its significance. Boarding school events were marked by a lack of family spirit. The community filed in and out with silent dignity and poise. At the close, the Superior spoke words of praise for the group, at which all smiled approval, and to which the first teacher probably added some comment, but the opportunity for friendly encounter was cancelled out by ideals of religious decorum and "downcast eyes." Recollection in God demanded an aloofness at which "outsiders," and that included students, were supposedly edified. Quite likely many were edified; they were surrounded by religious art that favored folded palms and heavenward glance. Anything like a photograph of the Sisters would have been unthinkable except for the information of the Mother House. Maria Lucas had her doubts about the wisdom of all this aura of sanctity in any era. Years later when she was shown a photograph of the community taken during her school days, she commented, "See, they wouldn't even let us know about this. They would have feared we would be scandalized. But it would have been so good for us just to know that it could happen. Every girl should have had one to treasure through life."

It seems likely though that even the young American Sisters of the early days accepted without demur the view of withdrawn religious life presented to them in their novitiate. In fact, there was no other view. At instruction, students sat with lowered eyes, totally receptive. They were quite the antithesis of today's groups seated at small tables, and at times threatening the flow of logical discussion with amazing non sequiturs.

The presence of at least three lay teachers in the early decades does perhaps indicate some little awareness of the dangers of completely intramural development in education, and the timidity in announcing their presence is, no doubt, due to Mère Constantine's grudging permission to hire them. In the prospectus of 1867 parents are told that the services of "a distinguished professor" have been secured "in the music department for those who prefer a Master," as though Professor Lawrie were some sort of necessary evil, subject to the condition mentioned on the same page in connection with fancy sewing, "hair work," and such accomplishments, which "were to be had." But to Mère Constantine, who had once counselled adaptation, these entries in the prospectus were merely oblique introductions to the customs of the country; it was "human reason" she said, to urge the need of adopting such customs. The Sisters had not gone to America to conform to what was done there, but to draw children to *their* ways. Declamations and representations nourished pride and gave rise to "love of theaters." It was not becoming for young ladies to amuse the public. Boarding schools of high standing did not do this. Belgian bishops had forbidden it. If girls are dissatisfied with these regulations, let them leave.

However, it is only fair to recall Mère Constantine's advice of twenty years earlier, and to note the general narrowness that was affecting those about her in her last years. She was not responsible for the attitude against the teaching of boys by Sisters that persisted through the decades following her death. It seems closer to truth to say that in her last years, when her resistance was weakened, she was surrounded by a narrowness which marked the thought of France and Belgium after the First Vatican Council, and it should be added, the thought of the Irish clergy, too. Yet despite Puritanic and Jansenistic influences, a perceptible liberalizing trend marked the close of the century. The Sisters themselves took lessons from art and music masters. Students were taken, properly chaperoned, to operas. An occasional lecture is recorded, and the note of apology for any bow to worldliness disappeared from the prospectuses.

From the outset, greater adaptability appears in studies and curricula than in social matters. The prospectus of 1857 indicates influence of the contemporary American pattern.[1] It lists all classes under the groupings Primary, Elementary, Junior and Senior, the first of these involving today's lower middle grades and including reading, spelling, writing, sacred history and the elements of arithmetic and grammar. This last included composition and, extending into the junior division, it entailed much descriptive writing and such practice in debate as made formidable adversaries out of shy 12-year-olds, while they wrestled with geography, elements of natural philosophy, astronomy and United States history. Besides, the junior learned "epistolary correspondence," a course guaranteed to reduce individuality as surely as did copperplate writing, that is until emotion revealed lurking reality. For the senior, grammar expanded into rhetoric; versification and argument, into elocution. Geography, "ancient and modern," ended for the senior with "The Uses of the Globes and the Projection of Maps." Sacred history, later known as Bible history, preceded "Profane History" with its subdivisions of "Universal-modern" and "Ancient," in that order, and a little later mythology was bracketed with these titles. Now the sciences, botany and chemistry, were added to astronomy. The only math course was algebra and it would seem that bookkeeping might be substituted for this course, either of them running through two years.

In all the early study lists, languages appear as departments, independent of the main divisions and appended, as were the fine arts and fancywork, as matters of culture. French soon acquired dominance, no doubt because the Sisters spoke it so commonly and recommended it as highly cultural. In fact, there were many who thought of Notre Dame as a French school, so that in the second decade the announcement that French was spoken at recreation, which meant at dinner, was followed by the note that the course of studies was pursued in English.

If languages shared nineteenth century honors with the fine arts, so did needlework, the arrangement being symbolic of what the well-bred young woman should know. And needlework, in the eyes of the Sisters, meant first of all plain sewing. When huge gold medals made their first appearance on closing days, a breathless moment preceded the awarding of the gorgeous dangling plaque engraved with the single word MENDING in high black letters. The Sharons and other heiresses arrived at Saturday morning class armed with workbox and passed up their darned stockings for Sister's exacting inspection. Those unable to "hold a needle" on enrollment day, both made and mended articles of "muslin" underwear before the year's end. Such essentials attended to, the feminine-minded were attracted by a battery of more artistic offerings. Bead, chenille, hair, shell, and waxwork were listed, and after a time, crocheting, and making of artificial flowers swelled the list. Almost all tried their hands at tapestry, actually needlepoint worked on patterns which appear in old academies with variations in color. But not even the most advanced and artistic of this work finds place in the "Course of Instruction." Like music and language, it was a finishing adornment, not basic to mental development. There is, of course, a pragmatic note, a range of usefulness. Plain sewing is essential; language was strongly recommended; the rest was "if parents desire."

The original division of studies came quite early to designate place in the boarding school, though the parallel is not exact. Seniors were older girls, who might on enrolling at 16 be receiving their first taste of the three R's. Juniors — they came later to be "juvies" — were at the awkward middle stage, not acceptable at senior table or recreation, happy to have at last escaped "Little Girls' Hall," babies' table and seven o'clock bedtime. But as these divisions in the boarding school became stabilized and traditional, scholastic nomenclature shifted about in the second decade in what seems at first confusion or carelessness, but is really an experimenting toward better definition. The senior class of 1857 appears in two divisions, the higher of which forms the first graduating class. Margaret Van Houten and Annie Fitzgerald were crown winners with equal distinction, in that little class of five, with Sarah Burnett coming in third. Below the senior classes, the elastic term "Elementary" appears as "First" and "Second," each with two divisions, all four years perhaps thought of somewhat as our junior high school. Below the two classes of the "Primary Division," the always small number of little girls formed an ungraded group regarded blessedly as individuals.

In the 1857 breakdown of prizes, the "Superior Class" in tall print, superseding all others, is of course the usual good conduct list, its two divisions referring only to degrees of perfection. And to show that day students could also, with effort, be ladies, there is a separate division for them, in which Sarah Burnett holds honorable distinction. Surprisingly, the name of Annie Fitzgerald does not appear in this noble list, nor does that of Margaret Van Houten. They may have been too busy winning scholastic renown to rise and open doors for Sisters, or perhaps the teachers thought they had achieved their quota of distinction. When years ago a Latin student inquired teasingly why she had been graded A-minus instead of the usual straight A, her teacher answered, "My dear, it is not good for the soul to have A's all the time."

In 1864 the first "Graduate Class" makes its appearance, though without candidates, in anticipation of the college charter of 1868. Two years later, the name Alice Lander appears beneath this new heading, and Alice goes down in Notre Dame history as first college graduate. From then on the title "Notre Dame Academy" designates the select day school built in 1867 and the expressions "Boarding school" and "College" become almost synonymous. Perhaps few Sisters of the last century thought of the title "College" as more than one of distinction and excellence. Notre Dame in San Jose was "our leading school." It was certainly all of that, because for one thing, of the effort of its teachers to improve it and to bring its plan of studies into logical sequence.

Curricular development was greater in the middle school. About the end of the second decade, four "Grammar Classes" emerge with the groundwork of arithmetic, grammar, and geography already accomplished in the new Preparatory Department. One entered the "Grammar Division" already proficient in spelling and then began orthography, which combined word analysis and proper use of words. Through these middle classes appears that smooth continuity, which became a strong characteristic of the school. A class in "Familiar Science" served as basis in Second Grammar. The regular sciences, astronomy, botany and chemistry, were given a good start in First Grammar and continued into Second Rhetoric. "Natural Philosphy" went on through First Rhetoric. Rhetoric classes were upper school, yet one would hesitate to equate them with the first two years of high school. Considering the study load, they were perhaps much more difficult. Above the rhetoric were two senior classes, the highest designated as "Graduate," but the curriculum for these was not announced before 1874, when the *Course of Instruction* in the prospectus was expanded beyond the original brief statement. Geometry, geology, zoology and "mental philosophy" were now listed as senior subjects. Those with courage for the second senior class received the college diploma.

The striking fact is recognition of mental development. The study of English is perhaps the best instance of growth. At the end of First Grammar, the good pupil must have possessed a ready vocabulary and a fair ability in expression. When rhetoric placed an array of fine excerpts before the two higher classes, their dual purpose must have been justified: analysis and excellent patterns for self-expression. Whether generally wise or not, the culmination of all this preparation was "Composition in Verse," though neither is this a sudden appearance; some verse writing began in First Rhetoric, before the usual thinning out of the less gifted. Rhetoric also led up to English literature in the two senior years. American literature, as a field of study, was unheard of, as was the term "world literature."

History had still to look to a far day for any sort of structural treatment. After two years of "Modern History," with Charlemagne as dividing line, First Rhetoric brought a year of ancient times. This was the last; there was no history in the advanced years. Thus it seems, younger children were given two years of sacred history while they were most easily impressed. United States history followed for the sake of the many whose school days would be brief. Ancient times, as more abstruse than the more recent, awaited the thinned ranks.

The course printed so definitely in 1874 was still in a fluid state; immediate alterations show that it was not considered final. With no idea of later divisions, grade school, high school, and college, the Sisters were unsure as to the point at which collegiate work should begin. Finally, in 1879, all knowledge was, like Gaul, divided *in partes tres:* primary, academic and collegiate. Now completion of the "First Grade," the highest academic class, and the earlier "First Rhetoric" was followed by academic graduation, an honorable goal attainable by more than the few attracted by zoology and solid geometry. At the same time, the term "collegiate" enhanced the college diploma. This was the true graduation, and its attainment stood now above all other awards, even Good Conduct; in fact, the few who reached it were not mentioned as award winners. They had arrived. Crowns, great, heavy ones, were bestowed upon them *ipso facto*, and the diploma took on the dimensions of the charter itself. There were distinctions, of course, even on the heights. The future journalist, Frances McClatchy, was accorded the note "With Praise of Excellence" when she and Alice Younger graduated together in 1879.[2]

Still the academic course did not carry entire classes through in later democratic fashion. Advancing difficulty still suggested learning and the eliminating process. Nor did the word "drop-out" carry a stigma. None met with discouraging treatment; the saturation point was met realistically by all concerned. Before 1890 eight of the classes conferring the college diploma numbered one or two students; seven was considered a bumper crop, despite the current high enrollment. And whether as cause or result of this paucity, teaching on the higher levels was virtually tutorial.

In 1885, the triple division was replaced by a *Course of Study*, the innovation consisting in a detailed classification of subjects. Chemistry, organic and inorganic, appeared on the collegiate level. Mathematics was more definitely planned but with no additional courses except a third year, or perhaps a third semester, of higher algebra. Political geography made its first appearance, but gone was "Uses of the Globes." History was more detailed but still as badly planned. The most revised and expanded subject was English. It now included elocution, taught in every class. Rhetoric and grammar held their places, and letter writing, still "Epistolary Correspondence," was coupled with essays. Now classical literature in translation led the list. This, "Principles of Criticism" and "Criticism of Modern Authors," were "collegiate" requirements. Foreign languages were merely entered, but all the array of drawing and painting, "if desired," were listed with voice and four instruments under the head Fine Arts. And in this first real breakdown of curricula, needlework, to say nothing of "bead, shell, and chenille ornamentation," no longer enjoyed scholastic listing.

Through the following half decade the plan of 1885 remains almost unchanged but the word "collegiate," is omitted, though the courses entered originally under that heading remain, and were followed by the few students possessing the necessary courage. The omission seems to indicate that the Sisters were becoming aware of developments in American colleges, that they realized their inability as yet to establish parallels in structure and curricula, but that they hoped to maintain advanced work for the time as a link with a future full college course. Unfortunately, in the absence of written evidence for such attitudes, one can only suppose.

The teaching approach on all levels was catechetical. From primary text to difficult tome, set questions follow chapters and divisions; student notebooks are filled with questions dictated by teachers. These are not thought-provoking inquiries, rather the type often beginning with "What are we told about . . .?" On the higher levels they are multiplied so as to make tremendous demands on memory. They can be comforting, of course, in their rich dividends of infallibility. This does not imply that reasoning had no place in the learning process. A fine teacher, could and did, point rational directions, which good students took up, keen on the scent. Less able teachers pounced more directly on ready answers. Everywhere then there were teachers who would not accept examples other than those in the text, and certainly many a pupil who could not offer any other. Few in any case would challenge the principle illustrated by the given examples. Supervisors praised the clear-cut question and answer as "bringing out" the less ready pupil, though it must have been plain that the same less-endowed children floundered in fractions, and were lost when faced with difficult reading.

If time was wasted memorizing printed answers and producing notebooks that were examples of order, there was no danger, on the other hand, of unreadable notes taken during lectures. The student's notebook was her prized possession; its questions, dictated by the teacher, or found in her text, were answered there, with strict fidelity to either, in her best penmanship and free from errors in spelling. These books were treasuries of detailed examples of parsing and prosody, of historical "tables," which were often pages of dates, centered on the page, with rulers and events of contemporary nations neatly paralleled at the sides. There are logical outlines, too, and the ever-present samples of "Epistolary Correspondence." Margaret Van Houten's letter to Elodie Hahn, probably her nearest neighbor in the classroom, is a winner. After one short sentence of concern about Elodie's health, Margaret launches into the verities. "Allow me," she says, "to say a few words upon filial reverence." Thereupon follows her little sermon, which she ends with a second reference to Elodie's well-being and congratulations on the near completion of her education, to which she adds appropriate warning against "temptations that are generally found in fashionable life."

A large notebook like Margaret's might contain scholastic memorabilia of several years. On the cover of hers is neatly pasted the school's first nameplate reading "Academy of Notre Dame, Pueblo San Jose," so that though dates, classes, and instructors' names are never given, this book must have been a repository of facts throughout her school days. She filled other books, of course, in various subjects, but this one presents the running core of her education. Owners of these books kept them always at hand, reservoirs of reference. For as greater continuity developed, teachers were more prone to require the total view. Thus only one's best, usually teacher-approved, went into those pages. Before entry there, the student's own verse and prose underwent such refining as to endanger what weak flicker of originality might have graced the first crude writing. Still it is safe to say that the refining almost never meant alteration by a teacher, a process which would have required far less time, and it seems likely that the thinning out in the upper classes bore some relation to the high degree of independence required.

The teacher would point out errors and weaknesses and suggest new models in the rhetoric text. It may be objected that this imitation of models was itself a form of dependence. Those inclined to think thus should try to express some fledgling argument on a Baconian pattern. And what if a schoolgirl's "Walk on The Alameda," should take a few turns mindful of "Gulliver's Travels," if it presents that tree-lined road in its pre-urban days? In art, in writing, in the management of a problem in arithmetic, norms and patterns seemed to those teachers safe modes of expression for yet half-formed thought, the better half to be rounded out by the form itself. To the end, Sister Anna Raphael valued the pattern. Ofter for her own poems she borrowed types that seemed most fitting, as when entranced by the movement of the first gas lights, she chose Shelly's "Storm" with its quick, breaking meter, and interline rhyme to convey her impression.

Certainly such respect for the model tried restless souls. As Maria Lucas checked entire sections of Bonnell's *Manual of Prose Composition*, the daily fare of rhetoric classes, she consoled herself by filling all blank spaces in the text with notes on astronomy, which was still her favorite "branch" in her late eighties.[3] Recalling her racy speech at that age, one can imagine her youthful impatience with such headings as "Inflectional Orthography," and "Propriety both Lexical and Decorous." She must have felt, in fact, rather an urge toward "Syntactical Violences," and "Provincialisms," under which lead the word "chore" is listed as a "barbarism because it is used only in New England." Tongue in cheek, Maria probably recited glibly that "decorous propriety requires that all the words and phrases of a piece of composition should be decent, and sufficiently dignified to put upon paper, though not stilted and difficult to be understood by persons of ordinary intelligence." In old age, Maria employed the most telling contemporary usage with a twinkle. Not so with her classmate, Marie Dillon. When she was close to one hundred years old, her speech was still marked by the "decorous propriety" of her graduation essay. And to account for her astounding vocabulary, one has only to turn to the fifty pages of synonyms in the fine print appendix of Bonnell's *Manual*.

Textbooks were loaded with difficulty and disproportionate emphasis. The girl emerging from First Rhetoric must have been appalled, for instance, by *The Student's Handbook of Literature*, edited by the Sulpician Fathers. Revised in 1880, it carried 52 pages for the period preceding 1250 A.D., and 92 for that preceding the age of Queen Elizabeth I, both sections furnished by interlinear assistance which made reading possible but not much less obscure. Its contemporary parallel would be a large freshman college anthology, in which fragments of better known selections from these eras are presented, to be studied very briefly, or omitted. In those days perhaps a semester was spent on the Anglo-Saxon and Middle English sections, the romances and Chaucer offering relief at last. And all literary selections are fitted into their historical setting as framework, so that one was responsible for stretches of English history as well. Contemporary rulers and great battles were seemingly considered as throwing light on the works of poets. Questions at each section end do little for interpretation. Aims of the editor are stated in order of importance. He wishes the student to consider: the historic setting of each work; the development of language, his evident reason for accenting the early period; the biographies of the writers, "who have portrayed the character of their times." His aim is also to awaken a taste for the works of the masters, for which reason he bans from his collection of "Polite Literature" all that is "merely technical or professional." In all, said Maria Lucas, it was a book for Mamie Sullivan; for herself, she eased her wretchedness by immortalizing Marie Dillon's classic nose again and again in the margins of this anthology.

In appearance and content, the history texts of the nineteenth century must have depressed the stoutest hearts. Preparatory classes carried around the ugly little *History of Sacred Scripture,* to which neither author nor publisher set his name, each division memorizing entirely its assigned portion of the text. Then followed the European series by Father Gazeau, S.J., with its lengthy treatment of the Middle Ages. Buying her texts at the school *dépôt* before each session, Maria Lucas at once marked the chapter nearest the center of the book with the words "Half done." That kept her, she said, in a more hopeful state of mind. At ninety she could still chant, "Nimrod laid the foundations of Babylon at the foot of the Tower of Babel," to which she added, "but I'm much more interested in Marxism."

In that encyclopedic era, the Notre Dame graduate's array of science textbooks included natural history, botany, chemistry, physics, zoology, geology and astronomy. As starting points for life pursuits, at least some of the owners of these texts treasured collections, classified according to their senior manuals. They also kept scrapbooks of scientific news clippings. Before a printed periodic chart was available, the chemistry laboratory boasted one made by Sister Mary of St. George and her classes. The third edition of Edward Youman's text in chemistry was in her students' hands immediately after it appeared in 1879, but she warned her girls that its latest findings would soon be out of date.

Santa Clara County's clear skies were the school's first textbook in astronomy. In the second decade sky manuals such as Norman Lockyer's *Astronomy* reached the school, its attractively written chapters making it Maria Lucas' favorite. Between its pages are her clippings and notes, including some on Halley's Comet in 1910. But even this text had its hurdles for Maria; one was the table of minor stars, 111 of them. "Page 146 is half the book," she wrote in the front, but still she loved it. Another of her favorites was *Fourteen Weeks in Zoology*, a reassuring book in that it explained at the outset that its extremely detailed "tables" were not intended for memorizing, merely for reference. After that, she said, no teacher would be likely to consider them grist for memory exercise. She liked the notion of "original research" recommended in the prefix, though she objected to preparation "of the skeleton of a cat, dog, etc." What the class liked best was the "biological approach" they were now expected to make to the animal world. Students were now asked how animals "act, think, and are mutually related," a more valuable achievement than to learn some "unpronounceable bone or muscle." The tables were there, however, and Sister Mary of St. George considered a great many of them indispensable.

Dana's *New Textbook of Geology* was in its third edition in 1882, the reason for revision being the new trend "to place dynamic geology before historic." Geology, however, was not Maria's field. She filled up the end pages with astronomical events of her last year at Notre Dame, including the Great Lunar Rainbow of January 16, 1883. On January 3, 1959 she folded between those pages *San Francisco Chronicle's* story of the Russ Moon Shots.

It was science, Maria thought, that most affected the lives of her schoolmates; but it was the pursuit of the classifier for the most part, or at best of one following with interest in the wake of discovery. Their preparation had not inclined them to work toward the breakthrough. That would have been dangerous and perhaps prideful. Their exact notebooks, their beautiful herbaria, lead to the already discovered; departures would have merited marginal correction. Their work is artistic and laborious. Irish girl Lizzie Lander's *Herbarium* is the work of an advanced botanist, and though she does not classify "unknowns," her collection indicates the best training in her era.

That the encyclopedic approach began early is evident from the reader used in the lower French classes, *Abrégé de Toutes les Sciences ou Encyclopédie des Enfants,* with its 116 "sujets graves." A full page of small print was required for the table of contents of this dreary catechism of universal facts. The tome was supposedly illumined by a few dismal drawings which today's child would be moved to improve with colors. Spacially, it presented the universe, temporally, the past. It was certainly not neighborhood-oriented. Its word lists made it seem a vocabulary builder, but of course, the nine-year-olds learned more French conversation at the dinner table.

The prize winner of all storehouses of facts is the third edition of Adrien Baldi's *Abrégé de Géographie,* with over 1300 double-columned pages in uninterrupted print, and its long discussion of "General Principles" in six-point. Maps are an almost solid mass of curved place names, the purpose, it would seem, being to omit nothing and to make all nearly impossible to find. This *Abrégé* — and one cannot help wondering at the title — was the sort of reference book found on corner tables for the convenience of teachers and senior students. "For the Use of Sister," is usually inscribed on the end page to discourage thoughts of ownership, or perhaps "Desk, First Rhetoric," to be more completely impersonal. At any rate, reference books were more numerous in French than in English through the early decades, a fact that offered no difficulty to most of the teachers and older students. Fortunately more interesting map models were available. One presents the European political divisions in colored inks. Another, entitled "Géographie . . . voyage des Israélites dans le Désert," is accompanied by a list of fifty items for identification.

Notre Dame girls of long ago, and of a later date, too, treasured their textbooks with almost pious sentiment. At the year's end they stored them, together with their "exhibits," in their large trunks. After the advent of Latin, it became customary for the Vergil class after its last session to bury their poet in a quiet spot near San Augustine Street, first drawing lots to decide who would sacrifice the beloved text. In 1907, the lot fell to top Latin student Hazel Nolting, who behaved, it was noted, with admirable detachment. Classmate Hortense White felt, however, that such courage was uncalled for, and so betook herself, armed with a shovel, to the funeral site at dawn next day only to find that the book no longer lay under the sign "Hic Iacet Publius Vergilius Maro." As she then surmised, it was safe in Hazel's trunk.

Books received as scholastic prizes also rated high as treasures, mostly by reason of the college plate inside the front cover, with its story of conquest, and Sister Mary Cornelia's signature. Usually these awards were pious novels, close cousins of the fiction signed out to the girls in the library on Sunday morning. At times, though, older girls received books in keeping with the subjects in which they had been won. Margaret Van Houten's grand prize in Spanish was the handsomely bound *Compendio de la Historia de los Estados Unidos*, its colored maps presenting something of a modern look.[4] But Margaret also treasured that parlor table favorite, *Flora's Lexicon*, an "interpretation of Language and Sentiment of Flowers," into which the author had slipped an unadorned outline of botany. Thus through the fanciful significance and verbiage, the unwary reader was lead to a consideration of cotyledons.[5] One of Margaret's last awards, *The Sphere and Duties of Woman*, had reached its third edition in 1852, despite its frontispiece of a doleful and unglamorous bride, and the strong advice of its author, George Burnap, an Anglican clergyman, to "The Ladies of Baltimore," to whom he dedicated it.

A favorite award for many years was the edifying little French novel, *The Castle of Roussilon*, which first appeared in English in 1850, to be reprinted several times for the libraries

of academies.⁶ Younger achievement was rewarded by stories
of impossibly angelic children, little introverts and self-con-
scious perfectionists. But if nineteenth century school libraries
were stocked with the purposely edifying, so were the current
magazines, and so even was the front page of the *San Jose
Mercury*. Building up a fiction library posed difficulties because
of the fears that circumscribed the choices of even so intelligent
a teacher as Sister Anna Raphael, whose class notes on criticism
indicate deep understanding of English poetry but almost complete avoidance of the English novel. It was little wonder. Retreat masters warned against the secular novel and Sister Superiors felt bound in duty to forbid their reading. When they
were finally included in the literary curriculum, they were still
not good fare for the religious mind. It is safe to conclude that
Sister Anna never read a Jane Austen novel, yet she was the one
of that group who would have best understood them. In an era
in which romanticism was running down to sentimentality in
any case, it was unfortunate that the weakest and most pietistic
fiction should have been selected for academy libraries.

The literary insincerity imbibed from such reading set its
stamp on student patriotic and allegorical flights and commencement valedictories. Biblical and early Christian heroism
often took an unbefitting sentimental turn. Scrapbooks filled
with the San Jose *Mercury's* printing of these were carefully
laid away in the library as jewels of literature, and as the *Mercury* gave of its space most generously, some of these collections were sizeable. Alice Lander's was considered very fine.
With it Margaret Dovak's *Delights of Romance, a translation
from the French,* was kept for posterity, witness to posing and
sentimental attitudes. Sister Anna Raphael indulged in the
sentimental, too, in occasional poems, but on the whole, her
note is very sincere. It was good fortune, said student Julia
Farney long afterwards, to have had the strongest influence in
the school so straightforward in an age inclined to fulsomeness.
That was true; not all schools of the time were protected by a
Sister Anna Raphael, or it may be added, by a Sister Mary
Genevieve or Sister Mary Xavier. Such collections as *Flowers*

in the Garden of Notre Dame, that gathered dust in the old library, were far from total evidence of their teaching.

The weakness of the system was lack of critical dialogue which might have punctured the pompous and verbose. But a ray of dawning strength is seen in the later editions of the old science texts, for these speak of change and searching. This may explain the general interest of the stronger teachers in science. These were in step with their time. One likes to imagine the progress they would have made with precision instruments.

A close look at the first four decades of Notre Dame in San Jose makes certain facts clear. This was not a finishing school; from the first the "branches" were emphasized, even though ladylike accomplishments were accorded so honorable a place. It could hardly be otherwise in a school that acquired at so early a stage so keen-minded a teaching group. Changes in curriculum point to a constant wish to increase the intellectual content. The Sisters did not subscribe to the current opinion expressed by the Reverend John Todd, that their students "would die in the process," or that they would turn out "to be puny and nervous."[7]

The year of the college charter, 1868, found the entire field of education in a state of flux and transition, and the Sisters on Santa Clara Street were aware of this fact. As at least some of them read the papers, they must have known about Vassar Female College, opening its doors three years earlier as a full-blown intellectual venture with no lower or secondary work to distract from its ranking with men's colleges.[8] They realized that the continental school pattern would hinder attainment of their goal. One thing emerges with clarity; those Sisters kept their eyes constantly on the college as a goal, nor did they wish to possess the title without the reality.

CHAPTER 11   BLESSING FROM A SOUTHLAND

*I*n their second decade the founding Sisters in San Jose thanked Heaven for scholastic progress far beyond their expectations; in the third, they enjoyed equal cause for gratitude when the paucity of their members was so completely reversed that Sister Mary Cornelia could "fill all the corners" and even share an overflow with houses in the East. Certainly membership had become a matter of grave concern; up to 1875 only twenty-nine novices had been professed in San Jose, and by that year the original Sisters were well on in middle life. The three daughter houses in Marysville, San Francisco, and Santa Clara were all boarding schools, built on the plan of the college itself in large and rambling units, which required a number of Sisters for maintenance, since their income did not allow for a staff of lay help, even if that expedient had been approved. And teachers were needed for the grade schools, for music and drawing and sewing; it was not enough to have the upper classes on Santa Clara Street well staffed.

An unsettled, money-mad population seems only one factor in this dearth of vocations. There was, besides, the fact that Notre Dame was considered a foreign order, not one fitted to the character of the American girl. It is possible, too, that the difficulty of reaching scholastic heights and the consequent small number in the upper division may have created an image of unattainability for the novitiate. Then there was the aloofness of novices and young Sisters who offered their former friends downcast eyes as evidence of dedication. Perhaps the chief cause was the Jansenistic emphasis in study hall and class "instructions," with their sometimes chillingly legalistic standards. Whatever the causes, the number of vocations from the college before 1875 was discouragingly small. Deplore it as she certainly did, Sister Mary Cornelia never for a moment considered any of the vocation "drives" of a later day. She and her Sisters looked to Providence for assistance, and saw an answer to their prayers in the closing in 1875 of the Notre Dame mission in Guatemala.

The Guatemalan mission was Mère Constantine's last, and the one which, before the gathering of clouds on its horizon, afforded her the greatest satisfaction.[1] Even when its sky was quite darkened, she refused to consider the cause hopeless; she died, in fact, believing that the threat would pass, that the Barrios revolution would fail. The outset of the project in 1859, it is true, had found her somewhat fearful because of the great distance of Guatemala from the nearest house of Notre Dame in America. Perhaps the "uses of the globes" helped her to discover that a mission group in Central America in 1860 would never know the isolation experienced by the Sisters whom she had sent to Oregon in 1844. At any rate, she yielded to the insistence of the Archbishop of Guatemala, Don Francisco de Paula García Pelaez. His offer of a financial start of some twenty to thirty thousand francs left him by his mother, Señora María Josefa Pelaez, was no doubt an incentive.[2] Certainly this offer was a new note to the Mother General, accustomed as she was to emptying her mission purse and making loans beyond its capacity that left the Mother House in monetary straits.

Another incentive was the promise of the Jesuit Provincial, Father D. Manuel Gil, to supply spiritual direction for Sisters and pupils in the new mission. And besides this, Belgian friends engaged in business in Guatemala hastened to assure Mère Constantine of whatever help might be needed. One of these, Juan Serigiers of Antwerp, who had established commercial interests in Guatemala City, became especially enthusiastic when he learned that his aunt, Sister Hermance Van Puyflick of the Notre Dame house in Jumet, had been chosen to lead the mission as its first Superior. This was in fact, a mission-minded family; when Josephine Louise, the sister of Juan Serigiers, entered the novitiate in Namur, just after the first Sisters had departed for Guatemala, her heart was set on following them, which she did as Sister Hermance Joseph, when the second group departed for that mission in 1862.

Among the seven who left Belgium for Guatemala, October 10, 1859, was the quietly forceful Flemish Sister Marie Béatrix de Cal, who was to become the very capable head of the mission on the death of Sister Hermance in 1870, a superiorship which she later continued through twenty years in California. Another also destined to play a leading role in California was gifted and beautiful Irish-born Sister Marie de Ste. Patrice Verdon, who set up the first novitiate in Guatemala and was later appointed to the same position in California, where she left a memory lovely with the little French *bon mots* which her novices never translated lest they might lose something of her spirit. She made herself well understood, however, in both Spanish and English, and with her varied experiences, came closer than did many of her countrywomen to a real understanding of the western world.

An unintentionally amusing member of that mission band was rotund little Sister Julie de St. Joseph Dur, a slow-going, unsubtle Belgian professed in Namur at the late age of 27. Arrived at, her decisions showed a flair for the unusual, a fact which may account for many things besides her volunteering for Central America. Her later life in California was dotted with escapades which sometimes still furnish western communities of Notre Dame with mirth. One of these tales presents her taking the small community of Sisters at Redwood City for a buggy ride on a Sunday afternoon, a thing unheard of in itself in those cloistered days, and rendered more conspicuous by the day chosen. Urging on a quite elderly horse, she must have presented a sight as wonderful as did Volscan Camilla leading her troupe, if so much less romantic. At any rate, the townsfolk gaped, though behind window curtains, and some took care to report the sight to Sister Mary Cornelia as unbecoming good Sisters. Sister Julie never suspected the smiles touched off by her doings, least of all by the memoir which she wrote in somewhat peculiar English in her last years, and which combined an

unreliable account of the Guatemalan mission with sanctimonious self-revelation.

To make sure that her missionaries would be well cared for,
Mère Constantine selected Sister Matthias Eckhoudt, a tall and
sturdily built Fleming, who loved to see her Sisters enjoy a
good meal and preferred sharing her culinary secrets to revealing those of her soul.

The other two of the seven were Sister Marie Aloysius and
Sister Marie Philippine Portemer. Almost nothing is known of
the first, but the other, a Belgian of stately poise and singu-
larly spiritual countenance, immortalized the first voyage and
reception of the Sisters in Guatemala in two long letters to
Namur. Unwittingly she carved out her own niche by her dedication to the orphans of the mission. One of the most persistent
traditions of the California Province of Notre Dame is her abiding sorrow at having to abandon her charges, homeless children, shown grouped around her in a faded photograph.

Arriving at Colón after an uneventful Atlantic crossing, the
Sisters found their journey to Panamá carefully planned for
them, and their passage up the west coast in the steamer *Shannon* as well. Sister Marie Philippine's letters are filled with
important names, and Mère Constantine should have been
pleased with her exact dates, for since 1844, length of time
required for transit of letters and movement of missionaries
from point to point had been one of her close studies. By 1860
she was beginning to know something of what to expect in
these matters, but if she was not surprised to learn that the trip
from Panamá to arrival in Guatemala City December 1 had
taken two weeks, she was certainly unprepared for the events
of their stop at Amatitlán on the last night. Here their carriage
was met by a military band and escort led by a trumpeter, and
next morning, after a royally appointed breakfast, General
Solar presented Sister Hermance with a superb bouquet of
almonds and raisins, whereupon the band reappeared and
played "Daughter of the Regiment" and other selections. It was
no doubt gratifying to the Mother General that the Sisters did
not accept all this display as honoring them personally; instead,

says Sister Marie Philippine, it was "chiefly to impress the people with the value of religious education." A grand cortege escorted the Sisters to Guatemala City, where a great crowd awaited them in the cathedral, which they entered with little children strewing flowers before them, as all the bells of the city rang a *Te Deum* with bass furnished by booming cannonade.

General Rafael Carrera, President of the Republic, came in person to present the greetings of his people. Prime Minister Don Pedro Aycinema and other important personages arrived presently with their wives to pay their respects, and to present their daughters to the Sisters as pupils. In every way Notre Dame's beginnings here were completely unlike those in Oregon and San Jose. Here the Sisters could begin their work at once in a house thoroughly renovated and prepared for them, while a former convent of contemplative nuns was being restored and converted to meet the needs of a future boarding school. For Guatemala, like all of Spanish America, had long been accustomed to orders of contemplative women, but was making a late start in establishing schools. The transformation of this old stone building, known as Belén, was chiefly in the hands of the Jefe Político, Don Luis Bartés, and his wife, Doña Luz, who with other members of the family, were the greatest benefactors of the Sisters throughout their years in Guatemala. But friendly concern proved general and besides, there was a wholesome promise of vocations. Here was a mission that would sustain itself with membership from cultivated native homes. There would thus be little language difficulty. A boarding school prosperous from the start would obviate the gifts and loans by the Mother House entailed by the earlier missions. The Sisters' energy would not be drained away by heavy carpentry work. Their spiritual life was cared for; the Coadjutor Bishop, Don José María Barratía, promised to officiate himself as convent chaplain. It was small wonder that Mère Constantine began almost at once to ask for a second band of missionaries for this Promised Land, nor that volunteers were numerous.

Letters from Guatemala now brought excitement to community hours in Namur. In this land in which the Church was historic, the Sisters were reporting that Christian practices and customs often formed mere additions to pagan superstitions. It should be noted here that the Belgian mind was likely to see little to be desired in "les moeurs du pays." The Sisters of 1860 would have been horrrified by the beat of tom-toms at mass. But certainly there was fanaticism to report, and that even among the better classes. As the Sisters of Notre Dame cleared debris from the long unused rooms of their convent, and explored the sacristy of the local church, they learned of the saintly Pedro de Betancourt and his founding of the Belemites (Bethlehemites), two centuries earlier.[3] They also found evidences of ancestral beliefs which shocked them. With no thought then of examining and understanding the native lore, music, and art, these first missionaries wrote to Namur of the need of teaching Sisters, which was, of course, very great. But the first of these letters had scarcely arrived before the second *colonie* was in formation, and the scribe of the mission, Sister Ludovic, saw this group depart April 10, 1862, with the promise that her turn would come next.

Three of the seven who set out on that spring morning were assigned to California in answer to Sister Mary Cornelia's pleas for help. Two of those en route to Guatemala were later to play important roles in her community, one being Sister Louise des Séraphines de Marneffe, daughter of a bell-caster of Antwerp. A stern soul, she developed a love of holy poverty which included having her shoes repaired so many times that their clatter announced her coming before her appearance. To prevent their falling off, she tied them around her insteps, and advised others to do the same. She disliked levity, which she declared typical of Americans. At a witty remark, she would look about in surprise at the general laughter; if she saw the point at all it was some minutes later, in which case she would explain it to all about in the manner of a solved problem. All loved her for her absolute honesty, a characteristic which prompted her to warn young Sisters whose lack of gravity she deemed it necessary to report. On her lips, "I just did tell Sister Superior," was a salutation devoid of animosity. Most admired her candor, even those who held reporting very rarely necessary. Believing that superiors might also profit by criticism, Sister Mary Bernardine when at San Jose in that capacity appointed this candid soul as her special monitor, and Sister Louise accepted the duty with her usual sense of responsibility. Her admonishings in this case one can only conjecture, but they could not have lacked the emphasis of her general statements. Though she made herself clear in three languages, the past forms of strong English verbs somehow eluded her. To younger Sisters, her repeated "dids" were a temptation to mimicry.

The second of this group later to play a leading part in San Jose was Sister Marguerite du St. Sacrament Kridelka, a graduate of Liége Conservatoire who had won prominence in European musical circles before entering the novitiate in Namur with the hope of becoming a missionary. Perhaps Mère Constantine relinquished her because she knew that the daughters of the upper class in Central America were in some instances already quite advanced in music; perhaps she was prompted by gratitude for her Sisters' reception in Guatemala; but these considerations would have been secondary to that of Sister's missionary aptitude and zeal. Certainly the choice of Sister Marguerite was ideal; when she was exiled from Guatemala she left there a group of dedicated young lay women who continued her combination of mission work and music.

The two other members of this group were Sister Marie Éléonore, a tall, fair Belgian remembered in the Cincinnati Province for her gift of mimicry and mirth, and the eager missionary, Sister Hermance Joseph. With this recruitment, the foundation at Belén began to take on the Belgian pattern, a *pensionnat* with its day and free school divisions, and a novitiate. Two aspirants were awaiting the erection of the novitiate. One of these, Margarita Gérard, though born in Belgium, was the child of a native mother, and so was rated a Guatemalienne. The other was native-born Jesús Castro of San Salvador, a child of "better family." In 1864 these two were professed as Sisters

Stanislaus and Marie Gonzague. From this beginning the novitiate grew rapidly, one of its first entrants, being Sister Clara du Sacré Coeur Zabadira, daughter of the official who had placed his house at the Sisters disposal on their arrival.

Expansion at Belén was phenomenal. Sister Ludovic compared it in housing and student enrollment with "Notre Dame's best schools." Only in California had numbers increased more rapidly. Perhaps no other beginning was so completely enveloped in friendliness, a blessing which helped the Sisters to close their eyes to such local customs as allowing children and family pets to wander unchecked about the church during mass, and keeping the church locked on weekdays.

Almost at once, too, the Sisters realized their hope of working for the very poor. They were not surprised, in fact, when Doña Luz Bartés asked them to take over her orphange with the promise of her assistance. When the cholera epidemic of 1853 had left many little ones homeless, Doña Luz provided a home for them with the rather haphazard aid of a lay diocesan group known as *Dames de la Congrégation*. Often the good lady had to face difficulties alone. Sister Hermance agreed to undertake care of the orphans, at which good word Doña Luz gladly announced the change in administration.

As this work would require further volunteers from the Mother House, Mère Constantine dispatched four additional missionaries in the spring of 1865. One was the young Sister Léontine Perwuolz, whose name later became a benediction among Notre Dame boarders in San Jose. A second was Sister Marie Pharaïlde Lamaire, a capable teacher in Guatemala, but past the age of adaptability when she reached California where English proved her first great obstacle. Still she loved her last mission and lived a useful life there, admired by all and never asking to return to her native land. The third of these, Sister Marie Augusta Lamberty, did return to Namur where she achieved the oblivion that used to be linked with sanctity. And there was Sister Ludovic, a natural recorder and interpreter of events, a collector of archival material. It grieved her later years to discover that certain relics of her loved mission had been lost in Namur.

Sister Hermance assigned Sister Ludovic to the orphanage as administrator, and Doña Luz withdrew completely, maintaining only a sort of development office connection, in which she discovered that patrons were more easily won to the cause when the school was staffed by Sisters. The assistance of a few lay teachers was still necessary, however, and Doña Luz pleaded for the retention of certain of the former faculty, an error, as the Sisters soon discovered. For one thing, these instructors, as well as the older girls, were addicted to smoking cigarettes. Even the good foundress, it seems, was given to "the vice," as were most Guatemaliennes. Still, when the teachers appealed to her, she declared for the Sisters, who with a first round won, felt they must attack another ingrained habit.

In corners of the kitchen, even on the stove, they discovered small dishes, pots, or pans of individual cuisine, the ancient protest against institutional cooking, bolstered often by convenient hypochondria. This custom the Sisters countered with a good and varied diet together with a bit of Belgian firmness.

Reform was further mitigated by the making of pretty dresses as a diversion from fancywork. Classes took on interest under Sister Marie Philippine's intelligent direction, and the orphans were soon "calm and tranquil." If the silent work hours seem exaggerated discipline, this was relieved by "sorties," fêtes, and daily singing around the organ, the gift of one Doña Lucile Roma. When General Vicente Cerna, successor to President Carrera, arrived in person to witness all the improvement, he was royally entertained, the little girls presenting him with a handkerchief, ornamented, "à la mode du pays," with huge initials.[4] A like gift, also "très jolie," was made to the Archbishop García when he called to assure himself that all the wonderful things he was hearing were true.

It was a fairy tale. Guatemala was a blessed land. Though to an extent aware of the undercurrent of revolution, the Sisters trusted in the tenure of their government. Thus Sister Hermance began to plan for a third educational venture, a *pension-*

nat de second ordre, in Ciudad Vieja, since the children of artisans and other plain people could not be expected, in that class-conscious land, to intermingle comfortably with the more opulent daughters at Belén. These *second ordre* girls were not orphans, nor were they actually indigent. Their parents desired for their daughters practical and vocational courses combined with the advantages of boarding school training under the supervision of Sisters.

Prominent Guatemalans at once promised assistance with this project. Don Juan Serigiers, who had been appointed Belgian Consul General for the Central American Republics in 1869, undertook chief responsibility, and before long the *Colegio de San José* was a reality. Sister Hermance planned the ceremonious type of dedication ceremony so pleasing to Guatemalans, and that over, installed Sister Marie Béatrix as Superior of the new community.[5] Three young native Sisters formed her faculty and Sister Marguerite came from Belén each weekend for music and catechetical work. In fact, all development seemed so rapid in Guatemala, that at the end of their first decade, the Sisters were turning their attention to a number of invitations for beginnings in more remote parts of the republic.

At the same time, a minor note of unquiet was gaining volume. The Sisters were coming to know that though "the leaves on the hedges seemed to join singing 'O Maria, Madre Mia,'" their most trusted friends might suddenly take sides with anticlerical forces, that not even the families of the native Sisters might be counted on in case of a coup. Then shortly after the death of Sister Hermance in May, 1871, all were brought to a sense of reality when a rebel group under Mexican leadership swept into Ciudad Vieja, which surrendered without resistance. True, the rebels held that center for only one day, but from that moment on each new report of atrocities perpetrated in the hills by the Barrios guerillas struck new terror. It was well that Sister Marie Béatrix succeeded Sister Hermance as head of the mission; there was need of her calmness and absolute refusal to be discouraged or disturbed. At Ciudad Vieja Sister Ludovic replaced her, keeping the school on an even keel, and taking deep interest in Sister Marguerite's three hundred catechumens. Here was true grist for her mill, and she jotted all down, including the arrival of a new little lad *con solamente un sombrero* of which he was very proud. He possessed no other wear, his sister explained as she helped him into whatever was at hand. From then on, trousers, rather than hats, were *de rigueur*.

For some time both Sister Ludovic and Sister Marie Béatrix thought they could ride out the storm. Even though friends should fail them, there were still such strong souls as Juan Serigiers, Doña Luz Bartés, and the many good and pious women who would intercede for the Sisters. But little Sister Julie of St. Joseph, now in charge of the orphanage, could foresee only the ruin of the work of Notre Dame in Guatemala, and so suggested leaving at once. Actually her work was the one least likely to be disturbed by a rebel government. Some of the Sisters argued that the position of the other schools was equally secure, and friends assured them that it would be impossible to replace them as teachers; even Barrios would see the folly of being opposed to the only available means of education of girls.

But when the Barrios victories at Santa Rosa and Los Nubes pointed to the end of the old regime, the Sisters began to notice a strange silence about these events on the part of the once loyal parents of their students. Soon even their pupils took on this noncommittal attitude. And parents of young native Sisters, who had been honored to see their daughters wearing the habit of Notre Dame, began to send worried messages begging them to return home. The insurgents, they warned, would presently be marching in the streets of the capital. But fear and vacillation stopped at the doors of Belén. As none of the native Sisters had taken final vows, Sister Marie Béatrix assured both them and their families that they were under no obligation to remain. She ceased to receive new aspirants, and allowed only two professions after February, 1873. Knowing the Latin American character, the Belgian Sisters would not have been surprised at a number of departures. In later years, in fact, they related with satisfaction the decision of the "Guatemaliennes" to remain and even to leave their country if necessary.

Departure began to loom as a necessity when news of the pillaging of the Jesuit property as Los Nubes reached the capital. And when next the Sisters learned that the city was receiving Barrios with smiles, that laurel wreaths and bouquets were being offered to "Héroe Barrios," they feared immediate expulsion. Presently, however, fear subsided, as one of Barrios' first acts was the placing of two of his young relatives in the boarding school. At this, Sister Marie Béatrix wrote to both Sister Mary Cornelia and Sister Louise, assuring them that their kind offers of hospitality in San Jose and Cincinnati would not be necessary. In Ciudad Vieja Sister Ludovic was completing an addition to her school. She had reached the conclusion that living amidst "continual alternatives," one must carry on as usual. Thus she sent an order to Belgium for "a good washing machine," and forty iron beds. When inspectors ended their visits in taciturnity, she kept her composure, as though friendliness could hardly be expected from them.

As Sister Ludovic came to realize, President Barrios was biding his time until he could win over the small landowners with loans from his Farmers' Bank. Finally, two officials called at Belén to forbid the reception of postulants, the taking of vows by novices, and conversions among the pupils. When Sister Ludovic reported a like visit in Ciudad Vieja, she felt it was time to leave Guatemala. With this decision came the rumor that the government would not allow native Sisters to depart. Families and friends began to call at Belén to escort them to their homes, and at this point some ten novices yielded to family persuasion. They had spent a longer than usual novitiate and profession was denied them in their own land. Besides, their Superior and Mistress made no effort to influence them. They were assured that if at some later time they should apply for admission in San Jose or Cincinnati, they would be welcome.[6] It was clear that the new government would not try to force the native professed Sisters to remain when the Belgians would leave.

Before that final day, there intervened a long period of strange contradiction. It was no secret that the government was staffing a school for girls with lay teachers from New York, an institution plainly intended to replace Belén. It was well known, too, that Catholic leaders who openly opposed anticlerical measures were being imprisoned and tortured. At last began the long months of questioning and of offers, refusal of which seemed to make the Sisters the offenders. Why, asked one official, did the Sisters refuse to dress as secular women, and if that were all, the Sister of today might ask, why not, indeed? And while the laying aside of their habit seemed a sign of betrayal to those Belgian Sisters, it was still a minor point, one which would not have satisfied the government.

The crux of the matter was Belén. If the Sisters would relinquish their novitiate and boarding school, they might retain the orphanage and their lower class school in Ciudad Vieja. At Belén teachers were being trained as well as daughters of the natural leaders, the intelligentsia. Thus matters dragged on until the Decree of Dissolution of Convents was issued on February 11, 1874, convents apparently meaning those of cloistered orders, of which there were 15 in the country in 1859.

To allow for a change of mind in their favor the Sisters decided to take no final step until the decree of February 11 should be extended to include them. Meantime they carried on the necessary communications with Namur and San Jose and arranged for storage of pianos and other objects, as well as articles of historic value, with their several constant friends. Thus when Minister Marco Aurelio Soto sent the President's order expelling the Sisters of Notre Dame on November 17, 1875, it found them prepared.[7] In accord with advice of the Belgian Consulate, Sister Marie Béatrix presented property claims only to have them completely ignored.

The Sisters left together on November 27, taking with them some eighty or ninety boxes and trunks, which at least, they laughingly said, should not fall into the hands of the Barrios government. For the 14 Belgian Sisters, the journey to the Guatemala port of San José was a Good Friday reversal, lighted though it was with one real joy; the 27 young professed native Sisters left with them. Persuasion and badgering on the part of relatives and officials had not affected them. Said one of them, "We just looked at the floor." They brought with them also little Teresa Solita, a girl who had been in the boarding school and whose desire to become a Sister of Notre Dame prompted Sister Marie Béatrix to place a postulant's cap on her head at the last minute, and that with no scruple about civil disobedience. Teresa had her family's approval, and if the Sisters did not receive her, she would board the ship with them, she declared, and apply in California in any case. This charming and determined native of Antigua had her way, though receiving her might have precipitated a crisis, but seemingly officials closed their eyes. Teresa became Sister Mary of the Cross and three years later was professed in San Jose.

In later years the Belgian Sisters always spoke of the "exiles" as heroic. For themselves leaving Guatemala was another step in a saga that in some instances led them back to Belgium. But the Guatemalans were leaving their native land as outcasts. They possessed the adaptability of seasoned missionaries though still young enough to enjoy the excitement of boarding the coast steamer *Colorado* at Panamá. Only one of them, Sister Angelina Sánchez, and she had sometimes shown signs of instability, succumbed to nostalgia in California. Her departure was a source of sorrow to the other exiles, who used to speak with pride of their almost unbroken record. Another sorrow was that Sister Rafaela de León lay buried alone under the wall of the parish church at Ciudad Vieja, where she had given great promise as one of the first community at the *colegio*. Sister Ludovic recalls the promise of Don Rafael Gonzales and his family to care for her resting place with its tombstone "in the shape of an urn," and reading that account, one recalls the story of Sister Renilde Goemaere at St. Paul in Oregon.[8] Costa Rican Sister Ignacia Gutiérrez was buried beside Sister Hermance in Belén.

It has often been asked whether the Sisters of Notre Dame could not have lived out the storm in Guatemala, yielded their boarding school, and perhaps "gone underground." Had they remained in the orphanage, it would have been as suspect in the eyes of the new government. The Sisters, even Sister Marie Philippine, with all her love for her charges, realized this. But Minister Soto's letter makes it clear that in the end the Sisters were no longer tolerated in any capacity.

Certain observations may be made from the vantage point of a century. Carrera was, for one thing, as certainly a dictator as was Barrios. That he was a conservative dictator happened to be an advantage to the missionaries. And while he strengthened the state by quelling the turbulent hinterland, he made enemies, on the other hand, by reestablishing church tithes. On the other hand, breaking the state-church bond failed to bring about the equality, the uplifting of the masses promised by the Liberals. Many decades later, the percentage of illiteracy was about as great as in Carrera's time. This may be partly due to Barrios' efforts to superimpose a Nordic culture on a Mayan-Christian background. But it was to a great extent the result of the overwhelming prevalence of ignorance. If leaders, conservative or liberal, wanted a reason for doing little, it was at hand in the frustration attendant upon doing anything. If many of the privileged class, and foreign businessmen as well, were pleased enough to leave the masses unimproved, they had at least the mountain of impossibility to offer as excuse. Doña Luz Bartés and her kind maintained hope and went to prison for it.

CHAPTER 12   NEW WORKERS IN THE FIELD

---

*T*en days after their departure, the 41 from Guatemala were welcomed in San Francisco by Archbishop Alemany, Sister Mary Cornelia and Sister Marie Catherine from San Jose, and Sisters from Mission Dolores. To their immense delight, everyone told them how much they were needed in "the States." For the notion of so much work to be done, so many posts to be filled was in strong and grateful contrast to that of being unwanted. But despite the great work to be done, Sister Mary Cornelia did not assign them at once.

The entire group boarded the train for San Jose and a good rest. Sister Marie Catherine tells of the exiles' utter astonishment at the train as a mode of travel; to be suddenly borne away on two rails at high speed required no little confidence in humanity. But what they all remembered about that journey's end was Sister Mary Cornelia and her Sisters bringing extra blankets to prevent ill effects from so great a climatic change, and being measured next day for warm garments suitable to Central California's winter months. Then through their days of rest, they were entertained by the students and taken in small groups to visit classes, all in an atmosphere of warmth that healed their recent memories of questioning visits and veiled threats.

In gratitude for earlier generosity of Sister Superior Louise of Cincinnati, Sister Mary Cornelia gladly shared her blessing. Within the next two years, 13 of the new arrivals, including five Belgian Sisters, were assigned to eastern houses of Notre Dame. Sister Ludovic returned to Belgium and there set about recording the saga of the Guatemala Mission. The remaining 29 furnished answers to many of Sister Mary Cornelia's problems. Besides, their presence made possible further foundations of Notre

161

Dame as need arose. For some, it is true, English remained a permanent difficulty. Increasing loss of hearing made it quite impossible for tiny Sister Catalina Aravalo, who developed, nevertheless, a lively sign communication understandable to all. Sister led a most useful life, not the least facet of which was the diversion offered by her pantomime to any who appeared over-serious. Aristocratic Sister Filomena de St. Joseph Sanchez de León, acquired a bewildering accent, though she read and wrote English with ease. As the accent disappeared when she sang, she employed her well-trained voice to good account, giving vocal lessons in her younger days, and always sustaining the choir. Among her "offices" was the large scullery in the old house in Santa Clara. Here she washed dishes after all meals, brushing aside any would-be substitute with tragic gesture and eloquent run of Spanish. Those who could follow her heard harrowing tales of the Barrios revolt. She had a few rousing ghost stories, too, hearing which it was wiser to appear credulous, since these tales were mostly personal experiences.

The always smiling Sister Maria Victoria Gonzalez, was according to Sister Filomena, the only peon among the exiles. But though the aristocrat made the statement almost as an apology, she still approved highly of her countrywoman. That approval was shared by all who saw this rosy-cheeked little Sister kneeling on a chair before the kitchen range as she canned endless jars of fruit. In her smile as she glanced up from her work was that singular reverence for each person which speaks in the eyes of those who treat simply with the Father of all.

Several of the exiles learned English quickly and became successful teachers of Spanish or music, usually combining these subjects with needlework or art. Some of the musicians among them had had "good masters," and in California kept in close touch with Sister Marguerite, as did the talented aristocrat, Sister Josefina Corzo de Sanchez, a fine teacher of piano up to her death in 1889. Sister Cecilia, about whom little else is known, was an excellent instrumentalist, but perhaps the ablest teacher of music was Sister Gertrude du Sacré Coeur Arzu, who brought prominence to the music school at Mission Dolores, and after 1889 to that of Marysville.

At Mission Dolores, Sister Sofia de Notre Dame du Sacré Coeur Giron, wrote all of those initials when she signed her name, but was known about the school as Sister Sophy. For many years Sister Sophy taught fine needlework to Latin Americans, but though she spoke English with a degree of ease, a certain aloofness marked her dealings with all Americans. For years she taught Spanish successfully enough but with some constraint. She was no doubt the least well-adjusted of the exiles.

In San Jose it was quite the opposite with tiny Sister María Josefa Muñoz whose embroidery classes were popular almost down to her death in 1917, and with the equally diminutive Sister Eulalia de la Cruz Zelaya who headed the Notre Dame Tabernacle Society, delighting members with her gay good humor. Sister Mary Bernardine called these Sisters her "two little birds," because of their quick, light movements as sacristans, an office which used to fall to the exiles on account of their ability to make delicate altar linens and the richly embroidered vestments so prized in baroque convent chapels. Sister Louise de la Trinidad Andreu was another petite embroidering sacristan, though not birdlike; her steps marked the quiet dignity of Spanish nobility. Her Sister exiles called her a saint, and spoke in whispers of her wealth and family, knowing that she wanted neither remembered.

While the Guatemalans were in their period of adjustment to American life, Sister Mary Cornelia made no use of their numbers for expansion of Notre Dame in the West. Then when Father William Gleeson, pastor of Brooklyn, the present East Oakland, requested teachers for his outlying parish of Alameda, she accepted the invitation as the typical work of Notre Dame. For Alameda and the adjoining Bay Farm Island were farmlands from which flatboats daily transported produce to San Francisco. Many of the farm workers were foreign and poor, and their children were growing up illiterate. But by 1880 Alameda, with its inviting climate and abundant live oaks, was also attracting lovers of beautiful homesites, some of whom, with park-like dreams, were investing in half, or even whole, city blocks. Among these new residents, two graduates of College of Notre Dame, Carrie Regan Nixon and Elizabeth Kane Buckley, added their petitions to that of Father Gleeson, and promised their assistance should the Sisters come to Alameda.

Father Gleeson had already established both Christian Brothers and Sisters of Mercy in Brooklyn, and himself rode horseback across the fields, Alameda not being as yet an island, to celebrate Sunday mass in his tiny outlying church on the southeast corner of Chestnut Street and Santa Clara Avenue.[1] It would have been difficult to refuse him but Sister Mary Cornelia experienced some doubt about which of a number of suggested sites would be most suitable for the school. This problem she placed in the hands of Sister Marie Catherine who was for once undecided, and the poetic Sister Marie Alenie, who found choice impossible since she discovered her beloved "venerable oaks" on all sides. Since they could reach no decision, Sister Mary Cornelia went herself and selected the future site on Chestnut Street at San Jose Avenue. Father Gleeson rounded out the block by moving the little church to the northeast corner of Chestnut and San Antonio Avenue. Within a year Notre Dame Academy in Alameda was completed and opened its doors.

The new academy was something of a departure from certain aspects of the pioneer foundations. For one thing it was planned in close cooperation with the pastor, though its ownership was completely in the hands of the Sisters. In the same block as the church, it seemed a part of the parish. And architecturally that first unit was closer to the large, high-ceilinged, compact residences of the day than to European-type convents with their long corridors and churchlike chapels. It was the first house of Notre Dame in the West headed by an American-born superior, Sister Marie du Sacré Coeur Barry. The first head teacher was young Sister Mary Veronica, daughter of Timothy and Anne Langen Dolan of Sierra County, who at once began a parish sodality and a First Communion class rang-ing from 16 years to 21, and whose radiant smile broke down walls of shyness and timidity.[2]

To help repay the loan made by the house in San Jose, a small boarding school had been planned, since there was no thought of parish support as yet. But though in its best days this division was never financially a great success, still the "house by the Bay" rendered great service to the community on Santa Clara Street in the years before the opening of the first Villa at Saratoga, furnishing rest and recuperation, they called it "rusticating," to sick and overworked Sisters. Sister Mary Cornelia and other pioneers spent weeks and months there in their declining years. And by reason of its nearness to the terminus of the Southern Pacific Railroad in Oakland, the academy gave hospitality to Sisters arriving in California from eastern points. From its opening day, the school brought joy to Father Gleeson. He rejoiced in his children's mass on Sunday and at their preparation for the sacraments. He spoke with pride of the school's progress. For the annalist's "uncouth" little illiterates, who "knew nothing of the creation, to say nothing of the deluge," were drinking in good manners with their letters. The greatest departure of all was the absence of a poor school; the disadvantaged were taught in one class with the boarders and the bright, well-mannered children who were daily increasing in numbers. This was Father Gleeson's wish; the Sisters were fulfilling it, and he could not thank them enough. His only criticism followed the honorific clichés read to him in the school's first Christmas greeting. That, he said, must not happen again. With the appointment of Father Michael McNaboe as first pastor in Alameda, the participation of the Sisters in parish work suffered a setback. Sisters, he announced, should remain in their cloister. They should direct neither the children's mass nor the choir. Sister Mary Cornelia counselled the patience and understanding which the Sisters displayed through the seven-year tenure of this well-intentioned but stern pastor. Then kind Father John Sullivan restored parish participation to the Sisters, and except for one or two "Belgian" restrictions, the community in Alameda looked to the future.

That a school with a French title and in a locale fast becoming elite should develop so strong a note of democracy may seem strange. Few of the resident pupils were wealthy or proud. Parents who looked for separation of their children from the common herd were told about the school in San Jose. Yet the academy on Chestnut Street possessed an air that satisfied most of the well-to-do of Central Avenue. In the minds of Sister Mary Cornelia, Sister Aloyse of the Cross, and Sister Anna Raphael, this school was to be a complete adaptation to the American scene. They wished its teaching to be second to none. For this end they were willing to assist it through the difficult years of street paving and borrowed money.

Even with augmented community, expansion from the central house could not be undertaken more rapidly than financial circumstances would allow. Thus the small beginnings made in Redwood City and Petaluma in 1885 and 1888 represent a generous and self-sacrificing effort on the part of Sister Mary Cornelia and the Sisters of San Jose. And generosity on the part of the San Jose community was possible because of increasing enrollment in boarding school, day academy, and music school, for these were benefiting by the current development which the newspapers were recording for the city and valley. They were expanding, too, because of emphasis on education in Santa Clara County. In 1885 it counted some eighty schools, and though these lessened Notre Dame's primary boarding list in both San Jose and Santa Clara, they greatly increased the numbers in the higher classes. The high school movement was on, and the notion of education for older girls was reflected in the *Daily Times,* as it quoted Ruskin on reading for girls. The *Times* was, in fact, devoting generous space to matters of education, to such discussions as the relative value of leading dictionaries, even to an interview with Thomas Edison on the possibilities of the record as a means of general reading.

Through the leadership of C. T. Ryland especially, good roads in the county were now making Notre Dame, as well as

San Jose's Normal School and High School, accessible to many. Good roads meant general economic progress, since lumber, New Almaden stone, and farm produce could be moved easily to market, and this progress brought to the boarding school many whose families could not have afforded that expense earlier. But pleasant travel seems to have been a more absorbing interest than economics; in the 1890s the county introduced the water sprinkler, spending half its annual income to make its roads worthy of its reputation as Paradise. In the wake of the sprinkler, the Notre Dame girl could step down from the family carriage at the lodge fresh as a daisy.[3]

The college itself was no longer one of the few bright spots in a community almost universally drab. For one thing, the great Electric Tower, erected at First and Market Streets in 1881, furnished "full moonlight to a radius of a quarter of a mile, and half moonlight to half a mile beyond."[4] That decade saw the new Auzerais House "entirely on the European plan," and the latest wonder of Levi Goodrich, the Phelan Block. But though the city was "bubbling over with electricity," it was another matter to have it installed on Santa Clara Street, which was still "out in the country," just as the Sisters had hoped it would always be. Thus the college blessed heaven for gaslight until after the turn of the century. "Gaz," as Sister Louise des Séraphines spelled it, was a major expense, and the supply not always dependable. For some years, in fact, the Sisters tried the expedient of home manufacture with a fair degree of success. But in either case, the evening task of Sister Mary Ignatius Love, and other lamplighters, grew more onerous as buildings became more numerous. In large rooms, lights were placed high for wider spread of light, so that the stepladder was an indispensible aid, to be returned by borrowers under pain of banishment from Sister Ignatius' good graces. Her charge was destined to retain its importance though everyone knew that through the efforts of Pierre de Saisset the Brush Electric Company had been incorporated in San Jose in 1882.[5] At Notre Dame electricity remained an academic matter to be demonstrated in physics classes with already outmoded instruments.

But with all this progress, Sister Mary Cornelia was still forced to defer opening a school for boys, a project which had been her first thought at the arrival of the exiled Guatemalan Sisters. Finally, Father Nicholas Congiato, S.J., obtained a reluctant permission from Namur; the Sisters might now teach little boys of the first three grades.

As parish funds were lacking, the Sisters erected a long, one-room building close to St. Joseph's School and opening on Santa Teresa Street, so that coming and going, the little unmannerly rascals might not disturb local decorum. In grandiose style, the *San Jose Times* announced the project,[6] but the polite interest which followed did not include offers of assistance until three years later, when C. T. Ryland discovered this branch of the Notre Dame apostolate and its need of further rooms. Straightway he donated the required sum of $12,000, adding in his will a bequest for improvements.[7] Thus St. Aloysius School started future citizens on their way, each year graduating a class of eight-year-olds to the boys' grammar school conducted in San Jose by the Jesuits. When finally the parish built its own grade school, and St. Joseph's became Notre Dame High School, the roomy classrooms of the little boys' school housed a succession of freshman and sophomore classes. Opposition to teaching boys was by no means ended, but in this experiment, Sister Mary Cornelia had at least given another proof of her unhampered spirit.

Seemingly a fair number of the Sisters approved of the "little gentlemen" and trusted at least to their good intentions. For these, stories of their doings enlivened recreation hours. Properly polished up, the third graders made angelic altar boys with loud but dubious Latin responses. These provided, too, an element of unexpectedness, as when young Aloysius Benoit remained in the sanctuary one Vow Day, kneeling in cherubic prayer through the holy formulas of consecration, an unheard-of departure in those days when not even parents were invited to the ceremony.

In general, perhaps, Victorian manners and restraints were not too well observed in the boys' school before the advent of

Sister Mary Baptist Hassett, whose Irish parents had stressed unquestioned discipline in her upbringing. Under her rule, the three grades took on the appearance of a Spartan camp. The same Aloysius Benoit described her method of maintaining order. At the first threat to unbroken discipline, Sister went down the rows, "giving each boy the ruler" without a word. Though the blows were light, the warning was not wasted, and if the just suffered with the unholy, the recipients were all nevertheless boys, and as such capable of any misdemeanor. It is not surprising that Sister spent her final years teaching little boys at Mission Dolores, where no doubt she "gave each boy the ruler," just in case, but gently. Her stance was that of a military officer, and her classes responded to her signals in the same ramrod fashion. But at the corners of her eyes and lips played controlled twinkles which caused grown boys to remember her kindly. At heart she was much less Puritanic than were some of her contemporaries, possessed of suave manner and exterior. With no little injustice, Sister Mary Baptist has been offered as an example of the Puritanic and tyrannic teacher of her time, a typical boys' teacher, too rough to handle girls. Those who recalled her ruler treatment said otherwise.

$\mathcal{A}$s the years of Sister Mary Cornelia's long provincialate passed by, she could see reflections of her own declining vigor in her companion pioneer Sisters. Sister Marie Catherine was growing crotchety, and Sister Marie Albine was administering her *médecines* with greater determination. As Maria Lucas put it, after their loss of Sister Mary Aloysia in 1880, the girls were fortunate that Sister Anna Raphael and Sister Mary Philomene were "so human," and that there was the studio of gentle Sister Joseph, S.H., as a relief from "Belgian strictness."[1] But this time of decline of the first Sisters was also one in which former loyalties grew stronger and fine new friendships were formed. And if students now seemed less dependent on their teachers, they were also more mature, and the founding of the first alumnae group was soon to prove their deep loyalty. As teaching was becoming more and more meticulous, graduating classes remained small; the largest in the 1880s counted only eight. But those who reached that summit brought honor to Notre Dame, marked as they were by Sister Anna's increased sense of intellectual values. Among those who absorbed an unusual share of her critical thinking was Frances McClatchy, whose appraisal of the first numbers of the *Notre Dame Quarterly* indicates high acumen and wide reading, as well as mature judgment.[2] Her classmate, Mamie Masten of San Jose, although somewhat less brilliant, won even more honors and set a pace that none of her many sisters could match.[3]

The most brilliant student of this time was Mamie Sullivan of the Class of 1882, daughter of pioneer John Sullivan and his second wife, Ada E. Kenna, who had swept honors before her at Notre Dame in 1857. Mary Dillon and Maria Lucas could never exhaust their praises of Mamie Sullivan. It was to be expected, they said, of the eldest daughter of John Sullivan,

who besides amassing great wealth, was first president of the
Hibernia Bank. Mamie added to all this distinction by her
marriage to Rudolph Spence, the son of David Spence and
Adelaide Estrada Spence. In the second number of the *Quarterly*, appears her long poem, "The Bugle of Memory," a simple
thought blown up into baroque design, mindful of the old valedictories yet lacking their bombast, which at least could be
hurled about with the "elocutionary force" that news reporters
used to admire when young speakers caused windows to rattle
with imitation of bell and wailing trumpet, at their best when
these were interspersed with groans of dying heroes.[4] Mamie's
audiences must rather have purred over the sentiment, as with
late Victorian sweetness she told of her days at Notre Dame as
of childhood protected by "hovering wings." Certainly there
was no stepping into the twentieth century for Mamie Sullivan.

Yet large doses of combined sweetness and prudery could
not dull the spirits of dedicated rebels like Minnie Urie, Lucia
Holbrook, and Maria Lucas, as they planned their pranks on
the southbound train from San Francisco after a holiday. That
even these were touched by the general romantic feeling is
plain from the fervor with which they threw themselves into
the weaving and rendering of their commencement offerings.
For Maria, the leader by her own account, confined her sub-
dued but cryptic remarks to the small area hidden from the
eyes of the presiding Sister by her open geology text, but in her
observed behavior rivalled the composure of Sister Mary Philomene through the entire spring semester, all to obtain the
miracle of being appointed valedictorian. In that role she be-
sought her listeners to consider the flight of Time on "golden-
tipped pinions" and then wept as friend Minnie transformed
herself with sorrowing eyes and elaborate phrases into the
Vestal Claudia. The *San Jose Times* printed every word of
Lucia Holbrook's original "Philippa," as if illustrating to what
length a romantic flight of fancy might be extended.[5]

After the next year's closing day the *Times* similarly quoted
honor student Mamie Dunne, a serious girl who lived, it seems,
more consistently in the presence of the Muse than did the

Lucia-Maria-Minnie trio.[6] Anticipating the first announced Latin courses at Notre Dame by eight years, Mamie Dunne entitled her offering "Non Nobis Solum." It was a lavish weaving of elaborate nature metaphors about the warp theme of unselfishness, a poem that ushered in a quarter-century of farewell odes ending in a "compliment" to the presiding dignitary.

This compliment came to be the grand finale with musical and dramatic numbers leading up to it. In the years after Mamie Dunne's 1884 offering, the effusion was often addressed to Archbishop Patrick W. Riordan, who accepted it with princely dignity, whatever he may have thought of it all. Things had been otherwise as long as the honored guest was his predecessor, Archbishop Alemany,[7] who was irked by such adulation. He preferred to be surrounded in the corridor by the juveniles, clamoring for a holiday. Archbishop Riordan was never encircled by juveniles and probably would not have understood their little game. Instead, the youngsters stood, also in dignity, and heard the fulsome words read by a senior, clear-voiced and otherwise worthy of the honor, careful to drop straight-backed little curtsies timed with her larger and more sweeping bows, not an easy matter since it required keeping an eye on the speaker when one was more interested in visions of princely purple.

Serious-eyed Crissie Watt, honor student of 1889, quite outdid all recent predecessors in her commencement sermonette in verse. Crissie was unsentimental, merely weighed down with an infallibility tinged slightly with the grandiose. After Crissie's graduation, the editors of the *Times* perhaps concluded that the public had had enough. Besides, newspapers were now beginning to devote more space to leaders of local society and to the large engravings that were the heralds of the society page photos. For a time the long commencement odes were copied out, by any who cared to preserve them, in bulging scrapbooks, but as this required a more laborious effort than clipping them from a daily paper, the importance of the grand effusion declined, to be replaced at last by the hastily prepared contributions to Class Day.

In contrast to the solemn-eyed angelic leaders, others were gay and prankish. The three-member Class of 1885, Mary Conway, Elizabeth Howell and Dollie McCone, styled themselves "The Funnies" and went through school happily, with no note of rebellion or sarcasm, despite restrictions which they seem hardly to have noticed. Dollie played the lead, talking the faculty and even Sister Mary of St. George, into more propitious attitudes. She and her sister Susan were completely unspoiled by their great wealth, coming to the college with sights set on the best it could give them, and both carried off the diploma with honors.[8] Stella Lion Blauer recalls holiday visits, arranged because of their distance from home, as especially jolly times.[9]

"The Funnies" were followed by a group quite as industrious, if less humorous. In the class of 1886 top honors were won by May Coolidge,[10] sister of the brilliant San Jose lawyer Clarence Coolidge, with Mary Dufficy of San Rafael and Mary Aloysia Byrne of San Francisco as close contenders, both daughters of leading pioneer families. Mary Aloysia was one of several second-generation Notre Dame girls named for their mother's beloved teacher.

A departure in writing was noticeable with this class, especially in the graduates' small bound volumes of original work.[11] While the sentiment was still Victorian, exuberance was now yielding to economy. Sister Anna Raphael herself had turned in this direction. In her classes prose writing was also becoming less ornate and stylized, more logically managed and somewhat more spare.

Representative of Sister Anna's prose training at its best were Gertrude, Emily, Beatrice and Genevieve Yoell of San Jose, writers by nature, whose scholarly ambitions were encouraged by their mother, Emelie Center Yoell. Gertrude and Genevieve won the diploma with honors, Genevieve's record being perhaps the highest known in the history of the college. Their older half-sisters, Eva, Harriet and Alice, were the society-minded daughters of "the most beautiful woman in Santa Clara County," Evaline Prothero Yoell.

The drive with which these Yoells approached scholastic duties must have greatly gratified their lawyer father, James A. Yoell; it was certainly accelerated by his growing impatience with anything short of perfection. In his youth he had worked against odds; he often reminded his family that he had been admitted to the Santa Clara County Bar before he had time to be naturalized as a citizen. His eye was constantly on report cards, and more than once he rushed coatless from his office on Santa Clara Street out to Notre Dame where all, from port-ress to the youngest faculty member, were instantly in a state of alarm. When younger Sisters objected to his stormy scenes, Sister Marie Catherine reminded them that he had moved out of his office and placed it at the disposal of the Sisters when they were getting settled in 1851.

Whatever fault their father might have found with their reports, prize-winning Gertrude and Genevieve became colum-nists for the *San Francisco Examiner* and *Chronicle,* respec-tively. Genevieve served on the editorial board of the *Pictorial Review.* Her poetry has the ring and marching challenge of Sister Anna Raphael's best occasional pieces.[12]

By contrast, the Taaffe twins, Mattie and Mollie, ranked in the lower half of their class, though they honored the memory of their mother, Elizabeth Yuba Murphy Taaffe, bringing to all tasks the considerable acumen and diligence required of gradu-ates. In their final year at Notre Dame, each produced a size-able sheaf of grammatically correct but uninspired verse which their doting father, merchant William P. Taaffe, had printed in twin volumes bound in leather. Sister Anna must have smiled indulgently at the efforts of her young relatives, especially since such diligence was not characteristic of the spoiled grand-children of the Murphy pioneers.

There was Diana, for instance, the daughter of Daniel and Mary Fisher Murphy. Diana spent rather less than two years at Notre Dame, distracted all the while by dreams of what her wealth could buy, aware of her beauty, which she complained was being wasted. Her marriage to Morgan Hill was unfortu-nate. At sixty, she realized her ambition for a noble title by her marriage to Sir George Rhodes, a British baronet. Like her brother, Daniel M. Murphy, she lived in luxury, forgetful of her early simple life, of her teachers, and even, it would seem, of Sister Anna Raphael.

But many besides actual graduates made up for her neglect. One of these was Betty Brenham, the very intelligent and studious second daughter of Charles J. Brenham, twice mayor of San Francisco. Her sister, Louise Brenham, had won distinction in music some time earlier and their musical mother, Betty Adair Brenham, had come to be a great admirer of the college. Many years later, Laura J. Brenham, a writer of note, who contributed occasionally to Notre Dame Quarterly, presented Mrs. Brenham's music collection in memory of Mrs. Brenham and her daughters.[13]

Two granddaughters of Notre Dame's early friends, Don Antonio Suñol and Dolores Bernal Suñol, Adele and Leontine Etchebarne, loved Notre Dame as had their mother Encarnación Suñol. These girls and their Bernal cousins call up the image of Sister Mary Aloysia's good señoritas much more readily than do the younger daughters of General Mariano Vallejo, Luisa and Maria, enrolled from Sonoma a little earlier. "Lulu" and Maria took life easily, won no prizes and must have disappointed Sister Maria Teresa Vallejo. Still they were happy at Notre Dame, and the general's high praises of the college seem based on his daughters' reports on their school.[14]

What pleased the Sisters in those second and third generation Suñols, Vallejos, and Bernals, was their family pride. In some quarters, there was a growing tendency to forget hacienda origins, and in cases of mixed parentage, to magnify the non-Spanish element. Student Harriet de Saisset continually lauded her father's distinguished French family, and scarcely mentioned her mother, María Palomares, a woman of local prominence. Yet it was common knowledge in San Jose that penniless Pierre de Saisset owned his success in the West to María's wealth. Harriet and her sister Isabel were not among the younger generation of old families that maintained lasting friendships with Notre Dame toward the end of the century.[15]

One of the finest of these friendships was with the White family of Watsonville, where pioneer William White had insisted upon raising his family in peace and quiet, somewhat to the annoyance of his lively wife, Frances Russell White. When Nellie and Genevieve White came to Notre Dame, they knew the story well. En route to the gold mines, their father had stopped in San Francisco. Finding it wild enough there, he reasoned that the mines would be wilder, and so settled temporarily in a profitable business in the new and unruly city. In their Watsonville home the boys, Edward and Stephen, and their bevy of younger sisters, read and studied constantly, so that the high honors appearing with the names of Nellie and Genevieve in the Notre Dame lists around 1875 are not surprising. Apparently both girls liked to write; both later contributed to the *Quarterly*, Nellie's prose and poetry fresh and graceful, her sister's unoriginal and pietistic. Nellie was a friendly soul, but stately, handsome Genevieve, who loved fine clothes and admiration, was serious and reserved. Putting off her vocation for years, she entered the novitiate in San Jose only in time to reach profession in 1889 at the age of thirty. Sister Mary Xavier, head of the school at Mission Dolores, discovered her ability and exploited it, attributing to her with customary generosity much of the success achieved by that school at the turn of the century.

In that era of Puritanic rigidity few paid so dearly for the life of dedication as Sister Genevieve. On the one hand, she loved, almost worshipped her family; her pride in the achievements of her brother, U. S. Senator Stephen M. White, knew no bounds. On the other, her perfectionist interpretation of restrictions built up in her mind an intolerable tenseness and aloofness. Accompanying the students on a walk, she would leave flowers from the convent garden on the steps of her mother's house and walk on without ringing the bell. Yet this coldness did not alienate the family. Senator White, whose wife, Hortense Sacriste, was the sister of the gentle Sister Louis de Gonzague Sacriste, became a staunch and admiring friend of the college in San Jose. At his death, the *Quarterly* bracketed his name with Governor Burnett's, both statesmen "with special prominence from their particular relations to our institution."[16]

A good friend in those later days was Rebecca Ord Peshine, an upper school girl in the 1870s, whose mother, Angustias de la Guerra Ord, was then writing a document on life in Hispanic California which she later dictated in Spanish to Thomas Savage. As a schoolgirl, Rebecca was ready at any moment to don full Spanish costume, the flowing lines in keeping with her soft utterance of her grandparents' names, Don José de la Guerra y Noriega and Doña María Antonía Carillo de la Guerra. But Rebecca was equally proud of her American inheritance. She would readily explain that her mother had lived under Spanish, Mexican and American rule, and that her father, Dr. James L. Ord, had come to California with the 36th Infantry. As a student Rebecca honored her forebears; as an alumna she led the pursuit of California history of which she considered Notre Dame an important facet.[17]

The names of the Austrian John W. Kottinger and his wife Refugio Bernal appear on Notre Dame's list of good friends at this time. Their younger daughters, Rose, Eva and Ann were among the Notre Dame girls who later attended San Jose Normal School and became successful teachers. Refugio Bernal, the daughter of Juan Pablo Bernal and Encarnación Soto Bernal, had been an early student and her admiration for the Sisters made her a frequent visitor to the college in her mature days. Sister Anna Raphael treasured an autographed photo of the elderly Kottingers, as well as some lovely Spanish shawls that were gifts to Refugio in her days as a bride at Rancho El Valle de San José in one of the first frame houses in the area.[18]

The college became, in fact, the mecca of pioneers grown history conscious and ready to talk to students and Sisters about their experiences and memories. One was that "cultured gentle-woman," Margaret Byrnes, the wife of State Senator James D. Byrnes and mother of alumna Margaret Byrnes. From tales of crossing the Isthmus, Mrs. Byrnes would pass to her husband's early days in San Mateo County politics, and the building of their palatial home there in 1875.[19] Another was the friendly

Mrs. Mary Bowden Carroll of San Jose, a leading clubwoman there and in the Bay Area, author of *Ten Years in Paradise*, social editor for San Jose newspapers, and contributor to various magazines. Her daughter, Agnes Carroll, a public high school teacher, entered Notre Dame novitiate in 1915 and was professed as Sister Agnes Gertrude. The rare visits of distant friends were celebrated by full assembly in Notre Dame Hall; the arrival of the much-traveled Margaret Van Houten Ditmars came to be something of a great occasion.

Mrs. Adelia Hickman McLaughlin, wife of banker Edward McLaughlin, was one whose friendship for the college had grown stronger over the years. Gentle and unassuming, she probably never felt inclined to entertain groups with the story of her girlhood in Kentucky and of her family's kinship with Daniel Boone, nor of crossing the plains as a bride to settle in Grass Valley. But she shared two interests with all the Sisters whom she came to know, and that was a number through the years when her daughters Minnie, Cecile, Agnes, and Winifred were students at the college. She loved to tell them about her conversion to their faith through the goodness of a little Irish girl whom she employed in Grass Valley as nurse for her first child, Minnie. The other subject dear to her heart was the private chapel in her new home at Seventh and Reed Streets. Planning this ornately beautiful room, she and Mr. McLaughlin came to the Sisters for suggestions. Mrs. McLaughlin's own interests, aside from her daughters' spectacular weddings, were chiefly charitable and that without ostentation.[20] A great event in her year was planning a fine Thanksgiving dinner for her "good Sisters," a work which came to require great secrecy as the somewhat possessive Mrs. Myles P. O'Connor began to play the role of Lady Bountiful for the community.

Archbishop Riordan himself became a great friend of the college, his stately mien ushering in a period of magnificent entertainment. For his reception in 1885, poet Marcella Fitzgerald composed a lengthy dialogue of personifications, including California, and angels of ocean, hills, and valleys, together with certain historic persons to the number of the senior class.

Resplendently costumed, Mamie Dunne, Belle Sullivan and others, addressing one another with varying ability, depicted Cabrillo regrettably missing the Golden Gate, and Drake as a pirate, a murderer, in fact, claiming the lovely land for his haughty queen. As these epithets slipped from maidenly lips, the angels, becoming very Michaels, assured His Grace of their readiness to do battle for the cause of justice.[21] In view of the new Archbishop's friendly attitude toward men of all races and creeds, one may guess his inward smile at such belligerence in the name of Holy Faith. Possibly he set it down as a manifestation of the narrow and assumed righteousness which allowed Notre Dame's fine new music hall no street entrance of its own, restricting its range of activities to the college, instead of dedicating its use to the encouragement of the arts in the surrounding area. One entered it through either the lodge or the Academy gateway, feeling in either case subject to enclosure. Yet its very stone walls made it a part of Santa Clara County, and with its fine acoustics it might have joined musical San Jose and Notre Dame Music Conservatory in a great common effort. Accustomed, however, to Notre Dame's secluded ways, the civic leaders accepted the hiddenness of the music hall, but hailed it as the crowning glory of the college and proudly accompanied noted visitors who were welcomed in it. One of these was John Cardinal Gibbons of Baltimore in 1887.[22]

As everyone realized that Sister Marguerite had supplied inspiration and initiative for the construction of the music hall, no one was surprised to see her second dream become a reality in the beautiful Lourdes Grotto just north of the building quadrangle. Through the years the Sisters had sung the Lourdes hymn and the Litany of Loretto on Saturday evenings, the latter in memory of its singing on the voyage of *l'Infatigable,* which had brought Sister Loyola, Sister Mary Cornelia and Sister Marie Catherine from Belgium to America. In fine weather, the gathering place had always been the shrine erected by caretaker Louis Pinard of stone which he himself collected and hauled from the foothills. Appearing on one of the first picture postcards made in San Jose, this first grotto falls somewhat short of the artistic, but the Sisters loved it with its statue of the apparition, and little Bernadette kneeling before it. But since Lourdes was Sister Marguerite's chief devotion, she insisted on a replica of the Grotto at Massabielle in its exact proportions, and as this devotion was running high at the time, she at once found herself surrounded by willing sponsors for her project, the most willing being Sister Mary Cornelia herself. It was this fact that hastened the project to its conclusion, and inspired Sister Marguerite's insistence on its completion before her Superior's Golden Jubilee in 1887.

For months the departments of art and embroidery bent every effort to produce elaborate copes and banners for the dedication procession. Beautiful statues of Our Lady of Lourdes and Bernadette were ordered from Paris. Skillful masons produced the grotto replica. Finally the community, the schools, donors, and invited friends assembled to accompany the life-sized statue of Our Lady of Lourdes on its tour of the grounds in a flower-covered chariot propelled by the white-gloved workmen who had fashioned it. The procession ended, the statue was placed in the grotto and blessed. By that time the small invited group had been augmented by hundreds of interested San Joseans who had found their way in through the school entrances, and their presence accounts for a sudden widespread interest in the "Lourdes of the West." Straightway the Sisters began to record cures, one of the first being in favor of Judge Bernard D. Murphy's small daughter Gertrude. None of these cures was ever attested by physicians; nevertheless, faith continued to grow in the Santa Clara Valley, a fact made evident by a large case of votive memorials that hung beside the grotto.

One unique petition was repeated daily at that grotto through the following weeks, one as sincere as might be expected from the character of the petitioner. In those days, when golden jubilees were observed in simple fashion as occasions strictly for the community, Sister Mary Cornelia was aware that unusual preparations were afoot in her case. True enough, she had long since thrown off the timidity that marked

her early years as a Sister, and she had learned how to accept
honors in the name of the office which she held. She knew that
she was loved by her community as few continue to be loved
after long years in office, but she felt that the Sisters were
building up a tradition about her which she did not deserve.
It was her lifelong friend, Sister Marie Catherine, who shared
the secret of her prayer at the grotto, to be somehow spared all
the fuss and honor. Every evening they prayed together, Sister
Marie Catherine assuring her Superior that she was asking that
God's will would be done, and all the while happily in the
possession of a letter from the Mother House with the order to
proceed with the celebration as planned. Besides, she said,
none knew as well as she how little vanity all the celebration
in the world could evoke in the mind of Sister Mary Cornelia.
Through her years as Superior and head of the college she
had insisted that celebrations on her feast day should be in
honor of her name saint. When the students presented tributes
in her honor, she thanked them in the name of her heavenly
patron.[23] These were occasions for bringing all present into
communion with the Saints of God. But a public jubilee was
another matter.

CHAPTER 14   DAWN OF A LOVELY DAY

*S*ome time before the celebration of her golden jubilee, Sister Mary Cornelia set down a condition in keeping with the "patron saint" motive. The occasion, she said, must commemorate the work of the Sisters of Notre Dame in the West through a span of over forty years. Amending that statement by the phrase "under the leadership of Sister Mary Cornelia," the Sisters completed arrangements for the great day, and the jubilarian reverted to her accustomed missionary intentions when she visited the Lourdes Grotto. But none referred to the coming feast as other than "Sister Superior's," as preparations went forward under the direction of the ailing Sister Mary of St. George, whose response to Sister Marie Catherine's admonition on the score of her health became a community classic. "How could one do less for one so deserving?" she asked. Besides, she explained, the celebration would draw the attention of younger Sisters to an extraordinarily fine example. It was part of that example that when all the grand "compliments" were read to the jubilarian on the great day, September 17, 1886, she could turn smiling to her companion Sisters, assuring them that all the fine things were being addressed to them. It was the same with the beautiful *Missa Cantata Solemnis;* it was offered for her Sisters' intentions. Again in the evening, when the college girls presented poet Harriet Skidmore's allegory, written specially for the occasion, it was in her Sisters' honor.[1]

Today, the yellowing pages of that allegory recall the poet's early friendship with Sister Mary Bernard Weber and the little group of penwomen that she encouraged. They call up the visits of Amelia Truesdell, Ina Coolbrith, and Marcella Fitzgerald, who gathered around Sister Anna Raphael and gave inspiring literary talks to her classes. True enough, most of these allegories written for girls' schools were a bit dull, and no doubt too many June afternoons were spoiled by impersonal Wisdom and Truth. But Miss Skidmore's drama, as she calls it, is more arresting than the general run, and if her work bears the Victorian stamp, as when she bids the cloister "deck the fair brow of safely sheltered youth," one must allow that the general saturation made escape practically impossible, and agree with Ina Coolbrith that her songs, at least some of them, are "free as wild bird lays . . ."

A significant outcome of the jubilee was the founding of the Cornelian Society, the original title of College of Notre Dame Alumnae Association. Headed by Geneva Brooks Robinson, a group of former students issued invitations to a preliminary meeting in San Francisco, its purpose to prepare for the golden jubilee and at the same time lay the plans for an alumnae organization. Mary Ann Murphy Carroll, who as a child had listened to her mother's urgent pleading with two strange Sisters from Oregon to remain and teach her and her sisters, was fittingly elected president.[2] On the first Board of Directors was the recently graduated Maria Lucas. Recalling this honor, Maria used to add that since she felt certain it was Sister Mary Cornelia who had "pulled her through," she was glad to have an opportunity to show her gratitude.

As preparations went forward for this golden jubilee, it became increasingly evident that the quiet, unassuming Sister Mary Cornelia had over the years acquired tremendous respect as a person, and this far beyond the boundaries of her religious community. For this reason when she suffered a severe stroke a few months after the jubilee, the news was received with widespread sorrow.

In the community itself, this common sadness resulted in an unwillingness to believe that her illness could be fatal. Where peace had once been disturbed, Sister Mary Cornelia had created great peace and maintained it for over thirty years. There was at the time, moreover, no canonical regulation on the tenure of religious superiors and the person, especially of a higher superior, had become sacrosanct. The very notion of expecting such a one to "return to the ranks" seemed a form of rebellion, or at least a sign of restlessness. Thus fear of change built up the unrealistic hope of Sister Mary Cornelia's recovery.

By virtue of her position as second in authority, Sister Marie Catherine was acting head of the house, but her failing sight left her at a loss, as did the death of Sister Mary of St. George. It was becoming clear that the invalid could hardly be expected to regain her former health, and the acting Superior was becoming increasingly aware of criticism that was causing cleavage in the once-united community. Whether she had doubts as to her own fitness or not, Sister Marie Catherine wrote to Namur, asking Mère Aloysie to send an experienced Sister to take charge.

When late in 1887 Sister Marie de St. Denis Fischer arrived in San Jose, Sister Marie Catherine felt that a troublesome chapter would soon be closed.[3] She had great esteem for this German-born Sister who had been so generally liked as head of the house in Marysville more than a decade before. Her appointment at this time suggests concern over Notre Dame affairs in California on the part of Mère Aloysie, whose letters reflected her worry over complaints made by dissatisfied members of the San Jose community. They also witness to her Jansenistic bent. She warned, for instance, against the use of illustrated textbooks in physiology, no matter how conservative, and ordered discontinuance of *The Souvenir,* a school publication started at Mission Dolores with the approval of Sister Aloyse of the Cross. It seems clear that this Superior General feared independence of the central government far more than had her predecessor, and that her insecurity demanded the certainty of unchanging custom.[4]

Sister Marie de St. Denis[5] was neither fearful nor likely to be unduly affected by discontent or complaints. She knew and loved the older Sisters in California, and they in turn looked to her for inspiring leadership and general peace. They trusted that her appointment entailed succession to the office of Sister Mary Cornelia, who herself believed it did and spoke of Sister Marie St. Denis as her higher Superior; in fact, when the Sisters visited her she assumed that their use of the accustomed title in greeting her was a mark of kindness. Her work was finished, she said, and the care of affairs was in capable hands.

For some time, unfortunately, Sister Marie de St. Denis had been suffering a deterioration of hearing which grew steadily worse, instead of improving in the gentle climate as she had hoped. She reported this to the Mother House and suggested the need of a skilled business administrator to replace Sister Marie Catherine who was gradually slipping into blindness.

In Namur, meanwhile, Mère Aloysie had been replaced by Mère Aimée de Jésus who, instead of recalling Sister Marie de St. Denis at once, sent Sister Amélie St. Joseph Caudron, a Belgian, to take over financial affairs in San Jose and to lighten the burden of government by acting as visitor to the other houses.[6] Her status, however, was not clear to the Sisters in San Jose. At New Years, 1889, the community tried to solve the problem in protocol by offering the customary greeting for the Sister-in-charge to both Sister Marie de St. Denis and Sister Amélie, and then proceeded upstairs to greet Sister Mary Cornelia.

It is quite clear that Sister Amélie lent an ear to the critical group, and in her energetic fashion called attention to what she considered a general remissness. It was well for the peace of the house that her duties often called her away from San Jose, for Sister Amélie's presence brought a tension which not even Sister Marie de St. Denis' deference could prevent, and this state of discomfort was only increased when she announced her intention to visit Namur in March. Many of the Sisters feared that Sister Amélie would report matters in the California Province unfairly, though the declared purpose of her journey was to accompany Sister Aloyse of the Cross on her first return to Liverpool where, unknown to her, a fine reception was building up in her honor. Besides, Mamie Tomb, a recent graduate, had been accepted for the novitiate in Namur, and her parents preferred her not to travel alone.[7]

At first Sister Amélie's cheerful journey letters tended to allay the fears of those who had felt her disapproval, but this relief ended shortly when Sister Marie de St. Denis announced her own return to the East in early April. An official visit by Archbishop Riordan followed on April 10, and at that, feeling among the older Sisters, and among all, in fact, except the dissidents, was that there had been no little misrepresentation. In June the blow fell when word reached San Jose that Sister Marie de St. Denis would not return, and that Sister Amélie St. Joseph would replace her in San Jose. This was "triste nouvelle." The community at large was in desolation when the word arrived. Yet all agreed with Sister Anna Raphael, Sister Marie de St. Patrice, and even Sister Marie Catherine, that as the arrangement was made by higher authority, all must accept it willingly. Apparently resignation was very difficult for Sister Mary Cornelia, who suffered two attacks, says the journalist, as a result.

It is clear that Sister Amélie's visit to Namur climaxed her series of reports and suggestions made in virtue of her role of visitor in California and certainly in confirmation of the complaints to which she had listened. It is equally clear that her judgment was highly respected at the Mother House. As might be expected, on her return to San Jose, her admirers gathered around her. Correction and change, much of it unnecessary and pointless, became the order of the day. Tapping her way around with her stick, Sister Marie Catherine sensed that the peace of the house had been disrupted. Soon she was aware that Sisters, even some still young and vigorous, and whose good sense she admired, were being ignored. Perhaps flattery prevented Sister Amélie from seeing her error and from noting the unrest that was becoming evident despite Sister Marie Catherine's counsel of patience. She should have perceived it at least on her visit to the house in Marysville, where her disapproval of Sister Marie Alenie's absent-mindedness was countered by the veneration accorded that saintly Superior by Sisters, clergy, students, and citizens.

In the absence of preserved correspondence, it can only be conjectured that Sisters in California expressed their opinions in letters to the new Mother General.[8] Certainly the death of

Sister Mary Cornelia, January 11, 1892, must have been an occasion to many for stating their minds. The election of Sister Anna Raphael as councilor on the following June 12 indicated consolidating thought in the community, and though Sister Amélie appeared to consider her appointment permanent, Sister Marie Catherine later referred to her recall to Belgium in October as expected "for a long time." The annalist at Namur described the recall as "definitivement," which after all is a more revealing word than most annalists, or writers of religious biography have permitted themselves to use. At any rate, as Sister Amélie prepared to depart, both community and classes organized elaborate farewell ceremonies, and with real gratitude on the part of the Sisters. For it was plain that she had been misled. If she had hurt good people, it had been in her mistaken desire to reform evils, which in most cases did not even exist. All recognized her financial ability and were grateful for the way in which she had cleared tangled business matters and disposed of debts. But all knew that Notre Dame in California had passed through a crisis, even though some genuine tears were shed at her departure.

Then, as both the annalist and Sister Marie Catherine recount, there followed "the dawn of a beautiful day," for presently two leaders of unusual understanding and great heart arrived in San Jose. One was Sister Superior Julia McGroarty, the major Superior of all American houses of Notre Dame.[9] Sister Julia's mission was to install the other leader, Sister Mary Bernardine Tivnan, newly appointed successor to Sister Mary Cornelia. Whatever misgivings Sister Julia may have had before coming, she was greatly pleased with Notre Dame in the West, and what pleased her most was the instant response of the Californians to Sister Mary Bernardine's outgoing approach, an understandable response, for in their new leader all recognized the generosity and warmth they had loved in Sister Mary Cornelia.

Perhaps the first in the community to experience Sister Mary Bernardine's way with suffering or sorrow, her glance of searching sympathy, was postulant Sadie Quinlan of Oakland, a recent honor graduate, who was finding the break with home and family a little more than she could bear until she was presented to the "pale and queenly" new Superior.[10]

The Sisters used to speak of her motherliness, since their notion of obedience kept the mother-child concept to the fore, but more important than this was the fact that she was one of the few heads of community at the time who met adults on the adult level. Her reverence for the person of each individual prevented classifying and judging. As the Sisters came to know her, the good news sped from house to house of Notre Dame.

In part, at least, Sister Mary Bernardine's fine qualities sprang from the setting of her early years. Born Catherine Tivnan at Roscommon, Ireland on May 1, 1839, she was child of a prosperous farming family. Out of her childhood, she brought love and trust, as well as a tremendous reverence of the faith of her fathers, though without the usual legacy of remembered persecution. Her recollections were lighted with glimpses of Irish countryside; to her last days, she spoke with feeling of whitethorn, and foxglove, of blackbirds and new-mown hay. But the great famine reduced family circumstances and drove the Tivnans from idyllic country life to a new home in Lancastershire, England, when ten-year-old Catherine had her first view of elegance as she watched Queen Victoria on a journey of state. At the death of Michael Tivnan, his family was again uprooted, this time at the persuasion of Catherine's elder brother, who had settled sometime earlier in Salem, Massachusetts. Here Catherine made the acquaintance of the Sisters of Notre Dame and, her schooldays over, asked to be admitted to the Institute.

In California Sister Mary Bernardine's varied New England experiences were assets of minor consequence compared with her lifelong habits of tact and of living simply in the face of reality. This latter quality led her to know that her presence as an outsider bore witness to the inability of the group of western houses to provide their own leadership; her tact was responsible for her quick and sensitive understanding of western points of view. Evidence of her great respect for her new home-

land was her immediate interest in pioneer families as well as
pioneer Sisters. To the older members of the community her
coming was a Second Spring. In the schools, descendants of
pioneers were roused to interest because of her questions. This
was, of course, only one phase of her ability to build up without
flattery the worth which she found in all. Meeting with discouragement in anyone, she quickly offered the pioneer Sisters
as examples, especially Sister Mary Cornelia, who became her
great ideal. When she discovered that little had as yet been
done to perpetuate the memory of early heroism, she asked the
now almost blind Sister Marie Catherine to dictate her memories. Thus young Sister Anthony, S.H., and others began the
custom of taking dictation in large writing on a blackboard so
that she might correct errors. In the midst of the project, however, Sister Mary Bernardine discovered Dr. Adolph Barkan
of San Francisco, who removed Sister's cataracts so successfully
that she completed the work in her large angular hand herself,
adding at the end her debt of gratitude.

Sister Mary Bernardine always confronted Sisters, students,
everyone without patronage. On the one hand, she expected,
and usually received, adult responses; on the other, she knew
that a harsh word or an injustice on the part of authority could
reduce the subject to the state of sub-person, or rebel. She
knew that the young religious, in an effort at sanctity, might
easily accept the sub-person status as a part of it all. In an age
when the concept of obedience was still too frequently com-
panioned by the corollary of unfailing direction of the superior
by the Holy Spirit, she was well aware that she might err in
judgment, or by reason of her naturally quick temper.

Circumscribed by the same minutiae of rule and customs
as were her Sisters, she bore the added responsibility imposed
on all superiors of her day of insisting on their being carried out
to the letter. Yet her distrust of herself and her great sympathy
would not allow another to grieve. When the Sisters were leaving the chapel after night prayer, she would stop the one whom
she felt she might have humiliated. In later years more than
one recalled her astonishment at seeing this stately woman

drop to her knees and ask forgiveness, as was the custom on being corrected. Said one, "I could never forget it; no wonder I loved her." Nor was it a wonder that, as Sister Anthony, S.H., used to say, "In no time, she held Notre Dame of California in the palm of her hand."

One cause of the general good will toward Sister Mary Bernardine was her own fondness for community and recreation hours. It was soon clear to all that these were the high peaks of her day because they brought her the presence of the Sisters. They knew that if she remarked a Sister's absence from the group, she was not checking on her; she sincerely missed her company. The community hour, known as "Holy Family," or "Six o'Clock," held daily before apostolic activity came to require so great a portion of the day, ranked almost with chapel exercises as a duty, its sanctity symbolized by statue and picture in the large community room, as well as by the always shining central aisle and the long rows of chairs arranged choirwise. Here the Sisters brought mending, or fancy needlework. Here older members listened to the younger, as they answered, with greater or less theological accuracy, questions put to them by the Superior or presiding Sister, who after each answer, made an application to Christian life suitable as a rule for use in teaching. There was no attempt at theological explanation, much less discussion.

But as Sister Mary Bernardine believed that something more than this was needed for teachers, she appealed to the Jesuits of Santa Clara College for lectures to the depth then considered proper for religious women. These, by Reverend Joseph Sasia, or some equally erudite Jesuit, were attended by most of the teaching Sisters and the more promising novices. But this was the extent to which Sister Mary Bernardine was in advance of her time.

There is arresting wisdom in the instructions and records written in her large, flowing hand. The content is straightforward, quite free from stylized phrases and picayunish standards. Her community hour was never the occasion of physical presence during which one got on with a bit of sewing. According to those who attended them, her "Six o'Clocks" were spell-binders. In her refreshing way, she stamped the hour with balance and reality. Sister Anthony, S.H., noted this, as well as her freedom from prudery and Jansenism, from addiction to sugary visions and pious tales, and other of the era's guaranteed marks of sanctity.

Making no educational claims, Sister Mary Bernardine left teacher guidance to Sister Anna Raphael, at whose request, however, she gave talks to the older girls with the same success that she had experienced in Massachusetts. In an era when convent schools were being accused, usually with justice, of failing to fit their students for life, alumnae of both East and West spoke of her wise personal counsels. This gratitude was, in fact, the common note in the hundreds of messages addressed to the Sisters in San Jose after her death.[11] And considering this frequent statement of personal loss, the appraisal of Sister Mary Bernardine by Archbishop John J. Williams of Boston is understandable. Boston, he wrote to Archbishop Riordan at the time of her transfer to the West had lost a mother.[12]

In practical management, Sister Mary Bernardine was a delight to Sister Marie Catherine, for while she expressed amazement at the accomplishments of four decades, she noted needed repairs, as well as the lack of development since Sister Mary Cornelia's vigorous years. Knowing the part that Sister Marie Catherine had played in construction, Sister Mary Bernardine consulted with her before beginning a building program which is the more remarkable because it coincided with the financial recession of 1894.[13]

Her first construction project was enlargement of the chapel, which despite former alterations was still too small for both community and students. The new plan bypassed the early dream of a completely separate church. Thus the entrance steps, leading down to the front corridor were merely widened and converted into a vestibule closed off from this main passageway by glass doors and from the chapel itself by panels and doors that formed a beautiful carved white grill. At the cost of over $16,000, the north end of the chapel was extended in length and width to produce a cruciform nave, a deep sanctuary, and large sacristies. To the general relief, the heavy, ugly side lofts were now removed to make way for large windows. Above the transcept, a great dome, raised through the deep attic above the chapel, added spacious dignity. Besides, both this and a smaller dome over the sanctuary served as lightwells.

When Archbishop Riordan dedicated the chapel, August 11, 1894, it was far from its final splendor, yet all were spellbound at sweep of nave, and majestic dome with graceful arches fanning out from its base. Except for its vestibule connection, it was now a church worthy of the Pontifical High Mass for which Sister Marguerite composed a special offertory hymn, with organ, harp, and violin accompaniment. Still, when a little later, the annalist recorded this completion of the chapel, she amended with "for the time," knowing as she did the characteristic tendency of Sisters to improve matters. Thus Sister Theresa, B.S., Spencer, a gifted arrival from Cincinnati, carved elaborate ornaments in wood for the main altar, and these were covered with rich gold leaf.[14] Next Mrs. Myles P. O'Connor donated a hand-carved Da Vinci Last Supper panel for the altar front, which became a sort of centerpiece for the colored statues that appeared later. Through the generous gifts of alumna Margaret Van Houten Ditmars and others, fine stained glass windows were made for the chapel in the studios of Thomas C. Butterworth in San Francisco.[15] And though gifts fell short of expectations, Sister Mary Bernardine placed an order with organ builder Louis Schoenstein. She had no worries about payment since Treasurer Sister Louise des Séraphines, the new head of the business office, astonished as she was at any failure to accept her own austere ideal of religious poverty, considered no expenditure too great when the chapel was in question. At her insistence, electric power was increased to accommodate an organ motor and brilliant chapel lighting.

The chapel was, in fact, the subject of constant improvement. After the considerable damage done to it by the earth-

quake in 1906, it received an elegant fresco. In Rome shortly
after that disaster, Sister Mary Bernardine ordered Stations of
the Cross done in oils in the manner of Raphael. At her golden
jubilee, she employed gifts from her family and friends to
round out her chapel dream. Now she added an oak inlaid
floor, tall, elaborate candlesticks of carved brass, and rich vases
and urns in gold and alabaster. Yet the ensemble was never
garish, nor unharmonious since all was selected so as to avoid
the appearance of accretion. There was a pleasing wholeness
about it even when feast days brought the treasures *en masse*
into the sanctuary. The younger generation, raised in post-
earthquake homes and accustomed to unadorned spaces and
the plainness of "mission" furniture, fell under the spell of that
chapel as novice or student. It was the distance, the vaulted
arches, the total view that impressed them: the altar that
glowed like a gem, the great urns and candlesticks.[16] Visitors to
the present-day Belmont campus, finding many of these objects
quite at home in the rococo setting of Ralston Hall, occasionally ask how one could have prayed in the midst of such
baroque splendor. Wasn't it all a bit sentimental? In a way it
was, as one considers the phrase, "a little bit of heaven," that
usually described the old chapel on feast days, when banks of
Christmas trees and tiers of candles lifted the eye skyward.

Shortly after the dedication of the chapel, the walls of
Notre Dame Music Conservatory began to rise. This fine, two-
story brick structure continued the line of the east wing some
300 feet, though architecturally it presented a departure with
its higher windows and ceilings. Theodore Lenzen must have
missed Sister Marie Catherine's helpful suggestions as he
planned this unit, the first in which she was not on hand for his
business meetings with Sister Mary Bernardine and Sister Anna
Raphael. Here at last was sufficient space for instruments and
ensemble work, and with an increased music faculty, income
was more than doubled in a decade; besides paying off the initial cost of this unit, it allowed the purchase of new grand
pianos and lovely harps. As Sister Marguerite explained, the
conservatory was the delayed half of the plan begun in Notre

Dame Hall; with it she could envision musical development that would be a credit to the college of the future.

The erection of Science Hall in 1905 bears witness to the hope for a college in the modern sense. This last building with its purely classic lines and pillars, was a complete architectural departure. Separated from the conservatory by an avenue, it was intended to be the first of a cluster of like buildings physically isolated from the older units, the nucleus of a western Trinity College. The presence in San Jose of Sister Mary Euphrasia Taylor, a prime mover in the initiating of Trinity, at this time, is probably explained by such a plan.[17]. The cost of Science Hall, $59,000, seems to include repair of damages caused by the great earthquake while the building was still under construction. One of the first buildings completed in San Jose after that disaster, it brought high praises to Architects Theodore Lenzen and his son, Louis T. Lenzen, whose photos, along with a small blueprint of the façade were placed in the cornerstone.[18]

Notre Dame Music Academy, facing diagonally on the corner of Santa Clara and Santa Teresa streets, seemed unrelated to cloister, yet it was in fact an expression of conservative thought. Intended for pupils of the parish school, it later separated music students of Notre Dame High School from those of the Conservatory, with resulting annoyance on the part of the former. The fact of separate closing exercises emphasized the undemocratic arrangement for several years, and this despite the attendance in the new high school of daughters of leading local families. Sister Mary Bernardine and others of democratic mind found this division regrettable.

With a three-story novitiate building completed in 1900, Sister Mary Bernardine set about redesigning the formerly crowded professed house. She was one of the first to see the necessity of airy and sunlit sleeping quarters as a means of combating tuberculosis, which she was astonished to find making inroads in the ranks of the young, even in California.

Her readiness to introduce laborsaving devices came as something of a shock to those who considered heavy work a source of virtue. One of her first reforms in this matter was to install a power washing machine and mangle, though Sister Louise des Séraphines raised strong objections to the cost of the motors. The institution-size washing machine was an innovation in convents. Hearing that the Dominicans in San Rafael had purchased one, Sister Mary Bernardine went there herself to see it. Pleased with it, she had the laundry in San Jose enlarged and ordered the machine. The mangle followed, an improvement on the first huge, noisy machine seen for many years in older convents. These improvements were a sort of community Christmas gift in 1895. No doubt the Superior enjoyed Sister Louise's almost lyrical entry in the convent journal later on as she noted that the washing had been cut to a single day. Higher bills for electricity, said Sister Mary Bernardine, were preferable to tired backs.

Convenience in the kitchen was another special interest. The thick-walled outkitchen, the walk-in cooler of that day, was her idea. One of her first acts was to increase the fitful water supply by installing a large tank and windmill. Next, a second new tank furnished abundant water for the garden, and Sister Mary Bernardine was not to be daunted by the discovery that artesian wells in that area had to be sunk lower from time to time. The dependable water supply prevented frayed nerves, which were as great an evil as tired backs. Another well which she had sunk for convenience near the kitchen door, supplied fine cold water which the novices took turns in pumping for table use, one of their first lessons being "priming the pump."

The very site of the college, however, made some improvements slow of attainment, for though the area had not remained "country," as Sister Marie Catherine had hoped it would, neither had it become part of either business or residential section of the city. More and more it came to be a down-at-the-heel section, its claims to any notice being the College of Notre Dame and its street leading into The Alameda. Thus though there was always talk of improvement in the future, the district as it was could not look for first attention

by public utilities. Electricity arrived late, and poor gas service
prompted the purchase of a gas generator in 1896.[19] And if life
became, as it did, a series of minor contests with her treasurer,
Sister Mary Bernardine met each with her guiding principle
that what promised help to the Sisters must be given a trial.

It was the same concern that prompted her to apply to the
Mother House for an experienced nurse to replace aging Sister
Aurelie, who had not in any case been specially trained. In
answer came the compassionate and capable Sister Marie St.
Pierre Frizzelle, daughter of a French family that had sought
refuge in Ireland during the French Revolution. From her first
days as a novice in Namur, Sister St. Pierre, as she was always
called, lived from one perfect adaptation to another. Though
she had always declared she would never become a nurse, she
discovered as a Notre Dame novice that she loved caring for
the sick, that she could now use happily her earlier training
with the Sisters of Mercy. Perhaps a greater adaptation was
her seemingly easy acceptance in San Jose of the crotchety
Sister Aurelie as head of the infirmary charge, since relieving
her of responsibility was easier said than done. With gracious
tact, the new assistant made use of her own superior knowledge, an accomplishment that won Sister Mary Bernardine's
great admiration. House Doctor George W. Seifert stamped her
work with high approval, for this once squeamish girl attended
him, to his complete satisfaction, when he performed serious
surgery in the convent infirmary.[20]

But it was Sister St. Pierre's sympathy that endeared her to
Sister Mary Bernardine. For at a time when convent infirm-
arians were overly guarded against "self-occupation," here was
one to whom the pain of another was real. She herself came to
know both pain and illness and Sister Mary Bernardine transferred her to the care of the gardens for sun and air, and because at the moment the gardens needed her. Other sisters
took over the general work of the infirmary, appealing to her
experience when necessary. Thus Sister St. Pierre could devote
her time to planning the grounds, directing the gardeners and

managing the large new greenhouse which furnished the altars with ferns, carnations, lilies, chrysanthemums and gypsophila.

Liturgical disapproval of flowers on altars was as yet unheard of and natural decor became a fine art in the hands of little Sister Catherine Josepha O'Brien, who with a deft turn of her wrist could crown a tall gold vase with long-stemmed beauty, and so perfectly that an added touch would have spoiled the picture. Sister Catherine loved to tell with gleeful satisfaction how Sister Mary Bernardine had received her. Frail little Josephine O'Brien, looking more like 15 than 20, rang the bell at Mission Dolores and announced to the portress that she had come to apply for acceptance in the novitiate of Notre Dame. Said the amused Sister Elizabeth Sinnot, "You are only a child. You had better finish school and then think about it." But Josephine held her ground and, as it turned out, Sister Mary Bernardine had no objection to either small stature nor youthful face. She questioned the aspirant for a few minutes and then observed to Sister Elizabeth, "Today is my birthday and this is my little birthday present."[21]

When the older and less pliant Sister Mary Bernard Stewart entered upon her belated vocation, she brought with her, besides experience in the business world, a practical hobby. As daughter of a printing family, she had spent many a fascinating hour assisting her father and uncle.[22] She had not expected to miss fonts, and handbills, and engraved cards so much, and decided that her yearning must be one of the attachments against which spiritual writers did verbal battle. But not so Sister Mary Bernardine. She had a large room below the chapel converted into a press room. In the center stood the press bearing the mark of Weiler's Liberty Machine Works and operated by a huge side-wheel and pedal until, years later in Belmont, it was fitted with a General Electric motor. As type families were added, there was soon little that the expert Sister Mary Bernard could not produce. Handsome announcements and prayer cards, dignified billheads and report cards, almost everything, in fact, came from Notre Dame Press. Only *Notre Dame Quarterly* and the annual prospectus remained in the hands of San Jose's printing firm of Popp & Hogan. And quiet Sister Mary Bernard followed another interest with the full blessing of Sister Mary Bernardine. She kept a list of poor missions that could not afford printing charges and supplied their needs on holidays and weekends. Said Sister Anthony, S.H., "That press played no little part in the missionary apostolate." It also played a strong part in the founding of Notre Dame in Belmont. Through the first decades there was always one dedicated printer in charge of the printing room in the rear end of the former Ralston Barn.

At times Sister Mary Bernardine's fondness for satisfying the inner needs carried her into humorous situations. When she heard Sister Theresa, S.H., Lang speak with enthusiasm of her native San Francisco, she made her her companion on her next errand to "the city" and business accomplished, treated her to a ride on a cable car. For better view, they sat outside, that is until a woman boarding the car tapped Sister Mary Bernardine on the shoulder and whispered, "The Archbishop doesn't approve of Sisters sitting outside." Looking up, the two Sisters saw the dignified prelate standing on a corner and apparently taking no note of their little holiday. Most Sisters of that day would have been mortified to have been seen, by an Archbishop at that, on the swaying end of that car facing the passing throng. Probably few Superiors would have related the incident. But for all her regal bearing, Sister Mary Bernardine loved to tell a good story on herself and to hear the Sisters laugh at her expense. Such laughter cut away distance that so often lay between superiors of lesser stature and their communities. She wanted her position to create no barriers in any case. On her last round of visits in the province, she asked to see a 15-year-old Alameda girl who had just won first place in a contest involving all the schools in the East Bay counties. Expecting to hear a dignified congratulation, the winner was almost speechless at the warmth of Sister Mary Bernardine's embrace.[23]

*F*our foundations were made possible by substantial donations during the years when Sister Mary Bernardine was
in San Jose. The first of these, Notre Dame Institute, became a
reality shortly after her arrival in 1892, through the generosity
of Mr. and Mrs. Myles Poore O'Connor, long-time friends of
Sister Superior Julia McGroarty, who was visiting from Cincinnati to install Sister Mary Bernardine.

East and west, the name of O'Connor was known for works
of charity. In the national capital their donations had helped to
make possible the Catholic University of America, which
opened in 1889. That same year their benevolence brought the
O'Connor Sanitarium to completion in San Jose, at a cost of
nearly half a million dollars.[1]

As Notre Dame's first donors of a sizeable amount, the
O'Connors deserve special mention. At the age of 14, Irish-
born Myles arrived in New York with his parents and accompanied them later to St. Louis, where in 1842 he began to study
law in the office of Major U. Wright. Four years later he graduated with honors from the law school at the Jesuit college in
that city. To improve his opportunities as a lawyer, he came
to the West Coast in 1849, became interested in mining, and
from then on led the life of a successful miner, lawyer and poli-
tician. Her served terms in both houses of the California Legislature and as justice of the peace, all the time building his
fortune to its highest peak in the quartz gold wealth of the
Idaho Mine in Grass Valley. There he married Amanda Butler
Young, a widow who shared his belief that the wealthy must
help the poor. They were not of the same religion, but behaved in present-day ecumenical fashion, she attending mass
with him and he going with her to sing in the Methodist
church. In time Amanda became an active, intense Catholic,

for she was intense about everything, including her desire to
make in San Jose a home spacious enough to include a large
art collection.

The O'Connors had adopted Annette Butler, the daughter
of Amanda's brother, Jonathan of Grass Valley. She came to
San Jose at the age of 18 when she realized the advantages of
a musical education at Notre Dame and of foreign travel with
her aunt and uncle. Ambitious and determined, Annette uti-
lized every opportunity to the full. At Notre Dame, she relates,
she found many scholastic courses far in advance of the curriculum of the Grass Valley high school from which she had
graduated. Finally with the college diploma and a foundation
for musical studies in Europe, she was ready for a continental
sojourn, with a piano provided for her on long stops to keep
her in practice.[2]

Judge and Mrs. O'Connor decided to offer their mansion at
Second and Reed streets in San Jose as a home for orphans and
half-orphans if the Sisters of Notre Dame would take over the
work. This was to be known as the Notre Dame Institute, and
before departing on their journey to Europe, Mrs. O'Connor
completed plans for it, leaving practical affairs to her old
friend, Sister Julia, to her new admiration, Sister Mary Bernardine, and to the first appointed head of the venture, Sister
Maria Teresa Vallejo. Perhaps her patient husband was now
weary of institutions; at any rate, he confided to Annette at
this time that he preferred helping people directly. But as his
wife preferred charity to be both organized and recognized, he
agreed to relinquish their fine home in the interests of needy
children and to take up residence in a suite at the O'Connor
Sanitarium.

To house some fifty girls the mansion at Second and Reed
streets would need some enlargement. Besides, an endowment
would be necessary, and the donors decided generously on
$100,000 in bonds. Then with what seems like a look into the
future, Judge O'Connor insisted on a clause in the deed of gift.
If care of orphans should cease to be the greatest need, the
Sisters of Notre Dame might transfer both home and endow-

ment to the necessity of the hour. The donors left the Sisters free in the matter of alterations, that is with the exception of the disposal of their now numerous oils, statues, and other works of art. And that seemed an easy task. Surely the civic and cultural leaders of San Jose, apparently so eager to see their city an art and music center, would accept the collection gratefully and erect a fitting museum for its display.

Though the city officials accepted with gratitude, Mrs. O'Connor had little patience with civic delays. She was annoyed on hearing a report that building of the proposed gallery was being postponed and that funds were being otherwise allocated; her annoyance turned to ire when she heard another rumor that certain critics considered her oils less than first rate pieces. That was enough.[3] She knew the paintings were reproductions, but to what pains had she gone to have expert advice on their selection! Straightway, the O'Connors withdrew their offer and asked their friend, Sister Julia, to accept their collection for Trinity College in Washington. Mrs. O'Connor could never quite forgive what she considered the ingratitude of San Jose. An art center would have rounded out the possible levels of O'Connor philanthropy there.

Her chagrin was assuaged, however, by her self-appointed role as fairy godmother to the forty or more girls at the Institute. Her frequent unannounced visits were a part of Sister Maria Teresa's order of the day. The house was on tiptoe as she flitted about with no need of guide, ending her tour with a crisp greeting to the cook and a demand to taste the food in preparation.

Sister Mary Bernardine treated her with lovely tact which included a round of social affairs at which Mrs. O'Connor, and sometimes the Judge, would preside. But the Institute was plainly Sister Mary Bernardine's darling enterprise. The Sisters and her friends as well had to see the wonder for themselves. On such occasions the "children" had to be assembled, so it was a wonder that Sister Maria Teresa could ever establish the sort of routine that the military side of her character demanded. But it was comforting that every visit should be followed by something that Sister Mary Bernardine had found wanting, whether kitchen supplies, blankets or bedspreads — just as comforting as the sight on the first page of the account book of Mrs. O'Connor's personal donation to meet house expenses until receipt of the first payment of endowment interest.[4]

To Mrs. O'Connor it was a matter of great pride that most entrants to the Institute improved in all respects. An old photograph presents a very healthy and happy group gathered around Sister Maria Teresa. Adding to the good care and smooth running of the house were a round of outings and other bits of excitement planned by Sister Mary Bernardine. Her friends, in fact, soon grew accustomed to her requests for chaperoned trips and picnics for the Institute children; with some good people, these excursions became a habit. Often Father William Melchers, S.J., pastor of nearby St. Mary's Church, furnished the transportation. Older girls took turns writing notes of thanks to "generous gentlemen" and "kind ladies," and Father Melchers was no doubt the most frequent recipient of such gratitude.[5]

Sister Mary Bernardine stationed ten or more Sisters at the Institute, including the four or five who taught at St. Mary's. In the house these Sisters supervised study hours, a fact which accounted for the scholastic standing of Institute girls soon being recognized in San Jose. As they finished the grades, they were given special business training, and a few advanced classes at the Institute. No one would have thought of their going to the Day Academy, which had its exclusiveness to maintain, but when Notre Dame High School opened in 1906 some Institute girls were enrolled there.[6] In all, the Institute for a time bore the marks of a well-kept nineteenth century orphanage. The children were orphans by the Will of Heaven, a fact that had to be impressed on their minds. Being drawn up for inspection by Mrs. O'Connor was outward sign of orphan status.

The clearest mark of that status is the "Constitution" drafted by Sister Julia for the Institute some months before her death in 1901. With the retired Sister Maria Teresa in her last illness, Sister Julia pondered "the uncertainty of life," and decided that while the three original witnesses to the O'Connor wishes still lived, rules for the future guidance of the Institute should be set in writing. This little document, legal in form, sets up "a board, the president of which will be the Superior of the college," and by which any change in management must be approved. The striking note is that the orphans must realize that they are such, and not mistake their status for "boarders." Thus they must work for what they receive, must earn the gift made in their behalf, since the O'Connors and the Sisters owe them nothing. Certainly here is no welfare state. Yet the manner of earning is itself mild and generous. A small sum, drawn from the endowment, is to be set aside for every child, the amount to be earned by "Good Notes," in other words ladylike behavior, homework well done, and household charge kept shining clean. The sum set aside for each girl was a small start in life; one could spend a little now and then and still have a neat sum at 18.

Before the "constitution" went into effect, Sister Julia and Sister Maria Teresa had both died. Perhaps the best fortune to befall the Institute girls, who later were no longer referred to as orphans, was the appointment of Sister Clare Callan, who established the atmosphere of a family home that marked the Institute's next 15 years. Sister implanted a feeling of importance and worth in even the youngest. Visitors in her office had to be patient with her habit of leaving the door slightly ajar so that the toddlers of the house would not feel excluded. Important business could wait while she greeted a tot with feigned surprise and real pleasure. Then followed the solemn introduction to the adult guest, and the quick inspection of little hands and shoes, prelude always to the award of sugar almond or chocolate from the unfailing supply in her desk drawer.

When she begged, and she did very often, it was rarely for funds, and never for "poor orphans." What she wanted most was interest of good people in her girls, persons who would supply some of the attention that is the lot of girls in good families, who would find pleasure in taking them on family outings. She talked to Mrs. O'Connor about the need of isolating cases of virulent diseases. The result was an endowed bed in the Sanitarium, a measure that prevented the spread of smallpox and other troublesome epidemics at the Institute. As might be expected, Sister Clare's fine leadership inspired a number of religious vocations among her girls. These became, like her, cheerful nuns and excellent teachers, almost every one of them possessed of a well-trained voice and love of singing.[7]

In 1915, when Sister Clare stooped to light a water heater, the gas exploded, bringing instant death to her and widespread grief in the community and city, especially to Mrs. O'Connor, who was still depressed by the loss of her husband in 1909. Following the death of Sister Clare the Institute began to decline, but Mrs. O'Connor was spared the knowledge that the endowment bonds were no longer yielding running expenses.

Notre Dame Altar Society, Sister Mary Bernardine's other beloved project, was also inaugurated in 1893 with the help of Mrs. O'Connor, who fitted up special rooms for its work in the O'Connor mansion. The roster of the society shows the names of almost all the prominent Catholic women in the area, a matter of high satisfaction to Mrs. O'Connor.[8] Photographs show these ladies, many of them former College of Notre Dame students, industriously operating sewing machines or embroidering vestments, with the O'Connor paintings looking down on them. For all their serious mien in the photos, the ladies formed a happy group under the direction of the merry-hearted little Guatemalan, Sister Eulalia of the Cross, who believed that needlework is improved by well-told stories, "chokes," as she called them. When new members remarked her jolly spirit, the others awaited her quick explanation: "Well, my mother is Irish." At the invariable look of surprise, she would continue, "She is Sister Mary Bernardine."

A foundation was begun in 1895 at Redwood City, nearly halfway from San Jose to San Francisco. It maintained a rather feeble existence until the 1906 earthquake, after which it was closed. It later reopened on a more secure footing.[9] The year 1898 brought a second generous foundress to Sister Mary Bernardine, making possible a new academy and parish school combination on the plan of Notre Dame in Alameda.

Josephine Moreland, a serious faced, studious senior student, died at the college after a short illness March 7, 1898. Her mother found some consolation in the sight of her teachers and friends praying beside her casket through the long hours preceding her Requiem, yet it seemed that nothing could heal her wound, not even the words of her friend, Sister Anna Raphael. Alone and disconsolate, Mrs. Moreland returned home and tried to find comfort in converting her daughter's room into a little shrine with the girl's favorite madonna surrounded by specimens of her perfect schoolwork and her bound volume of original verse. But candles and fresh flowers were not enough for one who had herself often reflected on the Will of God. Besides, Mrs. Moreland had sometimes considered the need for Sisters in Watsonville. Usually the thought had followed the expression of regret by parents unable financially, as she was, to send their daughters to the college in San Jose. An idea began to evolve in her mind and with it came a degree of peace. One morning she boarded the train for San Jose and laid her plan before Sister Mary Bernardine. She was not a wealthy woman; in fact, to invest in a school for girls the modest fortune which she had set aside for her "Josie" demanded heroic trust in God. Her gift was a sacrifice which left her only a home and modest livelihood, but as she often said, it brought her many daughters in the place of Josephine.

Sister Mary Bernardine referred her friend to Father M. Marron, pastor in Watsonville, who in turn advised her to write to Bishop George Montgomery of the Monterey-Fresno Diocese. The Bishop thanked her, took up the matter with Father Marron, and reported in July to Sister Mary Bernardine that the school would have to be an academy as the parish could not support it. Two days later, Father Marron confirmed this opinion, and stated that Mrs. Moreland was willing to build the school at her own expense. She had in fact on June 27 set in writing her promise to donate $10,000. There was some indecision about the property, a large lot opposite St. Patrick's Church, on account of its being diocesan, but finally Bishop Montgomery accepted Mrs. Moreland's offer to pay $1,000, about a forth of its value. All the terms are reviewed in his lengthy letter to the donor, including the obligation of teaching small boys. As the donor wished, the property was to be held in the name of the Sisters.[10]

Thus the Moreland Academy that opened its doors in 1899 was another regrettable instance of boarding school, convent, and classrooms all under one roof, and as it was clear that few affluent boarders could be expected, there would have to be special stress on the music department as a source of income. Actually, the tall, white house opposite St. Patrick's Church on North Main Street, an impressive sight to northbound travelers on the Santa Cruz Highway, gave no hint of the often harassed bookkeeper within, one cause of financial worry being Mrs. Moreland's ruling that day pupils would never be asked to pay more than a dollar a month. This restriction was observed for over four decades, until the parents themselves decided it was unfair to the Sisters.

Perhaps on the whole Mrs. Moreland's wishes were adhered to more on account of her admirers among the Sisters than of her own tenacity. Her visits were rare. She viewed each new teacher with calm appraisal, smiled graciously at all the well-prepared compliments which deafness prevented her hearing, visited the chapel and was gone, leaving all in wonder at her ability to rise from her knees without clinging to the bench. She was at her best on "Moreland Day," March 7, when the girls carried flowers to Josie's grave before going to the beach for a picnic. For some of the "foundation Sisters" her name and Josie's were sacred, and their oval-framed, unsmiling portraits might not be moved from their prominence just within the front entrance.

Sister Mary Bernardine herself set the example of high respect for those who provided homes for the work of the Sisters of Notre Dame. Until their last days, Mrs. O'Connor and

Mrs. Moreland were honored guests at college commence-
ments and other important functions. Little Mrs. O'Connor,
arriving in a wheel chair from her suite in the hospital in the
care of a Bon Secours Sister, and being gently fanned after so
much exertion by a Notre Dame infirmarian, seemed something
of an object of pity to straight-backed Mrs. Moreland. With a
nod of recognition that set her stiff front curls bobbing, she
would remark in a voice that grew louder with increasing deafness, "She seems to be failing." For to Mrs. Moreland, failure
of any kind connoted weakness; her curt remark when she
heard of a dropout from Moreland Academy was usually, "Non
compos mentis."

But she was also capable of admiration. Next to Sister
Anna Raphael and Sister Mary Bernardine, she esteemed Moreland's first Superior, Sister Mary Veronica Dolan, and Moreland's first head teacher, the capable and witty Sister Mary
Loyola Wynne. She paid little attention to young Sisters, who
were usually novices and not likely to remain at Moreland.
She esteemed those who remained for years, persuaded that
Sister Mary Bernardine, and after her, Sister Mary Veronica,
would allow only the best to remain in her academy. But then,
the "foundation" Sisters held firmly to the same idea, and no
doubt imparted it to their patroness.

Moreland Academy was little more than established when
the house in Alameda suddenly required Sister Mary Bernardine's full attention. There the need of a new unit was pointed
up by an early morning fire on April 11, 1902.[11] When Sister
Mary Bernardine reached Alameda, she found the Sisters setting up sleeping quarters in the parish hall placed at their
disposal by the pastor, Rev. P. A. Foley. But that, said Sister
Mary of St. George Harney, would be the extent of local assistance; unless a new unit could be started at once, it would be
impossible to continue the boarding school. Without hesitation,
Sister Mary Bernardine sent for contractor W. J. Smith, whose
firm and family were to become closely associated with Notre
Dame, and to cover both repair and new project, arranged for
a long-term loan from the central house.

Sister Mary Bernardine's determination to prevent foundations from failing is clear again in her assistance to the house
in Redwood City after the disaster of 1906. It seems little wonder that she should come to consider the academy system the
only certain means of maintaining them in existence. The boarding school and the music department, and a kind benefactor to
make the initial move, formed the correct combination. Parish
assistance could not as yet be counted on.

Suddenly a request from Santa Barbara seemed to offer a
departure from the pattern. In the summer of 1906, Father
P. J. Stockman, pastor of Our Lady of Sorrows Church, himself a Belgian and an admirer of the Sisters of Notre Dame in
his homeland, offered both convent and livelihood if Sister
Mary Bernardine could spare Sisters for a grade school in Our
Lady of Sorrows Parish.[12] It seemed a special blessing thus to
be invited into the diocese of Bishop Thomas J. Conaty, a
friend of the Sisters of Notre Dame and one dedicated to education. Thus Sister Mary Bernardine and Sister Louise des
Séraphines were happy to accompany the new community,
headed by Sister Paul, S.H., Kanady, to Santa Barbara.

Father Stockman met the group at the station with an
express wagon provided for themselves as well as for their
baggage. For lack of better seat, Sister Lucidie Kissane, youngest of the Sisters, had to sit at the rear end, feet hanging down,
not daring to enjoy the lovely scenery for fear of falling off.
The little brick convent which their new pastor had prepared
for them on Figueroa near State Street was Father Stockman's
idea of a house for Sisters, a little like a fort, with small windows of corrugated glass to exclude all worldly sights. A funeral
parlor next door added to the dismal impression, though as
Sister Paul observed, its solemnity failed to dim the jollity of
nighttime gatherings of the Order of Elks in their meetings on
the floor above it. Added to these inconveniences, the convent's
flat roof gathered winter rains which seeped down the walls,
as there were no drains. Fortunately the Sisters found a new
home in the renovated Santa Barbara Clubhouse across the
street.

As it became clear that parish responsibility was not to be counted on, Sister Mary Bernardine suggested a self-sustaining community in Santa Barbara. Bishop Conaty agreed gladly enough and pointed out a location for an academy on Santa Barbara Street in the Mission District. There, though Sister Mary Bernardine acquired the property, the matter stood for a time, partly for lack of building funds and partly because with the advent of Reverend Octavius Villa, S.J., as pastor, the needs of both Sisters and school began to take on parish importance, so that subsistence was possible with occasional help from the province and friends. Finally, in 1916, an aggressive local superior, Sister Juliana, B.S., Keegan, a firm believer in the boarding school as a means of livelihood, began to talk earnestly about erecting an academy on the Mission property. As a result, she soon found herself held in check on the one hand by Sister Mary Bernardine's successor, Sister Mary Veronica, and caught up on the other by a bit of excitement that rocked quiet Santa Barbara and gave rise to some tongue clucking in the local community and in San Jose as well.

Always sociable, Sister Juliana made the acquaintance at a school entertainment of the elderly David D. Walker, a gentleman accustomed to befriending charitable causes. She presented her community and their work as such to this "feeble old man," and soon received from him a token check and promise of further benefactions. What she did not know was that out of a penniless boyhood, Mr. Walker had built up a great and honest fortune in St. Louis, and that though he was alert at 77, his sons in Santa Barbara were attempting to obtain control of his fortune because of his supposed senility. In San Jose the case took on a humorous turn as Sister Juliana's faithfully mailed news clippings were read at community hour with her characteristic additions. Mr. Walker won his battle; his sons had to wait for the bulk of his fortune, and the Sisters were assured of a house on their long vacant holding.[13] But now Sister Mary Veronica limited the cost of that house to $10,000, partly because of the family litigation, and partly because she saw that the day of the strong academy was passing from the parish scene. Thus the new house could accommodate only a few resident pupils and these must attend the parish school.

The year 1906 brought a wave of requests for Sisters to staff parish schools. First came Father Edward P. Griffith's appeal from Sacred Heart Parish in Salinas. But Sister Mary Bernardine's visit to Salinas warned her against taking on too much too quickly. In constructing a very adequate school building, Father Griffith had exhausted parish funds and was in the process of vacating his tiny four-room residence for the Sisters' use. Looking at those little rooms, Sister Mary Bernardine stated briefly the least possible floor space for a convent, including that *sine qua non* of communities, a chapel room. Then seeing the poor pastor quite helpless, she offered a plan. Across the street stood two identical houses that answered to no architectural form. Said Sister Mary Bernardine, set the two houses wall to wall, designate the result as a "temporary convent," and hope for the best.

United, the two houses presented even a less pleasing effect than they had singly. On a visit to Salinas, Bishop Conaty dubbed it "the chicken coop," a title which Sister Flora Davie, the first Superior in Salinas, applied in her jolly fashion. It needed only a three-by-six rug, said Sister, to cover the sacristy floor, and to open the vestment press one had first to set the table and chair outside. Arriving before this odd little house was at all habitable, the Sisters slept for some nights on a classroom floor. As they had anticipated, a few fairy godmothers appeared, chief of whom was Sister Mary Veronica from Watsonville. From the start, Sister Flora said, there was always enough to eat in the "chicken-coop." What was most needed, she declared after the first rains, was a good supply of pans to set about under known leaks, with a reserve for the surprises that waited only for a change of the wind.

This humorous attitude gave way to discouragement after the death of Father Griffith. His successor, Father P. J. Browne, without thought of the Sisters' plight, declared the important thing was to build a new parish church. But help was at hand in the person of Mrs. Anita Hartnell Zabala, daughter of pioneer W. E. P. Hartnell and María Teresa de la Guerra, and wife of Don Pedro Zabala.[14] After a visit during a storm, she decided the community needed a proper house and built for them a comfortable convent on the site of the "chicken coop."

The addition of a few piano rooms in Mrs. Zabala's plan indicated that for some years at least the community in Salinas was expected to help pay its bills as well as to teach parish children. Sacred Heart in 1913 was not outstanding as a self-contained parish. Yet by reason of much patience, the generosity of a good alumna and a few music lessons, it was at least a foundation free from the duplication of duties that marked the boarding academies. The Sisters' strength could be conserved for parish work.

Aside from the parish apostolate, the health of the Sisters had always been of high importance to Sister Mary Bernardine. With this in mind she began a search for a country house in the hills near San Jose and soon found the Postelwaite home for sale in the foothill hamlet of Saratoga. Facing the wide sweep of the Santa Clara Valley, the house looked across a sloping lawn to a lovely sunken garden with "Trinity Oak," said to be the largest live oak in the state, standing guard beyond it. Farther out, the parklike beauty of Madronia Cemetery merged into stretches of orchard lands, a sight to remember in those smogless times, especially when spring turned the miles to soft pearly white in the sun.

To make sure of comfort and readiness for vacationers and those recuperating after illness, Sister Mary Bernardine stationed a small community in residence, the first group headed by Sister Paul, S.H., who was thus for the second time a foundation Superior. Her successor, the practical Sister Louis de Gonzague Sacriste, became a successful manager of prune orchard, vineyard and farm stock. She was an ideal hostess who assumed that guests arrived with plans made, and that hills were more than a symbol of freedom. When classes came from Santa Clara Street in quest of wild flowers, she welcomed them warmly, and added to her usual warning about poison oak, the dangers caused by winter rains along the route to the Cascades

and the upper reaches of Bohlman Road, as it used to wind
between a steep embankment covered with maidenhair, and
the drop down to the ravine, with danger hidden by chaparral
and low manzanitas. One might easily enough lose footing
reaching for brodiaea or mission bell, yet none would miss the
trek up to the end of that road and the former home of the
wife of the hero of Harper's Ferry, Mrs. John Brown, who lay
buried in Madronia Cemetery. It was a lonely road then before
homes began to appear on commanding viewpoints to share the
prospects of Notre Dame Villa and Senator Phelan's *Montalvo*.

In Sister Mary Bernardine's declining years this accomplishment in the Saratoga Hills was her great joy. A few days
at the villa was her prescription for tired look or frayed nerves.
She was herself the best of vacationers. Accompanied usually
by Sister Anna Raphael, she knew at last the Saratoga foothills
as well as she had once known the fields of Ireland. She loved
best the springtime sea of blossoms in orchards that had replaced the chaparral and mustard the pioneers had known.
Such a miracle the sight of the valley seemed to her that she
insisted on visitors sharing the view from the height above the
villa. One of these was Mère Marie Aloyse Van Laere, the first
Mother General of Notre Dame to visit California. A quiet
person, not given to rhapsody, she remarked the fitness of that
hilltop for a Christus of heroic size. Her gift of a beautiful
bronze stands on that spot, arms outstretched as in blessing
and plainly visible as one approaches on the Saratoga road.

Certainly one subject of conversation between the Mother
General and Sister Mary Bernardine during that 1910 visit
must have been the foundations in California during the preceding two decades, as well as guiding principles for further
extension. There was the question of accepting boys in the
upper grades, and on this point Sister Mary Bernardine must
have made clear the strong feeling of parents, as well as pastors, and in fact, many Sisters of Notre Dame, about such parishes as St. Joseph's in Alameda, where no provision had been
made as yet for boys above the lower grades. Neither could
envision the contemporary parish system with small convents

and salaried Sisters. Even the nearest approach to this depended on income from music lessons given by the Sisters and
gifts from the more generous or more affluent local friends.

St. Mary's in San Jose represented a degree of parental
responsibility, but the actual security of that school was, of
course, the Notre Dame Institute. Nor did that forerunner of
Sacred Heart School, the makeshift little building in which
three Sisters of Notre Dame began to teach Italian children in
1906, bear much resemblance to its successor. For years it was
Notre Dame's continued act of charity, and as the Sisters used
to say, "really Mother Julia's work."[15]

Long afterwards, Archbishop Edward J. Hanna remarked
that in California the Sisters of Notre Dame had spoiled the
people by not making them responsible. But it is also true that
many Sisters of Notre Dame, and superiors as well, clung to the
academy as a source of revenue and also as assurance of independence. Still it seems clear that Sister Mary Bernardine was
moving with the time, willing to make any adaptation toward
the parish organization as soon as it presented itself.

$\mathcal{S}$ ister Mary Bernardine's true worth was most evident in difficulty, and California's disastrous earthquake and fire of April 18, 1906 proved the point. Ironically, she had then just arrived in Namur bringing photographs and glowing accounts of foundations on the Pacific, the purpose of her journey being to represent Notre Dame of California in Rome at the beatification ceremonies of Blessed Mother Julie Billiart in May. In the face of her enthusiasm it was difficult to keep her in ignorance of the catastrophe until word from Sister Anna Raphael should come through, a message that had to wait its turn among hundreds of others that were being routed by unaffected telegraph lines. When at last the cable arrived, Sister Mary Bernardine said simply, "The Sisters, the children, all safe. God is good. Buildings can be rebuilt." By this time, too, the report that San Francisco was under water had been corrected, and the scattered community of the Mission Dolores convent was known to be safe.

When Mère Marie Aloysie visited the houses in California, in 1910, she recalled in each of them Sister Mary Bernardine's calm words, adding, "It is true. The buildings have been rebuilt, and in so short a time." She told also of the letters that Sister Mary Bernardine had shared with her, letters which throw light on the calamity as it affected the Sisters, and in some instances, even stronger light on the characters of the writers. With a sense of history, Sister Mary Bernardine kept them all.

Among the less emotional and more factual of these reports from San Jose were those of Sister Anthony, S.H., and Sister Mary Euphrasia. Sister Anthony recalls in clear-cut sequence the moments of the quake itself. Since a tremor of some three years earlier, there had been a general distrust of the third floor of the new novitiate, a building which many considered too narrow for its height. The few others who shared this quiet and airy quarter had already departed for the chapel. Thus Sister Anthony found herself alone in a narrow corridor, its floor twisting beneath her feet, its walls bending visibly. She made her way to the stairs, but at the sight of the moving steps, decided to try the fire escape. Mounting this "rocking ladder," she heard now the falling of walls that accompanied the roar and rumble of the earth. Across the campus the huge tank was swaying, the water rising in waves. The poplars were bending low as though in contrary winds; even the pines were bowing earthward. At the second floor level, she sought safety in the doorway, certain that another shock would bring down the brick wall. Instead great areas of plaster parted from the walls as she reached a window, from which she jumped down to the roof and made her way to the professed house. The novices had all reached safety, but in the Sisters' dormitory the elderly ones, in various stages of dress as well as shock, were praying aloud as they assisted the very feeble, with Sister St. Pierre directing matters in her able fashion.

On the ground level, Sister Anthony rushed to the long front corridor that led to the boarders' dormitories, but found all entrances locked until she reached the tower door at the far east end. Here with two other Sisters she forced back the beams that had fallen behind the door. Climbing in they saw heaps of fallen bricks and plaster. It seemed only a question of how many were lying killed or injured on the floors above. Then they saw the children, large and small, descending in night attire and picking their way between piles of rubble, the Sisters in charge bringing up the rear. Sister Anthony led them out on the lawn well away from the building, and then accompanied the other Sisters back upstairs to secure clothing that, in some alcoves, was pinned under bricks and plaster. On the upper floor, where a few minutes before the smaller children had lain asleep, heaps of bricks and mortar lay on the beds. A moment of delay in ringing the handbell would have cost many lives. Laden with blankets and clothing, the Sisters returned to the children and hurried them off to the boys' school, the only one-floor structure on the campus. En route, they heard the cry that San Jose was on fire.

Sister Anthony took on the duty of warning all comers away from the dormitory units, feeling certain that further shocks would level the walls. Any further disaster seemed possible as the air grew hot and smoke and cinders from nearby burning buildings were blown in on the lawn. The city's water supply was fortunately unimpaired and fires were under control in a few hours, but as friends stopped at the lodge, Sister learned the meaning of the crashes that had punctuated her flight down the fire escape, and as she sifted truth from exaggeration, she realized the magnitude of the destruction. But she realized, too, the deep concern of many for the welfare of all at Notre Dame. There were those who came running at the rumor that none had escaped. State Senator Charles Shortridge and Dr. George W. Seifert arrived, along with Father Filippo Mignacco, S.J., (with stole and oils to anoint the dying); they were relieved to find that not one person had been injured. Other doctors hurried to the lodge, certain of fatalities because of the brick construction. Professor Daniel R. Wood of San Jose Normal School, came on the run, offered his services, and left exclaiming, "It is miraculous." Shocks followed through the day and news from San Francisco became ominous.

Outdoor cooking and dining were distracting novelties, but sensing a certain tension among the girls as they settled down on improvised beds in the boys' school, Sister Anthony sat up that night to reassure them. All the other Sisters found corners in the 1851 House, for brick structures, even those that had withstood the quake, were considered untrustworthy as sleeping quarters.

Both Sister Anthony and Sister Mary Euphrasia remark the calmness of the girls, many of whom had heard nothing from ther families for days. The latter Sister found this behavior a wonder since she considered the young westerner "very excitable and nervous." To her it was beyond belief that rollicking Hawaiian Frieda Gay and spoiled Central Americans should take broom and dustpan and clear up the sanctuary, so that Father John Collins, S.J., might celebrate Mass that morning at nine o'clock. Other Sisters shared her astonishment at unwonted usefulness as the boarders peeled potatoes and made up temporary beds. But Sister Anthony was more impressed by their prayerfulness. As group replaced group before the shrine of Our Lady of Sorrows, they were an impressive spectacle to passers-by who detoured along Santa Teresa because of obstructions on Santa Clara Street.

Because stretches of the street wall had collapsed, classes started outdoors on Friday with a passing audience, but that mattered little. What distressed all was the intense heat from burning San Francisco which made concentration impossible as noon approached. Fortunately examiners soon declared the safety of some of the buildings, notably those constructed in the era following the great quake of 1868; earlier units and the more recent had suffered most. Thus classes soon found safe spots indoors, Sister Anthony finishing off the *Aeneid* and the Victorian poets in the dining hall. All were comfortable, she assured her Superior, whom she enjoined not to worry.

This letter presents Sister Anthony, slightly over a decade professed, a completely rounded character. Reading those easy-flowing, incisive words written in that legible and forceful backhand, one wishes that she had later avoided a certain ornate affectation in both. At any rate, Sister Anna Raphael, busy with "odd jobs" as head of the house and of the disorganized province as well, depended on Sister Anthony to send a clear account of events to Sister Mary Bernardine, and appended a note asking her to preserve it as such.[1]

Sister Anna's own letter a few days later serves as a scientific supplement, based on recordings at Mount Hamilton Observatory. She explains the period needed for the settling of the fault, during which time tall candlesticks could not be trusted on the altar. She treats in detail the points of greatest interest to Sister Mary Bernardine: the chapel and the Lourdes Shrine, the latter in utter ruin, and the lovely facade of the Conservatory opposite marred by falling chimneys. But by way of contrast, the roses in this area were at the height of their spring blooming, as though nothing had happened. This is a typical Sister Anna touch as is also her stress on the excellent morale of pupils as well as of Sisters. One feels her emotional restraint in her account of destruction. She hastens to tell good news: gas pipes have escaped injury; students taken away by anxious parents have returned; workers have fitted up electric lights in the girls' temporary quarters; the musicians accompany hymns with their violins at the parish Mass of St. Joseph's, celebrated in the playground because the church has been destroyed. Above all, the Sisters are wonderful.

Feeling that both she and Sister Anthony, with pressure of responsibility, might have omitted important details, Sister Anna asked Sister Mary Euphrasia to send a supplementary account, a task to which this delicate, precise little Sister brought her considerable narrative ability. Through her we learn that the ordinarily slow-going Sister Mary Editha Feely rang the third-floor bell at the first roar of the quake, that she and tiny Sister Julitta Doisron directed the safe and speedy descent of the children and that Sister Mary Regis Foley was, of course, quite in character as general marshal from then on. Sister Mary Euphrasia pieced together the story of Vice-President Ramon Corral's appeal in the Oakland newspapers for any news of his daughters, Carmen and Hortense. Then hearing of their safety, he sent a representative to charter a train and bring home the Mexican pupils at once, but had to be satisfied with reservations a week later. She told of twisted rails on the Southern Pacific, and of senior student Avis Sherwood's worried father paying $500 for the three hours' use of an automobile to drive down from Oakland, and his bringing word of the fire in San Francisco. It was this isolation, she says, and hearing of rumors, that made teaching and study trying until connections were established toward the end of the week.

Western girls rose in her esteem during that dreadful week, as they carried organ pipes from the chapel and stored them. She had never before seen one of them wipe a cup, but here they were stacking up bricks. She was equally astonished when

East Bay students, Hazel Foster, Gladys Emmons, and Avis and Mary Sherwood, returned calmly after the trains were running again at the week's end. The older girls in general were eager to resume classes and willing to put up with inconvenience, she assured Sister Mary Bernardine, whose Sunday morning "Lines" advice so often stressed the Valiant Woman as model. Sister loved such a determined attitude. And it seemed to her an evidence of noble spirit that in less than a week troops were clearing ruined San Francisco; that reconstruction of a finer city was under way.

It may be as well though that one humorous bit of testimony of the strong spirit seems not to have been presented to her rather strict judgment. For as it turned out, the girls, big and little, soon found "The Barracks," as they called their temporary sleeping quarters, something of a lark. As dormitories require rules, the more original drew up an eleven-point code of such injunctions as, "The candle is the only inmate allowed to go out at night." Acquiring a copy of this "Rules for the Barracks" from his daughters, Mr. Sherwood offered it to the *Oakland Tribune* much to the consternation of the over-proper mistress, Sister Mary Basil Gautier, whose chagrin, no doubt, added to the girls' fun.[2]

It would seem that the upheaval and general difficulty of the moment accentuated Sister Mary Basil's nervous tendencies. As others grew calmer, she became more fearful. A more terrible disaster seemed imminent; the location of the college was very dangerous; the boarders should all be sent to their homes. In dramatic phrases she described the unnatural quiet of the girls and their visible fears; when their parents took them home temporarily, she announced that they had fled. She questioned Sister Anna's wisdom in keeping the group together, allowing only for a slightly earlier closing in view of repairs when more workers would be available later on. But this is the one dissonant note in the praise of Sister Anna's leadership that marks the Sisters' reports to Sister Mary Bernardine.[3]

Perhaps little Sister Mary Annunciata McDermott paid the finest tribute. Uncluttered by harsh detail, her letter presents two brief observations which must have delighted Sister Mary Bernardine. Because of the disaster she finds herself caught up in a new chapter of community experience. Jolted out of routine, in which the best tend to drift off into the importance of their particular endeavors, the Sisters, and she might have added the students, have discovered their mutual dependence, and so risen to heights of charity.

Sister Anna found her resources taxed as news filtered in from the other houses. Through three days, vague and contradictory reports followed the first word of San Francisco's disaster. Then from Alameda came Sister Mary of St. George's play by play account. Like others in the East Bay, Sister had considered the big quake itself the end of the story, and settled herself that very morning to write a dramatic letter about it to Sister Mary Bernardine. The two high academy buildings, she said, waved like willows in the wind, but fortunately beyond fallen chimneys and broken plaster statues, there was no very serious destruction. Leaving the others to clear up the debris, she set out at once to comfort a very nervous Sister hospitalized some three blocks away. Warned by recurring slight shocks, and piles of fallen chimney bricks on the way, she kept to the middle of the street, thanking Heaven that no worse damage had been done. Returning to the academy, she found restored order. She was about to end her letter on that tranquil note, when suddenly from across the Bay came the sound of distant explosions, the first of the dynamiting by which fire fighters in San Francisco hoped to contain the flames. Joining the Sisters on an upper porch, Sister saw fire and black clouds mounting above the light fog that lay over the water. The letter forgotten for the time, she set about sending help to the community at Mission Dolores.

While she and her Sisters were discussing friends to whom they might appeal, Mr. Herman Scholten called at the Alameda academy with a plan that at least held some promise. As entry to San Francisco was forbidden, this good father of three academy girls, as well as of Notre Dame Sister Louise Marie of Watsonville and two Franciscan Sisters at St. Joseph's Hospital, had found a launch owner willing to convey him to a landing point on the Bay shore below the city proper. He was willing to pay the exorbitant sum demanded in order to reach his daughters and he would be happy to bear a message to the Sisters of Notre Dame at Mission Dolores. Sister Mary of St. George asked him to invite those Sisters to Alameda and at once began plans for their arrival.

The earthquake was on Wednesday; early Thursday morning the launch brought Mr. Scholten to his landing place, but only after a trek of hours, partly through ashes and cinders, did he reach the hospital, to find it crowded with sick and injured, and like everything else, under control of the militia. The Franciscan Sisters had at once given shelter to the three or four aged Sisters of Notre Dame, and now all the others were arriving in groups, asking to pass the night in the hospital gardens, some of them quite disturbed at the prospect of spending another night in the little neighboring park. Sister Mary Aloyse especially, with her habitual distrust of adolescent boys, felt certain that a "bad element" was about, a conviction which she shared with police officers and guardsmen. Through Wednesday as the Sisters sat on the curb opposite their house, forbidden to enter it and with no plan in view, Sister Mary Aloyse kept pointing out the stupidity of making no effort to save their furniture, and though she considered men in general helpless and illogical, she accosted passers-by, insisting that at least their 28 pianos should be saved. At last a patient policeman convinced her that it was impossible to move pianos. But she still maintained that the dynamiting was not being done scientifically, that it was spreading rather than containing the conflagration, and that destroying her convent was unnecessary. Finally a guard on duty at the hospital agreed with her; the work had indeed been bungling, but they had just brought in experts, and it was these who had ordered the demolition of her school. Sister was at last satisfied; experts as a rule were logical. Meanwhile her Superior, Sister Julia Theresa O'Connor, had met Mr. Scholten and accepted the invitation of the Alameda Sisters.

Martial law now made crossing the Bay impossible, but undaunted Sister Julia Theresa charged Mr. Scholten to have Sister Mary of St. George obtain a special permit from Governor George C. Pardee for her community of 42. She specified a large carryall, not realizing that few stablemen would want to risk vehicles or teams, which would likely be commandeered by the militia. But quiet Mr. Scholten was not one to back away from difficulty. When he returned to Alameda on Friday evening he had a plan to offer to Sister Mary of St. George. He would send his persuasive friend, Joseph Krieg, to obtain a permit from the governor who was then in Oakland. Meantime, Sister should appeal in person to a local liveryman whose three daughters attended her academy. Reluctantly this proprietor agreed to send a carriage, team, and driver, together with two wagons, if Sister could procure drivers for these. And of course he wished to see the governor's permit. Mentally enlisting Mr. Scholten and Joseph Krieg as drivers, Sister promised to have all in readiness at an early hour. All went well. The caravan reached San Francisco, took circuitous routes around burning areas, and finally reached the hospital and the waiting Sisters of Notre Dame.

In Alameda, Sister Mary of St. George spent that long Saturday mollifying the worried liveryman, who telephoned his fears to her at short intervals. . . . He was certain the soldiers would have taken his teams and he would never see them again. Adding to delay, Sister Julia Theresa insisted on the transfer by train from Oakland of six of her Sisters to the convent in Marysville, and of another six to Moreland Academy in Watsonville, houses which she believed not likely to have suffered earthquake damage. Arriving in Alameda, she discovered that this arrangement was unnecessary; hearing the rumor that Alameda was partly under water, the academy boarding pupils had feared to return after the Easter holiday, and their dormitories had been prepared for the entire Mission Dolores community. After midnight, the northbound Sisters reached the

Marysville house in a state of exhaustion, but as the night train to Watsonville was cancelled, the others accepted the hospitality of the Sisters of the Holy Names in Oakland. On the southbound train next morning, this group learned that Moreland Academy had also been stricken and decided to stop in San Jose, where they found "destruction equal to San Francisco, but without fire." At Sister Anna Raphael's direction, the six went on to Santa Clara.

In Alameda, Sister Mary of St. George presently found use for the extra twelve beds; in fact, she had to set up several more as the older Mission Dolores girls gathered there from all points, determined to finish out the school year in good standing. There were no idle hands at the academy during the following weeks. For as refugees flooded the East Bay, civic leaders turned to the Sisters for assistance. Suddenly Notre Dame Academy was a garment factory, with Sisters, mothers, and older girls giving their free time, and with Sister Mary of St. George directing all and enjoying the challenge. Hundreds came to the academy for food and clothing, local shops sending in daily contributions, and benevolent societies making the school a substation. For some reason, the very generous national aid was slow in reaching Alameda, but as Sister Mary of St. George remarked, the destitute were helped in that quiet city "without the delays of red tape." This woman of action, with her disapproval of "mediocre" responses to life, found channels for her zeal through those weeks following the great disaster.

In Marysville the earthquake seemed of passing moment until rumors from the south were confirmed by the Sisters from Mission Dolores. Then Sister Berchmans Joseph Murphy found contact of any sort with other communities, or with the families of her own Sisters impossible. Her telegrams were piled up with some ten thousand others in Sacramento. The six Sisters arriving at midnight on Saturday confirmed the day's report on Mission Dolores. They had not taken off their habits since Wednesday, and the exhausted six could never say enough about her goodness. That same day brought her letters from

Sister Anna Raphael in San Jose and Sister Mary Veronica in Watsonville.[4] At once she realized that the former, directing a boarding school and community in the midst of ruins, and acting head of the province as well, stood most in need of help. Illness in her own community at Marysville prevented her going to San Jose, but she arranged that Sister Anna might draw a sum at her disposal in a San Jose bank, and offered to send another amount from Marysville. Commenting on her "lovely, unselfish nature," Sister Anna forwarded this letter to Sister Mary Bernardine, adding that "this gentle soul" had been writing daily and managed dispatches for her when Sacramento lines were cleared.

Two other "gentle souls" came quietly to Sister Anna's assistance. The generally loved Superior of the house in Santa Clara, Sister Mary Joseph Hannan, received and cared for three of the refugee Sisters, all of them ill, whom Sister Anna had detained in San Jose on their way to Watsonville. The Santa Clara house had its own troubles; the chapel, a high, narrow, brick building, was closed, its east wall damaged and ready to crumble, so that the playground beneath it had to be roped off. The frame building that housed the children's dormitory was condemned. But the Sisters were proving ingenious, said Sister Mary Joseph, and actually difficulties in Santa Clara were comparatively light. Now if Sister Anna would agree to send two more refugees from the overtaxed house in Alameda, she would be happy to care for them. It was nothing that every chimney in her rambling house had come down with a crash. God was good. They had just removed a child from an infirmary bed the day before, and the quake had brought down a pile of bricks on that very spot. Gratitude for such protection took the instant form of charity. Sister Clare Callan at O'Connor Institute shared the same feeling as she assessed the minor damage in her house. Despite the thought of further quakes, she and Sister Mary de Sales Comerford made their way to the college among piles of debris on Santa Clara Street. Perhaps it was there that she learned of the destruction at the Myles P. O'Connor residence and of Mrs. O'Connor's great fears. At any rate, Sister Anna agreed that two Sisters should go at once and bring these benefactors to the Institute. The Sisters found them at last safe in a cottage at O'Connor Sanitarium, touched deeply by the Sisters' solicitude. What most impressed Sister Clare was the sight at the hospital of the patients, beds and all, in the grounds. Surgery even was performed outside, so great was the general fear of falling bricks. All San Joseans, she said, had taken to outdoor living. Returning to the Institute, she set about converting the porch and garden into an outdoor church for St. Mary's Parish, for though their church had not shared the destruction of St. Patrick's, there was still the regulation forbidding indoor gatherings.

Outdoor cooking was also in order at Moreland Academy in Watsonville where the first result of the earthquake was crashing of chimneys through inner walls and floors of that high frame structure. Sisters and boarders fled down stairways none too soon; at the foot of one staircase, some of the Sisters looked up to see bricks hurtling down after them. Sister Mary Veronica and first teacher Sister Mary Loyola decided that classes must continue, in safe places, mostly in the grounds. The real problem was sleeping quarters, it seemed; all feared to risk the upper floors even where they were undamaged.

Then suddenly fire erupted in the little chemistry laboratory. Finding the telephone disconnected, Sister Mary Loyola rushed to the street to call for help, and found that friends had summoned the fire department. None too soon. Fire had already spread from the corner to the large central tower. When it was finally under control, the beautiful white house was so badly gutted that all feared that it could not be reconstructed. Staunch Mrs. Moreland was grief-stricken; the academy represented her fortune. In a short time, however, Sister Mary Veronica wrote calmly that the fire had been a blessing; as a result, building defects revealed by the earthquake could be corrected. Besides, the insurance was fully paid and repairs were begun at once.

For the time, the former mayor of Watsonville, R. P. Quinn, arriving early that morning with a supply of coffee, bread and

butter, explained that he had obtained the shaky old Chalmers'
residence nearby as a temporary dwelling for Sisters and resident students. That saved the situation, though several slept,
fully dressed, on the floor for some nights lest with one more
quake the old house should collapse.

Because of widespread devastation in the San Jose area,
recovery could not proceed so quickly and smoothly. Scarcity
of skilled workmen seemed to increase with the weeks and
indecision about earthquake-proof reinforcements caused delay
in repairs. Delay finally caused discouragement, and added some
little support to Sister Mary Basil's dream of removing the
boarding school to a safer location, preferably Santa Barbara.
But the majority stood firm with Sister Anna, and to hasten
restoration, Sister Mary Bernardine, on her return from Namur,
made arrangements in New York with builders who were setting out to fill the need in California. After their arrival work
progressed speedily and courage returned to the few faint-
hearted souls excepting poor Sister Mary Basil, who still insisted that classes should be closed. Her state of mind probably
accounts for her becoming a member of the new community
in Santa Barbara.

When all was finished the chief signs of restoration were
the elegantly refinished chapel, a more richly ornate design
over the front portal, a few swinging doors, and painted sheet
iron ceilings in assembly rooms and auditorium. To obtain these
last the Sisters had invoked the aid of St. Expeditus, a mythical
Christian Roman soldier who perhaps stepped out of a church
goods manufacturer's mind to enjoy popularity for some years.
In gratitude the Sisters placed a large statue of this military
saint in the new Science Hall, where for years new freshmen
mistook him for Julius Caesar.

The most serious post-earthquake problem was, of course,
the complete rebuilding of the house at Mission Dolores, a
problem made initially more difficult by Sister Julia Theresa's
unwillingness to discuss it with any except Sister Mary of St.
George, whose notions of construction had recently proved

somewhat erratic. Through the month of May, the upper school
Sisters of the Mission began to hear, in their scattered locations,
that their Superior intended to build "as God inspired her," and
certainly not even her councilors were being consulted. They
discovered, besides, that she planned postponing the reopening
of school until October, when she hoped to have a new building completed on the old site. After a visit with Sister Anna
Raphael in San Jose, Sister Mary Aloyse Keegan wrote at length
to Sister Mary Bernardine, who received her letter in New
York and marked it for special attention, perhaps chiefly because it revealed the fact that as yet not even the pastor at
Mission Dolores knew what to expect. This letter is logical if a
little excited, and in one point mistaken; it presents the mind
of a Sister who wishes above all to preserve the high scholastic
reputation which she and her colleagues had worked so hard
to establish. While the property on Dolores Street is valuable,
Sister states, still the students are mostly from the "good families" of the Western Addition; thus a new site there might be
advisable. Otherwise, she says, their students might register in
a closer school and Notre Dame would have lost its opportunity
and prestige. It is clear that Sister shared the hope cherished
by her colleagues that College of Notre Dame in San Francisco
could easily justify its title. But her interest for the moment
was in retaining the type of student that made up her school's
roster.[5]

Sister Mary Bernardine was impressed with the advisability
of renting a house and opening classes at the usual time. Fortunately Mrs. Catherine Jones, widow of Dr. William Jones,
offered to rent her large residence on Guerrero Street for this
purpose. Lack of funds made it necessary to rebuild on the
former foundation on Dolores Street, where the concrete foundation stood as though waiting fulfillment. The new edifice
could not compare with the ambitious appearance of Sister
Julia Theresa's fine work of 1897, and like many hastily constructed post-earthquake houses, it soon succumbed to a rattling of windows that rendered life on its western side like a
long sea voyage. In general, though, it is still a sturdy house, a

credit to its architect-builder, Notre Dame's good friend, W. J. Smith.

For the time, Sister Julia Theresa continued in office; it seems to have been an error of Sister Mary Bernardine's declining years to see "lack of submission" wherever this Superior reported it. Finally in 1910 she was transferred to San Jose, where she acted, in a sort of temporary expedient, as Mistress of Novices, after which she was returned to New England, yet not without gratitude for her great labors, not the least of which was rebuilding the ruined Mission Dolores convent.

The character that emerges from these earthquake letters, in possession of tempered strength and fine sensibility is Sister Anna Raphael. This is the strength of great patience that goes hand in hand with great regard for the person of others. She tried to see reasonableness in "good Sister Mary Basil's" opposition, to believe that her viewpoint was unprejudiced. This and such problems as the difficulties in the community of Mission Dolores were Sister Anna's touchstones. She admired Sister Julia Theresa's "resignation" in the face of calamity. She saw good with willing eyes, and the good always required her telling. The comic needed telling, too. When some time after the big earthquake, a slight shock brought rushing downstairs some ten or more Sisters who had retired early, she asked the entertaining Sister Mary Gertrude Mogan to write to Sister Mary Bernardine describing the scene. One source of her patience was her optimistic view of difficulties. The crowded "temporary chapel" in the community room pleased her to the point of attachment. When others demurred, she thought it fine enough for two special events in honor of the new Beata, Mère Julie Billiart. Thus on May 13, the very day of the beatification in Rome, Reverend Richard Gleeson, S.J., celebrated solemn high Mass there as did Archbishop Riordan on the following day. As memorials, Sister Anna had their respective sermons printed. Both counseled courage and sacrifice in the work of restoration of the college. And when the Archbishop added the need of being "light-hearted and full of hope," he was describing, perhaps with reflection, the spirit of Sister Anna Raphael.

Returning to California in June, Sister Mary Bernardine was astounded at the restoration well under way in her Notre Dame houses. And in her glowing account of the beatification of the Foundress, the Sisters forgot their trials and fears. Through the ensuing year ceremonies were the order of the day, the culmination being the arrival in San Jose of the fine marble statue of Beata Julie. The sculptor, Michele Tripisciano, had required months to complete it, a work of love and joy, he said, and when Sister Mary Bernardine wrote her admiration of his work, he placed her letter among his "dearest souvenirs."[6]

Chapter 17 A SCHOOL'S ASSESSMENT

*W*ith Sister Mary Bernardine's fine leadership and the recognized ability of Sister Anna Raphael and others on her staff, it might have been possible to develop in San Jose an institution comparable to Trinity College, which other Sisters of Notre Dame opened at Washington, D. C., in 1897. Instead, the school on Santa Clara Street, chartered in 1868 by the State of California as the College of Notre Dame, failed to build a curriculum appropriate to its name until the middle of the twentieth century, when it finally attained recognized status as a four-year college.

Sister Mary Bernardine's purpose was to develop a fine religious spirit in her community and province and to provide the country with an excellent womanhood. She was not convinced, as were Sister Anna Raphael and Sister Mary Xavier, that intellectual attainment was essential to that excellence. Capable as she was of independent thinking, she was strongly influenced by the Mother House and accepted Belgian intransigence toward higher education for women. This attitude was not entirely Belgian, of course; Namur did yield in the controversy over establishment of Trinity College and many American Sisters were convinced that intellectual development was almost dangerous. No interest less than the spiritual was to them tenable. The sort of good that they anticipated was the conversion of Mrs. Leland Stanford, who came now and then to visit the Sisters, and offered railroad passes for their rare transcontinental trips.

This attitude toward higher education for women seemed to harden in the face of demands for acceptance of standards set by any organization outside the Congregation of Notre Dame itself. Many Sisters were opposed to direction by bishops as well as by the state. To be accepted by the academic community as a college, the religious community would be required to accept educational standards of other colleges and universities. This the majority of Sisters of Notre Dame were not prepared to do at San Jose at the turn of the century. Even the founding of Trinity College was a concession to the times.

Before 1890 there was little thought of seeking educational criteria from outside the community. College of Notre Dame was much admired; neither status nor charter was in question. Progress lay in internal criticism and resulting change, a development which led to a general overhaul of studies in 1892, with the hope of introducing the Bachelor of Arts degree, an admission that award of the school's diploma could no longer be considered the equivalent of a college education.

The list of fall semester examinations that year suggests the scope of the curriculum. Latin was now taught on six levels; Greek and trigonometry were listed, both taught by Sister Mary Aloyse Keegan, whose own education was more advanced than might be expected of a girl raised in the mining town of Jackson. At this time mathematics was also expanded; solid geometry made its appearance, and algebra was extended from quadratics through the course later known as college algebra. The array of weighty titles on the list included ontology, lithology, psychology and logic. Physics was begun in the "Third Science Class" which also included continuations of the study of botany and astronomy already begun in the earlier fourth class.

These two subjects were favorites of Sister Anna Raphael, likely to be taught wherever she happened to be and to anyone willing to listen, which usually included everyone. They again appeared in the second class, but now with nature poetry as a complement. Even rocks came in for this treatment: at the "Lithological Display" that year, Helen Petre of the Class of 1893 read her original poem, "Cosmea," and her classmates adorned the botanical exhibit with original verse on ampelopsis and asters, all in the manner of Sister Anna who considered the divorce of science and poetry a species of intellectual sin.

In those days at Notre Dame, the term "class" was used to refer to a unit of accomplishment in a given subject, and a good student might move on to a higher "class" when she was ready for more difficult work. The "class" was the predecessor of the numbered course, but without its limitation to the semester time length. One had merely to complete the work of the highest "class" in a subject; the notion of a stated duration of time for this completion had not entered the picture and there was no definite point of college matriculation. Subjects just flowed through from lower school. The time spent in the boarding school was measured in sessions or terms, but a teacher might complete the work of a "class" long before the end of the session; she might include the work of two "classes" in one term.

Actually all the subjects offered were studied by some few of the students; one who wished to reach the top must cut no corners. The college diploma was so difficult of attainment because it required completion of the highest "classes" of all subjects. The Bachelor of Arts degree would be even more difficult because of the added subjects required. Matters were far from settled when the B.A. was first offered. At the Commencement of 1892, Betty Tisdale appears as medalist in the "Post-graduate Course," with the explanation, "Classical and Philosophical," but at the same time this honor graduate with the Class of 1891 received the only B.A. degree conferred by Notre Dame from the time of its chartering in 1868 until 1953.

To understand this grant of a degree, one must recognize that Betty had been building up through her years at the college, well using her unthinkably long and numerous study hours, working ahead and skipping a "class" here and there. There was little those Sisters would not do for a girl like her; once her ability was recognized, the teaching would be tutorial. Betty presents that delight of nineteenth century teachers, the many-gifted student to whom all courses were majors.[1]

The degree experiment was not continued; perhaps Sister Superior Julia advised against it on her arrival, or it may be that Sister Anna Raphael and the others concerned saw the

need themselves of squaring the curriculum with the under-
graduate divisions of the universities. The decision was not for
want of high mentality in the Class of 1892, in which the four
winners of the college diploma, all "Cum Laude," drew lots for
the gold medal as of equal merit. That medal enhances the
photo of Sadie Quinlan, the future Sister Anthony, S.H., if
enhancing is possible in the case of that dignified, assured
young woman. And the stamp of excellence is on the nine of
the Class of 1893. Even aside from their grand totals of honors,
they have about them the look of young women equipped for
further search. In all, though Betty's degree was something of a
blunder, the school was on an excellent footing. Sister Anna
Raphael and Sister Mary Genevieve were perhaps at their best
as teachers, and were in full pursuit of learning and wisdom.
It is not surprising that Sister Anthony, S.H., considered 1892 a
very fortunate time to enter Notre Dame.

Yet Sister Anna Raphael may well have realized that a
complete change of curriculum would have been better advised
than mere expansion of the old system. She could easily have
known of the plan offered by Mrs. Alpheus Bull in "Radcliffe
Hall," as Ralston Mansion at Belmont was known in the decade
beginning 1890. Here some forty girls, including Mrs. Bull's
own three daughters, were instructed by graduates of Radcliffe and other eastern colleges. Mrs. Bull insisted on a home
atmosphere; classes were held in sun parlors, or under the oaks,
and the Chinese cook kept a cookie jar in readiness for hungry
girls who knocked at the kitchen door. But the Radcliffe Hall
prospectus was far from casual. Its detailed high school program offered both college preparatory and final courses. Here
is no slipping imperceptibly into more advanced work; this
preparatory course led definitely to matriculation and a new
beginning. Without college charter, and with no accepted
public image, Mrs. Bull had set up a contemporary program,
one certain of acceptance by the universities.[2] Through the
same decade, Sister Anna Raphael and her companion teachers
must have given thought to this sort of college preparation.

The very structure of Notre Dame's administration made radical change difficult. For there was no Board of Regents in touch with the outside world, and the Board of Trustees was composed entirely of members of the community. Actually, however, Sister Anna Raphael and her faculty were moving toward change and consulting Sister Mary Xavier all along. The last Notre Dame prospectus of the century listed the colleges from which catalogues had been received, and in its note of thanks it mentioned communications from the United States Commissioner of Education.

In May of 1899, the annalist recorded professors examining classes in mathematics, history and other subjects. These were, of course, "très satisfait," since annalists like sundials recorded, and some still record, only sunny hours. Less committed to happy results, the *Board Book* states simply that the members have commissioned Sister Anna to apply to the University of California for high school accreditation. Thus the visits of 1899 would seem to have been previews; the real test would begin in 1900. Sister Mary Xavier had been experimenting with a four-year high school plan in San Francisco and was happy to share her results with the Sisters in San Jose before the fall term of 1899. Substantially her program was now adopted in the boarding school and Day Academy, with high school a separate unit in each and with required and elective courses distributed through eight semesters. Sister Mary Xavier too had applied for accreditation and the schools in San Francisco and San Jose were both first listed with the University of California at the same time. The move was certainly due to her and to Sister Berchmans Joseph. It seems to have been the latter, no doubt on account of her public school experience, who asked for and obtained permission from Mère Aimée de Jésus to take this step.

In this framework the school at Mission Dolores and the two in San Jose were examined and accredited in the spring of 1900. During the following year, at Sister Anna Raphael's request, a delegation from the University's Academic Council visited the college and, it may be assumed, advised in the setting up of the new college curriculum, which appeared, together with the new high school plan, in the prospectus of 1902-1903. Henceforth the college diploma would signify completion of high school work in the boarding school, though as Professor W. Scott Thomas noted in his report of 1906-1907, the boarding school girls did much more work than could be accomplished in any day high school because of their long hours and supervised school routine. While abandonment of the earlier introduction and gradual evolution of subjects was a loss recognized by some of the Sisters, certainly the first students who matriculated to the universities under the new plan gave evidence of excellent preparation.

The Sisters may have at first been too eager that their students excel during those early years of accreditation. Some examiners remarked a sort of "military rigor" resulting in dexterity but not always in ability to think independently. This characterized the teaching of the nervously exacting Sister Mary Regis, who is described as "keen" but overanxious to make a good impression. It was less often noted by later examiners. A normal school graduate, she was considered well prepared, but her teaching in mathematics suffered in that she never lost the narrow view of the perfectionist. Sister Anthony, S.H., Quinlan, on the other hand, who made no claims in mathematics and whose only formal education at the time had been at Notre Dame, had acquired from her mother and Sister Anna Raphael that education of spirit that remains when facts are forgotten. A brilliant girl summed up the two teachers when she remarked, "You must give Sister Mary Regis only the example in the textbook; Sister Anthony is ready for anything." And in recalling her school days, Hortense White remarked not long ago, "Most girls took on a great maturity in Sister Anthony's classes."

The classes in French especially impressed those first examiners. They noted that only French was spoken in them and that Sister Mary Basil's success was outstanding; almost as highly praised was the teaching of Sister Marie Anne Charlier at Notre Dame in San Francisco, although on the whole that school came off less satisfactorily than did Notre Dame in San Jose.[3]

The examiners themselves, perhaps, were affected by the newness of their task plus their lack of experience in dealing with religious Sisters. On both sides the approach was sincere and cooperative. The examiner who withheld accreditation of a class in drawing because the students were merely reproducing other drawings instead of real objects, reported a year later that the same teacher had followed his suggestions and was doing very well.[4]

Perhaps the first completely reliable assessment was made in October, 1905, by Professor W. Scott Thomas. His typed report notes even the regulation black uniform worn by the girls, "with now and then a ribbon of gayer color to relieve it," but that, with a note of surprise, they seemed contented. All pupils, he notes, are required to take English, French, Latin, Greek or German, besides the usual amount of history, mathematics, and science, nor is it "observable . . . that the work is less well done than in High Schools." Then on second thought, "Indeed, I find in some cases it is distinctly better." First-year pupils, he adds, study both Latin and French, though most of them have begun French in the grade school. The library is "fully adequate for the school's needs." The tone of things is excellent, and the teaching "has less formalism than is usually seen in Catholic schools," The teachers are "evidently competent," and the pupils, "normal." Science seemed the less well-taught subject. There was not enough laboratory room for physics and chemistry, the same room being used for both. However, he noted an abundance of apparatus and supplies, and that plans were on foot for adequate floor space. And when a few weeks later, the Sisters reported a contract for Science Hall, he added the fact to his summary. He probably knew that this unit was intended to serve as first of a group of college buildings, but complete physical separation of college from high school classes had not then taken on its later importance.

In subsequent visits — and for over a decade he was the most frequent examiner — Professor Thomas ceased to be ner-

vously feared. As a just and kind appraiser and adviser, he was
certainly the greatest outside influence in the forming of the
two high school divisions. About Latin, not as yet an established tradition in the school, he was a little anxious. Thus
when Sister Anthony's Vergil class tripped itself glibly into
false quantities and inaccurate sense, he wondered "how this
sort of thing ever got accredited." But later he noted that
Sister's Ciceronians honored themselves and their teacher by
"exceptional regard for quantity," and general command of the
subject. And to confirm his altered opinion, he took the class
over himself for some minutes and asked "all the hard questions" he could think of on the assignment. They did not miss
one, he noted, and added his pleasure with Sister's Greek class;
in fact, he now felt "great faith in the thoroughness of this
woman's teaching."

Professor Thomas' comments on "keen-faced, critical, searching," Sister Mary Regis are kinder than those of earlier examiners. She is likely to do "first rate work if she knows the subject," and he sees no "sign that she does not." That was perfect appraisal; there was never a time when Sister failed to
know the subject, that is, in its time-honored guise. The alge-
braic formula was sacrosanct; she would have been horrified at
other than classical avenues to mathematical truth. But the fact
that Professor Thomas saw the values of her hard work and
exactitude adds to the trustworthiness of his total summary.

The same insight is evident in this examiner's account of
two English classes taught by Sister Margaret of St. Joseph
Sommers, whose unusual teaching ability, as well as the "sub-
dued enthusiasm" which she communicated to her pupils,
pleased him greatly. He noted special ability, too, in Sister
Mary Euphrasia Taylor, "a very cultivated woman, keen-
minded, wide awake, well read." In her history classes, Professor Thomas found perfect mastery of facts, but since thus far
no outside reading appeared in assignments, he wondered
whether, Sister being from Washington, D. C., she had "gotten
hold of our methods of history teaching." While his estimate
bears a faint trace of western suspicion of eastern attitudes, he

still seemed willing to trust this very intelligent woman to catch on. He was less sure about the timid Sister Marie de Ste. Thérèse Klausen, who had recently come down from Marysville to teach German, had never before seen an examiner, and was "scared out of her wits." Here was a native German, "still speaking English with a strong Teutonic twist," but so lacking in courage to use her advantage, that she clung to textbook exercises. Though her own German was good, "her class performance was not of much account." In fact, "very little attention was paid to German in the school." Then in extenuation, he adds, Sister, a music teacher, "has not yet learned much about handling classes." Yet the five pupils in this class "are good workers," and "the book translation is well done." And here one recalls this Sister's early difficulties with timidity and also Maria Lucas' remark that little attention was ever paid to German at the college.

But Professor Thomas confirmed the statements about the excellence of French classes. Sister Louise, S.H., André, "a large, jolly-seeming woman," was at home with her classes as well as with the language. Sister Mary Basil, "a woman of rare culture and native refinement," taught two upper classes, using only French. In fact, and the professor was well impressed by this practice, French was spoken at certain meals. This custom always seemed trying and unreasonable to the beginner in French, who found herself limited, for some time at least, to "Je voudrais du sel," and other strict essentials.

Sister Anna Raphael is not mentioned in Professor Thomas' reports, though as head of the school she represented it in all its contacts with the university, accompanied examiners from class to class, discussed their findings with them and reported their general suggestions at teachers' meetings. After the new program for high school work went into effect, her teaching function was limited to the few students who were enrolled in the college program. Sister Anthony helped out on that level when there was call for Latin; Sister Louise satisfied the almost constant demand for French; Sister Mary Regis taught bits of irrefutable logic. But it was merely tutoring, and they realized the fact as well as their own lack of degrees. They advised good graduates to enroll in San Jose Normal School and encouraged superior students to go to Trinity College, to the University of California or to Stanford. In 1910 the college program was removed from the prospectus, and the teaching potential focused on the high school program.

About this time it was clear that Sister Anna Raphael's robust health was rapidly declining, though until her final illness she exerted a telling influence on young teachers. In her casual way she enticed them into her little sanctum in the profesed house to share a news clipping on Halley's Comet, or the splendor of a fern spore under her microscope, her mind still the meeting ground of science and literature. She must have seen that their minds were set on special fields, that "English," or a foreign language, to say nothing of Latin, were to be their inland channels, and that their backs were turned to her open sea. Even Sister Anthony, writing nature rhapsodies, would approach no nearer to nature than the average Victorian; the batteries of her own phrases would prevent it. Where Sister Anna detected literary ability, she encouraged it, making unexpected assignments to the possessors and handing her selections to Sister Anthony for the *Quarterly*. Poets or not, all dropped in to that little office with their teaching problems. It is easy to see her eager attention, her kind eyes, her wide mouth puckered up a bit at the left corner as she thought the matter over, her unassuming expression.

Withdrawal of all claims of college work from the prospectus was Sister Anna's advice. Yet she was an optimist. Young Sisters must now be educated to staff a college faculty. Before her death, Californian Sisters were studying at Catholic University. Still, her last years were not all golden sunset. Jansenistic fears and narrowness were gaining ground. The burst of intellectual energy that had blessed the school in its second decade would not be entirely welcome in its sixth. That dismal fact was emphasized when at the Trustees' Meeting in February, 1912, Sister Mary Veronica read a communication from the Mother House calling for withdrawal from accreditation to the

State University, as opening the way to higher education in an atmosphere in which faith might be lost. The directive advised accreditation with the Catholic University of America instead. Sister Mary Veronica said simply that Sister Anna Raphael should notify the University of California at once. She obeyed "that same day," thus undoing, with a heartache, the work which she had initiated and sponsored.

The blow had fallen at a moment of general weakness. In California, Sister Mary Bernardine was totally incapacitated, and in Namur, Mère Marie Aloyse, who had approved of accreditation to the state university, was close to death. Sister Mary Veronica expressed no opinion except to counsel obedience.

In San Francisco, Sister Berchmans Joseph Murphy, the recently appointed and progressive Superior, postponed action for the time, no doubt in hope of a change of mind in Namur. Then, with the election of the unfettered and generally aware Mère Julienne Goffin, she and Sister Mary Xavier visited San Jose, where together with Sister Anna Raphael, they persuaded Sister Mary Veronica to present to the new Mother General the need and wisdom of affiliation with the state university.[5]

The request was granted. Sister Anna Raphael must have foreseen how the matter would end, since she had allowed the statement of accreditation to be reprinted in the intervening prospectus. The crisis had passed, though not all of the mentality which had produced it, nor did all the conservative thought in this matter emanate from Namur. To many Sisters in California, accreditation remained for long a necessary evil at best. As late as 1936, one of the sporadic episcopal pronouncements on the subject of secular eduation was interpreted, by the New Englander who was then head of the California Province, as forbidding Catholic Sisters to attend public universities.[6] Through the subsequent eleven years, the ban was lifted only in favor of a very few scientists and one school supervisor. This regrettable ruling was reversed by Sister Marie Frederica Kane in 1947.[7]

In 1915, a new four-year plan was announced, representing the enthusiasm of Sister Anthony, S.H., and Sister Mary Regis, then recently returned from Catholic University. But as both funds and faculty were lacking, only a junior college program could be attempted. Sister Anthony headed this department. The fact that the full curriculum continued to appear in each year's prospectus until the transfer to Belmont seems to indicate the hope that the two-year arrangement was only temporary. During this brief span, the faculty was strengthened by two or three very fine and properly degreed lay instructors, a gain unfortunately lessened by the employment of these and college Sisters as well, in the high school division.

The new college division was hindered by another unfortunate development. The combination of Sister Anthony's unintentional brusqueness and Sister Mary Regis' exacting manner were perhaps somewhat responsible for a sort of cleavage built up in those years between the tiny group of college Sisters and others. For at the time, some half a dozen brilliant younger Sisters were reaching maturity. The high recognition won by a few of these in the universities seemed more or less to go unnoticed by the college group. Had these been drawn into the circle, had their potential been realized, and had the college division been entirely separated from the boarding school, a full college program might have been on its way. As it was this potential greatly enriched the high schools of the province, for besides being brilliant, these Sisters were fine teachers. Notre Dame girls of that day still bless their good fortune in having been taught by the erudite Sister Xaveria Mulcahy, and the brilliant and witty Sister Mary Alexis Harrington. What was wanting was the generous and embracing spirit of a Sister Anna Raphael.

In her own teaching, Sister Anthony, S.H., continued much of Sister Anna Raphael's gift to her, adding besides her own special spicy quality, an edge of satire enjoyed by her keener students. Strangely enough she failed to move beyond a literary point in time. Facing their world, her students would require some adjustment, since part of her credo informed them that little of literary value had occurred since Tennyson. She made a few attempts at carrying students beyond the second year, since no authority had expressly forbidden this, but with the move to Belmont, she withdrew the upper division work from the program, and offered the degree of Associate of Arts instead.

Thus the program remained until mid-century, a not too assuring promise of things to come. But the work of accreditation of high schools developed into a strong and realistic educational movement. One has only to compare this type of assessment with the elaborate compilations of school work submitted in fine binding to the Columbian Exposition in 1893, to understand the role that was played by appearance in the late nineteenth century.[8] Characterized as "daily work," these pages are dress show, copperplate testimony, of which Notre Dame in San Jose had no need. It is a relief to find among those perfected and stilted exercises, a sheaf of notebook pages covered with rough penciling, the work of one of Sister Anna's natural science students on a field day at Mount Hamilton. Preparation of that grand exhibit is a far call from preparation for a professor's face-to-face examination on an unannounced date.

In time the examiner's visit came to be less of a nerve-racking experience and so an increasingly helpful occasion. The story of the worried Sister praying that the visitor would not discover the worst represents the total picture no more than does that of teacher and class "showing off" all they knew. Most were at ease and eager to profit by the examination.

There can be no doubt regarding the superiority of present methods of school evaluation; compared with these the annual visit, the examination of all subjects by a specialist in one, seems a haphazard arrangement. Yet that visit did much more than merely to establish standards; it brought the teachers into touch with a world of education much larger than their own. It is true, too, that criteria of evaluation have changed. On the whole, those examiners were demanding the use of knowledge as well as its possession. To the extent that they were, their visits raised the standards of the accredited schools. It was wisdom on the part of Sister Anna Raphael, Sister Mary Xavier, and others to stress high school accreditation, to see that the foundations of higher education lay in the strengthening of their secondary system.

*A*s scholastic matters at Notre Dame settled into a definite high school program, and college became a word used with modesty and caution, chiefly as an achievement to be hoped for, the school of music blossomed out with assurance and meteoric splendor. In the past it had attracted such artists as visited the Pacific Coast, but now with the turn into the new century, its concerts became much more numerous and dazzling; its publicity no longer consisted of home-produced programs and flowery comment.

Since her arrival from Guatemala in 1875, Sister Marguerite Kridelka had trained teachers, gathered a collection of fine instruments, planned Notre Dame Auditorium and, in her final year, supervised construction of the conservatory.[1] From the time she came until 1886 she enjoyed having as co-worker the silver-voiced Sister Marie de Ste. Thérèse Klausen, whose youthful experiences in Europe had so greatly resembled her own. Together, these two set about expanding the work begun by the gentle Westphalian, Sister Madeleine Mantell. Then in the 1890s the music faculty was augmented by a young group that recalls the eager members of the early school faculty. The year 1890 might well be named the year of music, bringing as it did four talented Sisters to profession in San Jose and an experienced musician from Namur. The last, Irish-born Sister Madeleine de Ste. Françoise Harbison, had studied and taught in the English schools of Notre Dame, no doubt with the zeal and habitual undercurrent of excitement that marked her life in the West. In her later years in Alameda, this small but sturdy Sister began many a morning with an hour in the laundry as prelude to a day of piano lessons, her directions and comment still spicy at the last, her brown eyes registering unbelief at an unprepared lesson. Then with morning freshness, she would con-

Notre Dame in Guatemala. Novice Mistress Marie de St. Patrice Verdon surrounded by the first Guatemalan novices (left) and Sister Marie Philippine Portemer, First Teacher at the orphanage (right).

The boarding school at Belén, Guatemala City. White uniforms were worn because of the warm climate, with the black sateen apron which came to be the boarding school symbol.

An orchestra of stringed instruments at Notre Dame in San Jose just before the turn of the century

Stella Light Eaton of San Francisco, violinist. First graduate of the Conservatory, 1900.

Aimée Auzerais of San Jose graduated in harp, 1906.

Hortensia Corral of Mexico City, one of six who received a B.M. in 1911.

Madame Schumann-Heink was visiting artist at the Conservatory in 1912.

Notre Dame Chapel at Christmas.

Notre Dame Music Hall.

Notre Dame Conservatory.

Views of earthquake
destruction at College
of Notre Dame in
April, 1906. Left, the
Chapel. Below, two
views of Notre Dame
Conservatory.

Theodore Lenzen and his son, Louis, were the architects of Science Hall, below, and other campus buildings in San Jose.

THE NEW NOTRE DAME HALL OF SCIENCE IN PROCESS OF ERECTION.

Theodore Lenzen & Son
Architects
110. S. 2nd Str. San Jose, Cal.

Demolition of Science
Hall, last unit on the
old campus, in 1966.

Contents of Science
Hall cornerstone.
Photos courtesy of
San Jose *Mercury-News*.

duct choir practice in the parish church, her sputtering remarks producing absolute attention, if not always absolute pitch, in the wearisome hours after classes. Sister Madeleine de Ste. Françoise was first assigned as assistant to Sister Marguerite, and in this office she met the gifted trio, Sister Irene, S.H., Siddons, Sister Cécile Marie Gerlach, and Sister Mary Gertrude Mogan.

From the first, Sister Marguerite admired the outspoken little extrovert, Sister Irene, S.H., whose incautious words were still not edged with bitterness. Her tactlessness, really a failure to note the slower intelligence of others, was always unintended. Her laughing remarks must have kept Sister Madeleine de Ste. Françoise in a state of wide-eyed shock. She enjoyed life, despite the contemporary Jansenistic trend. She loved to tell of her childhood in Carson City, where her father, jeweler L. L. Siddons, had brought her from South Carolina after her mother's death. Fascinated by gems but not at all by school and books, little Henrietta looked up one day from her favorite pursuit to find a hitherto unheard-of Siddons relative studying her closely but kindly. No kindred of the great actress, Sarah Siddons, should fritter away her youth, said the solicitous lady, and in no time Henrietta found herself spending time advantageously with the Sisters of the Holy Names in Oakland, and there discovering the joys of music. It was characteristic of Sister Irene to leave no clue to the Siddons relationship; certainly it was not direct descent. But as certainly the good lady was correct in supposing talent in little Henrietta, whose endowment probably bordered on genius.

Sister Cécile Marie's talent, and it was genuine, had to be recognized through a mist of somewhat grandiose self-assessment. As a child of four, Emilie Gerlach, daughter of a well-known family in San Jose, was entered in Notre Dame's Select Day Academy and met her future music teacher, Sister Marguerite. That Emilie was industrious as well as talented is evident from her frequent winning of school prizes in several departments, events which she noted in each current prospectus in her large and ornate writing. Years accented her desire for recognition. She assembled her musical compositions, labelled for posterity, together with her poems done in contemporary manner, but with nineteenth century spirituality poorly concealed by their obscurity. Yet in all this, as also in her patronizing and usually gratis advice to young teachers, was her sincere appraisal of her own gifts and accomplishments.

Daughter of the prominent Joseph R. Mogan family of San Francisco, Sister Mary Gertrude possessed a more extensive musical training than did either of her companions, as well as a talent that nearly rivalled Sister Irene's. Sister Marguerite recognized her ability, but probably knew from the start that with her quick, nervous reactions, she would do less for the department than the others. She could hardly be expected, for one thing, to agree on all points with Sister Cécile Marie. Thus it turned out that, as long as her fitful health allowed, Sister Mary Gertrude directed music at Notre Dame in San Francisco most efficiently, but devoted her talent to the conservatory at San Jose now and then in holidays when young Sisters gathered there for lessons. If her pronouncements on music seemed a bit crushing at times, that was because she was trying to discourage showy attempts by the poorly trained or incapable.

At the close of the century and later a strong individualism seemed the mark and privilege of the gifted musician, Sister Marguerite being perhaps the only one not permitting herself to indulge this characteristic, if indeed she possessed it. Thus with the resulting tension and its consequent transfers, temporary and otherwise, plans for a music conservatory moved slowly. However, an unexpected arrival in the summer of 1894 seemed a clear indication of Heaven's blessing on the undertaking. Among the occasional artist visitors who called at Notre Dame came an opera singer with the resounding name of Marie Ofelia Plisé de Losada de Richeblave, a 38-year-old Panamanian of French and Spanish parentage, with a formidable record of Parisian training, and European and American concertizing and opera roles.[2] Despite her prima donna contours and poise, however, Marie Ofelia had often experienced mystical yearnings; in fact, her occasional visits to convents were partly with an eye to their fulfillment. Now it would seem that as soon as the lodge door closed behind her, she was completely engulfed by a sense of Notre Dame's suitability to her spiritual needs. At any rate, she declared her desire, it was more like an intention, of remaining forever, and since her clerical recommendations were as formidable as her musical testimonials, it would have been less than tact on the part of Sister Mary Bernardine to demur, nor was her immediate acceptance of Marie Ofelia ever a matter of regret, for she was an honest soul, living in continual astonishment at the non-mystical aspects of convent life, her reactions a constant source of mirth.

In those days new postulants made their first entry to the community hour at the end of a line of novices, received a smile and word of recognition from the presiding superior, and were quickly seated behind a barricade of white veils, there to begin their hidden life. Not so Marie Ofelia, who with no warning to her novice guide, walked the length of the polished middle aisle, bowing graciously to the rows of seated professed Sisters on either side, who nodded with exterior composure at each "Good evening, Ladies." The grand entry over, Marie Ofelia set about the work of becoming a humble novice. Learning that a quick way to perfection lay in attempting assigned tasks unquestioningly, she decided to make up for her late start to holiness by not demurring at the impossible. Thus when a Sister in the laundry handed her a pile of wet towels telling her to take them to the laundry yard and place them on "the horse," she obeyed, only to return a little later, towels still over her arm, with the announcement, "Seester, I cannot find the animal."

Submission was, however, a matter of conventual life; in the music school, Marie Ofelia, or Sister Marie Aimée after she donned the habit, was every inch the prima donna; her approach to all musical situations was dogmatic, and her astonishment at challenge amounted to tragic magnificence. It probably never occurred to her to consider Sister Marie de Ste. Thérèse as a co-worker. Noting that Sisters, for love of poverty, write the monastic *ad usum* or its equivalent, in books which they were using, Sister Marie Aimée inscribed on her great tomes of voice culture, "This book is only for my private use." Clearly there were heights to which she could not expect others to ascend. Perhaps the eclipse was more than Sister Marie de Ste. Thérèse could bear.

Whatever the reason, Sister Marie de Ste. Thérèse was sent again to her beloved Marysville when Sister Marie Aimée was professed in 1896, and the latter took over the chapel choir as well as vocal classes. It was no doubt as well, since in any clash of minds, the self-assured young Sister Cécile Marie would certainly tip the international scales. And while Sister Marguerite admired both vocalists, she must have realized that Sister Marie Aimée possessed distinct musical advantages. Her taste tended, of course, to the grand polyphonic production so admired in that era, an accomplishment that demanded all her physical and emotional energy to which gifts she had added certain forceful expressions gleaned indiscriminately in her American contacts. It was a test of composure in a choral group to see her, solemn-faced, hands uplifted, and hear her compelling "One, two, three, bust!" And no one, it would seem, attempted to alter Sister Marie Aimée's eccentricities; or if anyone did, perhaps her reaction was too awesome, but that mattered little, for clearly her presence was a blessing, marking as it did the beginning of concentration on voice culture at Notre Dame, and no doubt hastening the realization af Sister Marguerite's dream, Notre Dame Conservatory.

This beautiful unit with high windows and ornate entrance, was completed in 1899 at the cost of over $12,000.[3] A few months later Sister Marguerite died suddenly while on a visit to Marysville. In San Jose her death meant more than ordinary loss; without her presence, tension in the conservatory increased. On the one hand, Sister Irene's natural talent, her almost effortless mastery, demanded no exhibition. On the other, Sister Mary Bernardine, impressed with Sister Cécile Marie's logical argument and suave approach, considered her the proper choice in replacing Sister Marguerite. It is a little surprising that with all her insight, Sister Mary Bernardine failed to see that the new head would not make allowance for talent greater than her own in one of her group, and that in the long run, her leadership would prove generally disconcerting. Departmental difficulties seem to have been the order of the day under the new regime. For Sister Irene especially it was a time of discouragement. On an impulse she asked for a change of occupation and suggested cooking, for which she possessed talent as well as liking. Sister Mary Bernardine assigned her to the new house in Salinas where her soul was at peace. And there as cooking gave her only part-time occupation, she continued her life as music teacher to her enjoyment and with no return of frustration.

Despite difficulties, however, the decade following 1900 wears all the marks of a success story. When Sister Cécile Marie inscribed her copy of the prospectus of that year "My First Exhibition," she was beginning a period of development and publicity. Notre Dame Conservatory of Music now became an institution in its own right, with special announcement of graduation in 1900, its first diploma granted to Stella Light Eaton in violin and its first gold medal to Winifred McLaughlin for harp. The curriculum was impressive with harmony and theory and with courses in Janko-Keyboard, an instrument that seemed promising at the time. As a rule, conservatory graduates were boarding school girls who had studied music at Notre Dame from ten to twelve years.[4] Classes were small, often one spectacular graduate, as Winifred McLaughlin in 1902; apparently Sister Cécile Marie believed that the prize was for the few. Among these distinguished ones were the local musicians Maude and Irene Campbell, Flora Thiltgen, and lovely Aimée Auzerais, second harpist in the McLaughlin-Auzerais family, who to Sister Cécile Marie's great satisfaction, went directly to Paris to continue her studies.

The conservatory's most telling publicity was the praise bestowed on its work in the pages of *Pacific Coast Musical Review*, by music critic Professor Alfred Metzger. In 1908 this review, "the only Musical Journal in the great West," featured graduates Grace and Geraldine O'Connell and vocalist Frieda

Gay, who as Sister Carmela soon became a bright star in the rising generation of Notre Dame musicians.[5] At the following commencement, the conservatory conferred the degree of Bachelor of Music on Carrie Goebel-Weston in violin, and on Rena Silverman and Sarah Lesser in piano. It seems incredible in view of the now accepted status of the college diploma as marking the termination of high school. Rena had completed that course a year earlier; the other two had not. Certainly all three had studied music for years, but the degree was as certainly a flight of fancy. But aside from falling short of academic standards, the music curriculum was itself wanting in unit value. Sister Cécile Marie was seemingly unaware of any risk in turning even a fine music department into a college without authorization. Separated from the academic faculty, she had merely to secure the approval of Sister Mary Bernardine, and it probably sufficed to show her the March *Pacific Coast Musical Review*, with its photo of Sister's large orchestra, with its six great harps flanking its violins and celli, and its assurance that the world of music now lay at the feet of Carrie Goebel-Weston. A degree more or less could scarcely make a difference.[6]

Perhaps none of the very distinguished artists who responded to Sister Cécile Marie's invitations ever thought of questioning the music curriculum. For most of these, the Conservatory appearance followed a more spectacular event as guest of San Jose's music lovers in the Victory Theater. Perhaps most of these artist guests, certainly Madame Schumann-Heink, preferred the "convent" reception. Like Maude Powell and others, this celebrity was touched when white-robed minims of the boarding school surrounded her with baskets of flowers.[7] In all it began to seem that a hitherto obscure institution had suddenly attained high recognition. Then a visit from Helen Petre, a graduate of 1893, revealed that fine things had been done in pre-Conservatory years. Helen had spent almost two decades abroad, and now gladly shared her exciting experiences as well as her magnificent soprano voice with a younger Notre Dame generation. Certainly the list of her instructors in Paris, Berlin, Rome and London was imposing, as was also her own opera and repertoire performances in many continental cities. Twice she had sung, by royal command, before Queen Victoria of England. But what Helen wanted most to tell the girls of Notre Dame was that Sister Marguerite had been her open sesame, and how her famous teachers abroad had praised her early training.

What these artists had to say about student receptiveness and ability was carefully dated and preserved for posterity in Sister Cécile Marie's elaborate hand; no other period of Notre Dame life is so well attested. And on the whole, Sister deserved high praise as a tireless and intelligent worker, who used her high degree of talent to its fullest. But time accented her unhappier characteristics, one of which was a tendency to illness when confronted with contrary opinion. Excepting Sister Marie Aimée, who in the absence of a competing vocalist, was quite untouched by departmental difficulties, the musicians of the province were finding the conservatory difficult.

One of Sister Mary Veronica's earliest adjustments concerned the music problem. Transferring Sister Cécile Marie to Watsonville in 1914, she appointed Sister Irene, S.H., head of the conservatory. Now began a period of realistic if less spectacular development, with Sister Marie de Ste. Thérèse replacing the ailing Sister Marie Aimée, and assisted by Sister Carmela, S.H., Gay, and Sister Marie Eugénie Balwick, both of whom were receiving lay professional training. The latter, a mature young person, with several years of voice culture before her entrance into the novitiate, directed the Sisters' choir even as a novice, leading the way from florid high mass through the beginnings of Gregorian Chant. Sister's artistic accomplishment was possible because of the other talented conservatory Sisters and because of the intensity and eagerness of musical pursuit under Sister Irene's leadership. In this picture there was no room for complacency. All were studying under more advanced musicians, and original masterpieces were not being attempted.

When professors of Ohio Conservatory of Music began to give instruction on the Pacific Coast, Sister Irene enrolled in a three-year course, during which lesson and practice hours were interspersed with "grueling" examinations. At last her examiners conferred on her their conservatory's Master of Music degree, now music at Notre Dame was brought fully abreast of current development. Music majors now were required to earn 120 units, exclusive of those acquired in the "Academic Course," and to give besides an "artistic recital." Notre Dame Conservatory now became Notre Dame College of Music.

The regrettable aspect of this fine music school with its dedicated teachers and students, its tremendous force and activity, was its continued separation, except for necessary work in physics and mathematics, from rounded intellectual life. For though Sister Irene bestowed the degree on few, many others actually reached advanced musical standing, working long hours at violin, harp, or piano, as though there were no interest beyond the walls of the conservatory. Still, to some degree, isolation has always been the problem of the music major; professional instruction in music and science have tended to exclude the humanities as though somehow these disciplines have no need of the great common integrating milieu.[8] It may have been this attitude on the part of the musicians that caused Sister Anthony's reaction to conservatory courses; no credit was given in the scholastic curriculum for music, just as there was no scholastic requirement in the conservatory; the separation was complete. Many academic students, of course, took music lessons and some became quite expert musicians, but it was always a matter of attending two distinct institutions with no interdependence. Still Notre Dame College of Music was an outstanding institution as long as the college remained in San Jose. It produced such vocalists as Eileen Costello, Sister Carmela, and the Smith sisters of Alameda, and such instrumentalists as Beatrice Mix, Madeleine Sterling, Yvonne Mitchell, Violet Bulmore, Margot and Virginia Matheu, Marguerite King, Marjorie Booth, and Maxine Cox.

The art studios, lodged spaciously in the conservatory, were as far removed as music from the academic curriculum, which allowed merely a minimum of credit to classroom drawing.

Nor could art be properly called a department; it gave no credit; it conferred no standing. Yet after the turn of the century, art was much more active than ever before, and the output was of much higher quality. In fact, the output, it would seem, was everything. Talent, especially Latin-American talent, flowed into the studios. In the case of the less gifted there was expert "touching up" as of yore. In any case, oils, water colors, and crayon drawings, set in heavy, elaborate gold frames, were on exhibit awhile, and then boxed and sent home to admiring parents. The studios were, in fact, on exhibit all year long, the crowning glory of all tours through the establishment.

In the studio there was almost no flicker of creativity, no knowledge of current artistic movements, or at least, no wish to understand them. Teacher or student might be seen before a new canvas, plotting on its lightly penciled squares the lines of a Carlo Dolci from tiny squares drawn on a picture postcard. Thus the student moved from one masterpiece to another, never setting on canvas or paper the outline of original form. Sister Joseph, herself, produced her large oils in this fashion, never quite mastering form, depending on the San Francisco artist, Edwardo Tojetti, to "do the hands" and straighten things out in general before bringing to the canvas her own phenominal gift of color. This gift at least she could and did share generously until the weakness of age ended her studio days. Those days were saddened for her by a desire for recognition, heretofore hidden in accord with that concept of sanctity which demanded nonentity in Sisters. In her earlier days, she had accepted that restriction, but there is a sense of satisfaction as well as humor, in her furtive request to a novice to write her name for her on all her oils. One feels inclined to applaud the novice for discreetly obliging her.

The character antithesis of Sister Joseph in the studio was Sister Mary Josephine, daughter of the pioneer San Jose family of Thomas E. Snell.[9] Professed in 1890, she was "destined" for the studio because of unfitness for classroom teaching combined fortunately with a decided artistic ability. As a frail and beautiful girl, Helen Snell had developed a throat affliction that reduced speech to little more than a whisper, a condition which conspired with her natural reticence to make her the ideal hidden soul of that time. An accomplished artist when she entered the convent, she made fine use of lessons from the "outside" teachers employed to instruct promising Sisters. Before and after studio hours, she performed the most laborious work in the kitchen. Seeing her wraithlike form lost in large kitchen apron and oversleeves, new arrivals supposed her the assistant cook. Her lovely paintings, still cool and refreshing today in their plain gold frames, might have been another's work as she turned quickly to the next task, to give a lesson in china painting or water color, or to brighten up a gift made by a beginning artist.

The studio's greatest service was perhaps the development of talent among Sisters of the province. Cultured and beautiful Sister Mary Angelica Cronin was one of these, a gentle woman who though unable to manage more than one or two young Americans at a time, still left in many an indelible impression of sweetness and light. Little Sister Veronica, S.H., Gelcich, daughter of an old family of Guadalajara, Mexico, learned, in her eagerness, every skill which the older Sisters could impart. Never losing her young enthusiasm, Sister became Watsonville's best-loved primary teacher. Three generations of Pajaronians learned to read in her little green schoolhouse, its corners oddly overflowing with partly finished pastels and chinaware in preparation for her kiln. Thus besides letters and numbers, those boisterous future citizens learned also to tiptoe about, dodging fresh oils and fine teacups.

Sister Stanislaus of St. Joseph Rademacher probably made a nearer approach to the underlying ideals of art than did any other Sister artist of the time. Sister Marie of St. Joseph Oddie, fresh from Paris studios at the end of studio days on Santa Clara Street, considered Sister Stanislaus Notre Dame's foremost artist.

Nominally, at least, a member of the studio staff, stout little Sister Amada Salazar maintained headquarters of her own in what was called the chapel attic. This daughter of Don Ramón

Salazar and Guadalupe Perrón of Sonora, Mexico, entered the novitiate at the age of 35 with little English and less aptitude for the ways of an active congregation of Sisters. For the latter reason, she was detained much longer than usual in the novitiate, and then "tried out" in some of the smaller houses in the hope of helping her to an understanding of the terms "common life" and "common work." Though she acquired a fine knowledge of English, these two terms in some way eluded her. Dishtowels and dusters were for the hands of Americans and other democrats; rotund as she was, she managed to drop quite out of sight at the onset of a cleaning party. Her piety tended to the audible and demonstrative; her prayer books were always bursting with holy pictures which she kissed in turn with sibillant endearments. Sister had her charities, too, one being a guided tour of her attic for each new arrival who admired sufficiently her very fine charcoals. Besides, Sister Amada taught the large drawing classes of Notre Dame High School, with success and a certain enjoyment, the latter being no doubt the cause of the generally good response accorded her unvaried arrangement of pyramids and cylinders. She was no more original than her colleagues, and as far removed from contemporary trends.

Still the most critical artists considered the work of Notre Dame's studio excellent. They did not expect to find there developments not as yet universally accepted. What they did appreciate was the mastery which the students were acquiring. And the fact that art was not integrated in the scholastic curriculum caused no worry; the weekly class lesson in "drawing" was all one might expect to find there.

To Sister Anthony the studio was perhaps a beautiful and elegant show piece; she enjoyed conducting visitors through those rooms, but she would not have presented the work done there as included in her program. The studio was valuable on the one hand, and on the other, harmless since it did not lead to an independent diploma. It was otherwise with music studies since the day in 1900 when Sister Cécile Marie had the new music building engraved on the new "Conservatory Diploma."

Sister Anthony and her colleagues saw in this a cavalier attitude toward things scholastic, an attitude exemplified in the grant of a music degree for music, however advanced, that was not oriented in a general collegiate plan. This orientation, Sister Anthony knew, would be the approved future status of music, though she herself was not quite ready to accept it; she was in fact, a bit cavalier herself where the fine arts were concerned. To the end, Notre Dame College of Music maintained a remarkably high standard.

*T*o complete the picture of College of Notre Dame in its final years in San Jose, one should peruse the pages of *Notre Dame Quarterly*. From its inception in 1908, this magazine presents, in its school and alumnae sections, both a revealing contemporary account and the flood of reminiscence which Sister Anthony, S.H., requested and welcomed. For a few years the school section bears the unmistakable character of Sister Anthony's own style; after that she entrusts it to such gifted seniors as Marie DiBernardi and Beatrice Mix, so that the columns become somewhat breezier, though the young writers keep an eye on their English teacher's correcting pencil. Anything too casual would not have fitted cozily into that austerely elegant format. For the *Quarterly* was the more ambitious successor to the short-lived *Woodpecker*, which seems to have been, though there is, sad to say, no extant copy for comparison, a slight booklet by and for the upperclassmen.[1] The character and purpose of the *Quarterly* are made definite enough in Sister Anthony's initial statement. As manager, she hopes the new magazine will serve as a bond between school and alumnae. As educator, she offers its pages for continued literary efforts of former students, believing as she does that too often the art of written expression is neglected after graduation. She invites especially the school's "bluestockings." Poetry, she says, is to be expected from those whose talent had been trained by Sister Anna Raphael. Yet the *Quarterly* must also become the voice of the school, its credo, evidence of its ambitions and accomplishments.

Almost at once the new journal, with its unchanging white cover and Notre Dame shield in gold, became a welcomed journal in a much wider circle than Sister had hoped. Lecturers, writers, poets, and educators sent in subscriptions.[2] And considering the names subjoined to commendations, among them David Starr Jordan of Stanford University, and the poet Charles Warren Stoddard, the anonymous "manager and publisher," had reason to feel encouraged. Press notices were complimentary, too, but perhaps Sister was happiest about the volunteer articles and poems by Frances Mace, Amelia Truesdell, Elizabeth Gray Lightner, Virginia Reed Murphy, and George Wharton James, besides such established alumnae writers as Marcella Fitzgerald, Rebecca Ord Peshine, and Frances Miller. Among these, recent graduates Dorothy Singer, Cecilia Kays, and Helen McKeever held their own.

Sister Anthony herself, as though to offset what might have turned out a plethora of sunsets and meadowlarks, began to produce such lengthy and profound blank verse poems as her "Prometheus," works that betray her close acquaintance with Wordsworth and Tennyson, a slight consideration in view of her verve and original outlook. For though one regrets the "Thou art's," the apostrophe better suited to Sister Anna's young days, and the tendency to the pathetic fallacy and personification, which becomes in her "Sister Seas" a dialogue pages long between two oceans, those long poems are marked by — she would have said "fraught with"— the power that enabled her to toss them from her typewriter like so much copy.[3] The grand sweep impressed many; Sister Mary Veronica was enraptured and Sister Mary Clothilde Evers considered it genius, on the basis of combined ease of production and fine word management. But young Sisters in the province, exploring twentieth century trends, found these stretches of blank verse uninspiring and suitable chiefly to the theatrical type of recitation on which Sister Louise, S.H., André, still insisted as commencement day offerings. It was ironical that Sister Anthony should have found Sister Anna's poems, which she otherwise admired, lacking in passion. Her own poetry is hardly impassioned; perhaps her grand manner and Victorian phrases prevent this achievement. One wishes that she had been impressed more deeply by Aeschylus than by Tennyson. As it was, Greek tragedy was later reading in her case; even her "Prometheus" lacks the stark dread that the subject should stir. Her attempt, too, to Christianize the subject, after the manner of too many nun poets, seems unworthy of her intelligence. Still, half a century ago, many a reader of the *Quarterly* would have considered these long poems the magazine's finest writing. Those especially who had experienced her forcefulness of mind in the classroom would have likely agreed. In general, it was fortunate that she should have been "manager" of the *Quarterly*. And if its allotment of space to alumnae and campus affairs seems relatively small, its literary purpose is thereby the better served. Reader or writer, the Notre Dame woman was presumably in a state of intellectual development; she would look to the *Quarterly* for proportionate satisfaction. To any who had lagged, the magazine brought fresh incentive as well as reminder of pristine ambitions. Its level was in keeping with that of their training. They were proud of it. To that cultured leader and alumna, Kate Blythe Cothran, the *Quarterly* was "a dream realized."

Still Notre Dame women, old and young, found special joy in the "school" sections, with accent shifting toward the contemporary as the early burst of reminiscences exhausted itself. Sister Anthony's touch lends a special vividness to her own teaching years with her gift of shrewd comment and telling soubriquet, though she never fails to establish historic links. She reprinted for instance, Alice Tisdall's schoolgirl poem "Valparaiso" commemorating the golden jubilee of Notre Dame on the Pacific Coast, and as well the long sojourn of the French Pillots in Peru.[4] Honoring three fine old families, Sister entered Elena Wolfskill's "A Californian Hero" in September, 1910, the ancestors of this beautiful graduate of 1896 seeming perhaps a more impelling cause of publishing than the poem itself.

In some instances friendship seems to have been responsible for rather weak selections. Minnie Livingston's effusion about pirates attacking *l'Infatigable*, and Mary Gallagher's romantic views of childhood might well have been omitted. Mary's three pages of sugary sentiment could hardly have pleased Sister

Anthony, but Mary was as general a favorite as her older sister, Sister Mary Rosario, whose poetic religious bits used to appear on pious cards as treasures in every religious prayerbook.[5]

A visit to the college, or perhaps merely a note or announcement, won very special treatment for "old families" in the *Quarterly*. Alice Graves of the Class of 1899, the beautiful daughter of the Jackson A. Graves family of Los Angeles, was one of these. Another frequent name is the "well loved child," Jennie Lathrop, entered early in the school by her famous aunt, Mrs. Leland Stanford, who shared her joys and sorrows with her friend, Sister Anna Raphael.[6]

Sister Anthony bestows a like touch of veneration as she enters the names of Anita Virginia Oreña and her sister Herminia, great granddaughters of Don José de la Guerra, Fifth Spanish Commandant of Royal Presidio in Santa Barbara. Sister's mood is understandable; she had enrolled the girls in 1906 amid the general rejoicing of Sisters who had taught their mother, Minnie Ortiz, and her sister Virginia. And as unlikely as she was to untangle genealogical connections, Sister Anthony knew that the girls' paternal grandmother, María Antonía de la Guerra, and the gracious if formidable María Angustias, mother of the literary Rebecca Ord, were sisters. Besides, the school's roster held the names of Delfina and Hermina de la Guerra, daughters of Don Pablo de la Guerra. Anita Hartnell and her daughter, Virginia Zabala, were also De la Guerra descendants. In all, the two Oreñas arrived at Notre Dame fortified with family ties outnumbered only by the Martin Murphys. And the joy caused by their arrival marks their *Quarterly* memories. Anita Oreña Dibblee describes old Notre Dame as "the loveliest enclosure of ten acres I have ever seen" where "dear loving Sisters" spent themselves in the "care and training that has remained through these many years."

An exciting era was beginning at Notre Dame, one reminiscent of the impetus of the 1860s. The change from seclusion and tradition was due partly to accreditation and partly to the increasing need of well-trained high school teachers. For some time preparation of these future teachers for their university

Sara Quinlan, class of 1892, at left above. Sara, later Sister Anthony, S.H., posed for the usual graduation photo with crown and diploma.

At left, the regal Marie Dillon (Lally) retained her poise as well as her almost astounding vocabulary into her ninety-ninth year. For decades she was a leader in the San Francisco Harp Association.

Luz Asturias, above, little Guatemalienne at Notre Dame at the turn of the Century, who still loves to share her memories of school and play, but most of all of her "good Sisters".

The lovely picture of Dolly
McCone, class of 1885, was
taken by John Noe of Vir-
ginia City, Nevada. A fine
student, Dolly, as leader of
"The Funnies", talked the
Sisters into more latitude in
the matter of uniforms.

At right: Innocent Wolfskill. Alice,
the third Wolfskill sister, in the
1890s became Sister Agnes, S.H.

Class of 1896. Four beauties enhanced by hats. 1. Elena Wolfskill.
2. Hortense Mangin. 3. Mary Wilcox. 4. Minnie Phelps.

Betty Tisdale at left, Class of 1892.
She captured many scholastic honors.

Architect's plan of the campus. (About 1885) East of the central quadrangle the Select Day Academy fronts on Santa Clara Street, with Notre Dame Hall directly behind it. To the west on Santa Clara is St. Joseph's Parish School, later Notre Dame High School. North of this is the Sisters' House. The dining hall and kitchen complex lie behind Sisters' House and Chapel.

Jennie Lathrop, niece of Mrs. Leland Stanford, in a typical First Communion photo.

Eugenie Pichon. As debutante in Washington, D. C., she defended western poets against eastern criticism.

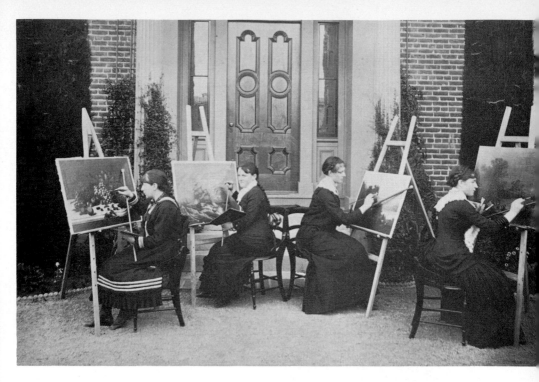

The Class of 1883 was strong in art. Here Minnie Urie,
Lucia Holbrook, Marie Dillon, and Maria Lucas perform
for the benefit of the photographer.

The play is forgotten, but the leading role is taken by
Betty Tisdale at her most assured.

Ina Coolbrith, friend of Sister Anna Raphael and Sister Anthony, S.H., occasional lecturer at Notre Dame and noted poet.

Margaret O'Brien (below) as Queen Esther, recalls the frequent biblical dramas.

Amparo Corral, student from Mexico City. First Communion was received at 12 or later.

Four later Notre Dame girls. Hazel Nolting, left, Class of 1907 and Clare Mc-
Namee, Class of 1918, were among the top rating Greek and Latin students and
became successful teachers of classic languages.

Marie DiBernardi, left, below, Class of 1913, carried on the tradition of dramatics,
art and music, was also "city editor" of *Notre Dame Quarterly*.

Daughter of Anita Hartnell, Virginia Zabala continued her mother's successes at
Notre Dame. She was the granddaughter of pioneer W. E. P. Hartnell.

training would be Notre Dame's mission and opportunity. Sister Anthony, certainly abetted by Sister Anna, became prime mover in this work of preparation. To what extent her heart was in it is clear from the reports of Notre Dame girls in the early numbers of the *Quarterly*. And to what extent Sister Anthony was setting her stamp on her girls is clear from the number who turned to the classics for their career. From her hands they entered the universities reading Vergil and Cicero with ability, with a sound foundation in Greek, and above all with a positive thirst for classical studies. The first of these was petite, golden haired Dorothy Singer, daughter of the J. A. Singer family of Goldfield, Nevada. Younger than her classmates, Dorothy graduated from the University of Nevada in three years, and spent a year of graduate study there. Sister Anthony reported that she won her M.A., then joined Isabel Duff at Stanford to pursue Greek while acting as teaching assistant. Sister Anthony was proud of her performance, and slightly complacent over the fact that her college grades in Latin and Greek had been higher than those she had given her, but it was also clear in these *Quarterly* notices that Sister's mind was set on degrees from the University of California and Stanford for Notre Dame girls.

Thus it was at the advice of Sister Anthony and Sister Anna Raphael that John C. Duff of Menlo Park sent his daughters Isabel and Margaret to Stanford University, its campus almost adjoining his former home on Kings Mountain Road above Woodside. Isabel's fine article, "Memories of Maro," in the *Quarterly* of December, 1910, indicates a maturity that must have delighted her relative Sister Anna Raphael.[7] Isabel became a valued lay teacher at Notre Dame. Her sister Carmelita took her degree the following year and then went to Chicago for special work in children's librarianship. Her recollections of "old Notre Dame" are not so merry in the telling as are those of her classmate, Hortense White, yet a keen humor flashes in her psychological insights.

Two somewhat more vocal about their achievements in their letters to Sister Anthony were Hazel Marie Nolting, and

Mary Florence Connelly. Phi Beta Kappa Hazel was perhaps Notre Dame's most generally fine student at this time, Sister Anthony commented happily on Hazel's enthusiasm over her Honors Latin course at University of California. Mary Florence, "our Thucydides," stayed on at the university for the teaching year. History is the usual subject of her letters. Reading them, one finds no surprise that as history teacher in the Alameda High School Mary soon became a leading educator in the Bay Area. It would seem, in fact, that the small classes of Notre Dame were contributing well to the public high school faculties, though a few, like Isabel Duff, returned to teach in their Alma Mater. Mary Grim of the Class of 1908, daughter of the Charles F. Grim family of Anaheim, was one of these. At the University of California Mary pursued Latin to her heart's content, "with Chinese for variation." Majoring in Latin becomes almost a refrain through these years. Mary's equally bright classmate, Cecilia Kays, daughter of the J. C. Kays family of Hollywood, took her degree in Latin at Trinity.

Sister Anthony, however, did not overstress Latin. She expected her "Thucydides" to be a history teacher; she also approved, albeit with some surprise, the choice of Ruth Grim, Mary's younger sister who elected agriculture. In general the attraction of Latin and also Greek for Sister Anthony's girls was due to her vital teaching. To read Vergil or Horace with her was to acquire a lifetime interest. Sight reading in Latin was the great desideratum and Greek was the reward. But Sister Anthony was inspiring on many levels, and though she had fewer keys to the universe than did Sister Anna Raphael, she still exercised a diversified and tremendously humanizing influence. Sister Catharine Julie Cunningham, President of College of Notre Dame in the 1960s, recalls her occasional announcement of a walk over the Belmont hills, instead of regular class, and the enlightening, if casual conversation along the old bridle paths.

School and alumnae notes in the *Quarterly* indicate that freedom from racial prejudice which characterized so strongly both Sister Anthony and Sister Anna Raphael, a trait the more remarkable since it was not too generally shared. There were Sisters who believed that both community and school would be better without "the dark races." To some it seemed regrettable that their presence, especially in numbers, should be financially necessary in the boarding school. But Sister Anthony shared no such misgivings. She wrote with real joy of the "golden record" of beautiful Abigail Campbell of the Class of 1900, when this eldest daughter of adventurer Irishman James Campbell and descendant of a long line of Maui warriors, Kuaihilani Maipine-pine, became the bride of Prince David Kawananakoa in 1902, with classmate Anita Christal as her bridesmaid. The falling of an island monarch meant nothing to Sister Anthony; "Abby" was a princess and the embodiment of royalty which she had matched with her "golden record." Her sister Alice also left a fine record, and their devotion to Notre Dame was no doubt responsible for the large number of registrations from Hawaii after 1900. Abigail's two younger sisters, Muriel and Beatrice came later to Notre Dame. The Princess brought her own daughters, Kapiolani Kawananakoa and Liliuokalani. Marion Dowsett of Honolulu graduated with Abigail in 1900 as did also Louisa Bradley, organizer of the Honolulu Notre Dame Alumnae Chapter, Rosalie Cunha, in 1901, Lucille and Isabel Mutch, in 1903, making with Irene Crook of Maui, a majority for Hawaii that year. Irene Wills, from Pahala Kau and Ada Rhodes from Honolulu appear often in the *Quarterly*. Their successors in the last years of "old Notre Dame" were Winifred Weddick and Dorothy Peacock.

The *Quarterly* preserves the memory of the school's Central Americans in such names as Asturias, Corral and Matheu. Luz Asturias Moreno arrived as a pre-school tot with her older sisters, Elisa and Raquel. She now recalls weeping when Sister Clare Callan was appointed Superior at Notre Dame Institute and thus left the boarding school. Sister Clare, she says, pro-cured lightweight uniforms for the Central Americans when the days turned warm. Sister Aurelie and Sister Léontine made eggnogs for her because she looked puny. Sister Ignacia carried her upstairs when she fell from a swing. Sister Flora told most wonderful stories. Father Alexander Mazzetti, S.J., reproved her for stealing grapes from the arbor, but fortunately there was also an apricot tree.

There was also five-year-old Domitila de la Rocha from Sinaloa, the school's darling, spoiled as tots always were by Sister Léontine. Like other Hispanic-American children, Domitila was greatly attracted by blue eyes and fair skin, and especially by angelic-faced Sister Monica Budde, who started the minims toward musicianship in the conservatory. Almost any time of day found this tiny admirer mounting step by step to the second floor, on each step calling "Seester Monica!" to the general delight.

On these pages are Guatemalans Virginia and Margot Matheu, who filled the last days of old Notre Dame with lovely music. Later came their friends, Mercedes and Concha Baucelles who moved to Belmont with the college and established the Guatemalan tradition there before returning to their homeland. Concha married Julio R. Matheu, brother of Virginia and Margot. She visits Belmont now and then, renewing each time her plea that the Sisters of Notre Dame return soon to Guatemala. Maria and Sara McManus, of the Classes of 1905 and 1906, bright girls of unmistakable Central American heritage despite their name, were loyal contributors to the *Quarterly* before Sara lost her sight. Social-minded Dolores Bonillas from Nogales in Sonora, with an eye on an early debut, persuaded *la Madre* to allow her to return home without finishing the conservatory course. Alas, Lola found training for coming out a bit gruelling. Agreeing with the family that she was far from prepared, she returned to graduate in 1907, regaling her classmates with the strict training required by society in Nogales and gaining poise by her daily promenade with a book on her head. Talented girls like Lola, María Harispuru and Rosita Tarriba were intensely proud of their heritage. They were well bred and patient, but they were justly annoyed by María Antonía Field's too frequent claims of *sangre pura,* made, they felt, at the expense of the native strain of which most of them were conscious. In the face of such racial condescension,

a Central American rebellion in the recreation hall was understandable. Sister Anthony was deaf to it, and María was wiser
for it.

The Far East was less well represented. From Hakodate,
Japan in 1914 came the four daughters of Englishman E. J.
King and his fabulously wealthy Japanese wife, and from Yoko-
hama, the two daughters of Irishman T. M. Laffin and his Japanese wife, seemingly also wealthy. It was apparently not the
intention of the Kings to be exploited intellectually, though
the eldest, Annie was bookishly inclined. All four were musicians. Marguerite graduated from the conservatory in 1918, a
harpist of high talent. Dorothy and Alice became accomplished
musicians and needlewomen as their mother had hoped. Eleanor and Myrtle Laffin followed the same pattern. The study
programs of their racial successors at present day Notre Dame
would have shocked any of these girls. They did, of course,
acquire a fair mastery of English. Ethel Laffin, younger sister of
Eleanor and Myrtle, translated so skillfully from the Japanese
that Sister Anthony included her offerings in the *Quarterly*.

The generous space devoted to the foreign student in the
pages of the *Quarterly* points to Sister Anthony's desire that the
magazine should assist the school itself in its efforts to lessen
interracial and international barriers. Yet in the last years of the
college in San Jose, the number of foreign students decreased,
and distance prevented most of them from participating in
alumnae activities. It was chiefly Californians, and especially
San Joseans of those later years who afforded alumnae leadership after the transfer to Belmont. Leading this list was Alice
Turel of San Jose. This sweet-faced girl of the Class of 1897
spent her life in charitable works. With the Altar Society as a
starting point Alice kept her hand in Notre Dame projects, her
generous gifts to the Memorial Chapel at Belmont stand among
many others to her Alma Mater.[8]

Anna and Estelle Kelly, graduates of 1898 and 1899, and
daughters of a prominent Watsonville family, should be noted
as strong alumnae leaders, as also Annie Hughes of 1898, of
Watsonville. And there were May Talbot and her sisters Jose-

phine and Maud, daughters of a pioneer Montana family, who wrote faithfully and spread the name of Notre Dame in the Northwest. Sister Anthony's "little Mormon of Salt Lake City," Frances McChrystal of 1908, another strong alumna, is the mother and grandmother of Notre Dame girls.[9] Beatrice E. Messmer, Class of 1910, who modestly claims "no distinction" in her school days, wrote for the *Quarterly* with real ability.[10]

Many formed the habit of sending contributions long after leaving Notre Dame. Eugénie Pichon, whose political connections necessitated life in the nation's capital, wrote delightful letters as a Washington debutante. Her bright humor, her knowledge of persons and affairs in the Taft administration, as well as the depth of her cultural understanding, flow along with the deep current of school memories. Her defense of Bret Harte and Marcella Fitzgerald in discussion with those who saw little of literary importance west of the Atlantic seaboard delighted Sister Anthony,[11] who was weighting the historic and literary content of the *Quarterly* quite heavily in favor of the West.

The frequent appearance of Ina Coolbrith's poems indicate her attraction for Sister Anthony, though they were also witness to the poet's long friendship with Sister Anna Raphael. The *Quarterly*, June, 1912, is dedicated to this poet of the West, with laudatory pieces by Charles Phillips, Elizabeth Lightner, Mrs. Norman Martin, President of Pacific Coast Press Association, and others. Sister Anthony's poem in honor of her friend is one of the best in a small collection entitled "A Valentine to Ina Coolbrith" found in the Coolbrith Papers in the Bancroft Library. The honors accorded Harriet Skidmore have been noted. These two noted poets were western and inspiring; besides, they were friends of Notre Dame.

Charles Warren Stoddard was almost an idol. There are frequent Stoddard articles and poems, and when Virginia Reed Murphy turned over to Sister Anna Raphael her Stoddard correspondence, Sister Anthony gave it full space.

When the popular writing couple, Edward Cothran and Kate Blythe Cothran brought their long nature effusions to

Sister Anna, Sister Anthony printed them, too. Both wrote solemnly beautiful cosmic thoughts, touched with mysticism, in run-on blank verse in the manner of William Cullen Bryant, the kind that Sister Anthony liked to read aloud in her classes.[12] What she looked for was exalted thought well turned. When she found it in the lovely poem by Florence Garesche Macauley of the Class of 1893, she entered it in March, 1912, in full.

Rebecca Ord, whose gift Sister Anna Raphael had polished to brilliance in 1877, was welcomed to the *Quarterly*. Rebecca wrote fine prose, chiefly about pre-American California, which appeared in other magazines as well. She wrote humorously, too; her "Parable from the Book of Days" is a clever forecast of A.D. 5900.[13] All *Quarterly* prose, in fact, makes good reading, even today.

Though Sister Anthony was pleased with the level of contribution, some contributors gave her special pleasure. Helen McKeever, 1906, delighted her with a humorous sonnet on the little wooden signals used in class until not too long ago by all Sisters of Notre Dame to give directions and to maintain silence that left no place for a busy working hum. What pleased Sister most was her girls' writing back after graduation. She savored their names: Edith O'Brien, Alice Griffin, Corinne Dolcini and Edith Watson. The list was lengthy, including names from her own school days: Louisa and Isabel Need, Elizabeth Murphy. There were the five daughters of the Charles F. Wilcox family of San Jose, Harriet, Mary, Hilda, Monica and Ruth, along with her first students, Pauline Ivancovich and Grace Buckley.

The *Quarterly* was a tremendous work, running to a hundred pages, its format elegant. But as Sister Anna Raphael read copy and Sister Anthony dashed off articles on her typewriter, neither perhaps realized the record it would afford of College of Notre Dame from its beginning, the special witness it would offer of a fine school in the early twentieth century, an orderly and completely teacher-directed school in which, however, the student milieu was expansion of thought and liberty of spirit.

Chapter 20   OLD SAN JOSE

*T*he last six and a half years of Sister Mary Bernardine's life were referred to by her Sisters as her golden sunset. Even materially things went well despite the depression that followed in the wake of the post-earthquake building boom. The boarding school income, which had risen from $16,000 in 1901 to $40,000 in 1906, levelled to a slightly lower average for nearly a decade. The conservatory, too, was an increasing financial asset; its income in the year 1912 was estimated as over its building cost. It seems little wonder that the cult of St. Expeditus flourished, and that Treasurer Sister Louise des Séraphines was among his leading devotees.[1]

The sunset was enhanced, of course, by the celebration of Sister Mary Bernardine's golden jubilee of profession. Had she been inclined to self-complacency, this occasion would surely have ministered to it. Every printed and written congratulation emphasized her high distinction, chiefly as leader of a united and enthusiastic group of teaching Sisters, a doubly notable distinction, as Sister Anthony remarked, because of her earlier three decades of leadership in New England. Archbishop Riordan celebrated the jubilee mass, July 31, 1912, and his sermon, inspired by the *Magnificat,* pleased the jubilarian with its emphasis on all dedicated Sisters. Her beautiful gifts from community, family, and friends, were a special joy, since they rounded out the treasure of the chapel. In its ornate way, that building stood now, an outward sign of her life's work. On her occasional good days through her final illness, she spent hours in it praying for the apostolate of Notre Dame.

When Sister Mary Bernardine died, January 3, 1913, friends thronged into the chapel for her funeral mass, and heard their Archbishop proclaim that hers "was no ordinary

life," that she had "built up a great work," and that she had
"ruled not by harsh measures, but by a mother's love." Her
good friend, Reverend Robert Sesnon, had come a great distance to celebrate an earlier mass for her that morning, using
the magnificent chalice which he had presented to her some
years before. The spring number of the *Quarterly* was given
entirely to articles, poems, and messages of condolence for
which its pages lacked sufficient space. Alumna Anita Christal
Purdy seemed to sum up many of them in her words, " . . . her
influence will continue . . . in the hearts of her girls scattered
the world over." Perhaps the most touching *Quarterly* tribute
is "Consecration," by Edward O. Tivnan, S.J., the nephew
whose priesthood had given so much joy to Sister Mary Bernardine. Sister Anthony's own nine-page paean, "Loss and
Gain," with gorgeous apocalyptical allusion, is clearly her attempt to express her personal feeling. A less expansive tribute
came from her onetime pupil, Ellen G. Moriarity, of Salem,
Massachusetts. Here is a picture of an unforgettable teacher,
and besides, "a model of easy grace. She had the stateliest
manners, and her speech was most dignified; but she was not
too proud for merriment."[2]

The appointment of Sister Mary Veronica as Provincial
followed the death of Sister Mary Bernardine. The first uneventful months of the new provincialate were a lull before the
outbreak of World War I, which for its duration cut off American Notre Dame from Namur. Then returning peace ushered
in certain canonical changes, and found Sister Mary Veronica
explaining regulations which canceled out long-standing articles of religious constitutions. Sister Mary Veronica moved
promptly with these changes.[3] In fact, some noted an eagerness
about her in these matters which was not always so easily dis-
cerned in persons of lesser authority. It was the same sort of
determination which she displayed in the matter of Sisters'
education. Today Sister Mary Veronica would certainly stand
among the more forward looking major Superiors, yet the most
progressive would not then have dreamed, for instance, of
changing the almost monastic structure of the house in San Jose,

a structure in which concentration seemed strength. Parish convents would have seemed a weakness, a serious division. Return to the central house was a blessing; on returning, the good religious maintained no correspondence with her former mission, for such contacts and progress in personal sanctity seemed incompatible.

Thus despite a growing divergence of activity, and the fact that actually the old distinction between boarding and day schools still existed, solidarity and *esprit de corps* flourished in the community. Frequent routine gatherings with all present helped to maintain this centeredness. And certainly proximity to the novitiate, with its emphasis on community spirit, was a factor, the more potent because of the succession of four novice mistresses of long tenure, all of them convinced that the welfare of the Apostolate depended largely on the ferver of community living.

Sister Mary Annunciata, last of these mistresses, took up her work after a broken five-year interval during which the office had been held briefly by three, the last, Sister Angela, S.H., her own younger sister. As Rose Anna McDermott she entered the novitiate, beautiful and utterly sheltered, the perfect 19th century symbol of womanhood. Loved by her family, she was also loved by every novice who came and went through the next 15 years. To the end she was always head of a community, if possible increasingly unbusinesslike with years, but always loved, the far-flung periphery of her peace enclosing the harrassed. When a former novice complained to her one day that she was finding the going a bit rough, she led her to a large framed list of deceased Sisters of the province and asked her to name the five or six whom she had most admired. Smiling approval at the Sister's choices, she asked her next to name the five or six who had suffered the most undeservedly. When Sister found herself naming the same half dozen, Sister Mary Annunciata smiled cheerfully and remarked, "My dear, I am happy to see you in such fine company."

Without benefit of Sister Formation, none of these mistresses had special preparation for their work other than directives found in the brief "Rule of the Mistress of Novices," and the writings of the foundress.[4] They knew little theology, Sister Mary Annunciata least of all. The *Codification of Canon Law* in 1918 was her only ecclesiastical adaptation; and to this she referred with wonder. When spiritual books began to present Thomistic fare, she considered them academic and useful for the very studious. Girls who came to the novitiate fresh from the hands of such teachers as Sister Mary Alexis or Sister Xaveria, were troubled by the childlike quality of her instructions. But these, too, came to understand her simple approach to their concerns. She made no claim to an understanding of all problems, nor did she minimize their possible complexity or importance. Her respect for the individual would not allow rapid and final analysis of novitiate troubles.

Perhaps Sister Mary Annunciata's attitude toward change inspired young confidence as much as anything else. For while so many around her considered anticipation of change in the Institute wholly anathema, Sister Mary Annunciata believed that some adaptation was in order. When a novice who considered deprivation of general reading the greatest trial of the novitiate, heard a retreat master utter strictures that threatened to extend it to her future life, Sister Mary Annunciata assured her that a change of view was in the offing in this regard, and should be. The custom of sending untrained novices out to teach was regrettable, especially since girls were entering younger than formerly. Her desire for proper teacher training struck a hopeful note at a time when superiors were counting on the help of Heaven to convert the inexperienced into teachers. So it was this unsophisticated little Sister, whose quaint speech often carried echoes of the current usage, misquoted or misapplied, whose efforts to straighten her bonnet usually left it more lopsided, was for so many a source of wisdom, at a time when cloying sentiment, with its appeal to the young, marked bits of poetry and retreat notes in which the Passion outweighed the Resurrection. The "Victim Soul" ideal was replacing the "Vow of Perfection," with a note equally certain to keep the spotlight on self. That the circle of the elect was narrow through those later years was perhaps largely due to the twinkle of Sister Mary Annunciata's eyes. Her instruction was oriented in the teaching apostolate.

Through its last two decades in San Jose the college was home for the faculties of three and finally four parish schools, as well as for weekend classes in outlying centers. Instruction in those schools benefited by the supervision of Sisters who entered with state certificates. Sister Mary Ignatia Callahan especially was a guide to generations of young teachers. From her profession in Cincinnati in 1862, her heart was set on going to California "as a missionary." When she died in 1916, the *Mercury-Herald* bestowed lengthy praise on this "gentle, patient, and saintly" Sister.[5] Her co-worker, Sister Mary Philomene Byrne, taught primary girls at St. Joseph's with equal success up to 1927, faithfully initiating each new young Sister in the lunchroom by extending the long handle of a saucepan and pointing to a hook a size too large for the eye in the end of the handle. After the newcomer had grappled with the problem for a few seconds, Sister Mary Philomene would hang the saucepan up by the loop in its other side. She laughed as merrily when fun was at her own expense, a fact, no doubt, which brought a crowd on the run when she appeared at lower grades' recess at St. Joseph's.

Perhaps the best loved of all those local parish school teachers was Sister Mary Vincent Burns. Both she and Sister Margaret Mary, her own bustling and excitable sister, were soon deeply involved in St. Francis Xavier's, the Italian School, as it was called. Its three poor, unadorned classrooms, with wide, rough floor boards, became chief interest of conversation in the community, as a center of Mother Julia's apostolate. Certainly this school was Sister Mary Vincent's apostolate. The several young Sisters who in turn kept pace with her rapid stride each morning and witnessed the mutual joy as her pupils welcomed her, knew why she always spoke of them as "beautiful." When she directed their singing, Heaven filled their eyes, as their high, clear voices melted into her rich alto. It was well for St. Francis Xavier's School that another such zealous soul should carry on the work in the person of Sister Mary of the Assumption Curry, an experienced businesswoman when she entered the novitiate in 1915. As completely dedicated as Sister Mary Vincent, she volunteered to work among the poor when the deadly Spanish influenza prostrated so many in Santa Clara County. This was the sort of challenge that appealed to her, yet like Sister Mary Vincent, she hoped for the improvement which the Italian families of San Jose were not long in overtaking.

Sister Mary Pauline Kennedy, represents the slightly aloof, dignified, but kind and gentle parish Sister of those final decades. As principal of St. Joseph's School, 1908 to 1920, she maintained a well-oiled discipline, never lost sight of yet requiring only infrequent recourse to her authority. Seeing her completing a pile of reports in the community room just at the stroke of the bell, one might well guess at the precision of life at St. Joseph's. A thorough teacher, she probably foresaw little change in education and less need for it. Her special achievement was school entertainment. She loved the pretty cantatas and Christmas plays that music houses were supplying and kept mothers busy making fairy and flower costumes and matching slippers, hose, ribbon, and dainty organdy in city stores. Without fuss the whole complicated production went like clockwork at the appointed hour and with utter smoothness, the one exception it seems, being the descent of a line of Christmas angels from on high by means of a plank concealed by trees and rocks. Hands folded and singing sweetly, each in turn discovered a slight wobbling in the plank and each in turn took on a look of unangelic horror. Then with feet securely set once more, each reassumed her interrupted bliss with a control which only a Sister Mary Pauline could instill. Behind the scene, she was fortunately spared the sight of this small fiasco, but not the young Sister Rita Marie Taylor, musical director of the cantata, who viewed it from the rear door and later regaled the community with hilarious re-enactment.

Two Irish-born parish teachers, Sister Mary Lucidie Kissane and Sister Mary of St. Anne Deasy, stressed the three R's, and both, by dint of praise and emulation, made homework somehow palatable. A "foundation stone" in Santa Barbara, Sister Mary Lucidie had long since learned how to deal with difficulties when she came to St. Joseph's. As Sister Mary Lucidie never quite abandoned certain speech characteristics of County Mayo, her pupils were soon easily recognized by an unmistakable merry lilt and by the transfer of stress in long words. This mattered not, since they were also known for orderly notebooks, long division "worked" correctly, and that *summum bonum*, sensibly stated paragraphs, albeit with the ornate capitals so completely out of conformity with Palmer Method of Penmanship, a matter of slight significance to Sister's lengthening list of friends.

Excepting a few years at Notre Dame Institute, Sister Mary of St. Anne spent her long teaching years at St. Joseph's and St. Leo's, which she opened as its first principal in 1915. With less of the Celtic in speech and manner she shared Sisiter Mary Lucidie's warmhearted humor, a gift appreciated most of all by her fellow novice, Sister Anthony, S.H. Thus it seems quite in order to find hilarious bits written by third and fourth grade boys in the distinguished company of *Quarterly* letter writers, together with the pleased reactions of the editor-in-chief. When a St. Joseph's fourth grade leader of men, quite innocent of spelling, presented Sister Mary of St. Anne with a set of rules for "The Sucity [sic] of Good Boys," Sister Anthony shared it straightway with readers of the *Quarterly*, especially since one section promised that members in good standing would have the right and duty to "beat up" unruly elements in the school.

Among the sprinkling of experienced public school grade teachers who became Sisters of Notre Dame were Sister Mary Albertus Traynor of Sierra County, and Sister Sylvester Arnoldy, who brought what her fellow novices called a trunkful of certificates. Later came Sister Marie Theresa, B.S. Bernhart, a Notre Dame girl and graduate of San Jose State Normal

School, with some years of public school experience. Another was May McCullough, a recognized leader in the public school system of San Francisco, who decided to unite her career with consecration. As Sister Mary Patricia, she continued her leadership as supervisor of Notre Dame grade schools. Her zeal gave tremendous impetus to the movement toward higher education for all teachers, but her best gift was her own teaching example. Her teaching of mathematics on any level opened for the onlooker hitherto undreamed of numerical meaning, and the marvel was how often her pupils themselves made the discoveries. Her quick wit and hearty laughter, however, left no cause for wonder about her pupils' attraction to her. As a white-veiled novice, she presented a novel sight surrounded on visiting day by a dozen or more young lads from San Francisco.

On the roster of parish school Sisters who set out on foot from College of Notre Dame each morning are such well-remembered names as Sister Mary Stanislaus Fennell, Sister Joseph Aloyse Kast, and Sister Alphonse Marie Kane. Sister Blondine, S.H. Keenan, pioneer at St. Francis Xavier School, spent many fruitful years at St. Leo's. Sister Regina Marie Schoen, has headed a succession of Notre Dame schools, usually as superior, and Sister Geraldine, S.H. Sinnott, teacher of phonics to a generation of first grade girls at St. Joseph's, has since shared her rich experience in other schools of the province. Sister Mary Callistus Ivancovich, who taught music at St. Joseph's School in those days, now heads the music department at Notre Dame Elementary School at College of Notre Dame in Belmont. There are besides, Sister Marie Ivan Kessler and Sister Marie Félicienne Ramazzina, who laid the foundation of fine teaching careers in those final years in San Jose. Sister Mary Perpetua Driscoll and Sister Elizabeth, S.H. Herzog were among the best known of Notre Dame's elementary teachers.

Outstanding high school teachers of the province, too, had their first experiences in the boarding school and in Notre Dame High School. There were Sister Mary Bartholomew Blake, honor graduate of Mission Dolores, whose fine teaching

San Joseans still recall, and Sister Julia, S.H. Hassett of Watsonville, a gracious but aloof soul who found mathematical problems good entertainment, and who kept in close touch with scientific development.

Another well-remembered teacher was Sister Cecilia Louise Shepherd, youngest daughter of an Oakland family which gave its three sons to the Society of Jesus and their three sisters to Notre Dame. Their naturalist father, William Shepherd, moved his family from the city to a secluded canyon in the Oakland Hills which came to bear his name. From accompanying her father on his scientific tours, Cecilia became at an early age a collector and classifier of California flora. Though she lacked Sister Anna Raphael's universal scope and synthesis, she was certainly her heir in creating scientific interest. The hills of the East Bay, Marin and Cupertino were to her open books which her students also quickly learned to read. Her older twin sisters were Sister Angela Marie and Sister Agnes Stanislaus Shepherd.

Sister Barbara Engs of Oakland, and Sister Aloyse Marie Reich of San Francisco, began their teaching careers in Notre Dame's last decade on Santa Clara Street. After the removal from Santa Clara Street in 1923, Sister Barbara became principal of Notre Dame High School in its new location at Second and Reed Streets. She succeeded Sister Anthony, S.H., as dean of the junior college at Belmont. Sister Aloyse Marie, first Doctor of Philosophy in the province, later joined the faculty as head of the history department. Sister St. James Doyle taught chemistry, physics, and botany with a gentle sort of thoroughness, and by reason of abiding poor health, spent weekends at the villa in Saratoga where she wrote much sweet but ineffectual verse.

Some of the Sisters professed in San Jose during those last years were never members of that community. Three of these, Sister Mary Aquinas Mehl, Sister Mary of St. Gregory Driscoll, and Sister Marie Eucharista Suber, should be mentioned here because of later leadership in the California Province. And among the novices who entered in San Jose but were professed in Belmont, were Sister Dolores Marie O'Connor, and her cousins, Sister Margaret Clare and Sister Patricia Marie O'Connor, and the future mistress of novices, Sister Joseph Marie Petar. Younger Sisters of the conservatory kept the community choir at an all-time high throughout the last years in San Jose. Besides those mentioned earlier there were the talented organist, Sister Maria Agatha Heinz, a musician discovered by Sister Irene, S.H., herself in Salinas, and Hawaiian-born Sister Marie Ernestine Vredenburg, descendant of an early Dutch colonial New Jersey family, who came to Notre Dame for a business education, but ended by following her musical bent in the conservatory. Sister Angela Bernardine Smith was fourth of the Alameda family of singing Smiths to graduate at Notre Dame. She was professed in 1921 with her cousin, Sister Mary Loretto Fealy.

Graduates of Notre Dame High School in the novitiate represented well-known Santa Clara Valley families. Besides those mentioned above there were Sister Mary of the Visitation O'Neill and her classmate, Sister Mary Letitia, S.H. Cunningham who affected each other mirthfully, but despite the soubriquet "gigglers," acquired in time a due gravity. It was otherwise with Sister Mary Anselm Sinnott, who abandoned her life-of-the-party manners at the convent door and became at once the sweet but grave Good Samaritan of the novitiate. Others were Sister Mary of St. Agnes Enright, a talented musician; Sisters Agnes Joseph and Claire Bernardine Voss; Sister Bridget Marie McKenzie, outstanding teacher of science; and Sister Loretto Julie Costello, member of the English faculty at College of Notre Dame in Belmont.

The prevailing good health in that large community was largely due to the skillful management of the kitchen by Sister Madeleine, S.H. McLean. Without electric oven or gadget, she served plentiful, wholesome, and most appetizing meals to some two hundred daily. Sister Mary Veronica's concern for health prompted the enrollment of Sister Bridget of the Immaculate Conception and others in whatever nursing courses were available, a first step toward the day of registered nurses in community and school. Sister Bridget was third of four Donnelley sisters to enter Notre Dame in San Jose. Sarah, Sister Mary Agnes, and Bridget, Sister Mary Columba, had preceded her. Her younger sister, Anna, Sister Julia, B.S. entered later with their cousin, Mary Donnelley, Sister Theresa, S.H. Excepting Sister Mary Columba, these Sisters were stationed in San Jose, ably heading one or other of the "charges." Novices and young Sisters became models of attentiveness and punctuality as servers under Sister Theresa's direction in the boarders' dining hall, where organization reached such heights as to win the unlikely accolades of both Sister Madeleine, S.H. and head mistress Sister Mary of St. George Harney. The least perceptive novice realized that her success in maneuvering in this Scylla and Charybdis situation was entirely due to Sister Theresa's management and her unobtrusive danger signals.

As head of the charge then referred to briefly as "The Black," Sister Joseph, B.S. Pollman did more than make and repair habits and veils, and that skillfully. A fitting in Sister Joseph's room was an experience in thoughtfulness, an example in action of Sister Mary Annunciata's injunction to perform services for the Sisters as one would for a person of great worth and dignity. And for this reason, no doubt, Sister Joseph's bits of pious advice, her kind little queries about one's family or work as she measured a skirt length, had the ring of tremendous sincerity. Today Sister Joseph would be classed "outgoing," and others in that community would share the epithet. Little Sister Mary Carmel Keeler, could scarcely have been a more affable assistant portress, despite certain small leanings toward primness. If her delicate handling of dishes, the result of her endless china painting, suggested restraint as she served a guest in the parlor, her ready flow of small talk dispelled the impression. Headportress Sister Borgia of the Nativity Starck, admitted comers with no touch of primness, her manner nicely balanced between the polite and the casual, her conversation unstudied. Between doorbells she made and repaired the large rosaries worn with the Notre Dame habit, an occupation which gave her somehow the absorbed look of an ancient hermit. Business received at the lodge often took Sister Borgia to the office of Sister Mary Catherine Quinn, successor to the charge of Sister Louise des Séraphines and Sister Angela, S.H. McDermott. Sister Mary Catherine's financial acumen reminded older Sisters of "the first Sister Marie Catherine." Her contemporaries wondered more at the unfailing fitness of her cryptic remarks; at least one of them thought these gems should be recorded as examples of this subtle form of Gaelic wit.

These and the many mentioned in connection with school and conservatory composed an extremely varied community as old Notre Dame on Santa Clara Street drew near its final days. The Victorian manner still won golden opinion; the zeal of Jansen now and then clothed an unbeautiful urge; sentimentalism canonized the tears of Father Richard Bell, S.J., brushed away by his blue bandana handkerchief. It was proper to call the annual retreat "grand," and unheard of to question the retreat master's fundamentalist dicta on evolution. Still a certain liberty of spirit began to prevail, especially after the Great War as international affairs became subject of reading and conversation.

And though Sister Mary Veronica tarried a bit at the crossroads in some matters, her shock for instance when she discovered interest among the Sisters in the Divine Office outside of Holy Week ritual, and her abiding distrust of mystical writings, she offered in most respects, a broadminded leadership. Without special talent herself, she valued it as God's gift to the individual and to Notre Dame. She led the way in outgoing friendliness. A grade school girl in Marysville summed up her approach briefly, "She likes us and she likes to come here. You can see it in her eyes." The first Provincial in California affected by the Canonical Code limiting tenure in that office, Sister Mary Veronica introduced her successor, Sister Berchmans Joseph, with the happy grace of the self-forgetting. Custom has made usual this limitation of tenure, but for those accustomed to the notion of superiorship, especially on the higher levels, as lifelong, Sister Mary Veronica's smiling abdication was impressive.[6]

As the new code also dictated that a provincial superior might not be at the same time a local superior, Sister Julia of the Passion Overend was appointed by the General Council to fill that office in San Jose. A superior in New England since 1890, Sister Julia hardly seemed the most adaptable choice. Yet she became shortly "a real Californian," an eager and always somewhat surprised enthusiast who "liked to be here."

*T*here are yet many in San Jose who remember the park-like front gardens of Notre Dame, guarded by the lodge with its arched windows, well barred, and metal doors which bespoke endurance as well as cloistered aloofness, impressions extended by the wall along the streets that enclosed the campus. Yet that lodge door seemed friendly enough when opened by a Sister who, like beautiful Sister Mary Angeline Kelly, took to heart the kind greeting recommended by the Rule of the Portress. Beyond a wide and sunny interval of roses and palms and wistaria, the almost massive central building set up again the note of permanence. In 1920 no visitor would have thought of those campus units as old or decrepit. Nevertheless, during the next two years the Sisters began actively to consider the possibility of relocating the college.[1]

While the brick buildings were in excellent condition, some of them less than half a century old, and the campus itself was as attractive as ever, the adjacent area of the city was by then deteriorating. Business expansion along Santa Clara Street was to be expected, and the resulting commercial activity might well render the present site unsuitable for a school for young ladies. Such a development, too, would surely be followed by a fabulous rise in the value of Notre Dame's acres in the heart of the growing city of San Jose. Enthusiasts estimated the worth of the property at three million dollars, conservatives at one million.

Some of the Sisters considered a change of site unnecessary and foolhardy; others accounted it folly to accept anything less than a million dollars for property on which so much had been expended. Sister Anthony, for her part, felt a bit impatient with both of these opinions. She was one of the most optimistic members of the community, financially, and her

281

confidence was such that she had no great worry about disposal of the old property, once a new site had been decided upon; nevertheless she felt that the valuation of even one million dollars did not square with reality. She considered it contrary to economic law that land should become so valuable by reason of position alone, without being fitted for its future business use. Still, she agreed with the other Sisters that the first bid was too low; a San Jose capitalist named Bean had offered $400,000 cash.

The Sisters' extensive property in the Saratoga foothills might have been a good site for an attractive college campus, but the water supply was dangerously low in dry years. The Stanford estate near Warm Springs, on the other hand, was blessed with a constant supply of water as well as a fine old home, but its location seemed too far from San Jose.

Then came word that the beautiful Ralston estate at Belmont was on the market.[2] It was suggested by the Reverend Michael Murray, headmaster of Archbishop Edward J. Hanna's Military School for Boys at Belmont. The mansion had been taken over by a family named Gardiner and was being operated as a sanitarium which then housed no more than a dozen patients. The story goes that on the Sisters' first trip to Belmont, Notre Dame's earliest chauffeur, the reliable Augustine Barbieri, departed too soon from El Camino Real, took the road over the San Carlos hills and thus added miles of lovely scenery to the approach to Belmont. With this breathtaking entrance, as it were, to Paradise, Sister Anthony begins her long, poetic description, yet her sharp eyes were quick to note excellent reasons for Father Murray's cordial reception and willingness to act as guide. The sight of patients from the sanitarium wandering about in such close proximity to his school must have been disconcerting to him as well as to the parents of his pupils. A ramshackle chicken house, too, stood at the site of Notre Dame's present main entrance, its inmates in a state of neglect. The fastidious headmaster knew well, concluded Sister Anthony, that as owners the Sisters of Notre Dame would soon remove this eyesore. Just as Father Murray hoped, neither this disgusting sight nor the "certain decay of beauty" that marked the stately mansion itself discouraged the visitors. He must have been pleased with the contrast between their enthusiasm and the discouraged attitude of the proprietor.

The visit to the Belmont property brought love at first sight to Sister Berchmans Joseph, according to Sister Anthony. It is quite clear from her poetic telling that she herself was certainly smitten. Here was rural elegance. Despite its comparative youth, the house at once became Sister Anthony's "historic Ralston Mansion," a title that since then has too often appeared in print. While some have in later years professed to see inconsistency between this enthusiasm and the objections to the other sites, it is safe to say that nearly everyone in the community fell under the spell of Belmont with its reliable cool afternoon winds through the summer months.

Sister Mary Veronica Dolan terminated her provincialate in the summer of 1921 and resigned as president of the college Board of Trustees; it was in keeping with her character to withdraw completely from affairs at this time, so her views on the change of site were not made public. She was succeeded by Sister Berchmans Joseph Murphy who, as the new provincial, became *ex officio* President of the Board.

As the Sisters made repeated visits to Belmont the challenge of the place assumed greater magnitude with new discoveries of neglect, and so did their attraction for the property and their planning to make the most of its possibilities. With her love for things Victorian, Sister Anthony declared that no amount of neglect could spoil "the intrinsic beauty of the place," the lightsomeness produced by skylights, the pale pink-and-ivory panels and pillars "in this day of dark-hued homes." This great house must now be changed from a "splendid tomb" to a place "of beautiful hope." Most of the Sisters agreed, though for some the greater attraction was the setting. Returning from an outing in the Belmont hills to the flat, high-walled gardens in San Jose, these talked of the afternoon orchestra in the giant trees and of the general benefits of bucolic life. One or two Cassandras, it seems, uttered warnings about four steep flights of stairs, but these voices were lost in the general approval. For the recently arrived New Englander, Sister Julia of the Passion Overend, the extensive lawn that sloped from the front entrance, the one well-tended garden area, offered the greatest aesthetic pleasure. It happened that this stretch of greensward held special appeal also for one of the hospital inmates, a Harvard genius with a strong compulsion for track. Back and forth he ran on his seemingly endless workout. First to object was Sister Julia of the Passion. When Sister Anthony overheard her lament, "He is ruining our lawn," she laughingly added that to the incentives for hastening the purchase.[3]

More urgent reasons for action were Father Murray's discovery of other prospective buyers for the Gardiner property. One of these, he learned, intended to convert the mansion into a roadhouse; another had plans for a tubercular hospital. Disliking both, of course, he urged the Sisters to proceed with the deal before demand for the place should increase its value. Hard upon this news came a warning from the Gardiners that they could not extend the Notre Dame option further. At this point, one cause of hesitancy on the part of the Sisters was suddenly solved. Adjoining the property was a 52-acre tract, low and suitable for building. This was now offered to them for $17,500. As the purchase price of the Gardiner property was $75,000, the Sisters borrowed $100,000 from the Hibernia Bank in San Francisco and proceeded with both purchases in February, 1922. Sale of even part of the San Jose property would pay off this debt. With all of it disposed of it would be possible to erect school buildings at Belmont.[4]

Though the year failed to bring a purchaser in San Jose, preparations for the transfer to Belmont were continued with assurance, Sister Berchmans Joseph leading activities herself, and prodding the disorganized Gardiners into action when they failed to vacate the house within a month after the deed was drawn up. It needed the arrival of a group of Sisters armed with cleaning materials to produce action. Then one inmate, rising from a late breakfast, scrawled a sign on the menu board in the kitchen, "Goodbye, Paradise. Our beautiful home is broken up." Perhaps he was the Harvard genius.

Thus the Gardiners were eased out, even old Mrs. Gardiner who, since the death of her husband, Dr. A. M. Gardiner, founder of the sanitarium, had lived in cranky grandeur in a suite now occupied by the business offices. Out went fine furniture, sold at a sacrifice, said Mr. Gardiner, since he believed the Sisters would not wish to keep it. With it went some of the Ralston pieces left from the Sharon occupation, though fortunately four fine relics remained, as high spots for the later "Ralston tour:" The koa wood piano made for Ralston by Jacob Zech, one beautiful marble done in Rome by Sculptor John Haseltine in 1868, and two magnificent paintings on the main stairway. Removal of these was, no doubt, too great a task for the Gardiners.

The first attack on the kitchen shelves made it clear that the cleaning of the mansion would require many hands, much time, and a leader of Sister Anthony's determination. Painting, repairs, and adaptation to boarding school and community use could not begin before the removal of quantities of debris. The Sisters themselves had to scrape off layers of dirt that covered the floors, recalled Sister Mary Regis. Still, the Gardiners could be thanked for their sense of historic beauty. The great mirrors, the cut glass chandeliers and almost all of the etched and carved glass paneling had been preserved.

Through the summer holidays all the strong and able of the San Jose community took turns in the almost daily "Belmont cleaning" trips. They combined an element of adventure with window washing and scrubbing accomplishments that extended to all parts of the mansion except the "Grant Room," built for the entertainment of that president by Senator Sharon, after the death of Ralston. Unfortunately it was over a cistern which held hillside seepage as a water supply in case of fire, and the moisture had rendered this once-ornate room hideous, with mouldy walls and loose floor boards. The Gardiners had had the loosened paneling removed from the walls as a fire precaution and the room was locked against entrance. The

wide stairway leading from the Grant room to the first floor
was also in a state of ruin approaching danger to life and limb.
Now this and the room itself were marked for reconstruction,
as was also the interior of Ralston's fortress-like stables, which
the Sisters referred to as the "barn," a name that still adheres
despite the present hanging signs "Museum" and "Little The-
atre." The immense greenhouse adjoining the barn was demolished as were other unsightly outhouses, including the old
Turkish bath and the chicken house. The greenhouse site was
perfectly fitted for the Lourdes Shrine.

But progress in transformation of the new site was offset
by failure to dispose of the old. A still heavier worry came at
the end of 1922, when Sister Berchmans Joseph died after a
recurring illness. To Sister Anthony, especially, the loss was
personal; her letter to the Sisters of the province was much
more than the customary eulogy. Perhaps she foresaw her need
of such a bulwark in the face of mounting crticism over failure
to dispose of the old property while interest accumulated on
the new mortgage.

She was happy that Sister Julia of the Passion Overend
succeeded as Provincial, although she knew she could not
expect from her the unquestioning confidence of Sister Berchmans Joseph. It was Sister Julia's nature to view the unexpected
with surprise, her first reaction to many manifestations of Western casualness; her considered responses, however, were based
on adaptation, as Sister Anthony was to learn in time. After a
long city life, she overcame her dismay at the constant falling
of eucalyptus leaves at Belmont by heading frequent "lawn
parties" at which she wielded a vigorous rake herself. But
capable as she was, and beloved by the community, she was
somewhat lacking in business experience, a lack which the
poetic and idealistic Sister Anthony as first councilor was
unable to fill. Thus, they and most of the trustees saw no
danger in what seemed an attractive offer early in 1923, one
which may have been made with honorable intentions, if not
with wisdom. In the end they turned to their good legal friend,
David Burnett, who averted disaster, when springtime brought

the Sisters recognition of their folly and the outspoken disapproval of friends. For the secrecy which surrounded plans and
negotiations for the removal of the college and disposal of the
Santa Clara Street campus could not keep the news from
spreading among the people of San Jose; it only added to their
indignation and feeling of betrayal, for they had been proud
of Notre Dame and considered it a civic asset that they were
reluctant to lose.

Commencement Day, June 14, was chosen as appropriate
for ceremonious announcement of already public knowledge.
For this occasion Sister Anthony had selected Longfellow's
masque "Pandora" with music score by the American composer
Rosalie Balmer-Smith Cale. As if in memory of early days, a
huge stage was erected under the elms, a perfect setting for
the choruses of Reeds, Trees, Eumenides, and Oreades. Violet
Bulmore, a recent conservatory graduate, sang the leading role.
Loretta Yaeger, a lovely golden-haired Santa Clara girl with an
equally golden voice, brought haunting beauty to the songs of
the Dream Spirit. The program was certainly Notre Dame's
largest mustering of talent democratically selected from conservatory, boarding school, and day school. Archbishop Hanna
spoke feelingly of the work of Notre Dame in San Jose, but
neither his words nor the ornate masque could lift the pall that
had somehow settled over the audience. Not even Sister Anthony's two-page effusion in the printed memorial program
seemed convincing; it had for many the air of too much pro-
testing. Many knew too well that "God's garden" would not
be "in one sweet summer pulsed by the power of commerce,"
that industry was not ready as yet "to strike steel roots" into
its soil. It must be said that Sister Anthony's faith in these
prophetic phrases was absolutely sincere; poet-wise she was
more concerned with final than immediate fulfillment. She saw
their fitness, as she did that of the fine Notre Dame Memorial
which she brought out in the format of the *Quarterly*, and
which presented the story of Notre Dame in San Jose in photo
and brief account, an introduction to the new college site
which indicates a writer impressed by Victorian grandeur, and

a long poem, "The Iris of the Years," by which she had marked
the end of the school's seventh decade in 1921. In all, the work
is a treasure, though at the time it may have increased, rather
than assuaged the general disapproval of the transfer.

Commencement over, moving was accelerated and a small
group of Sisters took up residence in the former Ralston bowling alley to direct disposal of arriving furniture. At the boarding school the Sisters packed everything detachable into the
huge van, dubbed Black Maria, which Augustine drove up to
Belmont each morning. It was remarkable what objects the
"heads of charges," and ordinary mortals as well, were coming
to consider as potentially useful, even essential, in their new
abode. While Lady Poverty is known to counsel traveling light,
the principle of the "common good," seems to indicate the
storage van rather than the suitcase. And until a recent date
the young iconoclast, envisioning a community hegira as an
opportunity to be rid forever of plaster statues looming life-
size in corridors, was doomed to frustration. Thus some four
decades and a good amount of grim determination have been
necessary to rid upper corners in Ralston mansion of a huge
painted Pietà group, mournful heavy-framed piety, and cum-
bersome presses filled often with forgotten treasures. For the
time Augustine and his helpers deposited these articles, along
with furniture of all descriptions, on front lawn and arcade
levels, while workmen hurried with repair work in the house
itself in preparation for the arrival of the first Belmont community, 32 in all, on September 10.

It was well that the beauty of Belmont awaited that community arriving fresh from the experience of their last mass
in "Old San Jose." They all faced bravely enough this ordeal
for which preceding mornings had prepared them, as main
altar, stations, benches, and even ornamental wainscoting disappeared, leaving elegance of arch and fresco to stress destruction. But courage faltered when 85-year-old Sister Marie Ste.
Thérèse, suddenly wept aloud; then all wept with her, stifling
their sobs. And one who wept was the chaplain of years, white-

haired Father John Collins, S.J. as he turned from the altar of
the Blessed Virgin to impart a last blessing.

When the community departed for Belmont, the Sisters
who taught in the parish schools and in Notre Dame High
School remained on the old campus until arrangements could
be made for them at Notre Dame Institute. Located about a
mile away, at Second and Reed streets, this now became the
center of Notre Dame life in San Jose. When no other solution
seemed possible, this house was enlarged to accommodate the
classes of Notre Dame High School, which opened there in
September, 1928. Notre Dame girls of the five intervening
years still recall the forsaken quarters, the gradual ruin of the
old campus, dangerous stairs blocked off, signs forbidding entrance, windows through which they looked at wrecked interiors. Worst was the chapel, emptied of all, its walls destroyed
by the removal of windows and fixtures. Yet classes gathered
in that chapel for lectures and retreats. Class after class asked
to have their graduation mass celebrated in it. Sister Teresita
Bihn of the Holy Family Sisters and Sister Anna Voss of Notre
Dame tell of covering those chapel walls with drapes to hide
the ugliness. They recall, too, presenting scenes from Shakespeare's *Merchant of Venice*, in Notre Dame Hall, enthralled
with matters of costume, and leaving reflections on the ruinous
state of things, the "big mistake," to their elders.

What perhaps worried their elders most was their own
inability to cooperate through their pastors with Archbishop
Hanna's plan for a Catholic girls' high school on the college
property, a plan which if premature, still indicated a deep
fatherly concern and sense of responsibility on his part. The
Archbishop proposed taking over the area of the college buildings and remodeling the more recently constructed units for
his new venture. The Sisters accepted his offer of $100,000,
retaining street frontage as more salable, but leaving a corridor to Santa Clara Street as entrance to the new school. Once
again hope was high; the Sisters of Notre Dame would staff a
fine interparish school on their old site; they offered the Arch-

bishop the equipment of Notre Dame High School and dreamed of paying off the Belmont mortgage at an early date.

The pastors involved in this plan at once, however, declared, their parishes unable to meet the shared indebtedness. They pointed out the additional cost of remodeling old buildings. They had already built parish grade schools, and were paying a salary of $40.00 a month to each Sister teaching in those schools. In fact, they felt overburdened as things stood. Explaining it later, Archbishop Hanna observed that it had been a matter of trying to alter a mental attitude too abruptly. For decades, he added, the Sisters had borne too great a burden themselves. He was right; they had applied too long the notion of a boarding school financing their apostolate; the new concept could not take root overnight. But though his plan had failed, the Archbishop discharged over half of the Archdiocesan indebtedness to the Sisters during the following year and the remainder before 1930, an act which set the college on a secure financial basis.

Failure of the Archbishop's combined parish high school plan made disposing of the whole property easier in the long run; its success would have made orderly subdivision of the tract impossible. Thus all concerned agreed to have it surveyed under the title "College Tract," the legend bearing the signatures of Archbishop Hanna, Sister Julia of the Passion Overend, and the recent buyers of the old Select Day Academy. According to this legend, the three holders yielded to the city the extension of Carlysle Street to the eastern line of the tract and the wide Notre Dame Avenue connecting Santa Clara and San Augustine Streets. Thus the tract became four rectangular blocks. Years later, the extension of Almaden Avenue cut off the old day academy which I. Krohn, his wife Etta, and three other owners had brought flush with Santa Clara Street by an addition so ugly that the constantly deteriorating assemblage became at last more than the city could bear. Yet such is human nature, that almost forty years later citizens bemoaned its passing, beyond reclaiming though it was.

While division of the property stirred up a few immediate prospects, nothing came of any of them. Since it was clear that provision must be made for Notre Dame High School, the Sisters turned to their friends in San Jose, and by means of donations and a large loan, erected classroom, library, science laboratory, and music facilities, adjoining Notre Dame Institute. As this beginning of the present Notre Dame High School was hurried to readiness for the fall semester of 1928, demolition played a sad accompaniment on the old campus. Destruction of the unused units and removal of trees had begun, in fact, with the plan to subdivide the tract. Falling of bricks and giant elms had reduced sensitive Sister Mary Angelica Cronin to tears many a time before the final onslaught, and like so many Helens of Troy, her sympathetic art pupils shed a few great tears with her. For months the wrecking company carried on the work of demolition until only the two last units remained. Driving through from The Alameda, one saw the music academy standing guard over piles of rubble. Beyond, Science Hall loomed large in its desertion.

Interest in the College Tract began to revive at the end of the decade with the sale of Science Hall to the Rosicrucian Press. Next followed the frontage area of the DeAnza Hotel. In 1944 the last buyers, W. J. Scilacci, and Y. Yarimie, brought the completed sales to slightly over $411,000. After deductions, the Sisters realized $383,000. That was little enough, but at least it meant freedom from years of financial worry.

Despite the delays and disappointments, despite the depression and the war, the Sisters of Notre Dame built a beautiful high school in Belmont and started the new Notre Dame High School in San Jose. More admirably, they had not complained. Young Sisters in that era heard very little about the worries and heartaches. Lay persons who knew how matters stood wondered at the Sisters' reticence. Archbishop Hanna, who suffered greatly himself by reason of it all, praised the Sisters' patience. And if Sister Anthony set down certain cryptic, almost caustic notes, she kept her *Belmont Annals* for those years carefully out of circulation, and much of its contents out of her *Harvest Fields*. Press accounts which she released from time to time convey the notion often repeated since, that commerce and business moved in and caused the Sisters to move away from the old campus, but instead of the boom which these words imply, both Sisiters and citizens recall the long stagnation, the last trace of which disappeared when early in February, 1966, the once beautiful Science Hall was demolished. The Rosicrucian Press had sold it to the City of San Jose to allow for an extension of Almaden Avenue. Citizens watched as the steel ball of 3500 pounds swung from a giant crane and crumpled the first pillar. One day's assault reduced to rubble the structure that had, under construction, withstood the 1906 earthquake.

For those who still experience a nostalgic twinge at the name "College of Notre Dame in San Jose," or just "Old Notre Dame," there is a delightful cure in the hills above Cupertino at the home of Mrs. Fremont Older, who a year or two before the transfer to Belmont, instituted an annual Shakespeare Garden Festival on the Santa Clara Street campus which pleased literary San Joseans and Sisters as well in the summer holidays. Mrs. Older continued this festival until the demolition made it impossible. A lover of historic San Jose since her writing of weekly features on the subject for the *San Jose News*, she was saddened by the change, and her regret was increased by the simultaneous destruction elsewhere of an old adobe. Not one to stand by idly, Mrs. Older purchased a Model T Ford truck in time to prevent the adobe bricks from being pushed into the Guadalupe river. Load by load, she had them transported to her "Woodhills Ranch" and there constructed into a lovely guest house with medieval turret and friendship stairs. From the Dolan Wrecking Company she purchased tiling from the long front corridor at Notre Dame. Told that she might then take anything else she pleased, Mrs. Older rescued the cornerstone set in 1854, and other treasures, including a graceful row of pillars for her garden. *Sunt lacrimae rerum*. And if one falls silent seeing these things, Mrs. Older graciously assists the moment with her bright remark, "I call it Little Notre Dame."

⁣ ⁣ ⁣⁣ ⁣ ⁣*

At any Notre Dame foundation, the most memorable date is that of the first celebration of mass. This occasion at Belmont had an added interest in its locale, the only possible one being the Ralston ballroom, converted into a temporary chapel.

The sanctuary was placed in a wide alcove with windows on the garden. Because no one thought of the lovely view as a proper backdrop for an altar, artist Sister Marie of St. Joseph Oddie painted cover screens for the window spaces in the delicate green, pink and gold which she used for arches and pillars. So that the states of prayer of other people might not distract the worshiper, the great mirrors were covered with light tan paper. The altar that had gleamed like a jewel in the large chapel at San Jose here filled the sanctuary, a blare of gold. High brass canonicals, tall romantic angels and other appurtenances much too large here had to be stored in a fourth-floor attic. The benches overflowed into an annex. The marshalled array of polished brown kneelers contrasted somberly with the gleaming chandeliers. Thus adapted, this scene of the Sharon-Hesketh wedding and of balls where royalty had danced, remained "the chapel" for Sisters and students for nearly forty years.

Classes opened, slightly later than usual, in a still disorderly setting, which according to all accounts, presented Sister Mary Regis with one of the greatest challenges of her life, a challenge that seemed to extend to all departments. Housing the four high school years in the Ralston barn was to her an engineering feat to be explained to all comers, as was also the setting up of a science laboratory in the end of the bowling alley. When the first nine college girls arrived a week later, Sister Anthony introduced them to intellectual life in the parlors and library. Now visitors seated in the long solarium wondered at such snatches as "Vide ut alta . . ." and "Odi profanum . . .". Thus began an era of community chapel prayer punctuated by the sound of heels on stairs and hardwood floors, and accompanied by conflicting pianos in the old Grant room. Living quarters, especially those of the Sisters, constituted an acid test of patience.

The first relief, the completion of Cuvilly Hall, came at the end of 1924. Here novices and postulants were housed until the novitiate was moved to Saratoga in 1937. On Cuvilly's opening day visiting Sisters remarked a note of continuity; stair railings and newel posts were those of the novitiate in San Jose. For many years Cuvilly served as library and junior college, with science, museum and music hall occupying the spacious barn. Through these years college girls lived happily in the Ralston guest rooms and dined in the scene of his banquets. Crowds of Sisters dined there, too, in the silence of summer retreat. For many of these, however, the real attraction of Belmont was "the hill," the height accessible by one or other bridle path, where solitude awaited to turn the pages of thought. There one might have encountered the spirit of Sister Anna Raphael and her *Weltanschauung*.

It remained now to bring alumnae and old friends to see the beauty of Belmont and to realize its astounding potential. Thus at the end of their first year, when things had fallen somewhat into a pattern, and treasures that proved purposeless out of their former setting had been stored in the "upper barn," as though time would produce the necessary metamorphosis, the Sisters announced their grand Inaugural Tea for October 7, 1924. Some five hundred attended that brilliant occasion, the largest Belmont gathering since the days of Ralston and Sharon. Among the alumnae hostesses were Maria Lucas and Marie Dillon Lally of the Class of 1883, also such recent graduates as Alberta Mooney, Margaret Johnson and Maxine Cox, of the class of 1921, and Evelyn Derby, Edythe Donovan and Catherine Canning of the class of 1922. Victorians and moderns joined in the celebration. Perhaps the final argument was the presence of the Sisters. It was satisfying, in a passing way, to learn that Ralston mansion somewhat resembled the first Palace Hotel, that the large painting of the Duke of Wellington was worth $10,000; that the hand-carved frame opposite was priceless and that fixtures were really silver. It was fine to see the paintings of Sister Joseph S.H. Burns in such a setting, to find Ralston's handsome daughters, Emelita Ralston Page and Bertha Ralston Bright, studying them with admiration. But when Sister Anthony laughingly told them that the Sisters occupied the servants' quarters,they saw again the image of self-sacrifice, the stuff of pioneering.

Notre Dame's Inaugural Tea ushered in a tradition of Ralston Hall events, the most memorable the grand opening of Ralston Ballroom in 1961, after its years of service as chapel for community and students. For that occasion interior decorators restored parlors, dining hall, and balcony to their early splendor, bringing back the spacious elegance that the "Builder of San Francisco" had planned for the entertainment of his friends. Since then the mansion has been a daily delight to visitors, who admire shining mirrors, chandeliers, beautiful furnishings, inlaid floors, and silver fixtures that speak of the Comstock. As a link with the present, the visitor finds at the eastern exit a master plan of the new campus. Since its inception in 1951, a large part of this plan has been realized in contemporary styled residence and classroom units. At the center of the campus stands Notre Dame Memorial Chapel, a triumph of twentieth century art and architecture, as well as a witness to Notre Dame's own creative genius.

As this story closes, College of Notre Dame is celebrating its Charter Centennial. With its many-sided leadership, its large lay faculty, its strong participation in current movements, the new Notre Dame may seem a far call from Notre Dame of long ago. But if the measure of success is intellectual awareness and energy, then the present era in the life of the college would seem to be repeating the brilliant one that produced its recognition by the State of California in 1868.

Notes

CHAPTER 1

[1]Pueblo San José was incorporated as "City of San Jose" March 27, 1850, sharing honors with Benicia and San Diego, only one month after the incorporation of Sacramento. But San Jose was actually the first civil settlement in the present State of California. Earlier settlements had been forts or missions, but Pueblo San José, founded in 1777 by Lieutenant Jose Moraga, under orders of Governor Felipe Neve, was established as an urban center, roughly midway between the forts of San Francisco and Monterey, both of which it was intended to serve as the fertile surrounding area would be developed.

[2]Frederick Hall, *History of San Jose*, 191; H. H. Bancroft, *History of California*, vol. 4, 772-3. For an interesting account of the Peralta Adobe, Rev. William N. Abeloe, in *San Jose Mercury-News*, October 20, 1963.

[3]The California State Legislature met for the first time December 17, 1849. The Act of Removal was passed February 14, 1851. The last meeting of the legislature in San Jose, at the close of its second session, was May 1, 1851.

[4]An account of the closing of the Oregon mission of the Sisters of Notre Dame is given in *Willamette Interlude*, by the author of this volume, beginning with Chapter 14.

[5]Hon. Peter H. Burnett, *Recollections of an Old Pioneer*, 188.

[6]The Murphy family, leaders in this famous party, arrived at Sutter's Fort late in 1844. As a reward for their assistance in the Alvarado-Castro rebellion, Governor Micheltorena promised them land grants. Among the holdings of Martin Murphy, Sr. were the two square leagues of Rancho Ojo de Agua de la Coche and Rancho San Francisco de las Llagas. Other holdings which passed into the hands of this pioneer family were Uvas Rancho, which Lorenzo Pinedo parted with for $200 and several barrels of flour, and La Polka Grant. By 1860 the family holdings included some forty thousand square acres. Generations of this historic family have been students at College of Notre Dame in both San Jose and Belmont.

[7]White's survey of the Davidson property was recorded March 21 in Santa Clara County, Map Book A, page 38.

[8]Land titles mentioned in this chapter are from the *Books of Deeds of Santa Clara County*.

[9]Charles White and his wife Ellen, overland pioneers of 1846, settled in San Jose and became extensive land owners as well as leading citizens. Charles White was killed in the explosion of the *Jenny Lind* in 1853. H. H. Bancroft, *History of California*, 5, 772.

NOTES 297

[10]Bishop Alemany's appointment of Father Nobili is dated San Francisco, March 4, 1851. Father Real, the Mexican Franciscan replaced by Father Nobili, departed for Santa Barbara, shortly afterwards left the Franciscans, and returned to Mexico. Father Piñero, of whom Sister Marie Catherine speaks, stayed on in San Jose until November, 1851.

[11]The story of Thomas Kell as related by himself is in *Pen Pictures of Santa Clara County*, 433.

[12]Frederick Hall, *History of San Jose*, 82.

[13]Born in Barcelona, Spain, Antonio Suñol entered the French Navy at an early age, but when that career brought him to Monterey, he decided to abandon the sea in favor of rural life in California. He became grantee of Rancho Valle de San José, some 4800 acres, and of other lands. In 1823 he married Dolores Bernal. H. H. Bancroft, *History of California;* and M. W. Woods, *History of Alameda County*, 983. Mrs. Frances A. Suñol-Angus, granddaughter of Don Antonio Suñol, and alumna of College of Notre Dame, gives her recollections of Suñol opulence and hospitality in M. B. Carroll, *Ten Years of Paradise*, 15-16.

[14]Levi Goodrich planned and constructed the old Court House and other civic buildings in San Jose. From 1870 on, his quarry at New Almaden supplied stone for several important projects including San Jose Normal School, Notre Dame Auditorium, College of the Pacific, and Stanford University.

[15]H. H. Bancroft, *History of California*, Vol. 5, 708-709.

[16]Mrs. M. H. Field, "Grandma Bascom's Story," *Overland Monthly*, May, 1887.

[17]At the age of seven, Johnny was placed in the care of the Jesuit Fathers in Santa Clara. In *Notre Dame Quarterly*, December, 1910, 82, is an account of Johnny's visits to Notre Dame as a member of the State Legislature of California. His wife always accompanied him and was, to her delight, listed as an alumna. Sister Loyola wrote of Johnny Townsend in her letter to Mère Constantine, August 30, 1851.

CHAPTER 2

[1]This chapter follows Sister Marie Alenie's *Journal* and her unsigned biography, as well as Sister Marie Catherine's *Memoir*.

[2]In a letter addressed to Sister Loyola in Oregon City late in 1850, Mère Constantine assured her that two of the missionaries who had left Namur that summer would proceed to Oregon, together with two Sisters from Cincinnati, who would know English, the arrangement being subject to change by Sister Louise, Superior of American foundations. Mère Constantine does describe her own two choices without naming them and certainly Sister Marie Alenie is one of them. Mère Constantine also states that Sister Louise had reported inability to pay the coast-to-coast traveling expenses of the four missionaries to Oregon. She had thus been obliged to borrow the amount from the bank, but hoped that the mother

house, being under great financial strain, would not have to assume the responsibility. Mère Constantine, Letters, December 12, 1850.

[3]The *Register Veritas* of Antwerp, describes the *Fanny* as a three-masted, full-rigged ship of 521 tons, built in Bremerhaven, Germany, in 1844, and known first as the *Frederick-Leo.* Her owners were Spilliaerdt-Caymax of Antwerp. Captain Schottey was master.

[4]Sister Mary of St. Francis, (Hon. Laura Jermingham Petre). After the death of her husband, Hon. Edward Petre, Mrs. Petre entered the Congregation of Notre Dame. She was professed at Namur in 1852. Her generosity aided greatly in establishing the English mission of the Sisters of Notre Dame.

[5]The first foundation of the Sisters of Notre Dame in New England was made in 1849 by Sister Louis de Gonzague and two other Sisters as a daughter house of "Sixth Street," for years the central Notre Dame house in America, often referred to as "Little Namur." At her own request, Sister Louis de Gonzague was succeeded at Sixth Street by Sister Louise Van de Schreieck, who had accompanied her to America, and is mentioned *passim* in these pages. Emmanuel College in Boston is successor to the first New England Foundation, still referred to as "Berkeley Street." Sister Helen Louise, S.N.D. de N. *Sister Louise.* Also *American Foundations of the Sister of Notre Dame de Namur.*

[6]The last letter of Sister Louise, O.S.D. to Sister Marie Alenie is appended to the latter's *Journal,* and dated Benicia, February 2, 1895, shortly before her death.

[7]*The Empire City,* a steamer built in New York in 1849, was modeled for speed and strength. She was said to be the first ocean vessel with deck house extending from stem to stern. Her maiden voyage was New York to Chagres, and she continued this run to 1856. She passed in succession from the Empire City Line to the Pacific Mail Steamship Company and then to the United States Mail Steamship Company. John Haskell Kemble, *The Panama Route,* 224.

[8]*The Sarah Sands,* a 1440-ton iron steamer built in Liverpool in 1846, for trans-Atlantic service, was chartered later by the Empire City Line for the run between Panama and San Francisco. She proved too small and too slow for gold rush demands, and was sold shortly after the Sisters' trip up the coast to British Australian purchasers. She was the first steamer to circumnavigate the globe. After a remarkable career, she ended her days as a sailing vessel in 1869. Erik Heyl, *Early American Steamers,* 383-84.

[9]Sister Catherine, (Catherine Marie Strubbe), born in Malgarten, Hanover, in 1824, was the daughter of one of the many German families that settled in Ohio early in the nineteenth century. N. D. Q.*, June, 1913, 65.

[10]Sister Aloysius, (Regina Richeat), born in Darmstadt, Germany, in 1825, entered the novitiate in Cincinnati, in 1841. In San Jose she taught mathematics for 23 years, as well as being accountant and sacristan. She held the post of Superior in Marysville 1876-1888.

---

*Notre Dame Quarterly

[11]Emma's younger sister, Henrietta Barry Byrne, was enrolled at Notre Dame a few years later. Their great uncle was the famous Commodore John Barry.

[12]Eugenie Van Damme Melville, mother of Alumna Marie Melville Russell, was first Public Librarian in Sausalito. She died in San Francisco in 1909. *N. D. Q.*, December, 1909, 81.

[13]*N. D. Q.*, March, 1914, 24.

CHAPTER 3

[1]For the running account, this chapter follows Sister Marie Alenie's *Journal* and Sister Marie Catherine's *Memoir*.

[2]Correspondence of the Rev. Isaac Owen, 1851-1853, dealing with work in California on behalf of the Methodist Episcopal Church. Transcript, p. 35. Statistical Report to Dr. Durbin, 1851. *Owen Papers*, Bancroft Library. The Rev. Ed Bannister arrived in the Santa Clara Valley in 1850. In December that year he opened the English and Classical School at San Fernando and Second Streets in San Jose. This educator founded a college, the forerunner of University of the Pacific. For many years its home was in Santa Clara.

[3]Lieutenant Governor John McDougal succeeded Governor Peter H. Burnett at the resignation of the latter in January, 1851. An account of this second governor is found in *Daily Alta California,* March 31, 1866, p. 2, col. 4. Ella McDougal died while still a school girl. Susan married William Tilgham. Her younger sisters, Lilian and Caroline, attended Notre Dame briefly. The author is indebted to Mrs. Samuel Hopkins Weston, granddaughter of Governor McDougal, who possesses an interesting collection of McDougal papers and photographs.

[4]Eva Bascom was enrolled at Notre Dame in the 1860s, and is listed as a senior in 1865. At the death of her father, Dr. Louis Bascom, in 1881, her name appears last of his five living children. *The Pioneer,* March 5, 1881. Dr. Bascom, as well as his friend and partner, Dr. Benjamin Cory, was attending physician at Notre Dame. Much to Dr. Cory's regret, Dr. Bascom later abandoned his profession to become a rancher. *The Pioneer,* April 23, 1881.

[5]The article in the *California Christian Advocate* was dated January 16, 1854. Sister Loyola's response appeared in *Daily Alta California,* March 2, 1854. She observed heatedly that the only truth in the article concerned needlework.

[6]Rev. Peter de Voss, S.J., to Martin Murphy, Sr., October 28, 1855.

[7]Martha Letitia Burnett, second child of Peter H. Burnett and Harriet Rogers Burnett, was born in Missouri in 1833. She had made the acquaintance of the Sisters of Notre Dame in Oregon, though her chronic poor health perhaps prevented her spending any length of time in school there. She married C. T. Ryland in Alviso, then the home of the Burnett family, in January, 1851. Her sister Romieta married W. T. Wallace in

Alviso in 1853. Peter H. Burnett, *Recollections and Opinions of an Old Pioneer*, 6.

[8]Letters of Mère Constantine, No. 38, June 21, 1851, and No. 39, Oct. 8, 1851.

[9]Letter of Mère Constantine, No. 40, Nov. 20, 1851.

[10]"Grandma Bascom's Story" in *Overland Monthly*, May, 1887.

[11]Papers and letters of Ysabel Ramírez Pelanconi-Tononi in Archives of College of Notre Dame. Ysabel married Antonio Pelanconi, who established one of the first wineries in Southern California, on Olvera Street in Los Angeles. He also erected the first brick house in that city, another state historical monument. After his death, Ysabel married G. Tononi.

[12]Sister Loyola's letter, August 30, 1851.

[13]Letter of Sister Mary Aloysia to Mère Constantine in Namur Archives. This letter was brought to Namur in December, 1853, by the Rev. Michael Accolti, S. J.

CHAPTER 4

[1]Sister Marie Catherine gives a detailed account of the arrival in San Jose of the last Sisters of Notre Dame from the Oregon mission.

[2]Letter of Sister Mary Aloysia to Mère Constantine, December, 1853.

[3]*San Francisco Daily Herald*, July 18, 1853. Judges, guests, prize winners, and an account of the program are given here.

[4]As daughers of four Castro families were enrolled during the first decade, identification is difficult. It seems certain that Dolores and Loreta Castro were sisters, daughters of Juan Castro and María Dolores Peralta. Hilarita and Inez Reed were daughters of John Reed of Marin and Hilaria Sanchez, daughter of Don José Antonio Sanchez. The two Valencia families registered in the first decade present the same difficulties as do the Castros, but the sisters Lucía and Tomasa were probably cousins of the Reed sisters.

[5]This broadside program is listed by Robert Greenwood in *California Imprints*, 1833-1862, No. 418. *N. D. Q.*, June, 1913, p. 10, quotes the list of prize winners in full, but is in error about the date. There was apparently no list nor program printed for the first closing, 1852. For many years, the annual *Prospectus*, printed just before closing day, was devoted chiefly to the prizes won and class standing of students. Brief information about the school was presented in fine print.

[6]Amanda Brannan may have been a relative of the famous pioneer, San Brannan, whose presence on this occasion is otherwise difficult to explain.

[7]Martin Murphy, Jr. no doubt spoke for many in the Santa Clara Valley when he told William Kelly of the falling off in sales of cattle for hides and tallow since the peak of the gold rush. William Kelly, *A Stroll Through the Diggings of California*, p. 226.

[8]Letter of Sister Mary Aloysia in Note 2 above.

[9]Frederic Hall, *The History of San Jose*, 259-261. A detailed description of this building, including the chapel. J. P. Munroe-Fraser, *History of Santa Clara County*, 492, describes the chapel as "a gem of chaste, artistic beauty. . . ."

[10]Sister Mary Bernard, (Emelia Weber), was born in Echternach, Germany, February 22, 1822. Her parents were John Weber and Catherine Reckingen Weber. She was professed at Notre Dame in Namur September 8, 1842, and was a member of the second group of missionaries to Oregon in 1847.

[11]Richard Henry Dana, *Two Years Before the Mast*, 427. Dana's visit to San Jose in 1859 is recorded in the section which he added to his famous book under the heading "Twenty-four Years Later." Here the author contrasts his former arrival on the *Alert*, which drifted into the Bay of San Francisco to find only one other vessel there, with his second arrival on the *Empire City*.

[12]There is some confusion about the names and dates of these two first Sisters. Both Sister Marie Catherine and Sister Anthony, S.H., are at variance with the Obituary, but comparison seems to indicate the conclusions here given. All accounts agree that Sister Julia died soon after profession, the first Sister of Notre Dame to die in California.

[13]Letters of Mère Constantine: Among the letters in which the Mother General expressed her opinions regarding certain faults in Sister Loyola's administration are those of June 2 and October 8, 1851, and May 2, 1855. Unfortunately, no letters from San Jose to the Mother General are extant for this period. Her letters, however, reflect complaints. The Blanchet letters here mentioned are No. 7 and No. 8, Archdiocesan Archives of Portland, Oregon. This subject is fully treated in the final chapters of *Willamette Interlude*.

CHAPTER 5

[1]Sister Marie Catherine recounts this incident in her *Memoirs*. She is probably quoting from a letter from Sister Loyola after her arrival in Cincinnati.

[2]*San Jose Times*, January 17, 1887. Obituary of Sister Mary of St. George. Mary Frances Redmond's appraisal of Sister Mary of St. George is in *N.D.Q.*, September, 1913, 57-62; "Reminiscences of School Days at Notre Dame."

[3]Mère Constantine was evidently concerned about the youth and impetuosity of Sister Mary of St. George. Shortly after the arrival of the two English Sisters, she advised Sister Mary Cornelia not to appoint her as first teacher. Here the Mother General was perhaps confusing the posts of head mistress of the boarding school and first teacher, or thinking of them as one. As a matter of fact, they were always distinct in San Jose, the former being for many years more important. From her arrival, Sister

Mary of St. George was first teacher. Letters of Mère Constantine, May 2, 1855.

[4]The *Annals* of the Sisters of Notre Dame of Mission Dolores in San Francisco, give a further account of Sister Aloyse of the Cross. She was Superior there from its founding in 1866 to her death in 1894. The *San Francisco Chronicle,* July 24, 1894, gave an account of her life in California. The S. F. *Evening Bulletin,* July 23, 1894, noted that "her mental attainments and talents brought her into prominence," and that she would be "widely remembered in California." Sister was 61 at the time of her death.

[5]Sister Aurelie was 26 when she entered the novitiate in 1851, a fact which may account for her somewhat set ways. *N. D. Q.,* September, 1913, 49, tells her story and quotes the *San Jose Mercury's* tribute to her life. *San José Mercury,* June 29, 1913.

[6]This journal, entitled, 4ième Colonie envoyée sur les Côtes de l'Ocean Pacifique," is in the *Annals of the Sisters of Notre Dame* in Namur.

[7]Sister Laurence tells this incident in her first Book of *Annals of the Sisters of Notre Dame in California.* Sister Laurence, Anne Lejeune, born in Belgium in 1819, arrived in Oregon with the second group of Sisters of Notre Dame in 1847.

[8]Letters of Mère Constantine, May 2, 1855. Here Mère Constantine assures Sister Mary Cornelia of the happiness of her community, "the first time in ten years."

[9]Margaret Elizabeth Von Aschen, (Sister Mary Gonzaga), born in Ohio in 1836, was professed in the novitiate in Cincinnati in 1856. In California she was appointed Superior of the foundation in Petaluma in 1888.

[10]Mary Dehan, (Sister Kotska), born in Boston in 1829, of Irish descent, seems to have had teaching experience before entering the novitiate in Cincinnati in 1853. She was 27 at her profession in 1856.

[11]Adèle Lefèvre, (Sister Marie de St. Albert), entered the novitiate in Namur in 1859 at the age of 23, and was professed there in 1862.

[12]Hedwig Klausen, *Sister Marie de St. Thérèse,* was born of a prominent family in Hainan, Silesia, in 1837. Mère Constantine's advice about this talented Sister is in her letter of July 18, 1862.

[13]Mère Constantine's letter mentioned in Note 12.

[14]An entry in the first Notre Dame Book of Accounts in California shows Annie Fitzgerald receiving $75 as salary for teaching at the school in 1864. According to Catherine Mahoney Nesfield she was already publishing poems, perhaps in local newspapers, at this time. *N. D. Q.,* June 1915, 63. Bret Harte included her poem, "Waiting for the Rain," in *Outcroppings,* 106. The following year, two of her poems appeared in *Poetry of the Pacific,* edited by May Wentworth. Her poems are, of course, scattered through *N. D. Q.,* notably: November, 1908, 6, 54, and 79; November, 1909, 53; September, 1911, 74.

[15]Judge Sheldon Wright was Probate Judge in San Francisco, 1868 to 1872. He became a kind benefactor of the Sisters of Notre Dame. His daughters, Elizabeth and Daisy, were students at the College of Notre Dame.

¹⁶The Comerford family has been well represented in the history of Notre Dame in California. The family of Michael J. Comerford and his wife, Sarah Jane Jordan, lived alternately in Ireland and London before settling in Sydney, Australia in 1844. Their second daughter, Margaret, married Charles de la Hautière, and their daughter, Marie Louise, became Sister Mary of St. Aloysius. The fourth, Catherine, married William S. Chandler. Her grandniece, Sister Janet Marie, is the present representative of the Comerford family.

<h2 style="text-align:center">CHAPTER 6</h2>

¹*Report of the First Industrial Exposition of the Mechanics Institute in San Francisco*, 1898, p. 100. Entry 200.

²Margaret Van Houten married Cornelius Ditmars of Brooklyn, New York. *N. D. Q.* records her visits to College of Notre Dame on her frequent trips to California, her correspondence with Sister Anna Raphael, and her generous gifts. *N. D. Q.*, Dec. 1911, 82; Sept. 1913, 76; June 1915, 79.

³Letter of Sister Mary Aloysia to Mère Constantine, December, 1853. Annals of Sisters of Notre Dame in Namur.

⁴Sarah Burnett was born in Missouri in 1841. The family migrated to Oregon in 1843 and came to California in 1848, but Sarah's name does not appear on the list at Notre Dame until 1855 when she was fourteen. She married Francis Poe, an easterner, in a double wedding in which her brother Armsted married Flora Johnson of San Jose. Mary B. Carroll, *Ten Years in Paradise*, p. 27. Peter H. Burnett, *Recollections and Opinions of an Old Pioneer*, p. 6.

⁵Elizabeth Yuba Murphy was born during the encampment of the Miller-Murphy-Townsend Party on the Yuba River, when its leaders went to Sutter's Fort to join the forces of Micheltorena.

⁶Ann Kell married pioneer Clement Colombet, who worked his way from his trade as tanner to great success in the Santa Clara Valley first as cattleman and then as vineyardist. *Pen Pictures of the Santa Clara Valley*, p. 559. Alumna Annie Colombet was their daughter, and Louise Colombet, their granddaughter. Ann Kell's sister, Mary Ellen, married T. A. Carroll. Their brother, Martin D. Kell, was grandfather of Alumna Margaret Kell Ryan, who died in San Jose in 1963. *N. D. Q.*, December, 1911, p. 82.

⁷Ophelia Gardiser married Charles Del Ponte of San Jose. Her sister Anna married William J. Del Ponte.

⁸*N. D. Q.*, *September*, 1911, p. 73. Account of the death of Mrs. James Kent Maddock, Sarah Hester. *N. D. Q.*, September, 1914, p. 86. The work of Laura Hester Phelps for the pioneer era in California. *San Francisco's Enchanted Palace*, pp. 68, 69.

⁹These names recur in the pages of Mary B. Carroll's *Ten Years in Paradise*.

¹⁰Shortly before his abdication in 1931, King Alfonso XIII of Spain conferred a noble title on María Antonía Field in recognition of the achievements of her ancestors in Spanish America. Subsequently Lady Field published the proud history of her family under the title, *Where Castilian Roses Bloom: Memoirs*. Through life she recalled the honor accorded her of unveiling the monument of Junípero Serra in Monterey as the "proudest moment of her life." *N. D. Q.*, December, 1910, p. 69. Villa Angelica at Carmel was the gift of Lady Field to her greatly admired teacher, Sister Mary Angelica. María Antonía also published *Chimes of Mission Bells: Historical Sketch of California and Her Missions*, and poems.

¹¹The report cards of the De Haro twins were presented to College of Notre Dame by Anita M. Truman of San Francisco, descendant of their sister Natividad de Haro. On these reports the school's title is given as "Colegio de Hermanas de Nuestra Señora." As yet the usual title was Academy, but "Colegio" was the Spanish title for almost any school in those days. An account of the shooting of the de Haro boys and their uncle, Don José de los Reyes Berryessa of Rancho San Vicente in Santa Clara County, is given in M. B. Hoover, *Historic Spots in California*, p. 169, with the comment that even admirers of Carson and Frémont cannot find an excuse for this act.

¹²See note 14, Chapter 1, concerning the family of Don Antonio Suñol.

¹³Bancroft, *History of California*, Vol. 4, 766. Palomares family of San Jose. And *Baptismal Records* of Mission Santa Clara.

¹⁴Bancroft, *History of California*, Vol. 4, 728. José de Jesús Noë.

¹⁵The children of Don Antonio M. Pico and María de Pilar Bernal in *Baptismal Records* of Mission Santa Clara.

¹⁶Bancroft, *History of California*, Vol. 5, 757-759. And *Annals of San Francisco*, 769-772.

¹⁷The author is indebted to Mrs. Louis McGee, *Ruth Wolfskill*, of Oceanside, California, for the genealogy of these interrelated families, whose story is constantly interwoven with that of College of Notre Dame. Elena Pedroreño married Joseph Wolfskill, and their daughters, Innocent, Elena and Ruth, at Notre Dame before the turn of the century, were thus grandchildren of the famous trapper, William Wolfskill and Magdelena Lugo. On the distaff side, their grandparents were Don Miguel Pedroreño and Antonía Estudillo. Joseph Wolfskill's sister Frances was an honorwinning student at the college. Her nieces, Alice and Isabel Wolfskill, daughters of Louis Wolfskill and Louisa Dalton, were also Notre Dame girls. Alice became Sister Agnes, S.H. Isabel married Henry Gunther Weyse.

W. H. Davis, *Seventy-Five Years in California*, p. 250, mentions Don Miguel de Pedroreño, the Spanish aristocrat, as going to the aid of Commodore Stockton in 1846, with Don Santiago E. Argüello and Captain Hensley.

[18]M. B. Hoover, *Historic Spots in California,* 40-41. Robert Livermore became a naturalized citizen under Mexican rule in 1844. Bancroft, *History of California,* Vol. 4, 715-716. Recounting Livermore's eventful youth, Bancroft adds that he was still thought honest. The children of the younger Robert Livermore are listed in *Baptismal Records* of Mission San Jose.

[19]Robert Walkinshaw in Bancroft, *History of California,* Vol. 5, 766. His four younger children, Josefa, Guadalupe, Robert, and Daniel, are listed in *Baptismal Records* of Mission Santa Clara. His eight children are listed in order of birth in *Santa Clara County Probate Records.*

[20]Rebecca Hanks married Manuel M. Galindo of Coyote. Anna Hanks married Thomas Fisher and Gertrude, Fiacro C. Fisher. These two Fisher brothers, sons of William Fisher, were awarded 20,000 acres at Coyote by U. S. Government in settlement of land. Hall of Records, Santa Clara County. The *San Jose Mercury,* June 26, 1907, carries the obituary of Isabel Montaña Hanks. Isabel and several members of the family were buried in Oak Hill Cemetery in San Jose.

[21]Katherine M. Bell, *Swinging the Censer.* The author is the eldest of the four children of Catarina Den and her English husband, Charles Bell. W. A. Tompkins, *Santa Barbara's Royal Rancho,* 66-166.

[22]Harriet was daughter of Peter G. Pambrun, head of Hudson's Bay fort at Walla Walla, an unusual position for a French-Canadian. *Willamette Interlude,* 121; and the family of William Glen Rae and Eloisa McLaughlin, p. 289, note 2 for chapter 13.

[23]The record of the marriage of Annie C. Burns, daughter of Patrick Burns, to Edward Cahalin of Portland is in Archives of the Archdiocese of Portland, 1867. *Willamette Interlude,* 252, for the charity of Hugh Burns.

[24]Charles A. Provost of San Francisco, nephew of Louise Provost Auzerais, compiled the story of the Provost family for College of Notre Dame in 1949.

Sister Anthony, S.H., is seemingly in error when she says that Louise Provost was a boarder in the Sisters' short-lived school in Oregon City. Her name does not appear in that connection. *N. D. Q.,* June, 1914, p. 65-66. Account of the death of Louise Provost Auzerais. The funeral, one of the most impressive ever held in San Jose, was from St. Joseph's Church. The Provost-Auzerais marriage had been solemnized in its predecessor, the adobe church of St. Joseph.

CHAPTER 7

[1]*San Francisco Business Directory and Business Guide,* 1864-1865, 254.

[2]Leo P. Kibby, "Union Loyalty of California's Civil War Governors," *California Historical Society Quarterly,* December, 1965, 311-319. This writer also notes that previous to the outbreak of the war, there was uncertainty as to the attitude that California should take, and that in the

election of 1860, though Lincoln won the state's four electoral votes, he received only 32 per cent of the popular vote.

[3]J. J. Owen quoted P. H. Burnett in a *San Jose Mercury* editorial, September 1, 1863.

[4]*San Jose Telegraph,* April 18, 1860, gives a dramatic account of the arrival of the Pony Express. *San Jose Mercury,* October 31, 1861, reviews all means of communication before the coast-to-coast telegraph.

[5]Letters of Mère Constantine, August 7, 1861, and June 24, 1862.

[6]Throughout 1864 the *San Jose Mercury* presented frequent items of interest about the San Francisco-San Jose Railroad, including the schedule, two trains a day, with a tiny train designed to call attention, as shipping schedules were indicated by little ships. Editor Owen's articles point to a great local interest in railroad development as well as his own. The proposed Western Pacific would be "the great work of the age." *Mercury,* May 21, 1863. And when a twenty-mile stretch of this road was completed, all San Joseans turned out for the offered pleasure trips. *San Jose Mercury,* October 4, 1866. And up to the completion of the overland railroad, this paper devoted much space to that venture, as in the issue of November 25, 1865.

[7]Bank of California ad in *San Jose Mercury,* June 30, 1864. And the same paper, December 21, 1865, for San Jose's freedom from debts; January 25, 1866, again states the city's readiness for a bank.

[8]*N. D. Q.,* September, 1909, 14, gives a glowing account of Mary Atchison's attainments.

[9]*San Francisco Chronicle,* November 20, 1874, gave a two-page spread to the Sharon-Newlands wedding. The often repeated story of Flora's romance is told intriguingly by Mrs. Fremont Older, *San Francisco: Magic City,* 183-184; Kroninger, Robert H., *Sarah & the Senator,* p. 67.

[10]Willa Okker Iverson, *The Strange Case of Constance Flood,* 29 and *passim.* An interesting presentation of Jenny Flood.

[11]Thomas F. Prendergast, *Forgotten Pioneers,* 183-188, calls the Donohue brothers "men of iron," and quotes Bancroft who designates Peter "the Irish Foundryman of California."

[12]Clara Hastings married Col. E. C. Catherwood, who died in 1893. In 1895 she married Col. John A. Darling. Her lengthy obituary in the *San Francisco Chronicle,* September 15, 1929, makes the error of placing Notre Dame Convent in Benicia, where Clara spent her earlier school days with the Dominican Sisters. Flora Hastings married W. S. Keyes in 1879. *The History of Napa and Lake Counties,* 1881, 475-476, gives a full account of the family of Judge Serranus Clinton Hastings.

[13]Brother Cornelius, F.S.C., *Keith, Old Master of California. San Francisco Daily Morning Call,* June 2, 1883, gave an elaborate account of the Keith-McHenry wedding.

[14]The author is indebted to Alumna Dorothy O'Brien Ryan for the story of Lizzie Landers. Mrs. Ryan has also given to Notre Dame the Steinway grand piano, gift to Lizzie from her father, who had it shipped around the Horn, as well as her exquisitely done Herbarium.

[15]James O'Meara in *N. D. Q.*, September, 1911, 34-36, an account of Major-General S. J. Hensley; also Frederic Hall, *History of San Jose*, 359-362, and Bancroft, *History of California*, Vol. 3, 781. Helen Hensley on early Notre Dame, *N. D. Q.*, September, 1909, 86.

[16]*N. D. Q.*, June, 1909, 78, Catherine Mahoney Nesfield's literary leadership, September, 1913, 65; and June, 1915, 63-64, her tribute to Sister Anna Raphael. The poetry of D. W. Nesfield and Catherine Mahoney Nesfield, appeared in San Francisco in *A Chaplet of Verse*.

[17]*N. D. Q.*, June, 1909, 71.

[18]Ellen Independence Miller was born at Independence Rock with the Murphy-Miller-Townsend party. Catherine Miller married John Keyes of Marin. The oldest daughter, Mary, married James Ross of the Ross Ranch in Marin. For an account of pioneer James Miller, Denis Donohoe, "The Story of James Miller," in *N. D. Q.*, September, 1914, 26-30.

[19]Mary Frances Redmond Zicovich in *N. D. Q.*, June, 1912, 11-15, "In the Light of Other Days," fascinating memories of early Marin County, San Francisco, and Notre Dame in San Jose; and September, 1913, 57-62, "Reminiscences of School Days at Notre Dame."

[20]The family of José Estudillo and Juana Martínez, daughter of Ignacio Martínez, appears in the Diary of Jesús María Estudillo, youngest of their children. Bancroft, *History of California*, Vol. 2, 749, is based on this document. The names are complete and in order of birth in Reginald R. Stuart, *San Leandro . . . A History*. Jesús María Estudillo speaks of his sister's going to Notre Dame to visit his niece and Grace Riddle, but Sophia's name appears only in 1864. Her mother, known as Concepción, was the eldest of the Estudillos. She married J. B. Ward in 1851. Her sister, María de Jesús, married William Heath Davis in 1847. William Heath Davis, *Seventy-five Years in California*, and Bancroft, *History of California*, Vol. 2, 777.

[21]Paul Frederickson, *The Authentic Haraszthy Story*, a full account of this historic family, with an extensive bibliography, this work was published by the Wine Institute of San Francisco, 1947.

CHAPTER 8

[1]The McDougal family, Chapter 3, Page .., and Note 3.

[2]Sarah's story was written by her daughter Zoë Fox, who married Fayette H. Thorpe of Tennessee. Zoë's granddaughter, Sister Julie Marie Thorpe is a Sister of Notre Dame of the California Province.

[3]In her charming book, *Ten Years in Paradise*, Mary Bowden Carroll presents Mary Rhodes and her sister Margaret, the Hesters, the Bascoms, Mrs. Coleman Younger and her daughters, as well as others whose names grace the lists of early Notre Dame, among the society buds of San Jose. Mrs. Carroll's accounts are the more delightful since she came to San Jose expecting to find a backward pueblo with no social life.

[4]*The Pioneer,* June 14, 1879.

[5]For many years C. T. Ryland was in charge of the San Jose Water Works. His holdings in Santa Clara County were extensive. When he died in 1897, his estate was set at about $3,000,000. He had served as senator, lawyer, banker, civic leader. O. T. Shuck, *History of the Bench and Bar of California,* 548; and W. S. Swasey, *The Early Days and Men of California,* 282 ff. Shortly after the death of Ada Ryland, *Notre Dame Quarterly* included in its September, 1910 issue, Norma Ryland's tribute to her father, p. 26, as well as those of both *San Jose Mercury* and Associated Charities of San Jose, 80-81, and an article on the Senator by Sarah C. Burnett, daughter of John Burnett of San Francisco, and granddaughter of Peter H. Burnett.

[6]An account of Francis Lightstone in the *San Jose Daily Times,* December 5, 1886, adds that he worked in Charles Weber's General Store in 1846 and was then associated with Josiah Belden in *Las Sirenas,* an adobe store near the plaza that featured sirens in its sign.

[7]For the story of the Pillot family, the author is indebted to Aloysius A. E. Benoit, son of Aloysius Benoit and Clorinda Pillot Benoit, of San Jose.

[8]The story of pioneer Eugène Veuve in *Pen Pictures of Santa Clara County,* 100-101.

[9]Charles Whiteman's story of his mother, Frances Jarboe Whiteman Messmer, is in the files of Florence Cunningham, late historian of the Saratoga area of Santa Clara County.

[10]*Pen Pictures of Santa Clara County,* 669. The Steirlin family and Lizette Steirlin Jansen, Mrs. Fred Jansen of San Francisco.

[11]*N. D. Q.,* June, 1912, 11-15.

[12]*N. D. Q.,* December, 1912, 19-28, "Across the Plains with the Donner Party," is a reprint of Virginia Reed Murphy's account in *Century Magazine.* C. F. McGlashan's story of the Donner Party was based on her recollections. Charles Warren Stoddard's correspondence with Mrs. Murphy began as a result of his reading the McGlashan account. *N. D. Q.,* September, 1909, 53-58.

[13]Ysabel Argüello's daughter is Mary Aloysia Den Warburton of Santa Clara. Bancroft's *History of California,* Vol. 2, 701-702. The Argüello family.

[14]Ed McGowan was a fugitive from the San Francisco Vigilance Committee in 1856. Walker A. Tompkins, *Santa Barbara's Royal Rancho,* 141-155.

[15]Mary Bowden Carroll says that James A. Lawrie was music instructor at University of the Pacific, then at Santa Clara College and College of Notre Dame in the 1860s. She also speaks of Mrs. M. A. Hamm as teaching piano at Notre Dame, and though no other mention is made, her name appears as a salaried teacher in Notre Dame accounts.

[16]Letter of Mère Constantine to Sister Aloyse of the Cross.

[17]San Jose *Mercury,* July 25, 1863.

[18]J. J. Owen's comment, San Jose *Mercury.*

[19]*N. D. Q.*, March, 1911, 13-17. The article in the *Leader*, February 26, 1910, based on an interview with Garrett Byrne was largely autobiographical. He was one of the first dry goods dealers in the West.

CHAPTER 9

[1]These regulations concerning visits and correspondence remained in the prospectus until the transfer of the college from San Jose to Belmont, and some persisted longer.

[2]Mollie Murphy's unsatisfactory report card is dated May 1, 1862. Her letter was written in the following November, and the "Testimony of Diligence" is dated February, 1863. These witnesses to Mollie's failures and successes are in a collection of letters written by Sister Anna Raphael Fitzgerald to Virginia Reed Murphy, Mollie's mother. *Pen Pictures of Santa Clara County*, 94, gives a sketch of Mollie Murphy Wright.

[3]This reply to the students at Notre Dame in San Jose, dated January 7, 1857 is in Archbishop Alemany's *Diary*.

[4]Mère Constantine's opinions and directives in these matters are found especially in her letters to Sister Mary Cornelia: December 6, 1860; June 29, 1861; and November 30, 1867.

[5]*Notre Dame Quarterly*, September, 1913, "Reminiscences of Early School Days, 57-62.

[6]The decree in question states that "all misunderstanding between the ordinary and regulars concerning temporal affairs will be averted if, at the founding of a new house, a document be drawn up expressing clearly all that relates to the foundation itself, to the rights thence flowing, and to the duties connected with it." Second Plenary Council of Baltimore, Title IV, *Catholic Encyclopedia*, Vol. 2, p. 237. (First Edition)

[7]Letters of Mère Constantine referring to titles of property held by the Sisters of Notre Dame are dated at Namur: October 23, 1863; November 1, 1864; January 21, 1865; May 7, 1865; April 13, 1865; and October 11, 1865.

In 1865 the Sisters of Notre Dame purchased part of their present property at Mission Dolores from the Archdiocese. Apparently they held a deed for this as they did later for added lots. As all papers were destroyed in the earthquake and fire of 1906, their claim to the entire property was acknowledged in 1910 in the San Francisco Hall of Records.

CHAPTER 10

[1]The Closing Exercises of 1854 and 1855 were honored by prize lists, printed by the *San Jose Tribune*. These carried no statement about the school or its curriculum, and seem to have been intended as a guide to visitors at the exhibits and at the distribution of premiums. They serve,

however, as a guide to school classes and divisions. The first extant "Prospectus of the Academy of Notre Dame," printed by O'Meara and Painter in San Francisco, marks the end of the Sixth Annual Session.

[2]Frances McClatchy Richardson, daughter of C. K. McClatchy, founder of the *Sacramento Daily Bee,* was well known as a literary critic. *N. D. Q.,* September, 1909, 85. She was also a distinguished painter of California flora.

[3]Textbooks mentioned in this chapter are chiefly in the collection of Margaret Van Houten and Maria Lucas. As Maria remarked, the science texts were "the most up to the minute." These include: *Fourteen Weeks in Zoology,* J. D. Steele, Ph.D., Chicago, 1872; *Geology,* J. D. Dana, Chicago, 1877; *Elements of Astronomy,* J. N. Lockyer, D. Appleton, N. Y., 1880; *Class Book of Chemistry,* E. L. Youmans, N. Y., 1875. The history texts of Rev. P. F. Gazeau, S.J., replaced the large but more attractively bound volume of William Russell and William Jones, *A History of Modern Europe,* Harper and Brothers, N. Y., 1853, while Maria was a student. The purpose of the change was mainly the orientation of history in the Catholic Faith. Gazeau's *Ancient History* and his *Middle Ages* were both published in New York in 1878. A note in the former states that the questions were composed by a pupil of the Sisters of Notre Dame. Gazeau's *Modern History* followed in 1880. Reeve's *Bible History,* with preface dated 1780, and with leather binding and clear type, may have been Margaret Van Houten's own book for chapel service; non-Catholic girls usually kept their own service book at their place in the chapel. Tooke's *Pantheon of the Heathen Gods, and Illustrious Heroes,* was revised in 1852 "for a Classical Course in Education, and adapted to students of every age and of either sex," by Cushing and Bailey in Baltimore. With 355 pages and index, it now included "Selections from the classic poets with translations." Tooke's *Pantheon* was introduced with ancient history and studied in the same year. It was replaced by White's *Mythology* in its year of publication, 1882.

[4]This *Compendio,* written in English by Emma Willard, and translated into Spanish by Miguel T. Tolón, was published in New York by Barnes in 1853. A beautifully bound volume, its price was $4.00. Margaret received it in 1857.

[5]*Flora's Lexicon* was first published by Fielding Lucas in Boston in 1832, under the title *Flora's Dictionary.* The author, "A Lady," had "not the vanity," says the preface, "to attach serious consequence to it." But this huge volume with fine leather binding and gold decorations, was entered "according to Act of Congress" in 1831, and accorded so wide a reading, or at least gift-giving, that Lucas persuaded The Lady, Catherine H. Waterman, to emerge from hiding in a second edition in 1854.

[6]*The Castle of Rousilon,* Eugénie da la Rochère, translated into English by Mrs. J. Sadlier, and published by D. J. Sadlier, New York, 1850.

[7]Thomas Woody, *A History of Women's Education in the United States,* Vol. 2, 154, quoted in George P. Schmidt, *The Liberal Arts College,* 129.

[8]George P. Schmidt, *The Liberal Arts College,* 130.

CHAPTER 11

[1]Sources for the account of the Guatemalan mission of the Sisters of Notre Dame: Annals of the Namur Province; Annals of the California Province, November, 1875; letters of Sister Marie Philippine Portemer, November 15, 1859, and December 1, 1859; memoir by Sister Marie Ludovic (family name unknown).

[2]Archbishop Palaez was ninth incumbent. Article on Guatemala, *Catholic Encyclopedia* (1907) Vol. 7, 54.

[3]Brother Pedro de Betancourt was considered the St. Francis of Guatemala. Early in the seventeenth century, he left his home in the Canary Islands to become a Franciscan in Central America. He dedicated his life to the sick and poor, finally founding an order known as the *Belemites*. Belén, in Guatemala City, was both monastery and hospital for these *Belemites*.

[4]President Carrera died in 1865 and was succeeded by General Vincent Cerna, who was in turn succeeded by General Miguel Garcia Granados in 1871. General Cerna was a Conservative. General Granados was himself a Liberal but did not inaugurate anticlerical measures during his two-year tenure of office.

[5]The *Colegio* was dedicated May 15, 1870.

[6]Letters of Mère Aloysia Mainy to Sister Mary Cornelia: October 25, 1875, the mandate to close the Guatemalan mission is quoted. Mère Aloysie was successor to Mère Constantine, and doubted the "solidity" of the "Guatemaliennes." The report of their loyalty must have proved a surprise to her.

[7]At the close of her account, Sister Ludovic quotes in full two letters of Minister Soto in reply to her queries. March 5, 1874, he informed her that the decree of February 9 of that year, did not apply to her congregation as yet, since the President had deferred its application to the Sisters of Notre Dame "per hora." The second, November 17, 1874, explains this phrase; as the scholastic year is finished, the decree is now applied to the Sisters of Notre Dame. *Catholic Encyclopedia* (see Note 2 above) mentions three decrees in 1872, which were probably signed by General Granados, but not put into force.

[8]Sr. M. Dominica McNamee, *Willamette Interlude*, 103-104, and photo opposite 110.

CHAPTER 12

[1]This church was dedicated by Archbishop Joseph Alemany, April 6, 1873. In 1885 St. Joseph's Parish, Alameda, was made independent of St. Anthony's in Brooklyn.

[2]Sister Mary Veronica, born in the mining town of Downieville in 1855, was educated at the Mission Dolores Notre Dame in San Francisco. She was professed in 1878.

[3]Before the 1880s, Santa Clara County roads had grown progressively worse. Perhaps to awaken minds to the state of things, *San Jose Mercury*, May 18, 1880, noted that a cyclist made the trip from San Francisco to Santa Clara cycling, but was forced to walk his bicycle the rest of the distance to San Jose because of the condition of the road. Running time was six hours.

[4]A description of this tower, "the largest in the nation," appeared in the *San Jose Mercury*, December 25, 1881. An account of the fall of the tower is in *N. D. Q.*, March, 1916, 68.

[5]In San Francisco, the first electric light was exhibited by Fr. Joseph M. Neri from the roof of St. Ignatius College, July 4, 1876. Three years later the Brush Electric Company held an exhibit at Mechanics Institute Fair, and California Electric Company was formed.

[6]*San Jose Times*, July 20, 1885.

[7]Some time later the Sisters placed a Ryland memorial window in their chapel in gratitude for this good friend's generosity. An account of this donation is in the San Jose Scrapbook, p. 74, San Jose City Library.

CHAPTER 13

[1]Sister Joseph, S.H., Burns, was professed in Cincinnati in 1867. She came to San Jose with Sister Mary of the Angels Burns, her sister, in 1871. She spent most of her religious life in San Jose building up its well-known art department.

[2]*N. D. Q.*, September, 1909, 85.

[3]The younger daughters of this family were Josephine Masten Dunne; Irene Masten Gordon; Georgia Masten Perkins; Alice Masten Spencer; and Jennie Masten Ewell. Josephine was the mother of the historian Peter F. Dunne, S.J. The Dunne family is of special interest in San Jose history. James Dunne married Catherine O'Toole, widow of Bernard Murphy who was killed in the *Jenny Lind* explosion. The children of James and Catherine Dunne were Mary and Catherine, alumnae of Notre Dame, and Peter J. Dunne who married Josephine Masten. Catherine O'Toole Dunn lived to a great age.

[4]*N. D. Q.*, March, 1909, 6, an account of the Sullivan family; and June, 1912, 77; as also T. F. Prendegast, *Forgotten Pioneers*, 88 and ff.

[5]*San Jose Times*, June 6, 1883.

[6]*San Jose Times*, June 5, 1884.

[7]Archbishop Alemany's last visit to the college was in the summer holiday of 1884 when he blessed the new Notre Dame Hall. He submitted his resignation toward the end of that year but learned of its acceptance only in January, 1885. Archbishop Riordan succeeded him.

[8]Dollie McCone McDonald and her sister Susan McCone of the Class of 1889 were registered from Virginia City, Nevada. Their brother, Alexander J. McCone, was the father of John A. McCone who became

head of the Central Intelligence Agency. Another brother was the prominent San Francisco surgeon, Dr. James McCone. Susan died unmarried in Virginia City a few years after graduation. Dollie died in 1918.

[9]In 1963, Mrs. William E. Blauer recalled her early school days at the Academy, where her aunt Estelle Lion, was an older student. Mrs. Blauer's grandmother, Zumela Martin Lion, had also attended Notre Dame; her father, Gustav Lion, was the son of Lazar and Zumela Martin Lion. The family was very prominent in San Jose.

[10]*N. D. Q.*, Sept., 1911, 89, gives account of the Coolidge family.

[11]These bound volumes, sometimes the work of an individual, sometimes the combined efforts of the class, came to be the same sort of memento as the later yearbook.

[12]Mrs. M. B. Carroll, *Ten Years in Paradise,* 29, an account of Evaline Prothero Yoell, *N. D. Q.*, March, 1912, 91, a memorial at the death of Emelie Center Yoell. *N. D. Q.*, December, 1913, Eva Yoell's recollections of Sister Marie Catherine. *N. D. Q.*, September, 1911, 6, poem by Genevieve Yoell Parkhurst. The other Yoell alumnae are listed as Beatrice Yoell Russell, Emelie Yoell Dunn and Alice Yoell who remained unmarried.

[13]Laura J. Brenham in *N. D. Q.*, December, 1910, 13-15, and several poems.

[14]In a letter dated March 16, 1972, General Mariano Vallejo recommended College of Notre Dame to his daughter Adela and her husband, Dr. L. C. Frisbie, for their daughter Lily. The original letter is in College of Notre Dame Archives.

[15]*Pen pictures of Santa Clara County,* 662. An account of Pierre de Saisset and his family. Harriet de Saisset married Dr. Eugene A Filipello.

[16]Nellie White's poems in *N. D. Q.* of March, 1912, 72; September, 1912, 26; September, 1913, 85. Her description of Yosemite, September, 1909, 83; and of Sonoma, June, 1910, 31, are examples of nature description taught by Sister Anna Raphael. Notre Dame's tribute to the Hon. Stephen M. White in *N. D. Q.*, June, 1909, 69. The Senator's daughter, Hortense, graduated from Notre Dame in 1907. She recalls unveiling the statue erected in honor of her father in Los Angeles. Rhoda, another daughter of the William White family, became Sister Mary Vincent of the Sisters of Mercy.

[17]Rebecca Ord's story of her family appeared in *Santa Barbara Daily News,* in a series entitled "Fifty Years Ago," in 1922. The manuscript dictated by Doña Angustias Ord in 1878 was translated and edited in 1956 by Francis Price and William H. Ellison and published under the title, *Occurrences in Hispanic California* by the Academy of American Franciscan History, Washington, D. C. See also Bancroft, *History of California.*

[18]M. B. Hoover, *Historic Spots in California,* 48. In 1855, the Kottingers moved to the future site of Pleasanton. Baptismal records for some of the children are thus in Mission San Jose. Refugio Bernal's uncle, Augustín Bernal, built an adobe on his section of Rancho El Valle.

[19]A tribute by Sister Anthony, S.H., is in *N. D. Q.*, March, 1915, 90. For an account of Hon. James D. Byrnes: Ray W. Cloud, *San Mateo County.*

[20]The author is chiefly indebted to the files of John A. Lennon, but see also under Auzerais and McLaughlin.

[21]The manuscript of Marcella Fitzgerald's pageant is in the College of Notre Dame Archives.

[22]Cardinal Gibbons' visit to San Jose was accorded detailed coverage in the *San Jose Daily Times*, October 19, 1887.

[23]Account of a college celebration of Sister Mary Cornelia's feast day in the *San Jose Daily Morning Times*, September 22, 1882.

CHAPTER 14

[1]In 16 handwritten pages, Miss Skidmore tells the story of the coming of the Sisters of Notre Dame to Oregon. The poem is the typical mixture of the Virtues and the Arts, together with the personifications of Belgium and Oregon. In *N. D. Q.*, December, 1909, the opening and closing lines of this Allegory appear on pages 1 and 11. This number of the *Quarterly* is a memorial to Miss Skidmore.

[2]The first issue of *N. D. Q.*, November, 1908, 19-26, gives the story of the inception of Notre Dame Alumnae Association. When the present title was adopted, the question of limitation of membership to actual graduates came up for discussion and it was decided to continue the policy of the Cornelian Society which granted membership to all who had been enrolled in the upper classes for a notable time.

A monetary problem that had been hanging fire was also settled when the society acquired official status. Before its first meeting, the group had collected the sum of $17,000 for the erection of a memorial to honor the jubilarian "within the walls," according to Geneva Brooks Robinson, Secretary of the Golden Jubilee Committee. She added that since Sister Mary Cornelia would object to a "trophy" in her honor, a marble, or carved wood altar had been decided on. The sum was placed in the bank in the name of the Administration. At once some difference of opinion arose about the use of the fund, but the "lady donors" discovered in an opinion given by Sawyer & Burnett of San Francisco, September 27, 1886, that they were not at liberty to change their minds after the acceptance of their gift. After the death of Sister Mary Cornelia, both administration and the "Corneliennes" agreed that an "obelisk" crowned with a cross should be erected at her grave. This time President Mary Ann Murphy Carroll appealed to the law firm of Garber, Boalt & Bishop of San Francisco, and obtained the opinion that since future controversy was unlikely, the fund might be used according to the unanimous desire.

[3]Sister Marie de St. Denis Fischer was born February 8, 1836, in Westphalia, was professed in Namur in 1857 and left almost at once for America. In 1871 she replaced Sister Mary Bernard Weber as head of the

house in Marysville, California and five years later was transferred to the Academy at Berkeley Street in Boston.

[4]Mère Aloysie granted permission for lessons in physiology if given "with prudence." But there were to be no "charts of figures" on the walls, and she enclosed a drawing of the type of illustration used in the Namur boarding school. Her letter to Sister Mary Cornelia, February 13, 1886. *The Souvenir* is of first importance in her letter of May 24, 1885. She has told Sister Mary of the Cross to stop it. The pupils "have sufficient to study without busying themselves editing a paper." Besides, she finds "this occupation contrary to our customs." Customs must be adherred to "in order that our successors may find them well established."

[5]The Annals of the Namur Province state merely that Sister Marie St. Denis was named "Assistant to the Superior of the house in San Jose" in 1886, but considering her ability and fitness and Sister Mary Cornelia's state of near prostration, it seems likely that the appointment included succession.

[6]Sister Amélie de St. Joseph, daughter of François and Marie Jeanne Van de Perre Caudron, was born in Wieze, Belgium, February 3, 1837. She was professed at Namur, April 8, 1859, died May 5, 1917. Sister Amélie's status in California is clearly set down in the Namur Annals; she was sent to straighten out the accounts and visit the houses in the name of the Mother General. Even after her visit to Namur in March, 1889, there seems to have been no thought in the Mother House of appointing her Superior. She was not named assistant as was Sister Marie de St. Denis. In fact, after the departure of the latter, Mère Aimée de Jésus expressed hope in her letters that Sister Mary Cornelia would recover fully and resume her charge. Thus Sister Amélie's "replacing" of Sister Marie de St. Denis must have been temporary in intention.

[7]Mary Tomb, brilliant and attractive graduate of 1888, remained for a short time in Namur, discovered the difficulties of novitiate life, and returned to Marysville, where she married George Harney. She was an active alumna for many years.

[8]Mère Aimée de Jésus Dullaert, who headed the Sisters of Notre Dame de Namur, 1888 to 1907.

[9]Susan McGroarty, who became the well-known Sister Julia, entered the novitiate upon completing the boarding school classes at the Sixth Street Academy. Her position as head of all the American houses of Notre Dame requires some qualification. Actually the foundations in the West were made from San Jose, not from Cincinnati, and Sisters in California looked to San Jose as their central house. Yet both Sister Mary Cornelia and Sister Mary Bernardine deferred to the provincial of Cincinnati, and Sister Superior Julia seems to have taken this attitude as a matter of course. When she could no longer travel to the West, the General Council took the "opportunity" of notifying Sister Mary Bernardine of her status as provincial in California, April 25, 1901.

[10]Sara Alice "Sadie," Quinlan, daughter of Maurice and Catherine McGinnis Quinlan, born in Boston, September 5, 1872, was one of the

four graduates of 1892. Catherine Quinlan, a close friend of Ina Coolbrith, wrote for the *Oakland Tribune*.

[11]*N. D. Q.*, March, 1913, 27-55. A number of these letters refer to Sister Mary Bernardine's gift of real understanding and friendship. As Sister Anna Raphael and Sister Anthony, S.H., selected letters for the *Quarterly*, they knew that an entire number of the magazine would not suffice for all the messages received.

[12]Archbishop Riordan quoted Archbishop Williams in his eulogy at the funeral of Sister Mary Bernardine. *N. D. Q.*, March, 1913, 24. Sister Anthony, S.H., included this eulogy in her own, though unsigned, tribute to Sister Mary Bernardine in that number, 7-21.

[13]This national crisis was the first to affect California seriously. The use of gold coin and avoidance of paper money had been sufficient protection before the West became involved economically with the rest of the nation.

[14]Sister Teresa, B.S., Isabella Spencer, daughter of Samuel A. and Maria R. Keating Spencer, was born in Hamilton, Ohio, August 2, 1851. She was professed in Cincinnati in 1875. As a result of a misunderstanding, she was transferred to California in 1894, where she headed the Day Academy and supervised its conversion into Notre Dame High School in 1906. She headed both boarding school and high school in Notre Dame in Marysville up to her last illness in 1914. By all accounts Sister Teresa was one of the ablest and most admired teachers of her time.

[15]The firm of T. C. Butterworth was located at 15 Polk Street near Market. In March, 1897, Sister Louise des Séraphines wrote hopefully that since the "galleries" were removed, windows would be donated by friends. When they were installed, Mrs. Leland Stanford so greatly admired them that she sought the advice of Sister Mary Bernardine about the windows for her Memorial Chapel at Stanford University.

[16]This same altar seemed to turn into a blare of gold leaf when it was moved to the ballroom of the Ralston Mansion in Belmont. There the urns and candlesticks took on a gigantic look and were wrapped and stored in the Ralston attic. With the erection of Notre Dame Memorial Chapel at Belmont in 1960, the famous ballroom which had served as "temporary" chapel for nearly forty years was restored to its original use. It was at this point that the exquisite brass and alabaster pieces were brought to light and adapted to use in the ornate halls and parlors of Ralston Hall itself.

[17]Sister Mary Euphrasia, Ella Taylor, daughter of Thomas and Mary Whitehead Taylor, was born in Richmond, Virginia, in 1851. Her ancestors were among the first English settlers of Virginia. Sister was a friend of John Cardinal Gibbons, who was responsible for her conversion to the Catholic Faith. The Cardinal greatly desired a Catholic college for women in Washington, and Sister's fortune helped to bring about the answer to his wish in Trinity College. In her voluminous letters, Sister never mentions this fact, though she does relate being honored on Trinity's opening night shortly before her transfer to the West. Tradition has

it that she came to San Jose "under a cloud," and her letters seem to indicate a sorrow, but a great loyalty to Sister Superior Julia as well.

[18]The Lenzen family was well established in San Jose in the 1870s. The architect Theodore and the contractor and builder, Jacob Lenzen, had offices at the southwest corner of Second and Santa Clara streets.

[19]The gas machine itself cost nearly $1300, though this amount may have included the year's gas supply up to November, or about $400. It was housed in a barn-like structure near the Santa Teresa Street entrance.

[20]Dr. G. W. Seifert, a native of Santa Clara County, and graduate of Santa Clara College, studied in the East and Vienna. Daniel D. Hruby, *Mines to Medicine*, an excellent account of San Jose's doctors. Mr. Hruby states that O'Connor Sanitarium offered no surgery during its formative years. Its change to a full-fledged hospital came at the end of the century.

[21]Sister Catherine Josepha O'Brien, daughter of John and Anne Judge O'Brien, was born in County Sligo, Ireland, in 1880. She was professed in San Jose in 1902. Sister was sacristan in both San Jose and Belmont. She died at Notre Dame Villa in 1965.

[22]Sister Mary Bernard was born in San Francisco, April 7, 1864. She was professed in San Jose in 1896, died in Saratoga in 1930.

[23]*N. D. Q.*, June, 1910, 91.

CHAPTER 15

[1]*N. D. Q.*, September, 1909, "Hon. M. P. O'Connor," 20-26. M. P. O'Connor endowed a chair for Catholic University and donated $50,000 to Trinity College at its inception. An account of the O'Connor benefactions is also given in Daniel D. Hruby, *Mines to Medicine*.

[2]Annette Butler Crimmins, of the Class of 1893, resides in Marysville and at 95 is an interesting conversationalist.

[3]Evidence as to the truth of this rumor is lacking, but according to Mrs. Crimmins, it was this annoyance that persuaded Mrs. O'Connor to withdraw her offer to the City of San Jose.

[4]This first account book of N. D. Institute in San Jose runs from April 12, 1893, to the end of 1902. Its first page "Notice" indicates that both home and endowment were to be in the hands of College of Notre Dame. Semi-annual interest on the bonds was to be cashed by the treasurer of "the Corporation," and disposed of according to the needs of the Institute. This explains the "cash" received at stated times by the Superior at the Institute for running expenses, though actually she determined what these would be. According to the then existing law, the Institute came under taxation; the first installment, November, 1902, was $237.53.

[5]Father William Melchers became resident pastor in the "German" parish of St. Mary's in 1894, and opened St. Mary's School, the teachers being stationed at the Institute. Thus both chaplaincy and school were provided for the orphans. *N. D. Q.*, September, 1912, "Churches and Schools of San Jose," 37-47.

[6]In a letter by Sister Thérèse de St. François to the Sisters in Namur, dated San Jose, December 20, 24, 1920, this traveling companion of Mère Marie Aloyse, described N. D. Institute and its founding. She added that the oldest orphans attended N. D. High School "for in this democratic country, they may become millionaires in a few years; it is a question of luck, not rare here."

[7]Sister Clare, B.S., daughter of Thomas and Mary Callam, born in San Francisco in 1861, was professed in San Jose in 1884. An account of her life is in *N. D. Q.*, March, 1915, 95-97.

[8]The first meeting of this society was held November 3, 1893. Its "Letters of Aggregation" were issued from Rome, March 16, 1895. Auzerais, Belden, Colombet, Suñol, and Turel, are among the recurring names through its early membership. The *Book of Minutes,* begun in 1899, reviews beginnings and previous meetings and events, many purely social.

[9]A more successful beginning in Petaluma was made July 26, 1888. There, because the Sisters of Notre Dame were not allowed to teach boys through the grades, they were replaced by the Sisters of Charity in 1892, though the reason is not given in the Namur *Annals*. The decision was unfortunate, since this foundation was the nearest approach to a true parish school offered to the Sisters in that era.

[10]In the Moreland correspondence in the Notre Dame Archives of the California Province are two final letters dated August 17 and 22, 1899 and addressed to Sister Mary Bernardine. In her crabbed, unformed writing, Mrs. Moreland, a woman of little formal education, displays here an unusual business sense and strong determination. Like most donors, she offers business advice, under the usual impression that nuns need it, though she hastens to admit Sister Mary Bernardine's experience.

[11]A graphic account of this nearly fatal disaster is in the *Annals* of Notre Dame Academy, Alameda.

[12]The account of this foundation is supplied by the *Annals* of the Sisters of Notre Dame in Santa Barbara, and by Sister Mary Lucidie's story written for the Golden Jubilee of the foundation in 1956. There is also the news story in *The Tidings,* December 14, 1906, p. 8. (Bishop Conaty's letters regarding the proposed foundation in Sacred Heart Parish in Los Angeles and the one in Salinas are dated July 16, July 20, and August 6, 1906.)

[13]All correspondence and legal papers connected with the Walker donation are in the Archives of Sisters of Notre Dame of Santa Barbara. Among these is the building permit, dated March 12, 1918. This house at 2225 Santa Barbara Street, was the Sisters' residence until the sale of the property in 1966.

[14]*N. D. Q.,* December, 1914, 87; and June, 1916, 45. Of pioneer descent herself, Mrs. Zabala was the wife of Don Pedro Zabala, a native of Spain who came to Monterey in 1849. Her daughter, Virginia Zabala, Mrs. W. G. Hudson, was also an alumna of the College. Her letters appear in *N. D. Q.,* June 1911, 92, and March, 1912, 81. Mrs. Pedro Zabala died in November, 1914.

[15]St. Francis Xavier School, was planned by Rev. Richard A. Gleeson, S.J., Rector of St. Joseph's Church, and completed by his successor, Rev. John D. Walshe, S.J. With Mrs. Graham as Principal, and Mary Collins and Julia Farney as teachers, it was dedicated September 17, 1905. On September 4, 1906, the Sisters of Notre Dame took charge.

Chapter 16

[1]Sister Anthony, S.H., wrote her lengthy undated letter within a few days after the earthquake. Sister Mary Euphrasia's letter to Sister Mary Bernardine is dated April 23. Her long documentary was addressed to the Superior of the community at Trinity College the following day, but she perhaps wrote these letters simultaneously. Sister Anna Raphael's letters are dated May 3, 9, 11, and 29.

[2]This schoolgirl humor appeared in the *Oakland Tribune*, April 19, 1906, with the note that the Notre Dame girls, who had escaped death in the quake, were enjoying life in "The Barracks." The humorous "Tour of the Campus," which Helen McKeever sent to Sister Mary Bernardine, May 6, is another sample of the girls' good spirit.

[3]Sister Mary Basil's fears were probably due to her poor health at the time. She wrote five letters to Sister Mary Bernardine between April 20 and May 10. One contains a list of the "remnants of the boarding school," but before it could reach its destination, most of the girls who had left were back and enjoying excitement of classes under unusual conditions.

[4]Sister Berchmans Joseph wrote these letters April 25 and May 2. Sister Mary Veronica wrote from Watsonville, April 26, but the circular letter from that house was the work of Sister Mary Loyola Wynne. The letter of Sister Clare, B.S., with its account of the destruction of O'Connor Sanitarium, is dated April 23.

[5]Sister Julia Theresa's letters, dated April 26 and 27 and May 8 and 25, are witness to her difficulties with her community. Before Sister Mary Aloyse had time to write her opinion, Sister Julia Theresa had already secured permission from the Chancery Office to rebuild on the old site, should her Provincial Superior agree. Her letter of May 8 states this permission, with her plan to build only a day school which she hoped to have finished in September. Sister Mary Bernardine agreed about the site but insisted on a boarding school.

[6]This sculptor's letter is dated September 5, 1908. His sculpture now stands in the foyer of Ralston Hall in Belmont.

Chapter 17

[1]Betty Tisdale was daughter of William D. Tisdale, a financier; she married Dr. Bryant. Her younger sister, Blanche, also a Notre Dame girl,

married Peter Weeks. Their mother Luella Gephert Tisdale, described Betty in *N. D. Q.*, September, 1912, 62.

[2]The "Radcliffe Hall" prospectus, 1895. Mrs. Bull's aim was "to secure for her daughters the training which is afforded in the best preparatory schools in the East. . . ."

[3]Sister Marie Anne du St. Esprit Charlier, a native of Luxembourg, was professed in Namur in 1873. She came to California in 1890. Known to all as Ma Soeur, she taught French for many years at Notre Dame High School in San Francisco.

[4]Schools were at first accredited according to subjects. In 1900 Notre Dame in San Francisco was accredited in five subjects. Both boarding school and academy in San Jose were accredited in six. Notre Dame in Marysville was rejected, as were other private schools not offering senior sciences. The author is grateful to Mr. Keith Merrill, Office of Relations with Schools, University of California in Berkeley, for making these records available.

[5]Sister Mary Veronica asked for reconsideration on behalf of the two schools in San Jose, making no mention of that in San Francisco. Her reason was that "institutions in California hold their standing through accrediting with state institutions." *Book of the Board of Trustees,* 79.

[6]Graduate studies were thus limited to six-week summer sessions conducted by Catholic University on the Pacific Coast, or to attendance at Catholic University itself in Washington, D. C. The ruling was discouraging for Sisters who had begun work in secular institutions.

[7]Sister Marie Frederica, S.H., Frances Kane, Class of 1917, daughter of Henry and Helen Wright Kane, was born in Gilroy in 1898. She was head of the California Province of Notre Dame, 1945-1951, and became the first Californian member of the Sisters of Notre Dame Generalate in Rome when she was elected Sister Assistant in 1963.

[8]These volumes are composed mostly of the work of the Class of 1893. They form part of a project submitted by Reverend Peter C. Yorke and representing the schools of the Archdiocese of San Francisco.

CHAPTER 18

[1]In her account of Notre Dame Conservatory of Music Sister Cécile Marie Gerlach says that besides being an honor graduate of the Royal Conservatory of Liége, Belgium, Sister Marguerite Kridelka had studied harp under Boscha, the greatest harpist of his time, and that she used his methods.

[2]Sister Marie Aimée, Marie Ofelia Plisé, daughter of Victor and Josephine P. de Losada de Rocheblave Plisé, was born in Panamá in 1856. She was professed in San Jose in 1896, died in San Jose in 1922.

[3]The plan adopted by the Board of Trustees, July 6, 1898, set the cost of Notre Dame Conservatory at $12,000. The total cost is difficult to assess, but was certainly a higher figure. Sister Cécile Marie gives a

detailed description of this building, as a two-story brick unit, 110 feet long, finished throughout in Oregon pine, its forty-three rooms sound-proof.

[4]Sister Cécile Marie included first years of instruction at Notre Dame, but girls who graduated from the Conservatory had usually had some years of music training before coming to the boarding school. Sister stresses the fact that all students at the Conservatory were obliged to reside at the boarding school, this in keeping with her belief that all practice should be under supervision. Sister was a firm believer in the great value of public quarterly competitions, at which all teachers were present, even those of the "Academy" who taught day students, the entire music faculty numbering about twelve. Two competitions were devoted to "Studies, Scales, and Technic." Harmony, Counterpoint, Original Composition, etc., were examined at the other two events, the last one being a preview of the "great public Commencement Exercises."

[5]Sister Cécile Marie treasured an evaluation of work done in the Conservatory, especially her own work, addressed by Alfred Metzger to the public and signed, September 12, 1934. Mr. Metzger was then Editor of *Pacific Coast Musical Review*, and Musical Critic of *San Francisco Chronicle*. His praise was certainly very high.

[6]Carrie Goebel-Weston studied under Nat Landsburger in San Francisco after graduating from Notre Dame. Next she continued her studies in Europe for some years. Finally she opened a studio in San Francisco. Her accompanist was Marian Provost, a 1907 graduate of the Conservatory and granddaughter of Alumna Louise Provost Auzerais. Her performances, with San Francisco Municipal Orchestra and otherwise, always received high commendation.

[7]The year 1912 was the high-water mark for artist visitors at the Conservatory. Madame Schumann-Heink sang there February 24, and violinist Maude Powell played December 5. Sister Anna Raphael wrote her last resounding welcome for the former, and singer Irene Smith of Alameda read it with appropriate feeling.

[8]In the conservatory program "Academic Course" referred to 52 units of music study; it had nothing to do with the academic studies. Some, mostly Americans, completed this work at the same time as their high school program, though in most instances it required one or two years of further study.

[9]An account of the San Jose Snell family is in *History of Santa Clara County*, 739.

CHAPTER 19

[1]Sister Anthony, S.H., recalls that Daisy Wright and Lita Robinson were co-editors of *The Woodpecker, N. D. Q.*, June, 1909, 80.

[2]Sister Anthony, S. H., included many of these commendations and press notices in *N. D. Q.*, of March, 1909, and subsequent issues. Repre-

sentative E. A. Hayes and Bishop Thomas Grace of Sacramento are quoted in the March number; in September, Professor Cornelius Bradley of University of California.

[3]Other examples of Sister Anthony's lengthy poems are "The Hymn of the Great Ship," and her stirring wartime poem, "Jesus of Nazareth Passing By."

[4]Alice Tisdall read this poem at the Golden Jubilee celebration of the Sisters of Notre Dame on the Pacific Coast, 1894. In *N. D. Q.*, June 1909, 6, it is followed by Father Peter DeSmet's story of the *l'Indefatigable's* stop at Valparaiso. This account is in H. M. Chittenden and A. T. Richardson, *Life, Letters, and Travels of Father Pierre Jean DeSmet, S.J.*, beginning p. 420.

[5]Mary Gallagher, a graduate of 1899, married Dr. Edward McKevitt of San Francisco. *N. D. Q.*, March 1915, 91. There are a few other instances of space in the magazine given to the sentimental, the reason being that the writers were well liked by alumnae. Minnie Livingston, 1894, was another favorite. *N. D. Q.*, September, 1910, 6.

[6]Jennie Lathrop Watson, who at school signed her name Jane Stanford Lathrop, gave general edification as a little convert by writing "intentions" on small pieces of paper and requesting the Sister Sacristan to place them in the tabernacle.

[7]"Memories of Maro" Isabel Duff, in *N. D. Q.*, December, 1910, 21.

[8]Alice Turel's father, Jean Turel, a French pioneer, early established a thriving merchant career in San Francisco. Her mother, Eugénie de Bettier Turel, descended from an old family of Savoy. The Turel home in San Jose was near College of Notre Dame which often experienced special kindness from this family.

[9]Frances McChrystal McNamee. Her daughters are Frances McNamee Moore and Marion McNamee, Sister Marion, Sisters of the Holy Family.

[10]Beatrice E. Messmer Standish admits that her classmates approached problems seriously. Her article, "The Influence of Slavery on American Literature," *N. D. Q.*, December, 1910, 27, is certainly very mature.

[11]Eugénie's reports run through the *Quarterly* from September, 1909 to March, 1912. Her defense of western literature, June, 1911, 89.

[12]An analysis of the poetry of George Sterling in *N. D. Q.*, March, 1910, 39, by Edward F. Cothran is followed by his selection of Sterling's poems.

[13]*N. D. Q.*, November, 1908.

Chapter 20

[1]Like other popular devotions, the cult of St. Expeditus was linked with the desire to obtain the impossible. This mythical saint was predecessor, among the devout, of St. Jude, saint of impossible cases. His very name indicated the speed with which he obtained petitions.

[2]*N. D. Q.*, March, 1913, dedicated to the memory of Sister Mary Bernardine.

[3]Matters of conscience are dealt with by Canons 520-527, and Canon 530. These canons are explained in Creusen, *Religious Men and Women in Church Law,* under Article 2, beginning p. 69. The codification of Canon Law was begun by St. Pius X and was almost completed at the time of his death. It was promulgated May 27, 1917 and went into effect May 19, 1918. The first revision of the *Constitutions of the Sisters of Notre Dame of Namur* after this codification was published November 27, 1921. Like the constitutions and rules of religious congregations and orders, canonical legislation is constantly undergoing modification.

[4]Like corresponding directives for the heads of "charges," the "Rule of the Mistress of Novices," had been drawn up in Namur more or less as the result of experience.

When the Sister Formation Movement began in 1954, it was sponsored by the National Catholic Educational Association. When two years later the Conference of Major Superiors of the United States was formed, Sister Formation became responsible to it as well, since the end of the movement was the formation of good Sister-teachers. The influence of Sister Formation on both the Sisters and their schools has been incalculable. For a full description of this movement, Sister Bertrande Meyers, D.D., *Sisters for the 21st Century,* Chapter 6.

[5]*N. D. Q.*, March, 1917, 45, carries the *San Jose Mercury-Herald* story and encomium of Sister Mary Ignatia Callahan.

[6]Canon 505. In *Religious Men and Women in Church Law,* p. 45.

CHAPTER 21

[1]*The Annals of Belmont,* a lengthy account by Sister Anthony, S.H., covers the years 1921-1929. Written in a few weeks, this compilation is more like a memoir. Compared with the same time span as presented in *Minutes of the Board of Trustees, College of Notre Dame,* Sister Anthony's story displays the benefits of hindsight. It ends on a triumphal note which was hardly justified in 1929. Legal documents and correspondence for the period of transfer of the college to Belmont are intact. Though the final chapter of this story is one of the best attested, prudence dictates silence on the reasons for abandoning the site of the college in San Jose, as well as on the debacle which accompanied the departure.

[2]In 1854 Count Leonetto Cipriani erected a country house on a ten-acre plot, which he had purchased from S. M. Mezes, a Spanish lawyer who had received the surrounding area and other portions of the Las Pulgas Rancho, three-twentieths of the grant, in payment of his services in defence of the Luis Argüello heirs. M. B. Hoover, *Historic Spots of California,* 428, 437; and F. M. Stanger, *South from San Francisco,* 48.

W. C. Ralston purchased this country house and a large acreage including the background hills, and erected his mansion around the Cipriani house. This and several smaller units were completed in 1868.

W. C. Ralston made the Cipriani house an integral part of his mansion by fitting it with the same elegant flooring and lighting. And here it could be said that the original house, was apparently not prefabricated, as stated on the title page of Ernest Falbo's *California and Overland Diaries of Count Leonetto Cipriani.*

[3]In 1924 this expanse of lawn was made more beautiful by a lovely Venetian fountain, the gift of Mr. Alfred Gump of San Francisco.

[4]*The Minutes of the Board,* January 3, 1922, shows the decision of the trustees to purchase the Gardiner Estate, as it was then called, and adjoining properties, by a mortgage of $100,000 on the Hibernia Bank of San Francisco. Official business was completed February 7, 1922. All deeds representing these transactions are in the files of College of Notre Dame, Belmont.

List of Mothers General of Notre Dame de Namur:

Blessed Mère Julie Billiart, 1805-1816
Mère St. Joseph, Françoise Blin de Bourdon, 1816-1838
Mère Ignatius Thérèse Josephine Goethals, 1838-1842
Mère Marie Thérèse Vandeputte, 1842-1843
Mère Constantine, Marie Jeanne Joseph Collin, 1843-1875
Mère Aloysie, Thérèse Josèphe Mainy, 1875-1888
Mère Aimée de Jésus, Elodie Dullaert, 1888-1907
Mère Marie Aloyse, Georgina Van Laere, 1908-1912
Mère Maria Julienne, Clotilde Goffin, 1912-1934

Note: Mère Maria Julienne resigned in 1934. The Superiors General of Notre Dame are now elected for a period of six years. The Generalate is now in Rome.

Bibliography

SELECTED BIBLIOGRAPHY

Many specific references are made in the Notes for each chapter. Books and other sources fundamental to the work as a whole, or appearing in the Notes pertaining to more than one chapter are listed here.

BOOKS

Bancroft, Hubert Howe. *History of California.* 1888.
Burnett, Peter Hardeman. *Recollections and Opinions of an Old Pioneer.* 1880.
Carroll, Mary Bowden. *Ten Years in Paradise.* 1903.
Catholic Encyclopedia. 1907, 1911.
Caughey, John Walton. *California.* 1953.
Dana, Richard Henry. *Two Years Before the Mast.* 1869.
Davis William Heath. *Seventy-five Years in California.* 1929.
Foote, Horace S. (ed.) *Pen Pictures from the Garden of the World, Santa Clara County.* 1888.
Hall, Frederic, *History of San José and Surroundings.* 1871.
Historic Spots in California. (Parts written by Mildred Brooke Hoover) 1937.
Hittell, Theodore Henry. *History of California.* (4 vols.) Vol. 4, 1897.
Hruby, Daniel D. *Mines to Medicine.* 1965.
James, William F. and McMurry, George H. *History of San Jose, California.* 1933.
McNamee, Mary Dominica, S.N.D. de N. *Willamette Interlude.* 1959.
Munro-Fraser, J. P. *History of Santa Clara County, California.* 1881.
Outline History of the Sisters of Notre Dame of Namur. 1938. Privately published by Trinity College, Washington, D. C.
Schmidt, George Paul. *The Liberal Arts College.* 1957.
Walker, Franklin. *San Francisco's Literary Frontier.* 1939.
Wentworth, May (Ed.). *Poetry of the Pacific.* 1867.
Woody, Thomas. *A History of Women's Education in the United States.* 1929.

OTHER PUBLICATIONS

Newspapers, including the *Oakland Tribune, San Francisco Chronicle, San Jose Mercury, San Jose Times* and the *San Jose Pioneer & Historical Register.*
Periodicals such as the *California Historical Society Quarterly,* the *Notre Dame Quarterly,* and the *Overland Monthly.*
City directories of San Francisco and San Jose.

DOCUMENTS

Autograph letters by or addressed to Mère Constantine, Sister Anna Raphael, Sister Loyola, Sister Marie Alenie, Sister Marie Catherine, Sister Mary Bernardine, Sister Mary Cornelia and others.

Bancroft Library collections of Coolbrith papers, correspondence of the Reverend Isaac Owen and Departmental State Papers of San Jose.

Archbishop Alemany's manuscript letters to Sisters of Notre Dame in San Jose, Diary 1855-1863, and *Libro Borrador*, 1850-1875, in archives of the Archdiocese of San Francisco.

Cornelian Society notes and legal papers, Notre Dame Archives.

Journal of J. M. Estudillo, 1862.

Baptismal records at Mission San Jose, Mission Santa Clara and St. Joseph's Church in San Jose.

NOTE ON ARCHIVAL MATERIAL OF THE CALIFORNIA PROVINCE OF NOTRE DAME

The historical record of the province is fairly continuous, the one significant break coinciding with the period of publication of *Notre Dame Quarterly*, a periodical of real merit described in Chapter 19 of this volume. Accounts, kept in large ledgers, are exact and almost complete. School prospectuses are in the same state of preservation. As an aid in interpretation, the letters are the real treasures, that is, when one subtracts the mass of seasonal correspondence, the trite, edifying, and fulsomely flattering sections. Even all this, of course, sheds light on mental and religious attitudes, and factual kernels are hidden in the maze. Because of European disasters, provincial correspondence with Namur is mostly one-sided; little remains of American letters beyond brief news items in the annals of the Mother House. But beginning with the faded blue letters of Mère Constantine to the Sisters in Oregon, the Namur correspondence is mostly extant. For preservation, these French letters were copied into *cahiers* in San Jose, and later translated into English.

A fine collection of photos, textbooks, schoolwork, awards, and other items present an unusual opportunity for reconstructing the past of Notre Dame in California.

Index

— A —

Accolti, Rev. M., S.J., 64-65, 71
Ainsa, Francisca, 48
Alemany, Archbishop Joseph
    Sadoc, 3-5, 8, 24-25, 35, 53,
    66, 97, 125, 128, 161, 172
Alta California, Daily, 35, 40
Argonaut, the, 100
Argüello, (Governor) Luis, Con-
    cepción, José Ramon, Ysabel
    (Mrs. Nicholas Constantino
    Den), 114.   Ysabel: Picture
Argüello, (Don) Santiago, 86
Asturias de Asturias, Luz, Elisa
    and Raquel, 263.   Picture
Auzerais, Aimée (Mrs. Milton B.
    Lennon), 90, 249, Picture
Auzerais House (San Jose), 90,
    95, 167
Auzerais, Mr. and Mrs. John E.
    (Minnie McLaughlin), Mr. and
    Mrs. John L. (Louise Provost),
    Louise A. (Mrs. Edward T.
    Sterling), 90

— B —

Bank of California, 95
Bank of San Jose, 95, 224
Bannister, Edward ("Brother") 34
Barrios, Justo Rufino, 147, 156-158,
    160, 162
Barry, Emma (see also Marie du
    S.C., Sister), 30, 90
Barry (Judge) P., 4, 25, 30, 73
Barstow, Mr. and Mrs. Alfred,
    (Mary Rhodes), 109
Bascom, Grandma (Mrs. Louis),
    12-13
Baucelles, Mercedes and Concha
    (Matheu), 264
Beans, T. Ellard, 95
Bear Flag Rebellion, 83, 101

Belén, 150, 152-153, 155-159
Belmont Annals, 291
Belmont Military School, 282
Benoit, Aloysius, 111, 168-169
Bernal, María de Pilar (Pico), 85
Bernal, John Pablo and
    Encarnación (Soto), Refugio
    (Mrs. John W. Kottinger), 177
Blanchet, Archbishop Francis
    Norbert, 25, 43-44, 58, 89-90
Blanchet, F. X., Vicar General, 00
Bonillas, Dolores "Lola", 264
Booth, Marjorie, 252
Bradley, Louisa (Mrs. E. M.
    Watson), 263
Branham, Isaac, 87
Brenham, Mr. and Mrs. Charles J.
    (Betty Adair), Betty, Louise and
    Laura J. 175
Browne, Rev. P. J., 210
Brush Electric Co., 167
Buckley, Grace, 267
Bull, Mrs. Alpheus, 233
Bulmore, Violet, 252, 287
Burnett, Peter H. and family,
    35, 46-47, 85, 92, 177
Burnett, Sally (Poe), 36, 47, 79,
    82-83, 110
Burns, Annie (Mrs. Ed Cathalin),
    89
Butler, Annette and Jonathan, 200
Butterworth, Thomas C., 192
Byrne, Bessie, 118-119
Byrne, Garrett J., 118
Byrne, Mary Aloysia, 173
Byrnes (Senator) Mrs. James D.,
    and Margaret (Mahoney), 177

— C —

Caedmon Club, 102
California State Legislature, 2,
    106, 199

327

Campbell, Maude and Irene, 249
Canning, Catherine (Mrs. S. J. Radley), 294
Carrera (General) Rafael, 150, 154, 160
Carroll, Mary Ann Murphy, 183
Carson City (Nevada), 97
Carson, Kit, 83
Castro, Guadalupe, 84
Castro, Isabel, 47
Castro, María Dolores Peralta and Juan, 7
Catholic University of America, 199, 239-241
Cipriani, Count Leonetto, 323
Charter, College of Notre Dame, 76, 100. Picture.
Chiles-Walker Expedition, 101
Christal, Anita (Mrs. William A. Purdy), 263, 269
Cobb, (General) H. A., Eugénie and Zoe, 101-102
Collins, Rev. John, S.J., 217, 289
Colorado, 159
Columbia (California), 97
Columbian Exposition, 242
Comerford, Michael J., Catherine (Mrs. W. J. Chandler) and Mary Ann (Sister Mary de Sales), 75
Conaty, (Bishop) Thomas J. 208-210
Connelly, Mary Florence, 262
Constitutional Convention, first, California, 1, 11, 85, 87
Coolbrith, Ina, 103, 182-183, 266. Picture
Coolidge, Mary and Clarence, 173
Cornelian Society (see also Notre Dame Alumnae Association), 183
Corral, Ramon and family, 218
Costello, Eileen, 252
Cothran, Edward F. and Kate Blythe, 259, 266-267
Cox, Maxine (Mrs. Raymond Pepper), 252, 294
Crosby, Elisha O., 7, 101

Crowley, Rev. D. O., 103
Cunha, Rosalie, 263

— D —

Dana, Richard Henry, 55
Danglada y Munras, Catalina (Field), 82
Davidson, Peter, 6, 48
Davies property, 7
De Anza Hotel, San Jose, 291
De Haro, Francisco and family, 54, 77, 83
De la Guerra, (Don) Jose and Doña María Antonía Carillo de la Guerra, 177, 260
De la Guerra (Don) Pablo, Delfina and Hermina, 260
De Voss, Rev. Peter, S.J., 35, 46
Den, Catarina (Mrs. Charles Bell), 62, 88, 105-106, 114
Den, Dr. Nicholas, 88
Den, Ysabel Argüello (Mrs. Nicholas C.), and Mary Aloysia, 114
Derby, Evelyn (Mrs. Frank Stockton), 294
Di Bernardi, Marie (Mrs. O. Seegelken), 257
Dillon, Marie (Lally), 60-61, 124, 139-140, 170, 294. Picture
Dillon, Patrice, French Consul, 25, 46-47
Dolcini, Corinne, 267
Donald, Sarah (Mrs. George Winthrop Fox), 108-109
Donohue, Mr. and Mrs. Peter (Anna Downey), Mary Ellen ("Mamie"; Mrs. Henry von Schroeder), 98-99
Donovan, Edythe (Mrs. Harold Toso), 294
Downey, (Governor) John G., 93
Downeyville (California), 97
Dowsett, Marion (Mrs. David Diggins), 263
Duff, John C., Margaret, Isabel, and Carmelita, 261

Dufficy, Mary (Tormey), 173
Dunne, Mamie, 171, 172, 179
Dye, Job F., 7

— E —

Earthquake of 1906, 119, 192-194,
214-229. Pictures
Eaton, Stella Light, 249. Picture
Electric Tower, San Jose, 167
Emmons, Gladys, 219
Empire City, 20-21
Estudillo, Antonio (Prefect), 86
Estudillo, Concepción, 85-86
Etchebarre, Adele (Calhoun) and
Leontine (Denson), 175
l'Etoile du Matin, 57

— F —

Fanny, 16-18, 57
Farney, Julia, 144
Fermor-Hesketh, Sir Thomas,
97, 293
Field, María Antonía, Munras, 82
Field, María Antonía, ("Lady
Field"), 264
Fisher, William, 87
Fitzgerald, Annie (see also
Sister Anna Rafael), 62-63,
70-73, 80, 92, 133. Picture
Fitzgerald, Johanna Murphy, 71
Fitzgerald, Marcella, 62, 70-71,
178, 182, 258
Fitzgerald, Mary, 48, 62, 71, 81
Flood, Jennie, 98
Foss, Irene Crook, 263
Fuller, Mary (Mrs. Charles
Watson Grant), 31

— G —

Gallagher, Mary McKevitt
(Mrs. Edward), 259-260
Gardiner, Dr. A. M. and family,
Sanitarium, 282, 284-285
Gardiser, Mr. and Mrs. Jacob
(Annie McGinnes), 81
Gareshe, Florence (Macauley), 267
Gibbons, John Cardinal, 179
Gleeson, Rev. Richard A. S.J., 228

Gleeson, Rev. William, 163-165
Goebel-Weston, Carrie, 250
Gold Hill (Nevada), 92, 97
Goodrich, Levi, 7, 10, 13-15, 49,
72, 115, 167
Grant, (General, President)
Ulysses S., 98, 285, 294
Graves, Jackson A. and Alice
(Stewart), 260
Griffin, Alice, 267
Griffith, Rev. Edward P., 210
Grim, Mary (Mrs. T. Heying) and
Ruth (Mrs. Richard Minor), 262

— H —

Haight, (Governor) Henry H.,
76, 101
Hancock, G. Allan, 107
Hancock, Major Henry, 106
Hanks, (Captain) Julian, Rebecca
(Galindo), Sofía and Ann
(Fisher), 87-88
Hanna, (Archbishop) Edward J.,
213, 282, 287, 289-291
Haraszthy, Agoston, Ida (Hancock)
and Otelia, 106-107.
Ida: Picture
Harispuru, María, 264
Hastings, (Justice Serranus Clin-
ton, Clara (Catherwood-Darling),
Ella and Flora, 99
Hastings College of the Law, 100
Hensley, (Major) and Mrs. Samuel
J. (Helen Crosby), Helen
(Thornton), 101
Hesketh, Sir Thomas Fermor,
97, 293
Hester, Judge and Mrs. Craven P.
(Martha), Sarah (Maddock-Kent)
and Laura (Phelps), 81-82, 109
Hibernia Bank, 171
Hill, Mr. and Mrs. Daniel (Rafaela
Luisa Ortega) and Rosa (Mrs.
Nicholas Den), 88
Hoppe, J. D., 10
Hughes, Annie (Mrs. G. Kennedy),
265

— I —

Infatigable, l' 27, 57, 179
Inskip, Florence, 109
Ivancovich, Pauline (Sullivan), 267

— J —

James, George Wharton, 258
Jarboe, Frances (Mrs. Charles Whiteman), 113
Jenny Lind, 81
Jordan, David Starr, 258

— K —

Kawananakoa, Mr. and Mrs. David (Abigail Campbell), Kapiolani (Mrs. H. M. Field), and Liliuokalani (Mrs. C. E. Morris), 263
Keith, William, 100
Kell, Ann (Colombet) and Mary Ellen, 80-81
Kell, Thomas and Margaret Murphy Kell, and family, 9, 11, 39, 54, 79, 80-81
Kelly, Anna and Estelle, 265
Kent, 88
Knox and Beans Bank, 95
Kottinger, John W. and family, 177

— L —

Lander, Alice, 100, 133, 144
Landers, Elizabeth "Lizzie" (Mrs. John O'Brien), 100-101, 142 Picture
Langlois, Rev. Anthony, 3-4, 24
Lathrop, Jennie Stanford (Watson), 260. Picture
Lathrop, Virginia (Mrs. Walter Turnbull), 101
Lawrie, (Professor) James, 116, 129
Lentzen, Theodore, 115, 193. Picture
Lewis, Jackson and William N., 112
Lightner, Elizabeth Gray, (Mrs. Joel, 258, 266
Lightstone, (Leuchtstein), Mr. and Mrs. Francis (Juanita Soto), Juanita and family, 111

Lincoln, (President) Abraham, 85, 92
Livermore, Robert and family, 86
Llebaria, Rev. John Francis, Vicar General, 46
Lucas, Maria, 30, 61, 74, 122, 124-125, 129, 139-141, 170-172, 183, 238, 294

— M —

Mackey, John, 125
Madronia Cemetery, 211-212
Mahoney, Catherine (Mrs. D. W. Nesfield), 102
Maria Theresa, 87
Marron, Rev. M., 205
Masten, Mamie, 170
Matheu, Mr. and Mrs. Julio (Concha Baucelles), 264
Matheu, Margot (Simon) and Virginia (Beltraneña), 252, 264
Mazzetti, Rev. Alexander, S.J., 264
McClatchy, Frances, 135, 170
McChrystal, Frances (Mrs. Frank McNamee), 266
McCone, Dollie (McDonald) and Susan, 173. Picture
McDougal, (Governor) John and family, 34, 85, 108
McGinnis, Rev. J., 4
McGowan, Edward, 88, 114
McHenry, (Justice) John, Bessie, Emma and Mary (Mrs. William Keith), 99-100
McKeever, Helen, 267, 258
McLaughlin and Ryland Bank, 95
McLaughlin, Edward and Minnie, 90
McLaughlin, Mr. and Mrs. Edward (Adelia Hickman), 178
McLaughlin, Dr. John, 89
McLaughlin, Winifred, 178, 249
McNaboe, Rev. Michael, 165
Mechanics Institute of San Francisco, 78
Melchers, Rev. William, 202
Menefee, Dr. J. J., 95

Messmer, Beatrice (Mrs. Allan M. Standish), 266
Metzger, (Professor) Alfred, 249
Mignacco, Filippo, S.J., 216
Miller, Catherine, Ellen Independence, Josephine (Mrs. Joseph Kirk), Julia and Theresa, 103
Miller, Frances ("Fannie"), 62, 70, 103-104, 258
Mills, Annie (see also Sister Mary Xavier), 62, 70-73
Mitchell, Yvonne, 252
Mix, Beatrice (Mrs. Henry B. Cheadle), 252, 257
Montgomery, (Bishop) George, 205-206
Mooney, Alberta (Mrs. Joseph E. Fitzpatrick), 294
Moreland, Josephine, 205-206
Moreland, Mrs. Margaret S., 205-207, 225
Mount Hamilton Observatory, 217, 242
Murphy, Bernard, 81, 180
Murphy, Daniel and Mary Fisher Murphy and family, 174
Murphy, Diana (Mrs. Morgan Hill, later married Sir George Rhodes), 175
Murphy, Elizabeth Yuba (Mrs. W. P. Taafe), 43, 80, 113, 174, 267
Murphy, Ellen (Nellie), 80, 113
Murphy, James and Ann Martin, and family, 80
Murphy, John M. and Virginia Reed Murphy, 113
John M: Picture
Murphy, Martin, Sr., 9, 35, 42, 48, 71
Murphy, Martin, Jr., and Mary Bolger Murphy, family of, 5-8, 11, 39, 54, 79-81, 113
Martin, Jr.: Picture
Murphy, Mary Ann (Mrs. R. T. Carroll), 80, 113, 183
Murphy, Mary Frances, 80
Murphy, (Don) Timoteo, 70

Murphy, Virgina Reed (Mrs. John M.), 258, 266
Murray, Rev. Michael, 282, 284
Mutch, Lucille (Dunbar) and Isabel (Munroe), 263

— N —

Neri, Rev. Joseph M., S.J., 312
New Almaden, 86, 112-113, 167
Newlands, Francis, 97
Nixon, Carrie Regan, 164
Nobili, Rev. John, S.J., 5-6, 8, 10
Noë, Guadalupe Gardano, Dolores and family, 84
Nolting, Hazel (White), 261-262 Picture
Notre Dame Alumnae Association, (see also Cornelian Society), 90, 98, 101, 183, 263
Notre Dame at Alameda, 163-166, 205, 207, 212, 220-223, 244
Notre Dame at Belmont, 241-242, 275, 281-295
Notre Dame at Marysville, 28, 53, 67-68, 74, 90, 94, 128, 146, 163, 184-186, 222-224, 238, 248, 279
Notre Dame at Petaluma, 166
Notre Dame at Redwood City, 166, 204-205, 208
Notre Dame at Salinas, 210, 249, 277
Notre Dame at San Francisco (Mission Dolores), 70, 73, 128, 146, 163, 169, 176, 184, 197, 214, 220-223, 226-228,234-236, 240, 246, 275
Notre Dame at Santa Barbara, 208, 226, 274
Notre Dame at Santa Clara, 70, 166, 223-224
Notre Dame at Saratoga, 211, 276
Notre Dame at Watsonville, 205-207, 210, 221-226, 251, 254
Notre Dame Conservatory (San Jose), 179, 193-194, 244, 248-252, 255-256. Pictures

Notre Dame High School (San
Jose), 168, 194, 202, 234, 255,
275-277, 289, 291
Notre Dame Institute, 200-204,
213, 224-225, 263, 274, 289
Notre Dame Music Academy, 194
Notre Dame Memorial Chapel,
Belmont, 78, 265, 295
Notre Dame Music Hall (San
Jose), 116, 179, 194, 244.
Picture
Notre Dame Press, 197-198
Notre Dame Select Day Academy
(San Jose), 110, 117, 118, 202,
245, 290
Notre Dame Tabernacle Society,
163

— O —

Oakland *Tribune,* 219
O'Brien, Edith, 267
O'Connell, (Bishop) Eugene,
20-23, 54, 128
O'Connell, Grace and Geraldine,
249
O'Connor, Mr. and Mrs. Myles
Poore (Amanda Young Butler),
178, 192, 199-204, 206-207,
224-225
O'Connor Sanitarium, 199-200,
204, 207, 225
Older, Mrs. Fremont, 97, 292-293
Orange Flour Mill, 112
Ord, María Angustias de la Guerra
177, 260
Ord, Rebecca (Peshine), 177,
258, 260, 267.   Picture
Oreña, Anita Virginia (Mrs. T. W.
Dibblee) and Hermina, 260
Ormat, Francisca and Mary, 105
Ortega, Encarnación (Sanchez),
40
Ortiz, Minnie (Mrs. Dario Oreña)
and Virginia, 260
Ortiz, Virginia, 260
Owen, Rev. Isaac, 34
Owen, J. J., 72, 95-96, 118

— P —

Pacheco, (Doña) Juana, 112
Pacific Coast Music Review,
249-250
Palomares, Mr. and Mrs. Francisco
(Margarita Pacheco), Rosaría
(Mrs. Narciso Suñol), 84
Palomares, María, Mrs. Pierre de
Saisset, 175
Pardee, (Governor) George C.
222
Parr, Jonathan, 7, 13
Peacock, Dorothy, 263
Pedroreño, Antonía, Estudillo,
Victoria, Elena and Ysabel,
85-86
Peralta, (Don) Luis, Gertrudis
and Trinidad, 1, 6-7, 29, 63
Petit, Eleanor Nugent (Mrs.
Eugène Veuve) and Mary, 112
Petre, Helen, 231, 250
Phelan Block, (San Jose), 167
Phelan, (Senator) James D., 212
Pichon, Eugénie, 266.   Picture
Pico, (Don) José Dolores, Antonio
M. and family, Petra and
Vicenta, 39, 85
Pillot, Julian, Emilia, Heloisa
(Mrs. James V. Tisdall),
Clorinda (Mrs. Aloysius
Benoit), 111
Pinard, Louis and family
113-114, 179
Pony Express, 94
Popp & Hogan, Printers, 198
Poulin, Mr. and Mrs. Auguste
(Eugénie) and Sidone, 112
Powell, Maude, 250
Prendergast, Rev. J., Vicar
General, 70
Provost, Louise (Mrs. John L.
Auzerais), 89-90
Pulsifer, Mary (Ames) and
Martha, 102

— Q —

Quinlan, Sadie (see also Sister Anthony, S.H.), 187-188, 233 Picture

Quinn, Mayor R. P., Watsonville, 225

— R —

Radcliffe Hall, Belmont, 233

Railroads, 94-95

Ralston Hall, estate, mansion, Belmont, 39, 97, 109, 193, 233, 282-286, 288, 291, 293-295

Ralston, William C., 109, 285-286, 293, 295

Ramírez, Isabel (Pelanconi-Tonani) 39, 40, 47, 78, 88. Picture

Redman, (Judge) Joshua, 7, 126-127

Redmond, John B., family of Marin County, 104

Redmond, Mary Frances, 61, 97, 104-105, 127

Reed, Hilarita, Picture

Reed, Inez, Picture

Reed, John, and Hilaria Sanchez Reed, family, 47, 54

Rhodes, Ada (Williamson), 263

Rhodes, (Judge A. L.), Margaret and Mary, (Mrs. Alfred Barstow), 109

Riordan, (Archbishop) Patrick, 172, 178, 186, 191-192, 228, 268-269

Robinson, Geneva Brooks, (Mrs. Luke), 183

Rosicrucian Press, 291-292

Ryland, Ada and Norma, 110-111

Ryland, C. T. and family, 47, 76, 79, 110, 167-168

Ryland, Letitia Burnett (Mrs. Caius Tacitus), 35-36

— S —

Sacred Heart Church, School (San Jose), 127, 213

Sacred Heart Parish (Salinas), 210

Sainsevain, Mr. and Mrs. Pierre (Paula Suñol), 8, 11, 39

St. Aloysius Boys' School, 168

St. Francis Xavier School (San Jose), 273, 275

St. Joseph's Union, 103

St. Leo's School (San Jose), 274-275

St. Mary's Church, Parish, School (San Jose), 202, 213, 225

St. Patrick's Church (San Jose), 225

Saisset, Harriet and Isabel de, 175

Saisset, Pierre de, 167, 175

Sanchez, (Don) José,María, and Encarnación (Ortega), Fermina, Refugia, Candelaría and Guadalupe, 40

San Francisco Daily Herald, 47

San Francisco Chronicle, 174

San Francisco earthquake and fire, 1906, 214-229

San Francisco Examiner, 174

San Jose Daily Times, 166, 168, 171-172

San Jose Mercury, 72, 92-93, 95, 96, 144

San Jose Mercury-News, 292

San Jose Normal School, 167, 216, 239, 274

San Jose Savings Bank, 95

Santa Clara College (University), 35, 76

Santa Clara County Pioneers, 110

Santa Clara, Mission, 70

Sarah Sands, 16, 23-25

Sasia, Rev. Joseph, S.J., 190

Schallenberger, Moses, 14

Schoenstein, Louis, 192

Schumann-Heink, Ernestine, 250 Picture

Science Hall (San Jose), 194, 226, 236, 291-292. Picture

Seabird, 88

Seifert, Dr. George W., 196,216

Sesnon, Rev. Robert, 269

Shannon, 149

Sharon, Clara (Mrs. Francis Newlands), 97
Sharon, Flora (Mrs. Thomas Fermor-Hesketh), 97, 293
Sharon, (Senator) William and family, 132, 285
Sherwood, Avis and Mary, 218
Shortridge, (State Senator) Charles, 216
Silver City (Nevada), 97
Silverman, Rena, 250
Singer, Dorothy (Mrs. Otto Andrew), 258, 261
Sisters of Notre Dame are listed separately following the main Index
Skidmore, Harriet, 182-183, 266
Smith, W. J., 207, 228
Soto, Marco Aurelio, 158, 160
Sparks, Isaac, Flora and Rosa, 105
Spence, Rudolph, 171
Stanford, Mrs. Leland, 230, 260
Stanford University, 239
Steirlin, Christopher C. and Lizette, 113
Stockman, Rev. P. J., 208
Stoddard, Charles W., 258, 266
Strawberry Farm, 127
Stull & Sonniksen, 125
Sullivan, Belle, 179
Sullivan, John, and Ada E. Kenna Sullivan, 170
Sullivan, Rev. John, 165
Sullivan, Mamie (Mrs. Rudolph Spence), 140, 170
Suñol, (Don) Antonio and Dolores (Bernal) and family, 9, 11, 29, 39, 47, 83-84, 175
Suñol, Encarnación (Etchebarre), 175
Suñol, Francisco, 83

– T –

Talbot, May (Linden), Josephine and Maud, 265-266
Telegraph, 93-94
Thomas, (Professor) W. Scott, 235-238

Tisdale, Betty (Bryant), 232-233 Picture
Tisdall, Alice, (Adams), 259
Tisdall, James V. (Chief of Police) and Heloisa (Pillot), 111
Tivnan, Catherine (see also Sister Mary Bernardine), 188
Tivnan, Rev. Edward O., S.J., 269
Tobin, Col. and Mrs. J. J. (Sophie Ward), 104-105
Tojetti, Edwardo, 253
Tomb, Mamie, 185
Townsend, Dr. John and Johnny, 14. Johnny: Picture
Trinity College, Washington, D.C., 194, 201, 230-231, 239, 262
Truesdell, Amelia, 182, 258
Turel, Alice, 265

– U –

University of California, 234-240
University of the Pacific, 34
Urie, Minnie, 124, 171

– V –

Vallejo, (Don) Ignacio and María Antonía (Luga), (Don) José de Jesús and Luisa Soledad (Sánchez), Encarnación and Guadalupe, 85
Vallejo, Luisa and María, 175
Vallejo, (General) Mariano, 2, 85, 175
Valencia family, 54, 84
Van Caneghan, Dr. Peter, 10, 14
Van Damme, Eugenie, (Melville), 30, 77
Van Houten, John, 78, 93
Van Houten, Margaret "Maggie" (Ditmars), 77-78, 93, 133, 137-138, 143, 178, 192
Veuve, Eugènie, Vida, William and Jenny (Williamson), 112
Viader, Rev. Jose, O.F.M., 9
Victory Theater, San Jose, 250
Vigne, Louis, 40
Villa, Rev. Octavius, S.J., 209
Virgina City (Nev.), 92, 97, 128

— W —

Walkinshaw, Robert and Francisca (Gamiz), Roberta, Francisca, Josefa and Guadalupe, 86-87
Ward, Arcadia Concepción Estudillo, 105
Ward, J. B. and family, 24, 104-105
Washoe (Nevada), 97
Watson, Edith, 267
Watt, Crissie (Mrs. H. H. Clarke) 172
Webb, Sarah, 100
Weddick, Winifred, 263
White, Charles and family, 7, 9
White, Elizabeth, 82
White, Hortense, 143, 235, 261
White, William and Frances (Russell), Genevieve, Nellie, Edward, (Senator Stephen) and Hortense (Sacriste), 176
Wilcox, Charles F. and Frances (Cahill), 267

Wills, Irene, 263
Witch of the Waves, 108
Woods, (Professor) Daniel R., 216

— Y —

Yarimie, Y., 291
Yaeger, Loretta (Mrs. B. P. Oliver), 287
Yoell, James A., Emelie (Center), Gertrude, Emily, Beatrice, Genevieve, Evaline (Prothero), Eva, Harriet, Alice, 173-174
Younger, Col. and Mrs. Coleman (Augusta Inskip), 109-110
Younger, Alice, 109-110, 135

— Z —

Zabala, (Don) Pedro and Anita (Hartnell), 210-211, 260
Zabala, Virgina, 260. Picture
Zech, Jacob, 285

MOTHERS GENERAL OF NOTRE DAME

Mère Aimée de Jésus, Elodie Dullaert, 185, 234
Mère Aloysie, Thérèse Josèphe Mainy, 184
Mère Constantine, Marie Jeanne Joseph Collin, 16-17, 26, 37, 49,
58-59, 60, 66-67, 69, 94, 117, 125-130, 147, 149, 152-153
Mère Julie Billiart, Blessed 127, 128, 214, 228-229, 272
Mère Marie Aloyse, Georgina Van Laere, 212, 214, 240

SISTERS OF NOTRE DAME

— A —

Agnes Gertrude Carroll, 178
Agnes Joseph Voss, 277
Agnes Stanislaus Shepherd, 276
Aldegonde Delpire, 37, 51-52
Aloyse Marie Reich, Ph.D., 276
Aloyse of the Cross, Hannah Jenkins, 61-65, 70, 73-75, 78, 82, 83, 88, 91, 117, 166, 184, 185
Aloysius, Richeat, 23, 26, 28-29, 69, 104
Alphonse Marie Kane, 275
Alphonse Marie Vermuylen, 53

Amada Salazar, 254-255
Amélie St. Joseph Caudron, 185-187
Angela Bernardine Smith, 277
Angela Marie Shepherd, 276
Angela, S.H., McDermott, 279
Anna Raphael, Annie Fitzgerald, 63, 71-75, 78, 81, 82, 102-104, 113, 119, 138, 144, 166, 170, 173-175, 177, 182, 186-187, 191, 193, 205, 212, 214, 217-220, 223-228, 230-235, 238-243, 257-258, 260-262, 266-267, 276, 294. Picture

Anna Voss, 289
Anthony, S.H., Sadie Quinlan,
    27, 78, 82, 90, 102, 119, 170,
    189-191, 214-218, 233, 235,
    237-239, 241, 252, 255-263,
    265-269, 274, 276, 281-287,
    291, 293. Picture
Aurelie, Jeannette André, 63-64,
    66, 196, 263

— B —

Barbara Engs, 276
Berchmans Joseph Murphy,
    223-234, 240, 279, 283-286
Blondine, S.H., Keenan, 275
Bridget Marie McKenzie, 277
Bridget of the Immaculate
    Conception Donnelley, 277-278
Bridgitte Van Houtvelot, 64

— C —

Carmela, S.H., Frieda Gay,
    249-252
Catherine Josepha, Josephine
    O'Brien, 197
Catherine Julie Cunningham, 262
Catherine Strubbe, 25-27
Cécile Marie, Emilie Gerlach,
    245, 248-251, 255
Cecilia Louise Shepard, 276
Claire Bernardine Voss, 277
Clare Callan, 203-204, 224-225,
    263

— D —

Dolores Marie O'Connor, 277

— E —

Elizabeth, S.H., Herzog, 275

— F —

Flora Davie, 211, 263
Francisca Gernaey, 50, 52

— G —

Genevieve White, 176
Geraldine, S.H., Sinnott, 275
Gertrude de Sacré Coeur Arzu
    162

— H —

Hermance Joseph, Josephine
    Louise Serigiers, 147-148, 152
Hermance Van Puyflick, 147-149,
    153-155, 159

— I —

Irene, S.H., Henrietta Siddons,
    245, 248-249, 251-252, 277

— J —

Joseph, B.S., Pollman, 278
Joseph Marie Petar, 277
Joseph, S.H., Burns, 253, 295
Julia, B.S., Anna Donnelley, 278
Julia McGroarty, 187, 199-203,
    232
Julia of the Passion Overend,
    280, 284, 286, 290
Julia, S.H., Hassett, 276
Julia Theresa O'Connor, 221-222,
    226-228
Julianna, B.S., Keegan, 209
Julie de St. Joseph Dur, 148, 156
Julitta Doisron, 218

— K —

Kotska Dehan, 67

— L —

Laurence Lejeune, 52, 66
Léontine Perwuolz, 153, 263-264
Loretto Julie Costello, 277
Louis de Gonzague, (Sister
    Superior), 19-20, 65
Louis de Gonzague Sacriste,
    176, 211
Louise de la Trinidad Andreu, 163
Louise des Séraphines Marneffe,
    151-152, 167, 192, 195, 208,
    268, 270
Louise Marie Scholten, 221
Louise, S.H., André, 238, 258
Louise Van der Schreick, 16, 20
    33, 59, 67, 94, 157, 161
Loyola, Duquenne, 1-15, 20,
    24-32, 35, 37, 40-49, 54,
    58-59, 60, 66, 114, 179
Ludovic, 151, 153-157, 159, 161

— M —

Madeleine de Pazzi, Léocadie
Pinard, 113
Madeleine de Ste. Françoise
Harbison, 244-245
Madeleine Mantell, 244
Madeleine Marie Brennan, 125
Madeleine, S.H., McLean, 277-278
Margaret Clare O'Connor, 277
Margaret Mary Burns, 272
Marguerite de St. Pierre Baltus, 64
Marguerite, du, S.S., Kridelka,
152, 155-156, 162, 179-180,
192-193, 244-246, 248, 251
Maria Agatha Heinz, 277
María Josefa Muñoz, 163
María Teresa Vallejo, 200-203
Marie Aimée Plisé, 246-248, 251
Marie Albine Gobert, 52, 170
Marie Alenie Thewissen, 16-30,
32-36, 39-40, 42, 54-58, 164,
180
Marie Aloysius, 149
Marie Anne Charlier, 235
Marie Augusta Lamberty, 153
Marie Béatrix de Cal, 148,
155-159
Marie Catherine Cabareaux,
1-15, 27, 29-32, 33, 38, 43, 45,
48-49, 53-54, 57, 89, 93, 99,
115-118, 126, 161, 164, 170,
174, 179, 181-182, 184-187,
189, 191, 193, 195.   Picture
Marie de St. Albert Lefèvre, 68
Marie de St. Denis Fischer,
184-186
Marie de St. Pierre Frizzelle,
196, 215
Marie de Ste. Patrice Verdon, 186
Marie de Ste. Thérèse Klausen,
68-69, 89, 99, 101-102, 238,
244, 247-248, 251, 288
Marie du, S.C., Emma Barry,
30, 73-74, 164
Marie Ernestine Vredenburg, 277
Marie Eugénie Balwick, 251
Marie Eucharista Suber, 276
Marie Euphrasie, 69

Marie Félicienne Ramazzina, 275
Marie Frederica Kane, 240
Marie Ivan Kessler, 275
Marie of St. Joseph Oddie,
254, 293
Marie Philippine Portemer,
149, 150, 154, 160.   Picture
Marie Theresa, B.S., Bernhart, 274
Mary Agnes, Sarah Donnelley, 278
Mary Albertus Traynor, 274
Mary Alexis Harrington, 241, 271
Mary Aloyse Keegan, 221, 227,
231
Mary Aloysia Chevry, 43-47, 49,
53-54, 56, 60-61, 79, 83, 85,
89, 91, 114, 124, 170, 175
Mary Angelica Cronin, 254, 291
Mary Angeline Kelly, 281
Mary Annunciata, Rose Anna
McDermott, 220, 270-272, 278
Mary Anselm Sinnott, 277
Mary Aquinas Mehl, 276
Mary Baptist Hassett, 169
Mary Bartholomew Blake, 275
Mary Basil Gautier, 219, 226,
228, 235, 238
Mary Bernard Stewart, 197-198
Mary Bernard Weber, 43, 45,
53-54, 69, 90, 128, 182
Mary Bernardine Tivnan, 152,
163, 187-202, 204-214, 217,
219-220, 224, 226-227, 229-230,
240, 247-250, 268-269.   Picture
Mary Callistus Ivancovich, 275
Mary Carmel Keeler, 278
Mary Catherine Quinn, 279
Mary Clara Pinard, 113
Mary Clothilde Evers, 258
Mary Columba, Bridget Donnelley,
278
Mary Cornelia Neujean, 37-38,
41, 44-45, 58, 66, 69, 73-74,
94, 98, 104, 115-118, 121-122,
126, 128, 143, 146-148, 151,
157, 161, 163-166, 168, 170,
179-187, 191
Mary de Sales, Mary Ann
Comerford, 75, 224

Mary Editha Feely, 218
Mary Euphrasia, Ella Taylor,
  194, 214, 216, 218, 237
Mary Genevieve, Mary Bridges,
  74-75, 99, 144, 233
Mary Gertrude Mogan, 228, 245
Mary Gonzaga Van Aschen, 67
Mary Ignatia Callahan, 272
Mary Joseph Hannan, 224
Mary Josephine, Helen Snell,
  253-254
Mary Julia, Annie Walsh, 56-57
Mary Letitia, S.H., Cunningham,
  277
Mary Loretta Fealy, 277
Mary Loyola Wynne, 207, 225
Mary Lucidie Kissane, 273-274
Mary of St. Agnes Enright, 277
Mary of St. Aloysius de la
  Hautière, 303
Mary of St. Anne Deasy, 273-274
Mary of St. George Bolton, 60-61,
  63-65, 70-71, 78, 80, 83, 88,
  94, 99, 101, 106, 115, 140-141,
  173, 182, 184
Mary of St. George Harney, 207,
  220-223, 226, 278
Mary of St. Gregory Driscoll, 276
Mary of St. James Doyle, 276
Mary of the Assumption Curry,
  273
Mary Patricia, May McCullough,
  275
Mary Pauline Kennedy, 273
Mary Perpetua Driscoll, 275
Mary Philomene Byrne, 272
Mary Philomene, Elizabeth Shaw,
  74, 104, 170-171
Mary Regis Foley, 218, 235,
  237-238, 241, 285, 293
Mary Rosario Gallagher, 260

Mary Stanislaus Daley, 56-57
Mary Stanislaus Fennell, 275
Mary Veronica Dolan, 164, 207,
  225, 269, 279-280, 283
Mary Victoria Barry, 67
Mary Vincent Burns, 272-273
Mary of the Visitation O'Neill, 277
Mary Xavier, Annie Mills, 71-73,
  144, 176, 230, 234, 240, 243
Matthias Eckhoudt, 149
Monica Budde, 264

— N —
Norbertine Vereux, 37

— O —
Odelie Godard, 50-52, 124

— P —
Patricia Marie O'Connor, 277
Paul, S.H., Kanady, 208, 211

— R —
Regina Marie Schoen, 275
Renilde Goemaere, 159
Rita Marie Taylor, 273

— S —
Stanislaus of St. Joseph
  Rademacher, 254
Sylvester Arnoldy, 274

— T —
Theresa, B.S., Spencer, 192
Theresa, S.H., Mary Donnelley,
  278
Theresa, S.H., Lang, 198

— V —
Veronica, S.H., Gelcich, 254

— X —
Xaveria Mulcahy, 241, 271